MASTER VISUALLY®

by Rob Huddleston

Visual®

Dreamweaver® CS4 and Flash® CS4 Professional

Wiley Publishing, Inc.

Master VISUALLY® Dreamweaver® CS4 and Flash® CS4 Professional

Published by
Wiley Publishing, Inc.
10475 Crosspoint Boulevard
Indianapolis, IN 46256
www.wiley.com

Published simultaneously in Canada

Library of Congress Control Number: 2008942700
ISBN: 978-0-470-39669-8

Manufactured in the United States of America
10 9 8 7 6 5 4 3 2 1

Trademark Acknowledgments

Contact Us

For general information on our other products and services please contact our Customer Care Department within the U.S. at 877-762-2974, outside the U.S. at 317-572-3993 or fax 317-572-4002.

For technical support please visit www.wiley.com/techsupport.

WILEY

U.S. Sales

Contact Wiley
at (800) 762-2974 or
fax (317) 572-4002.

Praise for Visual Books...

"If you have to see it to believe it, this is the book for you!"
—PC World

"A master tutorial/reference — from the leaders in visual learning!"
—Infoworld

"A publishing concept whose time has come!"
—The Globe and Mail

"Just wanted to say THANK YOU to your company for providing books which make learning fast, easy, and exciting! I learn visually so your books have helped me greatly — from Windows instruction to Web development. Best wishes for continued success."
—Angela J. Barker (Springfield, MO)

"I have over the last 10–15 years purchased thousands of dollars worth of computer books but find your books the most easily read, best set out, and most helpful and easily understood books on software and computers I have ever read. Please keep up the good work."
—John Gatt (Adamstown Heights, Australia)

"You're marvelous! I am greatly in your debt."
—Patrick Baird (Lacey, WA)

"I am an avid fan of your Visual books. If I need to learn anything, I just buy one of your books and learn the topic in no time. Wonders! I have even trained my friends to give me Visual books as gifts."
—Illona Bergstrom (Aventura, FL)

"I have quite a few of your Visual books and have been very pleased with all of them. I love the way the lessons are presented!"
—Mary Jane Newman (Yorba Linda, CA)

"Like a lot of other people, I understand things best when I see them visually. Your books really make learning easy and life more fun."
—John T. Frey (Cadillac, MI)

"Your Visual books have been a great help to me. I now have a number of your books and they are all great. My friends always ask to borrow my Visual books — trouble is, I always have to ask for them back!"
—John Robson
(Brampton, Ontario, Canada)

"I write to extend my thanks and appreciation for your books. They are clear, easy to follow, and straight to the point. Keep up the good work! I bought several of your books and they are just right! No regrets! I will always buy your books because they are the best."
—Seward Kollie (Dakar, Senegal)

"What fantastic teaching books you have produced! Congratulations to you and your staff."
—Bruno Tonon (Melbourne, Australia)

"Thank you for the wonderful books you produce. It wasn't until I was an adult that I discovered how I learn — visually. Although a few publishers claim to present the materially visually, nothing compares to Visual books. I love the simple layout. Everything is easy to follow. I can just grab a book and use it at my computer, lesson by lesson. And I understand the material! You really know the way I think and learn. Thanks so much!"
—Stacey Han (Avondale, AZ)

"The Greatest. This whole series is the best computer-learning tool of any kind I've ever seen."
—Joe Orr (Brooklyn, NY)

Credits

Senior Acquisitions Editor
Jody Lefevere

Project Editor
Jade L. Williams

Technical Editor
Dee Sadler

Copy Editor
Marylouise Wiack

Editorial Manager
Robyn Siesky

Business Manager
Amy Knies

Senior Marketing Manager
Sandy Smith

Vice President and Executive Group Publisher
Richard Swadley

Vice President and Executive Publisher
Barry Pruett

Project Coordinator
Erin Smith

Graphics and Production Specialists
Ana Carrillo
Carrie A. Cesavice
Andrea Hornberger
Jennifer Mayberry

Proofreading
Melissa D. Buddendeck

Indexing
Broccoli Information Management

Media Development Project Manager
Laura Moss

Media Development Assistant Project Manager
Jenny Swisher

About the Author

Rob Huddleston has been developing web pages and applications since 1994, and has been an instructor since 1999, teaching web and graphic design to thousands of students. His clients have included the United States Bureau of Land Management, the United States Patent and Trademark Office, the States of California and Nevada and many other federal, city and county agencies; the United States Army and Air Force; Fortune 500 companies such as AT&T, Wells Fargo, Safeway, Coca-Cola; software companies including Adobe, Oracle, Intuit and Autodesk; the University of California, San Francisco State University, the University of Southern California; and hundreds of small businesses and non-profit agencies. Rob is an Adobe Certified Instructor, Certified Expert, and Certified Developer, serves as an Adobe User Group Manager and was named as an Adobe Community Expert for his volunteer work answering user questions in online forums. He has been a beta tester for the last few versions of Dreamweaver and Flash, and now serves as an expert moderator on Adobe's Community Help system. Rob lives in Northern California with his wife and two children.

Rob is the author of *XML: Your visual blueprint™ to creating expert websites using XML, CSS, XHTML, and XSLT* and *HTML, XHTML and CSS: Your visual blueprint™ to creating efficient websites.* You can visit Rob's blog at www.robhuddleston.com.

Author's Acknowledgments

This book is dedicated to my wife Kelley and my children, Jessica and Xander. Without your love and support, I couldn't possibly do this. I love you all.

I also would like to thank Jody Lefevere for letting me take on this project, Jade Williams for all of the help and support as my Project Editor, Marylouise Wiack for the phenomenal copy editing, and Dee Sadler for the keeping my honest with your technical editing. You were a fantastic group of people to work with.

As always, I need to thank my parents for their support and for being the "proud parents" who keep the rest of the family informed of my goings-on when I get too involved writing to do so. To Brian and Laura Armstrong: thank you for allowing me to use your wedding photos in the Flash chapters. I wish you all my best in your life together.

Finally, thank you to Gordon Clarke for introducing me to the user group world and for trusting me with your group when you left, as well as a great big thank you to Ted Fitzpatrick and the members of the Sierra Adobe Multimedia User Group for continuing to show up every month. I would urge all readers to visit http://groups.adobe.com to find and join your local Adobe user group.

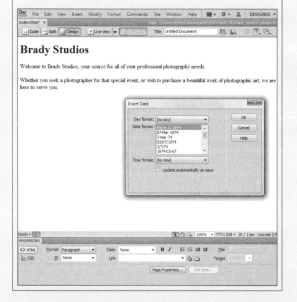

WHAT'S INSIDE

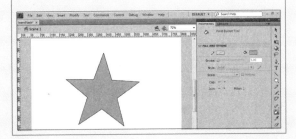

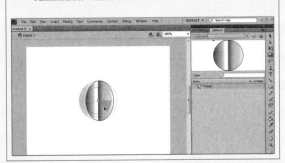

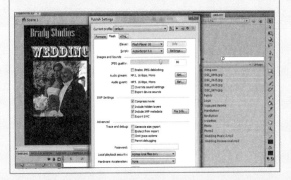

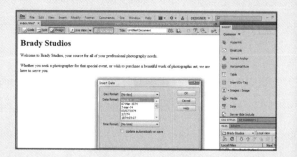

TABLE OF CONTENTS

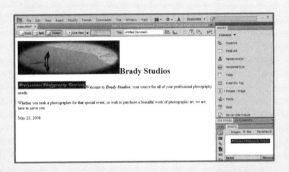

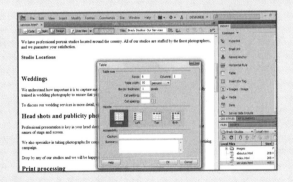

7 Format with Style Sheets

8 Lay Out Pages

PART III Advanced Dreamweaver Features

9 Reuse Web Page Components

TABLE OF CONTENTS

10 Attach Behaviors to Web Page Elements

11 Add Web Page Elements and Effects with the Spry Framework

12 Work with (X)HTML Code

13 Manage a Web Site

⑭ Work in a Team

⑮ Customize Dreamweaver

PART IV   Create a Dynamic Site

⑯ Set Up a Dynamic Site

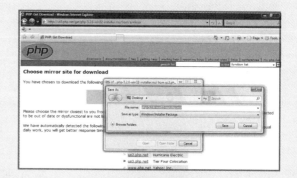

TABLE OF CONTENTS

⓱ Create Forms

⓲ Validate Data with Spry

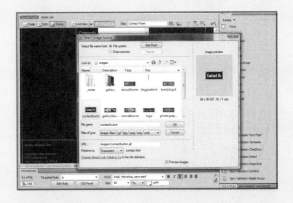

⓳ Integrate a Database with a Site

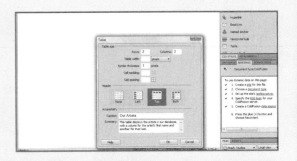

20 Work with Data-Driven Pages

21 Modify Database Information from Your Site

22 Advanced Dynamic Topics

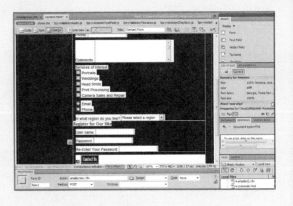

TABLE OF CONTENTS

PART V — Mastering Flash Basics

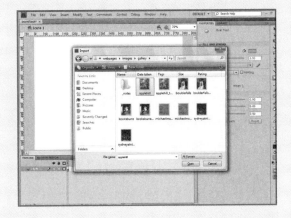

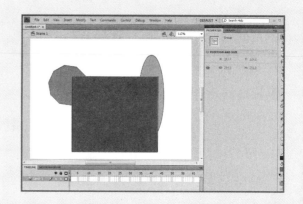

26 Work with Text

PART VI Adding Movie Elements

27 Work with Layers

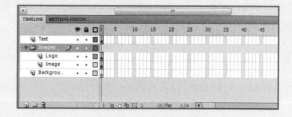

28 Work with Symbols and Instances

TABLE OF CONTENTS

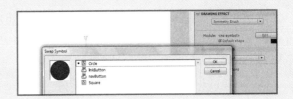

PART VII — Animate in Flash

29 Create Basic Animation with Flash

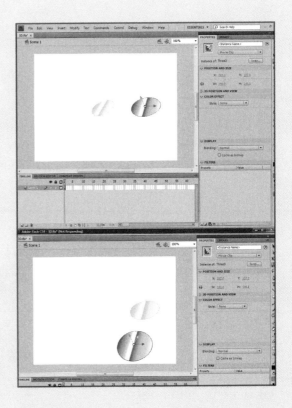

30 Modify Tweens

PART VIII Add Sound and Video

PART IX Implement Actionscript in Your Movie

TABLE OF CONTENTS

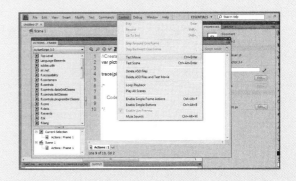

34 Use ActionScript in Your Movie

35 Work with Text in ActionScript

PART X   Finalizing Your Project

36 Publish Your Project

37 Integrate Flash and Dreamweaver

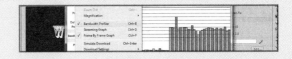

How to Use This Master VISUALLY Book

Do you look at the pictures in a book or newspaper before anything else on a page? Would you rather see an image than read how to do something? Search no further. This book is for you. Opening *Master VISUALLY Dreamweaver CS4 and Flash CS4 Professional* allows you to read less and learn more about the Dreamweaver and Flash programs.

Who Needs This Book

This book is for a reader who has never used this particular technology or software application. It is also for more computer literate individuals who want to expand their knowledge of the different features that Dreamweaver and Flash have to offer.

Book Organization

Master VISUALLY Dreamweaver CS4 and Flash CS4 Professional has 37 chapters and is divided into 10 parts.

Part I, "Dreamweaver Basics," introduces the reader to the Dreamweaver application. You will learn how to create a new Web page, discover the Dreamweaver interface, and work with each of the views in the program that allow you to work with your pages. You will also gain understanding of the importance of setting up sites in Dreamweaver and learn how to do so.

Part II, "Add Design Elements," covers the basics of adding content to your Web pages. You will see how you can add paragraphs, headings, lists, and other text elements. You will learn how to add images, including graphics created in Adobe Photoshop CS4, and how to link your documents to other pages you create and to other pages on the Web. You will also explore the use of tables for displaying data, and learn about Cascading Style Sheets and how that technology allows you to format and lay out your pages.

Part III, "Advanced Dreamweaver Features," shows how to reuse page components through Dreamweaver templates, library items and snippets. You will also learn about adding JavaScript to your pages through behaviors and Ajax components through the Adobe Spry framework. You will also look and editing (X)HTML code and how to upload your pages to a Web server. The section also shows how Dreamweaver can be used in a team setting, through its check-in and check-out feature and its integration with Subversion, Adobe Contribute, and Adobe InContext Editing. Finally, you will look at how to customize the program.

Part IV, "Create a Dynamic Site," shows how you can set up a development testing server on your own computer by installing a Web server and either the PHP or Adobe ColdFusion application servers. It shows how to create forms to collect information from your users and validate that data with Adobe Spry. It then details how to use a database online and how you can use Dreamweaver to create pages that display information from the database as well as write new data to it. You will also learn about including external files, using cookies and sessions, and allow your users to upload files to your server from your site.

Part V, "Mastering Flash Basics," introduces Flash CS4 Professional. You will learn about the Flash interface and how to create and save new Flash movies. Then, you will learn about the Flash drawing tools and how to import graphics from Adobe Photoshop CS4. You will also learn how to select and modify objects that you have drawn or imported into your Flash document, how to use Adobe Kuler to choose colors, how to create and modify gradients, and how to work with text in Flash.

Part VI, "Adding Movie Elements," teaches how to work with layers to organize your movie's elements. You will then learn about symbols, the basic building block for creating animation. You will discover the differences between the various symbol types and be shown how to create examples of each.

Part VII, "Animate in Flash," covers the principles of animation in the program. You will learn about the basic ideas behind Flash animation and how to determine settings such as the frame rate, or the speed at which the movie will play. Then, you will learn about frames and keyframes and how to add each to the timeline. Finally, you will discover how to create frame-by-frame, motion tween, and shape tween animation. You will also explore animating in three dimensions and using the new bone tool to create realistic character animation.

Part VIII, "Add Sound and Video," shows how to use sound and video assets in your movie. You will learn about how Flash handles sound files, how to import sounds and how to start and stop them. You will also learn about Flash video, how to convert movies to the Flash video format using the Adobe Media Encoder, and how to embed and play that video in your Flash movie.

Part IX, "Implement ActionScript in Your Movie," introduces you to the concepts of using ActionScript. You will see how to open and use the ActionScript panel. You will also learn how to create and use variables and functions, and learn how to have ActionScript make decisions based on run-time criteria. You will look at using events to trigger code as your movie plays, how to allow your users to drag and drop elements in your movies, and how to animate through code. You will also learn how to work with text through code, populating text fields based on text input by your user.

Part X, "Finalizing Your Project," shows how to publish Flash movies. You will learn about the various Flash file formats, publish a SWF, and change publishing options. You will also learn how to integrate your Flash movie in Dreamweaver to create a Web page that contains both (X)HTML and Flash content.

On the Web site (`www.wiley.com/go/mvdreamweaver flashcs4`) that accompanies this book.

Chapter Organization

This book consists of sections, all listed in the book's table of contents. A section is a set of steps that show you how to complete a specific computer task.

Each section, usually contained on two facing pages, has an introduction to the task at hand, a set of full-color screen shots and steps that walk you through the task, and a set of tips. This format allows you to quickly look at a topic of interest and learn it instantly.

Chapters group together three or more sections with a common theme. A chapter may also contain pages that give you the background information needed to understand the sections in a chapter.

What You Need to Use This Book

In order to complete the steps in this book, you will need a copy of Dreamweaver CS4 and Flash CS4 Professional. Either can be purchased individually or as part of one of the Creative Suite 4 editions. You can also download a 30-day trial of Dreamweaver at `http://www.adobe.com/products/dreamweaver`, and a 30-day trial of Flash at `http://www.adobe.com/products/flash`.

The minimum recommended system requirements for Dreamweaver CS4 on Windows are:

- 1GHz or faster processor
- Microsoft® Windows® XP with Service Pack 2 (Service Pack 3 recommended) or Windows Vista® Home Premium, Business, Ultimate, or Enterprise with Service Pack 1 (certified for 32-bit Windows XP and Windows Vista)
- 512MB of RAM
- 1GB of available hard-disk space for installation; additional free space required during installation (cannot install on flash-based storage devices)
- 1,280x800 display with 16-bit video card
- DVD-ROM drive

The minimum recommended requirements for Dreamweaver CS4 on Macintosh are:

- PowerPC® G5 or multicore Intel® processor

- Mac OS X v10.4.11–10.5.4
- 512MB of RAM
- 1.8GB of available hard-disk space for installation; additional free space required during installation (cannot install on a volume that uses a case-sensitive file system or on flash-based storage devices)
- 1,280x800 display with 16-bit video card
- DVD-ROM drive

For either platform, a broadband internet connection is required for using online services such as Adobe InContext Editing.

The minimum recommended system requirements for Flash CS4 Professional on Windows are:

- 1GHz or faster processor
- Microsoft® Windows® XP with Service Pack 2 (Service Pack 3 recommended) or Windows Vista® Home Premium, Business, Ultimate, or Enterprise with Service Pack 1 (certified for 32-bit Windows XP and Windows Vista)
- 1GB of RAM
- 3.5GB of available hard-disk space for installation; additional free space required during installation (cannot install on flash-based storage devices)
- 1,024x768 display (1,280x800 recommended) with 16-bit video card
- DVD-ROM drive
- QuickTime 7.1.2 software required for multimedia features

The minimum recommended requirements for Flash CS4 Professional on Macintosh are:

- PowerPC® G5 or multicore Intel® processor
- Mac OS X v10.4.11–10.5.4
- 1GB of RAM
- 4GB of available hard-disk space for installation; additional free space required during installation (cannot install on a volume that uses a case-sensitive file system or on flash-based storage devices)
- 1,024x768 display (1,280x800 recommended) with 16-bit video card
- DVD-ROM drive
- QuickTime 7.1.2 software required for multimedia features

In addition, some of the tasks in the book use Adobe Photoshop CS4, which is also available separately or as part of the Creative Suite packages. A 30-day trial of Photoshop is available at http://www.adobe.com/products/photoshop. In order to complete the steps in Chapter 19, you will need an active internet connection in order to download the required software and administrative privileges on your computer in order to install the programs. Detailed instructions on downloading and installing the files are contained in the chapter.

Using the Mouse

This book uses the following conventions to describe the actions you perform when using the mouse:

Click

Press your left mouse button once. You generally click your mouse on something to select something on the screen.

Double-click

Press your left mouse button twice. Double-clicking something on the computer screen generally opens whatever item you have double-clicked.

Right-click

Press your right mouse button. When you right-click anything on the computer screen, the program displays a shortcut menu containing commands specific to the selected item.

Click and Drag, and Release the Mouse

Move your mouse pointer and hover it over an item on the screen. Press and hold down the left mouse button. Now, move the mouse to where you want to place the item and then release the button. You use this method to move an item from one area of the computer screen to another.

The Conventions in This Book

A number of typographic and layout styles have been used throughout Master VISUALLY® Dreamweaver CS4 and Flash CS4 Professional to distinguish different types of information.

Bold

Bold type represents the names of commands and options that you interact with. Bold type also indicates text and numbers that you must type into a dialog box or window.

Italics

Italic words introduce a new term and are followed by a definition.

Numbered Steps

You must perform the instructions in numbered steps in order to successfully complete a section and achieve the final results.

Bulleted Steps

These steps point out various optional features. You do not have to perform these steps; they simply give additional information about a feature.

Indented Text

Indented text tells you what the program does in response to you following a numbered step. For example, if you click a certain menu command, a dialog box may appear, or a window may open. Indented text may also tell you what the final result is when you follow a set of numbered steps.

Notes

Notes give additional information. They may describe special conditions that may occur during an operation. They may warn you of a situation that you want to avoid, for example, the loss of data. A note may also cross reference a related area of the book. A cross reference may guide you to another chapter, or another section within the current chapter.

Icons and Buttons

Icons and buttons are graphical representations within the text. They show you exactly what you need to click to perform a step.

You can easily identify the tips in any section by looking for the Master It icon. Master It offer additional information, including tips, hints, and tricks. You can use the Master It information to go beyond what you have learn learned in the steps.

Operating System Difference

Dreamweaver CS4 and Flash CS4 Professional are mostly the same on both Windows and Macintosh. While all of the screen shots in the book were taken on a computer running Windows Vista, readers using other versions of Windows or those on Macintosh should find that their screens closely resemble those shown in the book. The only key differences between the programs running on Windows or Macintosh are in how each handles standard operating system dialog boxes such as Open and Save. Also, keyboard shortcuts vary between the systems, but wherever possible, the Windows shortcut is given with the Macintosh shortcut provided in parentheses.

1

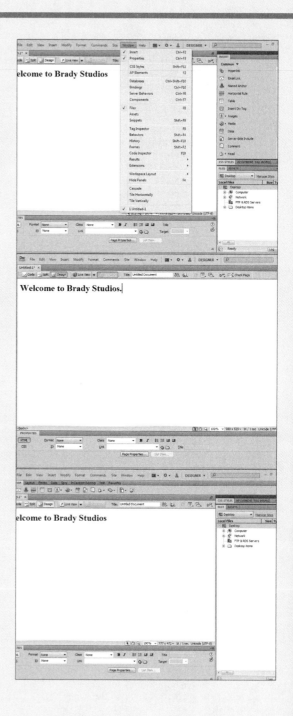

PART I
DREAMWEAVER BASICS

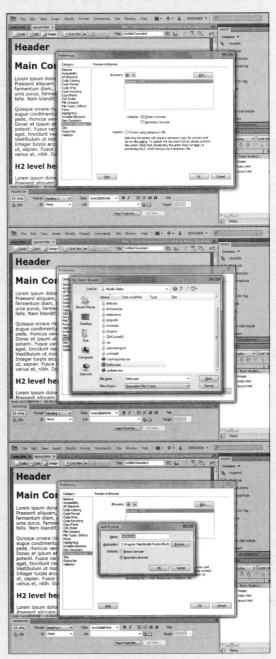

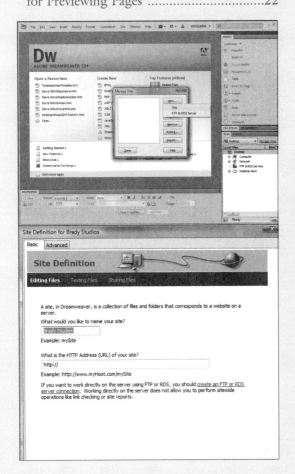

Introduction to the Dreamweaver Interface

With Dreamweaver CS4, Adobe has radically reengineered the Dreamweaver interface to provide a more unified experience across all of the Creative Suite applications. If you are familiar with Photoshop or Illustrator, many of the interface elements will be familiar to you.

The Dreamweaver interface is made up of three basic elements: the menu bar, the panels, and the main workspace. When you first launch Dreamweaver, the main workspace displays the Start Screen.

A Start Screen

Provides a central location to select recently opened files, create new documents in various file types, or create documents from samples.

B Menu Bar

Provides access to menus and commands.

C Layout Menu

Allows you to switch layouts.

D Extend Dreamweaver Menu

Accesses online tools to add additional features to Dreamweaver.

E Site Menu

Provides commands for setting up and modifying site definitions.

F Workspace Menu

Allows you to switch between Dreamweaver's various workspace layouts.

G Search Box

Search Dreamweaver's help files directly by typing a term here.

H Collapse Panels to Icons

Collapses the panels to icons.

I Panels

Collapsible panels provide most of the functionality in the program.

J Property Inspector

Allows you to change properties of objects on your Web page.

Open a Blank Web Page

Y ou can get started creating Web pages in Dreamweaver very quickly by creating a new, blank page. You can then add content and design to your page as you like.

For example, in Windows Vista, Dreamweaver can be launched by clicking the Start button, and then clicking All Programs. Depending on whether you purchased Dreamweaver as a stand-alone product or part of one of the Creative Suite packages, you will find an appropriately labeled Adobe folder from which you can click Dreamweaver CS4.

The Start Page, which displays when Dreamweaver first opens or when you have no other documents open, provides quick links to create a blank page in a variety of formats. HTML creates a basic blank document. ColdFusion, PHP, and ASP VBScript create pages that allow you to start building dynamic sites, a topic that is covered in detail in Part IV of this book. XSLT is a special format that works with XML documents. The final three page options create a Cascading Style Sheet, JavaScript, or an XML document. The final option in the column lets you set up a Dreamweaver site, which is covered in Chapter 2.

Open a Blank Web Page

1 Open Adobe Dreamweaver CS4.

2 Click HTML.

● A new, blank document opens.

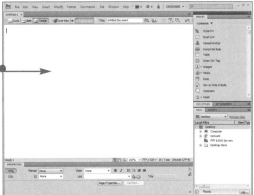

Add Text in Design View

You can use Dreamweaver's Design view to see a representation of what your page may look like in a Web browser. You can create entire pages, and even entire sites, in Design view without ever touching the underlying code. As you insert objects into your page in Design view, Dreamweaver writes the code for you, using proper (X)HTML, Cascading Style Sheets (CSS), JavaScript, or other languages based on the document type and your preferences. Conversely, any items you delete from Design view have their corresponding code deleted as well.

The Property Inspector, the panel that runs along the bottom of the screen, allows you to modify the properties or settings of objects after you have inserted them. These changes are immediately reflected in the Design view interface, as are any other changes that you make through other panels.

While Design view gives you a representation of what your page will look like in a Web browser, it also displays additional page elements that may assist you in designing and working with your documents but that would not normally appear in a Web browser.

Add Text in Design View

① Click Design from the Document toolbar.

The document displays in Design view.

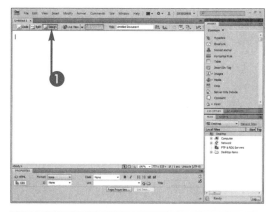

② Type some text in the page.

The text displays as it would in a Web browser.

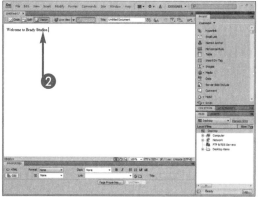

Enter Code in Code View

You can accomplish most of your work in Dreamweaver in Design view, but there may be times when you need to edit the underlying code of a page directly. For these situations, Dreamweaver provides a powerful code-editing environment.

Code view allows you to enter (X)HTML, CSS, JavaScript, or other code. It provides code hints for all of the languages it supports, as well as line numbers and customizable color-coding to make reading and editing code easier.

All of the panels that you use in Design view to work with your pages are available in Code view. Any changes made in Code view are reflected in Design view, and vice versa, and so it is possible to freely switch between the two views as needed while editing pages.

The Code view toolbar gives you additional functionality when working in this environment. Running down the left edge of the screen, the toolbar lets you open pages, expand and collapse blocks of code, turn line numbering on and off, insert and remove comments, and more.

Enter Code in Code View

① Click Code in the Document toolbar.

The document switches to Code view.

② Type < to begin a new HTML tag.

③ From the code hints, select an element you want to use and then press Enter.

● Dreamweaver inserts the tag name.

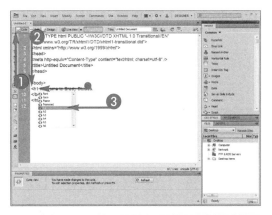

④ Type > to finish the tag.

⑤ Type the text to be marked up by the tag.

⑥ Type </.

● Dreamweaver inserts the closing tag.

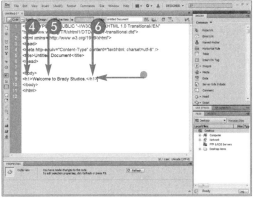

Explore Split View

Dreamweaver offers a third view that provides the best features of both Design and Code view. Split view divides the screen in half, showing Code view on the top of the screen and Design view on the bottom, although you can switch these if you prefer. A divider bar that separates the two allows you to give more screen space to either view as needed.

Clicking in the Design half of the screen allows you to work in the same way you would in Design view, but you are now able to see the underlying code as

Dreamweaver writes it. The reverse is also true: if you click in the Code half and type code, you see the results appear in real-time in Design view.

The disadvantage of Split view is that, except for very large monitors, you do not have much room in either of the two sections to work effectively, and so many designers use it sparingly. However, it is a good way to have Dreamweaver help teach you the code, as you can focus on your work in the Design section but then immediately see the associated code.

Explore Split View

1 Click Split in the Document toolbar.

The document displays in Split view.

2 Click-and-drag the gray bar that separates the two sections to resize them.

Dreamweaver resizes the sections.

3 Click View.

4 Click Design View on Top.

Dreamweaver swaps the position of the Code and Design views.

5 Click in the Design view and type some text.

● The text also appears in the Code view.

Can I select the same portion of the page in both the Code and Design sections of the Split view?	Can I split the screen vertically as well as horizontally?
▼ Yes. Any page element you select in the Design pane automatically has its code selected in the Code pane, and vice versa. There may be times when you need to edit a piece of code in a particularly long page where it can be difficult to find the specific block of text. Using the Split view, you could scroll the Design section to the section you need to edit, and immediately the Code view scrolls to that same section of the page and places your cursor in the code that matches the Design selection.	▼ Yes. In Dreamweaver CS4, you can orient the split to show the pages side-by-side, rather than having one on top of the other. When you are in Split view, click View, and then click Split Vertically. Dreamweaver will remember this setting until you deselect it, and so if you switch back to Design or Code view, your screen will still split vertically next time you switch to Split view. When you are using the vertical split, you can choose on which side the Design screen and Code screens appear by clicking Edit, and then clicking Design View on Left.

Explore the Panels

You can access most of the features of Dreamweaver through panels along the sides of the window. Each panel provides a specific set of functions, and related panels are grouped together.

You can expand or collapse a panel by double-clicking the tab that contains the panel's name. When in a panel group, individual panels can be accessed by clicking the tabs. You can move panels to other locations on the screen or into other groups by dragging their tabs.

This set of panels that runs along the right edge of the screen can be collapsed to icons with labels so that it takes up very little room, a feature that is particularly handy for designers working on small screens. The set can be further resized to show only icons as well. Once the panels have been collapsed to icons, you can access a panel temporarily by clicking its icon. The panel collapses again as soon as you click elsewhere on the screen. The Window menu provides a list of every panel available in Dreamweaver, and allows you to open panels that are not currently visible.

1 Click Window.

- Dreamweaver displays a check mark next to each panel that is currently open.

2 Double-click a panel's tab to expand or collapse it.

- In this example, the panel expands to show its features.

3 Click the Collapse to Icons button.

- The main panel set collapses to show icons and labels.

4 Drag the left edge of the icons to the right.

The icons collapse further, hiding the labels.

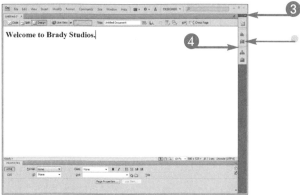

⑤ Click the Expand Panels button.

The panel set expands.

⑥ Click-and-drag the Insert panel to the top of the screen, just below the menu bar.

The panel repositions itself.

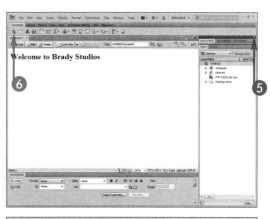

⑦ Drag the tab of a panel.

The panel floats on the screen.

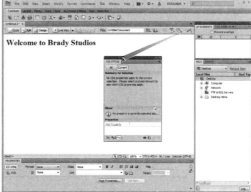

Can I quickly show or hide all of the panels at once?

▼ Yes. Simply press the F4 key on your keyboard, which hides all of the panels. Pressing F4 a second time brings them all back, in the positions in which they were when you hid them.

Is it possible to hide all of the panels and then have them simply appear when I need them?

▼ Yes. If you hide all of the panels using the F4 keyboard shortcut, you see a gray bar where the panels were. If you simply move the mouse over that bar, the panels in that area reappear, and then disappear again when you move your mouse away from them.

Can I put panels on the other side of the screen?

▼ Yes. You can drag panels to any edge of the screen. When you see a thin blue line appear, release your mouse and the panel docks along that edge. You can also have two columns of panels along either the right or left edge, or two rows along the top or bottom.

View
Workspaces

Dreamweaver provides a set of panel layouts called *workspaces*. You can use the workspace menu in the upper-right corner of the screen to switch between workspaces whenever you want.

Eight workspaces are available by default in the program. Designer, the default workspace, shows those panels most likely to be used by Web designers creating static pages. App Developer and App Developer Plus display the panels used by those creating dynamic Web sites, a topic covered in Part IV of this book.

Classic provides the panels that were available by default in older versions of Dreamweaver, and places the Insert panel along the top of the screen. Coder displays a set of panels along the left edge of the screen, while Coder Plus adds several more along the right edge. Designer Compact shows the same panels as Designer, but collapses them to icons by default. Dual Screen undocks all of the panels so that they are floating and can be easily moved to another monitor. If you select a workspace, change its panel layout, and then want to revert to the saved version, you can do so by reselecting the workspace from the menu.

View Workspaces

1 Click Designer to access the Workspace menu.

2 Select Classic.

● Dreamweaver rearranges the panels.

3 From the Workspace menu, click Designer Compact.

The panels are rearranged.

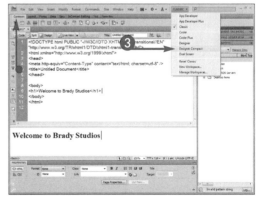

④ Click-and-drag the Insert panel into the middle of the screen.

The panel floats on the screen.

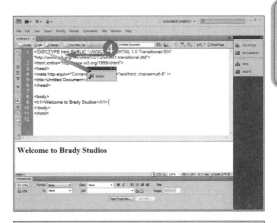

⑤ From the Workspace menu, click Designer Compact.

The panel layout is restored.

Can I create my own workspaces?

▼ Yes. You should begin by selecting the pre-installed workspace that has the panel arrangement closest to the one you want. Then, you can move panels to other locations on the screen, close those panels you will not be using, or open and position additional panels. Once you have the panel arrangement you want, you can click the workspace menu, choose New Workspace, and then give it a logical name. It then appears with the other workspaces so that you can switch to it whenever you want.

Can I delete workspaces?

▼ You cannot delete any of the workspaces that are preinstalled with Dreamweaver, but you can rename or delete workspaces that you create by clicking the workspace menu and selecting Manage Workspaces. This displays a dialog box that lists all of the workspaces you have created. When you select one, you can rename or delete it.

Create a Site in Basic Mode

You primarily use Dreamweaver to create and edit Web sites — collections of related pages. While it is possible to work with individual pages, you will find that many advanced features only become available when you define a site.

Before you begin defining a site, you need to create a folder on your computer that will contain the files to be used in your site. This folder, called the site root, can be placed anywhere you normally store files; for example, in a Microsoft Windows environment, you would probably place the folder in My Documents.

Defining a site in Dreamweaver basically allows you to tell the program where the site's files reside on your computer, so that it can locate them and enable its site-management features.

One method of creating a site relies on Basic mode, in which you simply follow a wizard and answer a series of questions about your site. The only piece of information you need before you begin is the location of the site files.

Create a Site in Basic Mode

① From the Files panel, click Manage Sites.

Note: If you do not see the Files panel, click Window, and then click Files.

The Manage Sites dialog box appears.

② Click New.

③ Click Site.

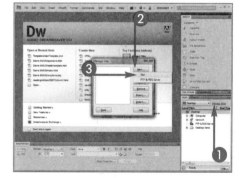

The Site Definition dialog box appears on the first page of the wizard.

④ If necessary, click Basic.

⑤ Type a name for the site.

Note: You can leave the HTTP address blank, or type the address for your Web site.

⑥ Click Next.

The next page of the wizard displays.

⑦ Select No, I do not want to use a server technology.

Note: Server technologies are discussed in Part IV.

⑧ Click Next.

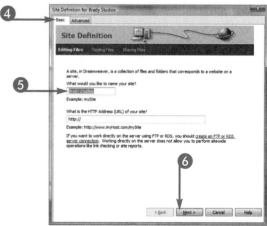

The next page of the wizard displays.

9 If necessary, click Edit local copies on my machine, then upload to server when ready (recommended).

10 Type the path to the folder that contains your files.

11 Click Next to display the next page.

12 Choose None from the drop-down list.

13 Click Next.

The next page of the wizard displays.

14 Click Done.

The wizard closes and the Manage Sites dialog box reappears.

15 Click Done.

The site is created and the Files panel updates to show the site's files.

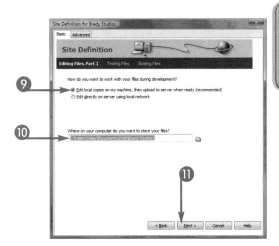

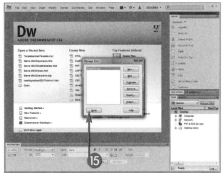

What if I need to store my files on a network drive?

▼ Dreamweaver always refers to a local path for the site files, but it is okay if they are on a shared network drive. If you use Windows and the drive is mapped to a letter, simply type the path as you would; for example, you might type **s:/files/website** if the network drive was mapped as the *S* drive. If the drive is not mapped, you can type the address in the format **server_address\directory**.

What name should I use for the site?

▼ The name for the site can be anything you want. Most often, it will relate in some way to the name or purpose of the Web site, but it does not necessarily have to. The site's name is purely for your own reference when using the program.

Create a Site in Advanced Mode

While you can quickly create sites using Basic mode, Dreamweaver also allows you to create sites in Advanced mode. Advanced mode presents its settings in the form of a dialog box with selectable categories instead of the wizardlike approach used in Basic mode.

Defining a site in Advanced mode offers several advantages over Basic mode. You can define a default images directory, which ensures that if Dreamweaver copies images into your site, they will be properly placed. You can define whether you want the site to

use document or site-root relative paths, which is explained in Chapter 5, and instruct Dreamweaver to honor case-sensitivity when checking links. If you are using a server technology such as ColdFusion or PHP, you can define the settings required to test your pages.

If you work with a team of developers or designers, you can set up and control Design Notes, type the settings to communicate with a Subversion server, and set up the site to use Adobe Contribute. Each of these topics is discussed in Chapter 14.

Create a Site in Advanced Mode

① From the Files panel, click Manage Sites.

Note: If you do not see the Files panel, click Window, and then click Files.

② In the Manage Sites dialog box, click New.

③ Click Site.

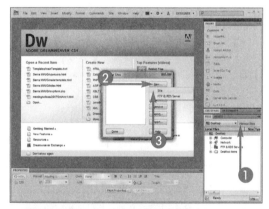

The Site Definition dialog box appears.

④ Click Advanced.

⑤ From Categories, click Local Info.

⑥ Type a name for the site.

⑦ Type the path to the site's root folder.

Note: You can also click the folder icon to browse to the root.

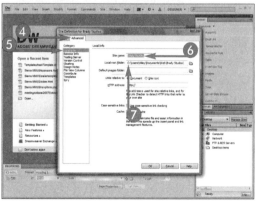

8 Type the path to the default images directory.

9 Click OK.

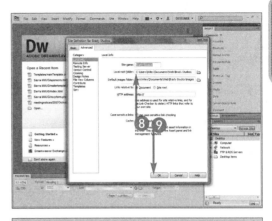

The dialog box closes and the Manage Sites dialog box reappears.

10 Click Done.

The site is created and the Files panel updates to show the site's files.

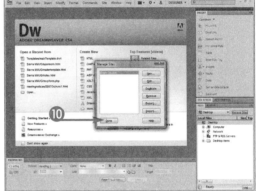

Can I edit sites in one mode if I create them in another?

▼ Yes. In fact, many designers use Basic mode to create the site, and then edit the site's settings as needed in Advanced mode. Any information you type in one mode is copied into the appropriate sections in the other, and you can freely switch between them if you want.

What does it mean if Dreamweaver displays an error that says that the root folder of my site is inside the folder for another site?

▼ Each site should have its own root folder, independent of other sites. However, it is possible to define a site within a site. The vast majority of features within Dreamweaver work in this situation, but you can run into problems with some of the more complex site features such as synchronization.

How many sites can I create?

▼ There is no limit to the number of sites that can be defined in Dreamweaver. You simply need to ensure that each site is given a unique name.

Create a Web Page

You can create new Web pages in many different ways in Dreamweaver. If you are familiar with other programs, the most obvious way is to select New from the File menu. The New Document dialog box allows you to create a basic, blank page in one of 17 file types, a new blank template, a new page based on an existing template (Dreamweaver templates are discussed in Chapter 9), a page from one of several dozen starter pages, or a document using several other programming languages, such as C# or Java.

If you have a design in mind that you plan to create from scratch, you can choose a new, blank HTML page with no layout. You can also choose a document type definition, or DOCTYPE, you want to use for the page. DOCTYPEs tell the Web browser which version of HTML or XHTML you are using and how you want the page to be interpreted. The most common DOCTYPE used by Dreamweaver is XHTML 1.0 Transitional. You can choose to use a different DOCTYPE by selecting it from the drop-down menu in the corner of the dialog box.

Create a Web Page

1 Click File in the menu bar.

2 Click New.

The New Document dialog box appears.

3 Choose Blank Page.

4 Choose HTML in the Page Type list and choose <none> in the Layout list.

5 In the DocType drop-down list, select XHTML 1.0 Transitional.

6 Click Create.

Dreamweaver creates a new, blank Web page.

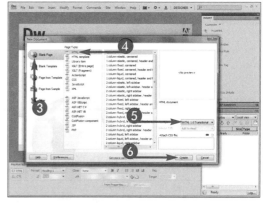

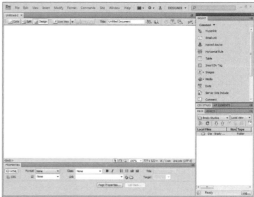

Save a New Web Page

Y ou should get in the habit of saving your new Web page in Dreamweaver before you do any other work. Certain features of the program, such as creating hyperlinks and inserting images, generate extra dialog boxes and warnings if the page has not already been saved.

Your pages need to be saved in your site folder. Certain pages, such as the home page, need to be directly in the root folder. Beyond that, you can feel free to organize your site in any way that makes sense to you. Some designers like to create many layers of subfolders, while others prefer simpler

structures with only one layer of subfolders. The only thing that is really important in that regard is that the site's organization be logical to you.

You must follow some rules in naming your Web pages. Your filenames cannot contain spaces, and filenames should begin with a letter, not a number, and can be made up of only letters, numbers, underscores, and dashes. Depending on the operating system of the server to which you upload your files, your filename may be case-sensitive, so it is a good idea to always use all lowercase letters.

Save a New Web Page

① Click File.

② Click Save As.

The Save As dialog box appears.

③ If necessary, navigate to the folder in your site into which you want to save the file.

④ Type a filename.

⑤ Click Save.

The file is saved.

Create a New Page from a Starter Layout

You can use one of the almost three dozen page layouts that come with Dreamweaver to jump-start your design process. All of these layouts rely on Cascading Style Sheets and the latest Web standards, while being compatible with older browsers as well.

The starter layouts cover many of the most popular layouts used on the Web today, including one-, two-, and three-column designs with and without headers and footers, organized into four basic categories. Fixed layouts use widths set in pixels for their page elements, and so the columns always remain at their preset size, regardless of the size or resolution of the user's screen. Liquid designs use percentages for the widths, and so the columns expand or collapse based on the user's screen size and resolution. Elastic layouts rely on a unit called an *em* for their measurements, which means that the size of the column expands or collapses based on the current font size. Hybrid layouts combine elements of both elastic and liquid designs, where one of the columns uses percents and the other ems. You can also choose one of the two layouts that use absolutely positioned columns.

Create a New Page from a Starter Layout

① Click File.

② Click New.

The New Document dialog box appears.

③ Choose Blank Page.

④ Choose HTML in the Page Type list, and select the layout you want to use in the Layout list.

⑤ Click Create.

Dreamweaver creates a new Web page based on a starter page.

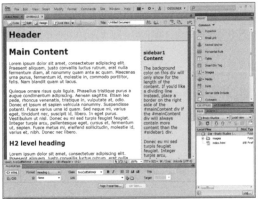

Preview a Web Page in a Browser

You can get a good idea of what your page will look like in a Web browser while using Design view in Dreamweaver. However, you also need to preview the page in an actual browser on a regular basis, as there are times when Design view does not correctly render pages.

The most important reason to preview in a browser is that since the early days of the Web, browsers have never absolutely agreed on how Web pages should display. Microsoft Internet Explorer, Mozilla

Firefox, and Apple Safari — the three most popular browsers — each use a different underlying rendering engine that provides the instructions as to how pages should look, and as such there are always variances in display. Sometimes these differences are minor, but at other times your layout may appear radically different, and some elements may fail to appear at all. The only way to effectively test for this is to view your page in each browser, and then return to Dreamweaver to make the necessary changes to fix problems you see.

Preview a Web Page in a Browser

① From the Document toolbar, click the Preview in Browser button.

② Click Preview in IExplore.

Note: If you see a different browser, select it instead.

Note: If necessary, click Yes to save the page.

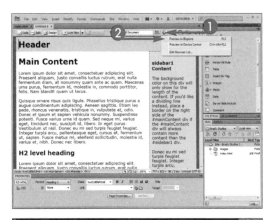

Internet Explorer opens and displays the Web page.

Add Additional Browsers for Previewing Pages

You can set up Dreamweaver to recognize as many Web browsers as you want for previewing. You need to designate one of those browsers as the primary one, which means it will be listed first on the Preview in Browser button and be accessible through the F12 keyboard shortcut. You can designate another browser as your secondary one, which you can open through the Control+F12 shortcut. Any other browsers you install are only easily accessible by selecting them from the Preview in Browser button.

If you are using Microsoft Windows, you already have a copy of Internet Explorer on your computer, and when you install Dreamweaver, it should detect that browser and set it as primary. At a minimum, you should also download and install Mozilla Firefox, which you can get for free from www.getfirefox.com, and Apple Safari, which is also free from www.apple.com/downloads/macosx/apple/windows/. Both provide simple installation wizards, and a default installation works fine for previewing pages. Any browsers that are installed after Dreamweaver are not available automatically, but you can easily add them to the list of browsers.

Add Additional Browsers for Previewing Pages

1 Click Edit.

2 Click Preferences.

   The Preferences dialog box appears.

3 Click Preview in Browser.

4 Click the Add button.

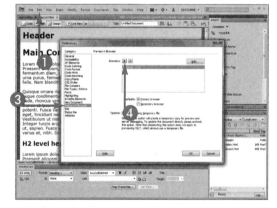

5 Click Browse from the Preferences dialog box that appears.

6 Navigate to the EXE file for the browser.

7 Click Open.

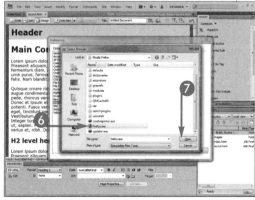

8 If you want, change the name that will display for the browser.

9 Click the Secondary browser option (☐ changes to ☑).

10 Click OK.

11 Click OK.

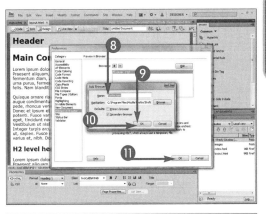

12 From the Document toolbar, click the Preview in Browser button.

The new browser appears in the list.

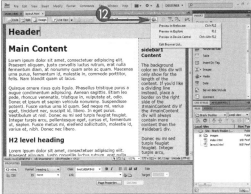

How can I test my page in more than one version of Internet Explorer?

▼ Unfortunately, Microsoft has always made it very difficult to run more than one version of its browser at a time. You can use its Virtual PC software, which allows you to run a second version of Windows, but that can be difficult to set up and requires that you buy another Windows license if you want to use it beyond a 120-day trial. There are hacks available that allow you to install more than one version of Internet Explorer at a time, but they can make your computer unstable and require that you edit the Windows registry. Some designers use a second computer with an older version of the browser, while others ask friends or co-workers who use a different version to test for them.

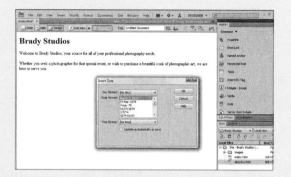

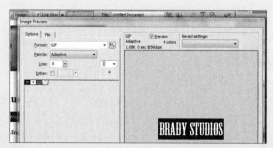

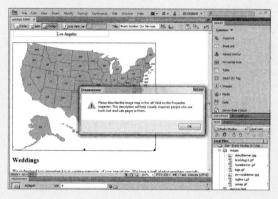

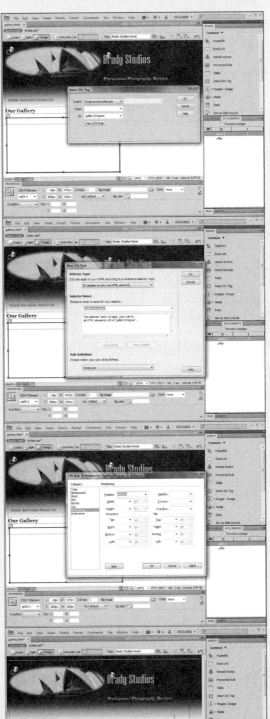

Add Paragraphs

I n (X)HTML, the basic unit of text is a paragraph. To create a paragraph, you simply begin typing in the Design view window. When you are done with the paragraph, you press Enter on your keyboard. Dreamweaver wraps the (X)HTML paragraph tags around the text you just completed typing, as well as creating a new set of tags for the text you will be typing next. You cannot see these tags unless you switch to Code view or Split view, but they are there.

You may find it odd that pressing Enter creates an extra space between the paragraphs, and that the first line of the text is not indented. This is actually due to the fact that in (X)HTML, paragraphs are designated with a default amount of space above and below and no indentation. You may be expecting the indentation because that is what you were taught in school, but in fact, outside of most fiction and newspapers, very few publications today still use first-line indentation for paragraphs and instead use space before and after paragraphs.

Add Paragraphs

① Click in the Design view window.

② Type text.

3 Press Enter.

Dreamweaver creates a new paragraph.

4 Type more text.

The text appears on the page with space between the paragraphs.

Can I do anything about the amount of space between the paragraphs?

▼ Yes. You can use Cascading Style Sheets to control the amount of space, so that you can either increase or decrease it to fit your design needs. You are shown how to do this in Chapter 8.

Can I change the font being used by the paragraph? How about the size and color of the text?

▼ These and all other formatting issues can be handled easily by CSS, and this is discussed in Chapter 7. There is a natural tendency to want to rush ahead and start making your pages look nice as you create them, but you should try to resist this as much as possible. Ensuring that you have content that is readable and logically structured is more important to the success and usability of the site than any formatting. You will find that if you focus first on content and structure, and then later on visual design, thereby making sure that your design follows your content, you will end up with a site that can be very usable and visually interesting.

Add Headings

S tudies have shown conclusively that most people scan, rather than read, Web pages. You can make your pages much easier to scan by dividing the content into logical sections, with each section set off by a heading.

(X)HTML provides six heading levels. Heading 1 is for the main topic on the page. Any subtopics below that should be marked as heading 2, with subtopics under heading 2 being marked as heading 3, and so forth. Every page should at least have a heading 1, preferably at or near the top. You should not skip heading levels, so do not place a heading 4 directly under a heading 2 without a heading 3 between them.

You can convert any block of text to a heading in Dreamweaver by clicking within the block and selecting the appropriate heading level from the Property Inspector. You can also create headings by first clicking on a new line and then selecting the heading from the Property Inspector before you start typing. Because it is considered to be a bad practice to have consecutive headings without body text between them, when you press Enter after typing a heading Dreamweaver automatically switches to a paragraph for the next line.

Add Headings

1 Click in the Design view window.

2 Type a line of text to serve as a heading.

3 Click the HTML button on the Property Inspector.

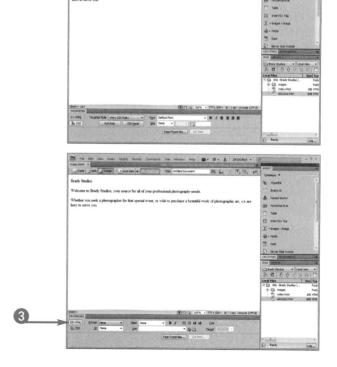

④ Click the Format drop-down menu.

⑤ Click Heading 1.

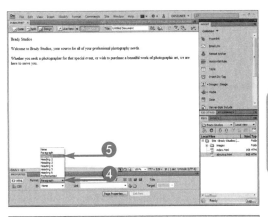

The text is formatted as a level 1 heading.

The size of the text for heading 1 seems far too big. Can I just go ahead and use a heading 2 or 3 instead, because they are smaller?

▼ You should always use the appropriate level of heading based on the context in the page, so the main heading needs to always be heading 1. Do not worry about the size of the text, as that can be changed through CSS. You will also note that the text of headings is bold by default, which is another property that you can alter later through CSS.

I heard somewhere that headings help with search engine rankings. Is that true?

▼ Yes. Modern search engines scan your page in much the same way that your readers will, picking up on the important words in your text. One way that they can distinguish what is important is through the headings — they can assume, for instance, that words in a level 1 heading are very important, because you have chosen to make those the main heading on your page. Text within a heading 2 is less important than the heading 1 text, but more important than words found in a regular paragraph.

Insert Objects Using the Insert Panel

While the majority of your page will likely be text, and much of that will be formatted as paragraphs or headings, you can also use many other elements on your site, including images, tables of data, hyperlinks, and more. One of the most common ways of inserting these elements is through the Insert panel.

The Insert panel is divided into a series of categories, which you can access from a menu at the top of the panel. You can insert items from the panel by clicking

most of the buttons. Some, however, provide a menu of additional items. These are denoted by a small arrow to the right of the icon for the button. When you first view the Insert panel, these buttons display a generic name, such as Images, but once you select an item from them, they change to show the most-recently used button and label.

Like all other panels, you can reposition the Insert panel so that it sits along any edge of the screen.

Insert Objects Using the Insert Panel

1 Click the Insert panel's category menu.

The menu appears.

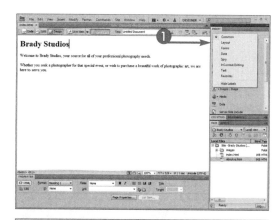

2 Click Common.

The Common category's buttons appear.

3 Click Date.

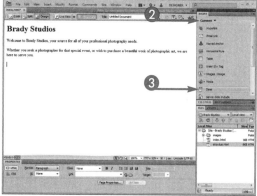

The Insert Date dialog box appears.

④ Select a date format.

⑤ Click OK.

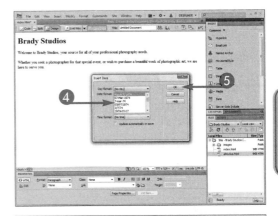

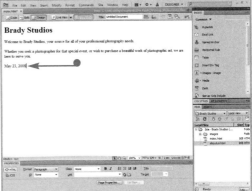

● The current date is inserted into the document.

I notice that the last category in the menu is Favorites, but it does not appear to have anything in it. What is it used for?

▼ The Favorites category allows you to customize the menu to suit your needs. Any button from any of the other categories can be added to Favorites. To do this, right-click anywhere in the Insert panel and click Customize Favorites. This opens a dialog box with all of the available commands from the Insert bar in a list on the left. Click one of the items and then click the button in the middle of the dialog box to add that command to the Favorites category.

Favorites is useful if you are constantly switching between two or three categories to access one or two buttons in each, as all of those could be added to the Favorites category and then accessed together.

Apply (X)HTML Formatting with the Property Inspector

You can emphasize text on your page by applying bold and italic formatting using the Property Inspector. You can apply bold or italic to any text on your page, including entire paragraphs, individual words, or even selected letters.

When you click the Bold button on the Property Inspector, Dreamweaver adds a `<strong>` tag to your code. Clicking the Italic button adds an `<em>` tag, which is short for emphasis. Both of these have logical meaning in your page: They tell the browser — and other devices that may be accessing your page, such

as a screen reader for the visually impaired — that you are emphasizing that text if you apply italics, and strongly emphasizing it if you apply bold. Therefore, these should only be used for those pieces of your text that you want to emphasize. If you are merely trying to make text such as a company name stand out on a page, you are better off using CSS to apply the formatting, which is discussed in Chapter 7.

Like all panels, the Property Inspector can be moved around on the screen, although it always appears along the bottom in any of the preset workspace layouts.

1 Click and drag across some of the text on your page to select it.

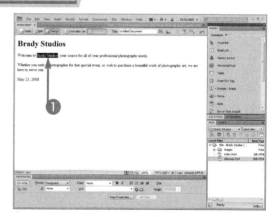

2 Click the Bold button.

The text is formatted as bold.

③ Click the Italic button.

The text is italicized.

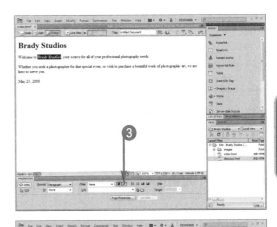

④ Click in another place in the text to deselect it.

The text is deselected.

Why is there not an Underline button along with the Bold and Italic buttons?

▼ While it is technically possible to underline text on your page, you should never do so. Web users have become accustomed to assuming that any underlined text is a hyperlink, and will become confused when they encounter text that is underlined but is not a link. Many users will try to click the text anyway and may get frustrated, wondering why the text is not functioning as they think it should.

Because it is universally agreed that underlining should be avoided on Web pages, Dreamweaver does not provide a button to apply it. Hyperlinks, by the way, are underlined automatically, as you see in Chapter 5.

How can I apply other formatting, such as changing the font or color?

▼ All other formatting options, such as changing the font or the size or color of text, is done through Cascading Style Sheets (CSS). Using CSS and applying these and many other format options will be covered in Chapter 7.

PART II

Create Lists

Another element that is used often in a site is lists. For example, you may end up listing your products or services or employees. If your business has more than one location, you may have a list of those offices. Less obvious but more common, you will have hyperlinks to the pages in your site — your navigation — which is ultimately a list and is most often marked up as such.

(X)HTML provides for three types of lists. The two most common are unordered lists, which denote each

item with a bullet, and ordered lists, where each item is numbered. You can create either of these list types by clicking a button on the Property Inspector. You can change a preexisting set of paragraphs into a list, or click the button before you start typing and create the list as you go. Dreamweaver automatically adds a new list item each time you press Enter. The final type of list, a definition list, is less common, but can be created from the List submenu of the Format menu.

Create Lists

① Click to create a new line of text in a document.

② Click the Unordered List button on the Property Inspector.

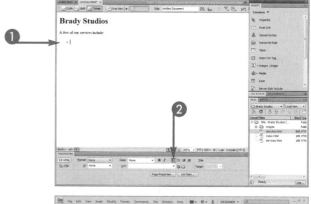

③ Type a list item.

④ Press Enter to create a new item.

⑤ Repeat steps **3** and **4** for each additional item you want to add to the list.

⑥ Press Enter twice to end the list.

Can I have lists nested within lists?

▼ Yes. If you click the Text Indent button on the Property Inspector, your current list item is indented below the last one, creating a nested list. The nested list uses a slightly different bullet if you are using an unordered list. Clicking the Text Outdent button returns you to the outer list if you need to add more items to it. You can have as many levels of nesting within a single list as you want. You can also combine list types, so an unordered list can contain a nested ordered list.

Can I control what the bullet looks like or the numbering system used by the list?

▼ Yes. CSS allows you to change the bullets on unordered lists. You can have a filled-in circle, an open circle, or a square, or you can create your own graphic and use it. You can also change the numbering system for ordered lists through CSS, which actually provides 17 different numbering schemes. Using CSS to format lists is covered in Chapter 8.

Insert a Line Break

When you add a paragraph to your page, it spans the width of the browser window by default, and the browser automatically wraps the lines of the paragraph at that point. There may be times when you want to force the Web browser to break the lines of a paragraph at a specific point, rather than the edge of the window. This can be accomplished by adding a line break to your page.

When you separate content into distinct lines with a line break, that content is still part of the same paragraph, and so formatting applied to the

paragraph as a whole affects lines both before and after the break. For this reason, you should not use the line break as a substitute for paragraphs simply to avoid the extra space that normally appears above and below the paragraph. (As you see in Chapter 8, you can easily use CSS to control this space.) Instead, line breaks should be reserved for those times when you need content that is logically related to simply appear on separate lines, such as with a mailing address.

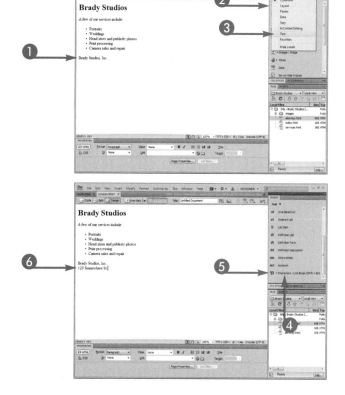

1 Type the first line of the content that will contain the break.

2 From the Insert panel, click the category menu.

3 Click Text.

The Insert panel changes to display text objects.

4 Click Characters.

5 Click BR.

A line break is inserted.

6 Type the second line of content.

Insert a Horizontal Rule

There may be times when you want to visually separate the content on your page. For example, you may have a footer that contains the copyright and contact information for your site, or you may simply have two or three distinct blocks of information on the same page.

(X)HTML includes a horizontal rule tag, which instructs the browser to draw a visible line across the page. By default, the rule has a slightly raised appearance, is dark gray, and stretches across the width of the page. All of these properties, as well as other formatting options for the rule, can be precisely controlled through CSS.

While the rule can be useful in visually separating content on the page, you should be careful to avoid overusing it, as was frequently done in the early days of the Web to substitute for the lack of borders on any elements of the page other than tables. Today, CSS allows you to set borders — both horizontal and vertical — on any element, and so horizontal rules should be limited to times when you need to physically divide different logical blocks of content.

Insert a Horizontal Rule

① From the Insert panel, click the category menu.

② Click Common.

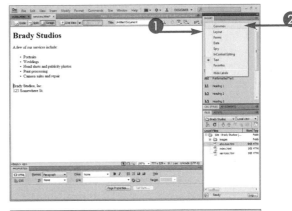

The panel updates to show the Common category's buttons.

③ Click Horizontal Rule.

A horizontal rule is inserted in the page.

Understanding Image File Formats

B efore you can begin to insert images into your pages, you need to understand the file formats available to you. Web browsers support three file formats for images, while Dreamweaver allows you to use a fourth in your design work.

Graphics Interchange Format

The Graphics Interchange Format, or GIF, is perhaps the most common image format on the Web. The format actually predates the Web, having been invented by CompuServe in 1987. GIF images are limited to 256 colors, and so you most often see them used for line art and images with large blocks of solid color.

A GIF can be saved with a series of individual images within the same file, which the browser can then play back in sequence, creating the illusion of animation. However, the popularity of animated GIFs has declined sharply with the increasing popularity of Adobe Flash and the need for animation that is more complex and interactive.

Your GIF can have one color on the image designated as transparent, which allows designers to display a nonrectangular image on a colored background. In fact, transparency support is perhaps the most important feature in maintaining support for GIFs.

Joint Photographic Experts Group

In the early 1990s, the Joint Photographic Experts Group published a new graphics standard, which was named after the group: JPEG. Technically, the format is the JPEG Interchange Format, although common convention simply refers to it as JPEG. Unlike GIF, the JPEG format allows the image to contain up to 16.7 million colors. Thus, JPEG is ideal for continuous-tone images such as photographs.

Portable Network Graphics

Portable Network Graphics, or PNG, is a file format developed as an alternative to GIFs. As such, the format features many improvements on the older standard. In particular, a PNG can support up to 16.7 million colors like JPEGs, but the format also supports transparency.

PNGs do not directly support animation, leaving this to the realm of the GIF, although several extensions to the format do. To date, browser support for these extensions varies widely, and so animated PNGs are rarely used.

Adobe Photoshop Files

Images created in Adobe Photoshop and saved as native Photoshop files, with a .psd filename extension, are not supported by browsers and so cannot be used directly on Web pages. However, Dreamweaver does allow designers to insert Photoshop files into their pages, and it then handles the conversion to Web-safe formats such as GIF, JPEG, or PNG. This technique is examined later in this chapter.

Choosing the Appropriate Format

Which format you choose mostly depends on your intended use for the image. GIFs, with their limited palette but support for transparency, are commonly used for line art, logos, and buttons. JPEG is the best format for photographs as those images need the deeper color palette and are expected to be nontransparent and rectangular.

A PNG can be used anytime a nonanimated GIF is used, although its support for millions of colors also makes it a suitable replacement for JPEG. PNGs are particularly useful when a richer color palette is needed along with transparency, in cases such as images with gradients, shadow effects, or complex logos.

Understand Image Optimization

PART II

When you create an image in a graphics program, take an image with a digital camera, or scan an image into your computer, most are far too large, both in pixel dimensions and in file size, to be appropriate for use on the Web. Therefore, you need to optimize the image, which is simply a process of reducing the file size while attempting to maintain the quality.

Optimization Techniques

The techniques you use to optimize your images depend on the file format you are using.

Optimizing GIFs

A GIF contains a specific palette of colors, which is called its *color table*. As a designer, you can remove colors from the image. Every color you remove reduces the size of the file. At the same time, removing colors may reduce the quality of the image, as the image now needs to substitute the removed color with one that still exists in the image. This can create a blocky or banded appearance in the image. Most graphics programs allow you to set the total number of colors you want to preserve, and then let the program choose which colors to remove, or allow you to manually select and delete colors from the file.

Optimizing JPEGs

JPEG files do not contain a color table because they generally contain too many colors. Instead, JPEGs are optimized through compression.

Unfortunately, JPEGs use a technique known as *lossy compression*, which means that the file size is reduced by deleting data from it. Therefore, the more you compress a JPEG, the worse its quality. Overcompressed images may contain *noise* — areas of the image, usually along any well-defined edges, that contain noticeable blocky pixels.

Most programs present JPEG compression rates as a percentage of the original image, with 100 percent being completely uncompressed and each number below as a level of compression;

so, the lower the number, the higher the total amount of compression in the image.

Optimizing PNGs

You can save PNG images as either 8-bit or 24-bit. Eight-bit PNGs contain a maximum of 256 colors and so are optimized in a manner similar to GIFs, where you can access a color table and reduce the color palette. Twenty-four-bit PNGs can contain up to 16.7 million colors and are thus optimized through compression similar to JPEGs.

Programs for Image Optimization

For the most part, you will not use Dreamweaver to optimize images. Instead, the process needs to be completed in a graphics program such as Adobe Photoshop or Adobe Fireworks. However, Dreamweaver CS4 does allow you to insert images directly from Photoshop and optimize the images upon insertion.

Many graphic designers are more comfortable with Photoshop than with Fireworks and thus do most, if not all, of their work in Photoshop. However, Fireworks was originally designed for Web work, whereas Photoshop was not. While Photoshop still contains many tools that make it a more powerful overall image editor, the Web graphics optimization in Fireworks is more efficient and results in smaller files. Therefore, if you have both programs, you should consider doing your primary editing in Photoshop, but use Fireworks to optimize the image. When you insert a Photoshop image into Dreamweaver and have it perform the optimization, it uses the Fireworks engine.

Insert an Image from the Insert Panel

You can insert images into your pages by using the Insert panel. Using this technique, Dreamweaver allows you to browse your file system to find the image you want to insert.

Images and other assets that you place on your site need to be placed somewhere under the site's root folder. Most designers create a specific images folder in which they store all of the pictures to be used on the site, but very graphics-intensive sites may require more organization, either through subfolders in the images directory or by placing images folders in subdirectories under the root.

When you insert an image in Dreamweaver, the program prompts you to enter alternate text. This provides a text description of your image so that blind or visually impaired users can understand what the image represents. Any image that matters for the content on your page should have descriptive alternate text. For images used purely for visual flair on the page that are not important content, you should select <empty> from the alternate text's drop-down menu, which causes the image to be ignored by screen readers, the software used by the visually impaired.

Insert an Image from the Insert Panel

1 Click Images.

2 Click Image.

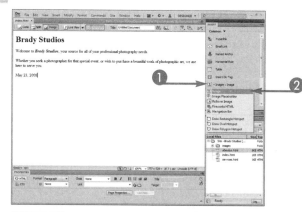

The Select Image Source dialog box appears.

3 Browse to the directory that contains your image.

4 Double-click the image.

The Image Accessibility dialog box appears.

⑤ Type a description of the image in the Alternate Text box.

⑥ Click OK.

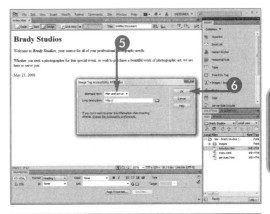

The image is inserted into the page.

Does *every* image need to contain alternate text?

▼ Yes. Providing alternate text is the only way blind and visually impaired users can understand what the image represents. If you do not provide it, the screen reader reads the image's path and filename, which is not only useless but also confusing. Of course, when you include alternate text, you should ensure that it accurately describes the image.

Internet Explorer displays the image's alternate text as a tooltip when you move your mouse over it, but you should be aware that it is the only browser that does this, and so there is nothing wrong with your page when you view it in Firefox or Safari and do not see the tooltip.

Does alternate text help my search engine rankings?

▼ Yes. Any text on your page that can be read by search engines will help your ranking. However, alternate text is given fairly low priority with search engines, so do not use it as a way to embed keywords merely to try to improve your search ranking.

Insert an Image from the Assets Panel

I nstead of using the Insert panel, you can insert images from the Assets panel. As with other panels, this can be opened from the Window menu if you do not see it, but it is most often docked with the Files panel. This can potentially save you from having to navigate through many levels of subfolders in the Select Image Source dialog box that appears when you insert from the Insert panel.

The panel is divided into nine sections, indicated by a column of icons running down the left side of the

panel. You can view the images category by clicking the topmost of these buttons. The Assets panel displays every image in your site, regardless of the directory in which they may reside, and so it can be particularly useful for very large sites with images scattered throughout multiple folders. It also includes a preview window to see the image before you insert it.

You can insert an image by simply dragging it from the panel to the Display view. Dreamweaver prompts for alternate text before placing the image on the page, as this is always required.

① Click Assets.

The Assets panel displays.

② Click an image.

The image displays in the preview window.

③ Click-and-drag the image to the Display view.

The Image Tag Accessibility Attributes dialog box appears.

④ Type appropriate alternate text for the image.

⑤ Click OK.

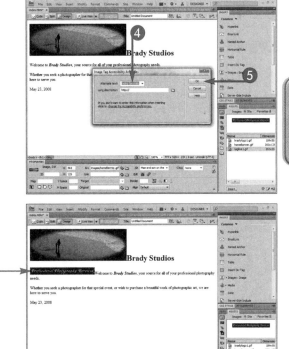

● The alternate text displays on the page.

Why did my image appear in the top-left corner of the screen instead of where I dropped it?

▼ Web pages display all of their content in a single column down the left side of the screen by default, with each element you place appearing below the last. The Web does not easily support placing images at random spots on the page, and you should also keep in mind that your page will be viewed on many different sizes of screens, so precise placement can never be guaranteed. Techniques for controlling the placement of elements on the page are covered in Chapter 8.

In the dialog box for alternate text, it also asks for a long description. What is that?

▼ Some images, such as charts or graphs, cannot be adequately described in a few words through alternate text. In these cases, you should create a separate Web page that describes the image in detail and then enter the path to that page in this area. Normal images do not need long descriptions, so unlike alternate text, you do not need to provide it for every image.

Insert a Photoshop Image as a Smart Object

Adobe Photoshop is the most-commonly used graphics editor among professional designers. In the past, designers who wanted to use Photoshop to create images that could be used on the Web faced a multitude of steps in order to optimize the image, save it in an appropriate format, and then place it on their Web page. If the original image was changed, then you had to repeat all of those steps.

In Dreamweaver CS4, however, you can eliminate this hassle by inserting Photoshop images directly into the

program. When you select a Photoshop image, Dreamweaver prompts you for the optimization settings you want to use in order to convert the file from Photoshop PSD format to a JPEG, GIF, or PNG. Keep in mind that images with many colors, such as photographs, usually need to be saved as JPEGs, while images with few colors, such as logos or buttons, should be GIFs. PNGs are most often used in place of a GIF where the format's alpha transparency is needed. You are then asked to save the new copy of the image in a location in your Web site.

Insert a Photoshop image as a Smart Object

① Click Images: Image.

② Select a Photoshop PSD file.

③ Click OK.

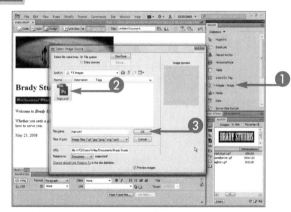

The Image Preview dialog box appears.

④ Select your desired format.

If you selected JPEG, you can set the quality.

● If you selected GIF, you can select the palette you want to use.

⑤ Click OK.

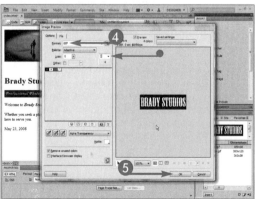

The Save Web Image dialog box appears.

6 If necessary, navigate to your images directory.

7 Type a filename for the image.

8 Click Save.

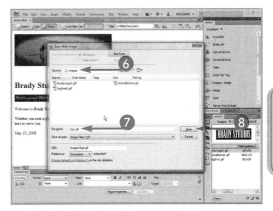

The Image Tag Accessibility Attributes dialog box appears.

9 Type alternate text for your image.

10 Click OK.

The image is inserted into the page.

What if my Photoshop image is too big for my page?

▼ In the same dialog box where you set the optimization for the image, you can click the File tab to set size properties. You have the option of scaling the image by percentage or by setting exact pixel dimensions. You can also crop the image by using the Crop tool, located at the bottom of the dialog box.

I noticed that when I insert images from Photoshop and optimize them in Dreamweaver, they end up as smaller files than if I use the Save for Web feature in Photoshop. Why is this?

▼ Even though you are inserting an image from Photoshop, Dreamweaver is actually using the optimization engine from Fireworks, which is more efficient for optimizing than Photoshop. Note that this is built into Dreamweaver, and does not require that you have Fireworks installed.

Update a Photoshop Smart Object

Dreamweaver creates something called a *Smart Object* when it inserts Photoshop images, which simply means that while it creates an optimized JPEG or GIF, it also retains a link back to the original PSD file. This allows you to make changes to the image in Photoshop and have Dreamweaver revise its optimized copy from the updated source.

Smart Objects show in Dreamweaver with an Images synched icon in their top-left corner, which lets you know that Dreamweaver is keeping a link to the original file. You also see the path to the original

source file displayed at the bottom of the Property Inspector.

When you make changes to the file in Photoshop, you simply need to save the file — you do not need to do anything special in order for the updating to work. After saving the changes, you can return to Dreamweaver to update the image. The changes are not applied automatically. Instead, you need to click the Update from Original button on the Property Inspector. Dreamweaver then overwrites its optimized copy of the image with the new one, using the same settings as before.

Update a Photoshop Smart Object

① Click the Smart Object on the page.

② Click the Edit button.

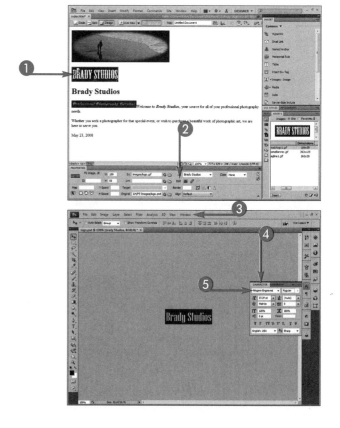

The image opens in Photoshop.

③ Click Window.

④ Click Character.

⑤ Select a new font.

The font changes.

6 Click File.

7 Click Save.

The changes are saved to the file.

8 Return to Dreamweaver.

Dreamweaver regains focus.

9 Click the image on the page.

10 Click the Update from Original button.

The image updates to show the changes made in Photoshop.

If I do not like the optimization settings on the modified image, can I change them?

▼ Yes. The Property Inspector has an Edit Image Settings button, which looks like two small gears, just to the right of the Edit button. You can click this button to reopen the Image Preview dialog box and make any necessary changes to the size, cropping, or optimization of the image. Dreamweaver then automatically saves a newly optimized version of the image.

I renamed the original source file from Photoshop, and now Dreamweaver displays an error when I try to edit the image. How can I give the new filename to Dreamweaver?

▼ You see a box at the very bottom of the Property Inspector labeled Original that contains the path to the Photoshop image. You can simply type the new filename in this box, being careful to ensure that the path is also accurate, or you can click the small folder icon to the right of the box and browse for the file.

Insert an Image Placeholder

There may be times when you need to create your layout in Dreamweaver before the graphical assets of the page have been created. This is particularly true for Web designers who work in teams or with contracted graphic designers.

When inserting a placeholder, Dreamweaver writes the appropriate (X)HTML tag into the document for an image, but displays a blank box on the page where the image will be placed. You can give the placeholder a name, which you can then use as a reference to

remind you of the purpose of the image. You want to set the width and height that you anticipate using for the final image, and you specify a color for the box. You can also enter the alternate text at this time if you know enough about what the image will look like.

When the final image is ready to be inserted, you can simply double-click the image placeholder. Dreamweaver prompts you to browse to the actual file, which it then uses to replace the placeholder. Any attributes you set on the placeholder, including the alternate text, are retained for the final image.

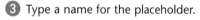

Insert an Image Placeholder

① Click the drop-down arrow next to Images.

② Click Image Placeholder.

The Image Placeholder dialog box appears.

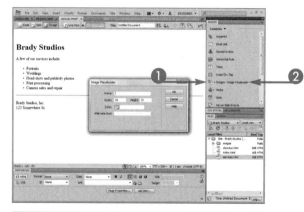

③ Type a name for the placeholder.

Note: *The name cannot contain spaces.*

④ Type a width and a height.

⑤ Type alternate text.

⑥ Click OK.

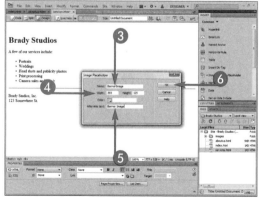

A placeholder is inserted into the page.

7 Double-click the placeholder.

The Select Image Source dialog box appears.

8 Select the image you want to use.

9 Click OK.

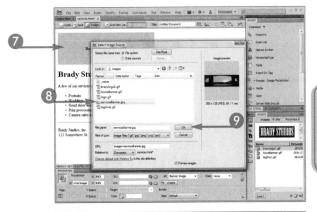

The placeholder is replaced by the image.

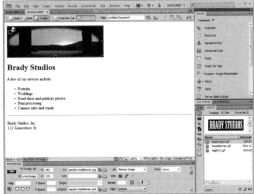

If I am unsure as to what the final image will look like and cannot enter alternate text in the placeholder, can I add or modify it later?

▼ Yes, you can always change alternate text on any image. All you need to do is click the image. In the Property Inspector, you see an entry box labeled Alt. You can either enter appropriate alternate text or choose alternate text you have already used from the drop-down menu.

I do not I see the colored box for the placeholder when I preview the page in a browser. Why is this?

▼ Dreamweaver is creating an (X)HTML image tag in your code, and the colored box only appears in Dreamweaver Design view. If you preview a page with a placeholder in the browser, you see a broken image icon, as the only thing the browser sees is an image with an empty source path.

Insert a Hyperlink with the Insert Panel

Every Web site is made up of a series of related documents that are linked to one another. Many sites also provide links to external sites. When designing your pages, you can create these hyperlinks directly in Dreamweaver.

A hyperlink is made up of two parts. The first part is the clickable content. This is most often a piece of text, but images are often frequently used. The second part is the path to the resource to which you are linking. You can create links to just about anything.

Most of the links on your pages will probably be to other Web pages on your site, but you can also link to other resources such as Adobe PDF files.

In Dreamweaver's Design view, you can create text links by clicking the Hyperlink button on the Insert panel. This opens a dialog box in which you can type the text to be used for the link and the path to the file to which you are linking. You have the option of either typing the path and filename to the link's target page, or clicking the folder icon to browse to the file if you are linking to a page within your site.

① Click Hyperlink.

The Hyperlink dialog box appears.

② Type the text for the link.

③ Type the path to the file to which you are linking.

④ Click OK.

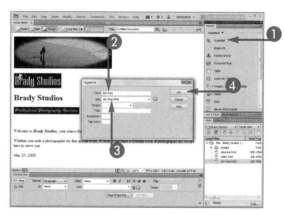

Dreamweaver creates the link on the page.

⑤ Click the Preview/Debug in Browser button.

⑥ Click your primary browser.

The page opens in the primary browser.

7 Click the link.

The target page appears.

I see four additional fields in the Hyperlink dialog box. What are the Target, Title, Access key, and Tab index settings used for?

▼ The *Target* of a link specifies the window in which the new page will open. It was only designed to be used in frames pages, which is essentially an outdated method of creating sites, so many designers avoid using Target today. *Title* allows you to add text to the link that appears in a tooltip when the user moves his mouse over the link. *Access key* sets a keyboard shortcut for the link, which can assist disabled users who cannot use a mouse. *Tab index* allows you to set the order in which the links on the page will be selected should your user be navigating the page with his Tab key instead of a mouse.

Do I always need to add descriptive titles for my images?

▼ All four of these settings are optional, although always adding a descriptive title can help disabled users better understand the link's purpose while also providing additional information to sighted users. Pages that contain forms usually rely on Tab index.

Add a Hyperlink to Existing Text

You can choose to create hyperlinks by first typing the link text in your page and then converting that text to a link. This method is probably used more often than the Hyperlink button on the Insert panel.

Any text on your page can be converted into a hyperlink by typing the path to the page to which you are linking in the Property Inspector. Most of the time, you use what is called a relative path. You can think of a relative path as giving someone directions: You provide the path to the new location based on where you already are. Therefore, for instance, if you have two pages in the same directory, you can simply list the filename of the page. If the page to which you are linking is in another directory, but that folder is in the same parent folder as the page with the link, then you would type the directory's name, a slash, and the filename of the page within the directory.

Add a Hyperlink to Existing Text

① Type text in the page.

② Select the text by clicking-and-dragging the mouse over it.

③ Type the path to the page to which you will link.

Note: *Be sure you are in the HTML category of the Property Inspector.*

④ Press Enter.

Dreamweaver creates the link to the page.

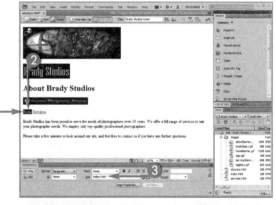

⑤ Click the Preview/Debug in Browser button.

⑥ Click your primary browser.

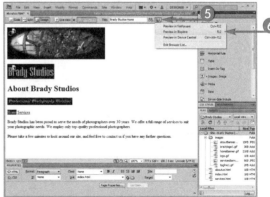

The page opens in the primary
browser.

⑦ Click the link.

The target page appears.

Do I always have to type the path?

▼ No. Just to the right of the Link box on the
Property Inspector are two buttons that
will assist you. The first button is the Point-
to-File icon. You can click-and-drag this
icon to a file on the Files panel to create a
link to that page. The second button, the
folder icon, opens a Select File dialog box
that allows you to browse for the file and
have Dreamweaver create the appropriate
path.

**Do I always need to use relative paths for
my links?**

▼ No. You can also use site-root relative
paths, which provide the location to the
file by giving the path from the top-level
folder of the site, represented by a slash, to
the new page. Site-root paths always begin
with a slash, and can be useful in very
large sites where it is difficult to keep track
of the precise paths from one page to the
next. You can also use absolute links,
which are discussed in more detail later in
this chapter.

Add a Hyperlink to an Image

While most of your links will be text based, you can also use images for links. (X)HTML allows you to wrap tags around other tags; so, if you were writing the code, you could simply wrap the tag for a hyperlink around the tag for an image.

Of course, you can also have Dreamweaver create the link in Design view without worrying about the code. The process of creating an image link merely combines the process of inserting an image, discussed in Chapter 4, with the processes already mentioned in

this chapter for creating a link. You can use any method to insert the image, and use any of the formats previously covered for images. Once the image is inserted, you can click to select it and then create the link by typing the path to the file or browsing for it from the Property Inspector.

Another possible method for defining the link's target resource is to use the Point to File icon. This tool, which is immediately to the right of the Link box on the Property Inspector, allows you to click-and-drag to select a page from the Files panel.

Add a Hyperlink to an Image

① Click an image on the page.

② Press and hold your mouse button on the Point to File icon.

③ Drag to the file to which you will be linking on the Files panel.

④ Release the mouse button.

The image is linked to the selected file.

⑤ Click the Preview/Debug in Browser button.

⑥ Click your primary browser.

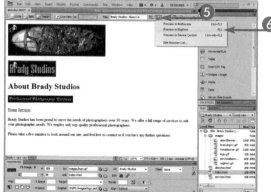

The page opens in the primary browser.

7 Click the image.

The target page appears.

Why does my image now have a blue border around it?

▼ Originally, it was thought that it would be necessary for browsers to designate in some way that an image was a link, and so from the very early days of the Web, linked images have appeared with a border, which is actually using the same colors as normal hyperlinks — first blue, and then purple when the link has been visited. Most often, however, it is clear from the context or the appearance of the image that it is a link, and so this border is very rarely desired. You can remove the border using CSS, as shown in Chapter 8.

Can my images be linked to other sites on the Web?

▼ Yes. You can link to anything from an image or from text. Linking to external resources such as other Web sites is discussed later in this chapter.

Can I have my image change its appearance when a user mouses over it?

▼ Yes. There are several different approaches to creating roll-over effects for images. You can use CSS, which is discussed in Chapter 7, or you can use JavaScript by inserting a Dreamweaver Behavior, which is shown in Chapter 10.

Link to a Place in a Document

While most links take the user to another page, either in your site or on the Web, there may be times when you have long pages and want to create links to specific places on the page, such as subheadings. (X)HTML provides two methods for creating links such as these.

The first, older method is to create a named anchor. In this technique, you define a place on the page to which you want to link and give it a specific name. Dreamweaver displays a yellow icon at that point.

Then, you can create your link as normal, using either text or an image, but you can use the Point to File icon to point to the yellow icon instead of another file.

The second method is to use an existing page element's ID. Every element you place on the page can take an ID, which is a unique identifier for that element. You can define these IDs on the Property Inspector. You must make sure that each ID is unique on a page. Then, you can link to it by typing a pound or hash symbol (#) followed by the ID in the Link box.

① Click in Design view at the point at which you want to link.

② Type an ID for the element.

③ Press Enter.

④ Select the text you will use as the link.

⑤ Press and hold your mouse button on the selected text.

⑥ Drag to the element to which you added the ID in step 2.

The link is created.

⑦ Click the Preview/Debug in Browser button.

⑧ Click your primary browser.

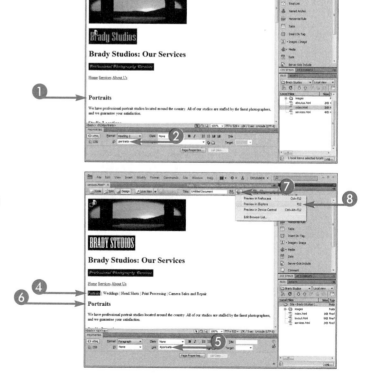

The page opens in the primary browser.

9 Click the link.

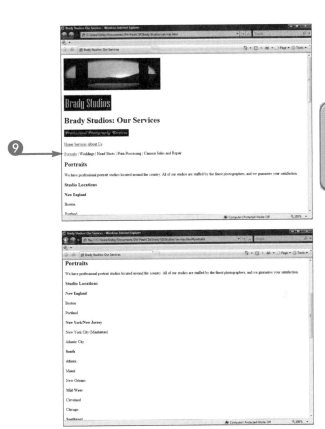

The browser jumps to the target of the link.

Are there any special rules for what I can use for the name or the ID?

▼ Yes. Perhaps the most important is that each name or ID can only exist once per page, although you can link to the same name or ID as many times as you want. However, you must also be sure that the name or ID follows the rules for Web filenames, and so you cannot use spaces and you need to begin with a letter. You will also find that maintaining the site is easier if you ensure that your names or IDs are clear and descriptive.

Is there any real difference between using the named anchor and using an ID?

▼ If you are only trying to create the links, then there really is not. Named anchors are the older method, having existed since the very earliest days of the Web, while linking to IDs is comparatively new. Therefore, some very old browsers may not support the links to IDs, but the chances of encountering significant numbers of users who rely on these ancient browsers are slim. IDs can also be used for JavaScript and CSS, whereas named anchors cannot.

Link to an External Web Site

While most of the links you create will be to pages within your site, there may be times when you want to create links to other sites on the Web. For the most part, the process for these links is the same as for internal links: You create some text or insert an image, and then provide the path to the target page.

Internal links can be created by typing the path, browsing for the file, or using the Point to File icon. External links, however, can only be created by typing the path to the page in the Link box. Here, you must use an absolute path, which is the complete address for the page, as you would normally see on the Address bar in your browser. This path *must* begin with the protocol to access the site, which is most often http://, but may sometimes be https://. Following that, you provide the domain name for the site, and if necessary the file path to the page in question. An absolute path may be something simple, such as http://www.robhuddleston.com, or it may be complex, such as enter_path_to_this_book's_website_here.

Link to an External Web Site

① Select the text on the page that you want to use for the link.

② On the Property Inspector, type the absolute path to the page or site to which you are linking.

Note: *Do not forget the http:// or https:// at the beginning of the path.*

③ Press Enter.

The link is created.

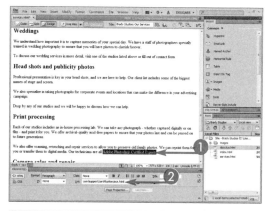

④ Click the Preview/Debug in Browser button.

⑤ Click your primary browser.

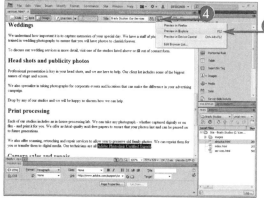

The page opens in the primary browser.

6 Click the link.

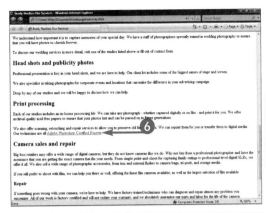

The target site appears.

If the address for the page is particularly long or complex, is there a way I can create it without typing?

▼ Yes. Use your Web browser to navigate to the page to which you are going to link. Then, select the address in the browser's Address bar — most browsers allow you to do this by simply clicking once in the Address bar. Then, copy the address, which you can normally do by right-clicking the address, and choose Copy. Return to Dreamweaver, right-click in the Link box, and choose Paste.

Can I really link to *any* page on the Web? Can some pages not keep me from linking to them?

▼ According to Tim Berners-Lee, the inventor of the Web, "The ability to refer to a document (or a person or anything else) is in general a fundamental right of free speech to the same extent that speech is free. Making the reference with a hypertext link is more efficient but changes nothing else." You can read more of his thoughts on issues and myths surrounding hyperlinks on the page from which the quote was taken, at www.w3.org/Design Issues/LinkMyths.html.

Create a Hyperlink to an E-mail Address

In addition to creating links to other Web pages, it is possible to create links to e-mail addresses to allow users to contact you from the site. In Dreamweaver, you can create these links by simply clicking the Email Link button on the Insert bar and providing the text for the link and your e-mail address.

When the user clicks the link, his e-mail program generates a new message, with the To: field prefilled with the address you specified in the link. Be aware that this means that these links only work for users who have a properly configured e-mail program such as Microsoft Outlook on their computer.

Unfortunately, purveyors of spam, or junk e-mail, can find the e-mail address you set in the link very easily, and so you can expect to see a sometimes-dramatic increase for spam that you receive if you put one of these links on your page. You can prevent this by using a contact form instead and having a server-side script e-mail the form data to you. This process is covered in Part IV of this book.

Create a Hyperlink to an E-mail Address

① Click Email Link.

② Type the text you want to display on the page.

③ Type the e-mail address you want to use.

④ Click OK.

The link is created. The Property Inspector shows mailto: and the address.

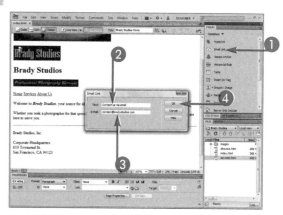

⑤ Click the Preview/Debug in Browser button.

⑥ Click your primary browser.

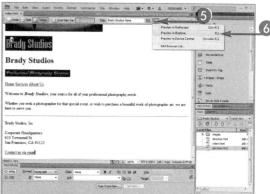

The page opens in the primary browser.

⑦ Click the link.

A new e-mail message appears.

Note: *You must have an e-mail program such as Microsoft Outlook installed and configured on your computer in order to test this link.*

Can I prefill any of the other fields in the e-mail, such as CC or subject?

▼ Yes. You can add additional fields when you create the link by typing a question mark after the e-mail address, and then inserting the name of the field, an equal sign, and the value you want to set. For example, if you wanted to add a CC address, you could type:

info@mysite.com?cc=admin@mysite.com

If you want to add another field, type an ampersand, the field, an equal sign, and the value:

info@mysite.com?cc=admin@mysite.com&su bject=test

You can list these additional fields in any order.

What if the data I need to use contains characters such as spaces?

▼ If you will have spaces in the values of a field like subject, you need to use a plus sign instead of a space:

info@mysite.com?cc=admin@mysite.com& subject=Reply+from+Web+site

You will need to use special escape sequences for other characters. You can see a list of these at community.contractwebdevelopment.com/ url-escape-characters.

Create an Image Map

Most of the time, you want to have an entire image link to a single resource. However, there may be instances where you want a large image to have links to different resources. For example, you might have a map of the United States, where the user can click different states to get to information about each one.

This kind of image that links to multiple resources is called an *image map*. Attempting to create an image map in code is extremely difficult, but Dreamweaver simplifies the process by giving you tools that allow

you to draw the clickable areas, or *hotspots*, directly on the image and then type the path for the link on the Property Inspector.

You can draw three types of shapes: rectangles, circles, and polygons. All three of these tools can be found in the bottom-left corner of the Property Inspector when an image is selected. You can click-and-drag to draw a rectangle or circle, or click at each point where you want a corner to draw a polygon. Shapes can be resized by clicking the arrow tool and dragging one of the square control handles.

Create an Image Map

① Click an image.

② Click the Polygon Hotspot tool.

③ Click the image.

A hotspot point appears, and a dialog box appears, reminding you to set alternate text.

④ Click OK.

The dialog box closes.

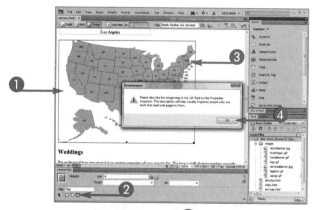

⑤ Continue to click the image to create the polygon.

⑥ On the Property Inspector, type a path to the target path in the Link box.

⑦ Type alternate text for the region.

⑧ Repeat steps **2** to **7** to create additional hotspots.

⑨ Click the Preview/Debug in Browser button.

⑩ Click your primary browser.

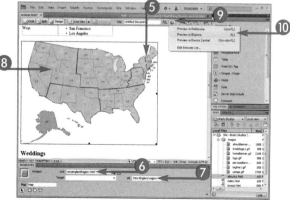

The page opens in the primary browser, showing the image map.

⑪ Click in a hotspot area.

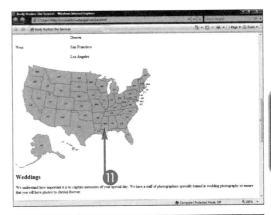

The target page appears.

I am having a hard time seeing the points on the page to create the hotspot. How can I see them better?

▼ Dreamweaver has a Zoom tool that allows you to magnify the page, which is often helpful in creating hotspots around complex areas, such as tracing states. The Zoom tool is the magnifying glass in the lower-right corner of the Design view window. You simply click the image to zoom in, and you can press and hold the Alt key and click to zoom back out. You can also click-and-drag to define an area of the page to zoom in on, at which point Dreamweaver magnifies the page to fit that area on the screen.

If I zoom in on the page, how can I move around to see other areas of the page?

▼ When you are zoomed in, you can switch to the Hand tool to move around on the page. You can also select a preset magnification from the drop-down menu next to the Zoom tool. Double-clicking the Zoom tool immediately returns you to 100 percent magnification, and clicking the Select tool — the arrow next to the hand — returns you to Dreamweaver's normal tools so that you can resume your work.

Insert a Table with the Insert Panel

Many Web sites need to present tables of data, such as product lists or employee phone directories. You can insert tables into your pages in Dreamweaver by simply clicking the Table button on the Insert panel, which allows you to set your initial parameters for the table.

When you first insert a table, you are asked to specify the number of rows and columns you want, but you can very easily add or delete either later, and so you only need a rough idea at the start. You can choose to specify the width of the table, the thickness of its borders, and the whitespace contained in the table through cell padding and spacing; however, you will find that you can better control these aspects of the table through Cascading Style Sheets (CSS), and so you may want to leave them blank.

Most of the time, you want to specify a row along the top of the table or a column down the left side as a header row. By default, text in table headers is bold and centered, although these properties can be changed.

① Click Table on the Insert panel.

The Table dialog box appears.

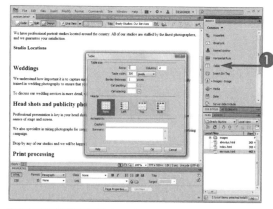

② Type the number of rows you want to use for your table.

③ Type the number of columns you want.

④ Either type a width for the table or delete the default value.

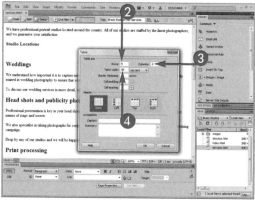

5 Delete the value in the Border Thickness box.

6 Click Top.

7 Click OK.

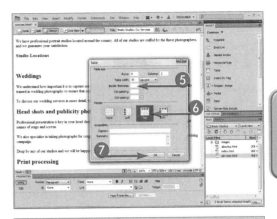

The table is inserted into the Design view.

If I enter a width or border for a table when I insert it and then later change my mind, how can I modify the setting?

▼ You can change the number of rows and columns, the width of the table, the border thickness, the cell padding and cell spacing, and other properties of the table at any time by selecting the table and modifying the appropriate settings on the Property Inspector.

I deleted the value from the width, but my table is tiny. How can I work in it?

▼ Tables with no width are only as wide as their content. If you carefully click inside the table, you can insert text into it, which causes the table to expand. However, some designers prefer to enter a width for a table in the Table dialog box to avoid this problem, and then delete the width using the Property Inspector once it contains enough content to be usable.

Insert Content into a Table

Once you have the basic structure of the table on the page, you can begin to insert content. You can put just about anything inside a table. Both text and images are allowed, and the text can be formatted as headings, paragraphs, or lists. Either text or images can be made into hyperlinks inside the table. You can even insert tables into tables. You insert content into a table in exactly the same way you insert it into a page without a table.

You can navigate through the cells of a table by using the Tab key on your keyboard. Each time you press Tab, you are taken to the next cell to the right. When you reach the end of a row, you are taken to the first cell in the next row. Pressing Tab from the bottom-right cell of the table inserts a new row. You can move to the left along a row by pressing and holding the Shift key while you tab.

① Click in the first cell of a table.

② Type text for the header.

③ Press Tab.

The cursor moves to the next cell.

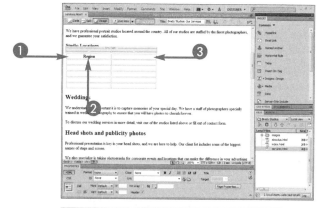

④ Type more header text.

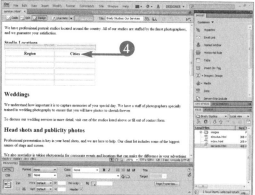

5 Press Tab.

● The cursor moves to the next cell or row.

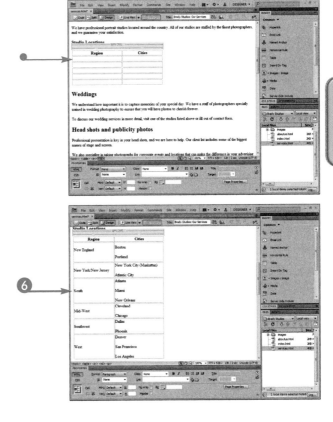

6 Continue adding text to complete your table.

How do I move the text in a cell farther from the cell's edge?

▼ The cell padding attribute determines the space between the content and edge of a cell. If you have a good idea as to how you want your table to look, you can set cell padding in the initial Table dialog box; otherwise, you can select the table at any point and set or modify the cell padding on the Property Inspector.

Cell spacing is the space between cells. If your table is set to not show borders, then you will not be able to tell the difference between adjusting cell spacing and cell padding.

Why is my text vertically centered in rows with images?

▼ The default alignment of content in a cell is both horizontally and vertically centered. When you insert an image, it forces its row to be at least as high as the image itself, and so this vertical alignment becomes obvious. You can control it by clicking in a cell and using the Vert setting on the Property Inspector.

Select Tables and Table Parts

I n order to change the basic properties of a table, such as its width or border, you need to select the entire table. Changing the alignment of contents requires selecting specific cells.

You can select a cell that contains text by simply clicking anywhere within it. Its changeable attributes appear in the lower half of the Property Inspector. However, if you have an image in a cell, you may find it harder to select, as clicking the image does not show table cell properties. Instead, you need to use the Tag Chooser. In (X)HTML, tables are represented by the `table` tag, rows by the `tr` tag, and cells by the `td` tag, which is short for table data. Dreamweaver displays all of the tags that make up the current selection's hierarchy along the bottom of the Design view window. You can click any of these to select that element. So, in the case where you have an image in a cell, you can select the cell, rather than the image, by clicking the <td> button in the Tag Chooser.

① Click in a table cell that contains text.

   The cell properties are displayed on the Property Inspector.

② Click-and-drag to select all of the cells in a row.

   The row is highlighted and its properties display.

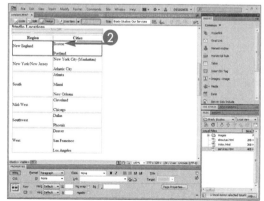

③ Click <table> in the Tag Chooser.

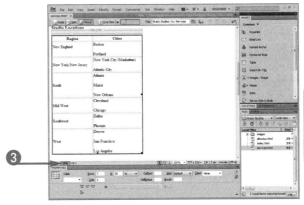

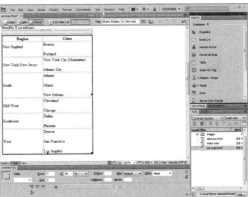

The table is selected and its properties appear.

What does it mean when I see a pound sign or period displayed in the Tag Chooser?

▼ If you see a pound sign followed by a word after the (X)HTML element in the Tag Chooser, that means that the element in question has an ID associated with it. IDs can be used as the targets of links, as discussed in Chapter 5, or more commonly for applying CSS formatting, as discussed in Chapter 7. A period with a term following the element means that it has a class attribute assigned, which is also used for CSS formatting and is discussed in Chapter 7.

What do the green bars that span along the bottom of my table represent, and can I remove them if they get in the way?

▼ Those bars display the widths of the table and each column. They are one of the ways that Dreamweaver helps you design your page, as you can tell how wide a table is by simply moving your mouse over it. However, they often cover the content immediately below the table, and so you can turn them off by clicking the View menu, selecting Invisible Elements, and then clicking Table Widths.

Insert Rows or Columns

Often, you have a good idea of how many columns your table needs before you start working on it, but not precisely how many rows you want. Other times, you may discover that you forgot to account for some important piece of information and need to add additional columns.

You can insert a new row at the bottom of your table by simply clicking in the lower-right cell and pressing Tab. If you need a row inserted into the middle of your existing data, you can right-click anywhere within that row and choose Insert Row from the Table

submenu of the context menu. The new row is inserted below the row in which you clicked. Columns can be added using the same submenu, with the new column appearing to the right of the selection.

You can also select Rows and Columns from the right-click context menu; you are presented with a dialog box that allows you to insert a specific number of rows either above or below the currently selected row, or a specific number of columns to either the left or right of the current selection.

Insert Rows or Columns

① Right-click in a cell in a table.

The context menu appears.

② Select Table.

The Table submenu appears.

③ Select Insert Row.

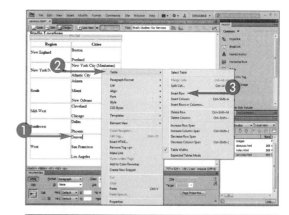

A new row is inserted above the current row.

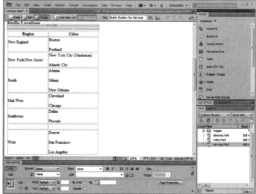

Delete Rows or Columns

If you insert a row or column that you do not need, you can delete it. When you choose to create a table with no borders, extra rows at the bottom of the table or columns to the right may not be visible, but they still take up space on your page and can create problems for your layout.

You can delete rows and columns in much the same way as you insert them, by using the Table submenu when you right-click, which gives you options to delete the current row and the current column.

You can also select the row or column and press the Delete key on your keyboard. You can select a row by simply clicking its `tr` tag in the Tag Chooser. To select a column, you need to click-and-drag either from the top cell of the column to the bottom, or from the bottom up.

Any content within the row or column that you are deleting is also deleted. If you delete a row or column from the middle of the table, the cells either below or to the right shift to fill the empty space.

Delete Rows or Columns

① Right-click in a cell of the row you want to delete.

The context menu appears.

② Select Table.

The Table submenu appears.

③ Click Delete Row.

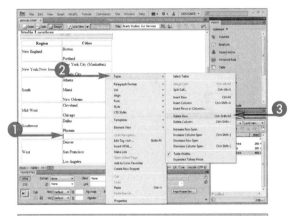

The row is deleted.

Merge Table Cells

Sometimes, you may have content in your table that needs to span more than one row or column. For example, you may have a table that is displaying a phone directory for your company. Assuming that the list is organized alphabetically, you might want a row that spans all of the columns of your table to show that the following listings are the *A* names, and the later listings the *B* names, and so forth.

You can merge cells in a table into bigger single cells by selecting the cells you want to merge and clicking

the Merge Selected Cells Using Spans button at the bottom of the Property Inspector. You can merge any number of cells along a row or in a column. It is even possible to select a set of cells that span multiple rows and columns and merge them into a square block.

If you merge a cell with content and a cell without content, Dreamweaver combines the content of the cells, so that you will not lose any information; however, the new content will not have any whitespace, and so you may need to click in it and add spaces between words.

Merge Table Cells

① Select two or more cells in the table.

② Click the Merge Selected Cells Using Spans button.

The cells are merged into a single cell.

Split Cells

If you merge cells that you later discover should be separated, you can split the merged cell back into its original individual cells. You can also split cells that have not been merged, thereby creating new columns or rows within the cells.

The button to split cells is on the Property Inspector next to the Merge Cells button. To split a cell, simply click inside the cell you want to split and click that button. A dialog box appears, where you can specify whether you want to split the cell into rows or columns, and how many resulting cells you want.

You cannot split more than one cell at a time. If you have a row or column where you need to split most of the cells, it is probably easier to insert a new row or column and simply merge the cells you would not have otherwise split.

If you split a cell with content, the content is placed in the right most cell if splitting into columns, or the top most cell if splitting into rows, but no data is lost.

Split Cells

① Click in a cell in a table.

② Click the Split Cells into Rows or Columns button.

The Split Cell dialog box appears.

③ Choose whether you want rows or columns.

④ Choose the number of rows or columns.

⑤ Click OK.

The cell is split.

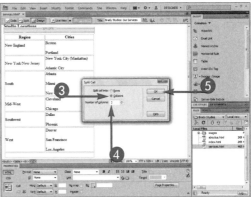

Sort a Table

If you enter data into a table directly in Dreamweaver, you often end up with data in a random order. As you receive additional data points to add to the table, it can be difficult to keep it organized. To avoid these issues, you can sort your tables in Dreamweaver.

You can sort the table on up to two of its columns. You have the option of sorting each column either alphabetically or numerically, and in either ascending or descending order. You can choose to include the first row if you do not have headers, or leave it in

place if you do. If you have more than one header row or if you have footer rows, you can sort them along with the data. If you have designated alternating row colors, you can have Dreamweaver rearrange the colors so that the alternating pattern is retained.

You can sort the table as often as you need to, but there is one big limitation of which you need to be aware: You cannot sort a table that contains any merged cells, whether they are columns or rows. It may therefore be necessary to split merged cells, and then sort and remerge them.

① Click in a table.

② Click Commands.

③ Click Sort Table.

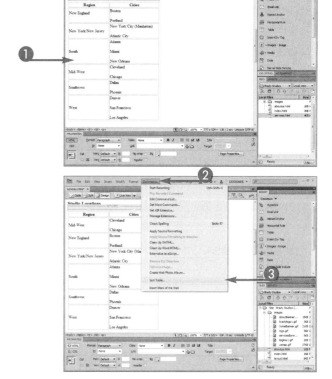

The Sort Table dialog box appears.

④ Select the first column to sort.

⑤ Choose to sort alphabetically or numerically.

⑥ Choose ascending or descending order.

⑦ Click OK.

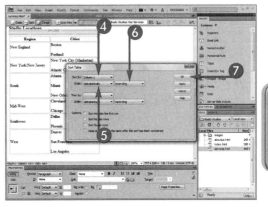

The table is sorted.

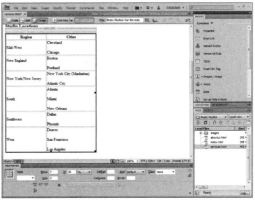

How do I designate footer rows?

▼ (X)HTML includes three elements to designate the sections of a table: thead, tbody, and tfoot. You can wrap the thead tag around the rows that make up the head of your table, the tfoot around the rows that make up the footer, and the tbody around the remaining rows.

Most browsers ignore these tags. A few have the ability to automatically include the header and footer rows at the top and bottom of each page if the user prints a very long table, but this behavior cannot be guaranteed. Dreamweaver recognizes them for sorting, but nothing else.

Unfortunately, there is no way in Dreamweaver to add these in Design view — they must be typed directly into Code view.

Import a Table from Microsoft Excel

I f you already have a set of tabular data in a spreadsheet program such as Microsoft Excel, you can import it directly into Dreamweaver. This obviously saves you the time and trouble of creating the table and entering the data. You can import a file from Excel by simply selecting the file in the Import Excel Document dialog box. Dreamweaver can import XLS files created in Excel 97 or later, or XSLX files created in Excel 2007.

When you import the file, you can choose to have the data imported as completely unformatted text; text

with structural elements such as paragraphs, lists, or most commonly tables; text with structure and basic formatting, in which case Dreamweaver preserves bold and italic text from the original; or text with structure, basic formatting, and styles. If you select this final option, Dreamweaver generates CSS styles to mimic as closely as possible the original formatting of the document, including fonts, text sizes, and text and background colors.

You can only import Excel data when you are in Design view. If you are in Code view, you need to switch to Design view.

Import a Table from Microsoft Excel

1 Click File.

2 Click Import.

3 Click Excel Document.

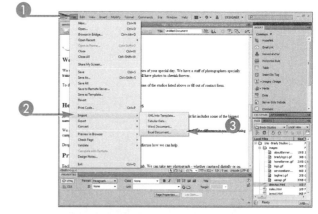

The Import Excel Document dialog box appears.

4 Click the document you want to import.

5 Click Open.

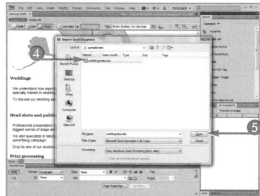

PART II

The document is imported.

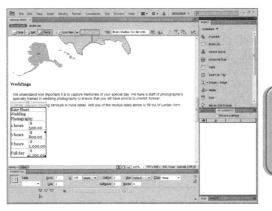

6 Click <table> on the Tag Chooser.

7 Delete the width.

The table's width resets to properly display the data.

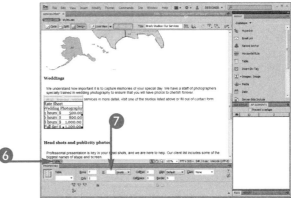

Can I import tabular data from programs other than Excel?

▼ Yes. Dreamweaver supports importing documents from any delimited file, meaning any file where the contents are separated by some predictable character such as a tab, space, or comma. Most spreadsheet and database programs allow you to export files in one of these formats.

When you have a delimited file that you want to import, you click File, select Import, and then click Tabular Data. You can select the file you want to import, the delimiter used in the file, and basic table settings such as width, cell padding and spacing, and borders.

Can I import tabular data from Microsoft Word documents?

▼ Yes. You can click File, select Import, and then click Word Document to select a file to import. Importing Word documents gives you options similar to those when importing from Excel — you can choose to import as plain text, text with basic structure, or text with basic formatting, or have Dreamweaver create styles to match the more complex formatting from your Word document. If the Word document contains tables, they are converted to (X)HTML tables, just as they are when importing from Excel.

Introducing Cascading Style Sheets

Cascading Style Sheets, or CSS, were developed in an effort to provide a more robust formatting language for the Web. CSS can be used with any Web page.

Versions of CSS

The original specification of CSS, version 1.0, was released at the end of 1996. It introduced text formatting, including bold and italic typefaces, indents, and spacing; the ability to add foreground and background colors to elements; alignment for most elements; and margins, padding, and borders on elements.

Version 2.0 was adopted about 18 months later. Its most useful additions were many of the positioning properties used for page layout and media types that allow designers to target style sheets to specific uses.

Browser Support for CSS

For many years, browser support for CSS provided a roadblock to its adoption, and even today, the most commonly cited reason for not adopting CSS is concerns over browser support. While these concerns were at one time justified, today few browsers lack significant support for CSS.

Of the major browsers on the market today, all fully support CSS 1.0, and all support most if not all of the properties in CSS 2.0. However, not all browsers implement CSS exactly according to standards, and so there are still significant differences in how pages may display. It is absolutely imperative that, as a Web designer, you test each of your pages on a variety of browsers to ensure that they function properly. Remember that Dreamweaver's Design view is not intended as a replacement for browser testing.

CSS and Dreamweaver

Dreamweaver has supported working with CSS in Design view for the last several versions, but in each new release, that support has increased. Dreamweaver CS4 uses CSS by default for any formatting you want to add to your pages. The primary method of working with CSS is through the CSS panel, although the Property Inspector also includes many tools for formatting with CSS. You can also create and modify your CSS in Code view.

CSS Selectors

CSS applies its formatting to elements on your page by way of selectors. While many different selectors exist, the three most commonly used are element or tag selectors, classes, and IDs.

A tag selector allows you to apply the formatting to every portion of the page that shares a common (X)HTML element. For example, if you wanted to change the font used by all of your first-level headings, you could add a CSS style that uses the h1 tag selector.

Often, you will want your styles to apply only to portions of the page. For example, you may have a set of second-level headings in a sidebar that you want to look different from the second-level headings in the main content area of the document. In this case, you can apply your style through a class selector. Class selectors use a name that you define when you create them, and they are then applied to the page elements through the (X)HTML class attribute.

If you have one specific element on your page that you need to style, you can use an ID selector. IDs function in much the same way as classes, and so you can give them whatever name you choose when you create them. Unlike classes, however, which can be used many times on a document, IDs can only be applied once per page.

Advantages of CSS

While it is more difficult to learn CSS formatting than (X)HTML formatting, there are many advantages to using it:

- **CSS provides many formatting options not available in (X)HTML**. For example, CSS gives you the ability to add borders and background colors to any element, control the spacing between lines, override default formatting options, and implement layout controls.

- **Pages that use CSS load and render more quickly**. Because your (X)HTML documents do not contain code purely for formatting, they are smaller when you use CSS; as a result, the browser can download the pages more quickly, and, because they contain only the code needed for the content, they render more quickly as well. Subsequent pages in your site see an even bigger speed increase, because the CSS document has already been downloaded and cached by the browser.

- **You can reformat an entire site**. By separating your content and your presentation, you can change the formatting on your entire site from a central location — your CSS file. Therefore, it is possible to reformat your site without having to dig into individual content pages. You can find an example

of this capability at www.csszen garden.com, which is a site that presents a single page with many different formats, all using CSS.

- **You can repurpose your site without rewriting it**. These days, more and more users are viewing pages on alternate devices such as cell phones. This creates both a unique challenge and a unique opportunity to designers. The challenge is in designing pages that can look good on a 19-inch widescreen computer display and a 3-inch cell phone screen. By having all of your presentational code in CSS, you can switch layouts dynamically as your users move from one device to the next, again without having to rewrite any of your underlying (X)HTML. Dreamweaver includes a companion program called Device Central to help in this process by showing you your page in a cell phone display.

The Cascade

CSS information can be added directly to a page in your site, or placed in an external document that can apply to many pages. This can create situations where you have more than one style rule applying to the same element on your page. In these cases, the *cascade* specifies how conflicts are resolved. Style rules that are closer to the element in question take precedence over those farther away, and so, in general, rules in a style sheet on the page override conflicting rules from an external style sheet. More specific rules override less specific rules, and so an ID selector that targets one specific element takes precedence over an element selector as IDs are considered to be more specific.

Set Styles for a Page

You can add some initial styles to your page through the Page Properties dialog box. Dreamweaver writes the code needed to format the page through element selectors, which are added as an embedded style sheet to the current document.

The dialog box contains three main categories: Appearance, Links, and Headings. The Appearance category allows you to set a font, a base size, and the color for the text on the page, as well as a background color or image for the document as a whole. You can

also define margins — the space between the edge of the browser window and the page content.

The Links category lets you establish a font and size properties for hyperlinked text on your document. It also allows you to create different settings for links that have been visited or ones that your user moves his mouse over.

Headings let you set a font to be used by all of the headings on the page, and establish a size and color for headings by level. You can also choose whether you want your headings to be bold or italic.

Set Styles for a Page

❶ Click in Design view.

❷ Click Page Properties.

The Page Properties dialog box appears.

❸ Click Appearance (CSS).

❹ Select a font family from the Font drop-down menu.

❺ In the Size box, type **100**.

❻ Click % in the units drop-down menu.

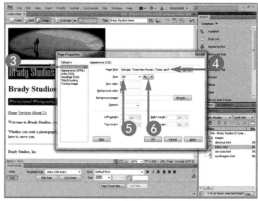

⑦ Click Headings (CSS).

⑧ Type a size for heading 1.

⑨ Type a size for heading 2.

⑩ Click OK.

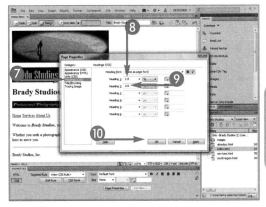

Dreamweaver applies the styles on the page.

What happened to all of my fonts?

▼ Your Web pages do not contain any actual font information. Rather, they merely contain instructions as to which font the browser should use on a particular block of text. Therefore, you must limit yourself to the font that you can be reasonably sure will exist on your user's computer.

Arial, Times New Roman, Courier, and Verdana are the four most popular fonts in the world, and so you can usually trust that a user will have them. However, you should provide a backup just in case. The font selections in Dreamweaver reflect this by listing a choice of fonts. The browser reads this list left to right and uses whichever one it first encounters.

What do serif and sans-serif mean?

▼ *Serifs* are the feet on letters in fonts such as Times New Roman. *Sans* is Latin for without, and so a *sans-serif* font is one that does not have feet, such as Arial. A common design practice is to use a sans-serif font for headings and a serif font for body text, or vice versa. Having your headings use a different font helps them stand out on the page.

Create a Style for an (X)HTML Tag

You can apply formatting to all instances of a particular (X)HTML tag by creating a style rule for that tag. For example, if you create a style rule for the p tag, you will have a style that applies to all paragraphs on the page.

The primary interface in Dreamweaver for creating and managing styles is the CSS Panel. You can create new style rules from here by clicking the New CSS Rule button at the bottom of the panel. This opens a dialog box that prompts you for the type of selector you want to use, which is followed by another dialog box where you can add initial settings for the style.

Once you have created the rule, you can modify it by simply selecting an element to which the rule is applied and then adjusting its settings in the Properties section of the panel. You can add additional properties, change the values of existing properties, or delete properties directly in the panel.

The panel also contains a section that defines the CSS properties that are currently being modified. You can use this to help teach yourself CSS.

① Double-click CSS Styles.

② Click the New CSS Rule button.

The New CSS Rule dialog box appears.

③ Choose Tag (redefines an HTML element) from the Selector Type drop-down menu.

④ Type **p** in the Selector Name box.

⑤ Click OK.

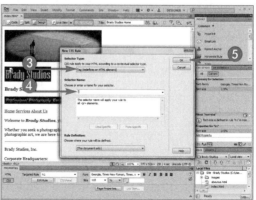

The CSS Rule definition dialog box appears.

6 Select a font from the Font-Family drop-down menu.

7 Type **90** for the font size.

8 Select % for the unit.

9 Click OK.

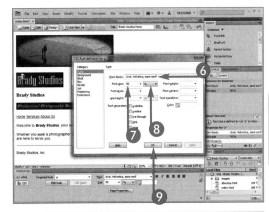

The CSS rule is created, and all paragraphs are formatted.

Can I add additional font choices?

▼ Yes. You can add fonts to the font list by clicking Edit Font List from the Font-Family drop-down menu on the Property Inspector. This displays a dialog box that shows all of the font choices currently listed in Dreamweaver, as well as all of the fonts installed on your computer. You can create a new list of font choices by selecting the desired font and clicking the button with the two left arrows. To create another new list, click the Add button (the plus sign) at the top of the dialog box. You can also rearrange the order in which the fonts are listed in Dreamweaver's other dialog boxes by using the arrow keys at the top of the dialog box.

What units of measurement are available for font sizes?

▼ You can set your text size using inches, centimeters, millimeters, points, picas, ems, exes, pixels, or percents. However, computer monitors do not consistently display inches, centimeters, millimeters, points, or picas, as their definition of these sizes varie, depending on the screen resolution and physical monitor size. Therefore, the best units are pixels and percents. However, Microsoft Internet Explorer does not allow users to resize the text in their pages — an important accessibility feature — unless the size is set in percents or ems.

Create a Class Style

You can create class styles to format individual instances of elements. Once created, class styles can be applied to any element on the page.

Class styles are created in the CSS panel. When you click the New CSS Rule button, you can create a class by typing a name for the class in the Selector Name box. Class names must begin with a period followed by a letter, and can contain letters, numbers, underscores, and dashes. Class names cannot contain spaces. You should give your classes names that describe their purpose or use on the page, and not

just their formatting properties. For example, if you want to create a class to format instances of your company name in orange, bold text, you should use .companyName instead of .orangeBold; this gives you the flexibility to change the formatting properties later while maintaining the logic behind the name.

You can apply classes to elements by selecting the object or text on the page and then selecting the class from the Targeted Rule drop-down menu on the Property Inspector's CSS tab. You can also select the name from the Class drop-down menu on the HTML tab of the Property Inspector.

① Click the New CSS Rule button.

The New CSS Rule dialog box appears.

② Click Class (can apply to any HTML element).

③ Type a name for the class.

④ Click OK.

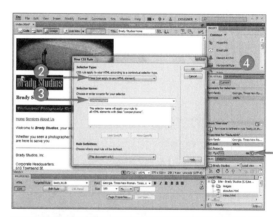

The CSS Rule Definition dialog box appears.

⑤ Select bold.

⑥ Click OK.

The class style is created.

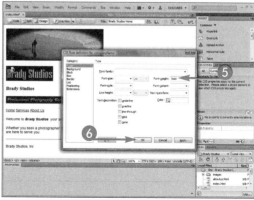

⑦ Select the text you want to format.

⑧ Select your class name from the Targeted Rule drop-down menu.

The text is formatted.

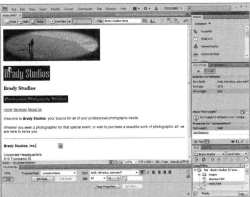

How are classes applied to the elements?

▼ You can apply a class to an (X)HTML element by adding a class attribute to the element's tag, using the name of the class without the period at the beginning. For example, if you had a class of `.companyName` and wanted to apply it to a second-level heading, you would type:

<h2 class="companyName">

How does Dreamweaver apply a class to a selection of text if there is no (X)HTML element around it?

▼ If you select only a word or words within a line and apply a class, Dreamweaver wraps the text using a `<span>` tag with the appropriate class attribute:

`<span class="companyName">`

The `<span>` tag was created for just this purpose. Unlike most other (X)HTML elements, `<span>` does not have any predefined formatting, and it can be used to apply styles to text that does not have any other tag around it.

Create a Style Based on an ID

You can create styles that target one specific element or object on the page by using an ID selector. Unlike a class, which can be used repeatedly on a page, an ID can only be applied to a single element per page.

Many designers who are new to CSS are confused by the difference between classes and IDs, and unsure when it is appropriate to use one over the other. Indeed, to a point, they can be used interchangeably, as there is no problem with only using a class selector once on a page. ID selectors are usually reserved for

identifying an element that defines a section of a page, rather than particular page content, as page sections are generally unique by definition.

You can give an ID any name you want, following the same rules as you did for class names, with the exception that instead of beginning with a period, an ID name begins with a pound or hash sign (#). It is thus possible to have an ID and a class with the same name, only differentiated by the initial symbol, although this should be avoided as it can be confusing and more difficult to maintain.

Create a Style Based on an ID

1 Click the New CSS Rule button.

The New CSS Rule dialog box appears.

2 Click ID (applies to only one HTML element).

3 Type a name for the ID.

4 Click OK.

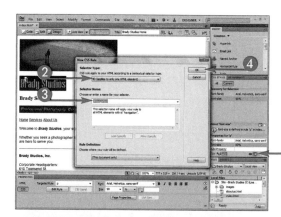

The CSS Rule Definition dialog box appears.

5 Select bold.

6 Click OK.

The ID style is created.

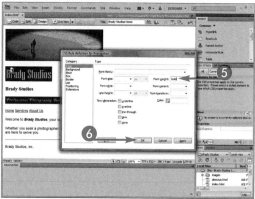

⑦ Select the text you want to format.

⑧ Click HTML.

⑨ Click your ID name from the ID drop-down menu.

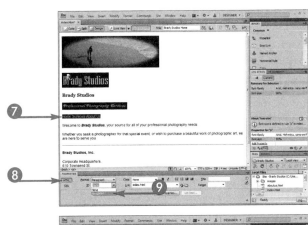

The text is formatted.

Does it matter how I capitalize the name of a class or ID?

▼ No, you can use any capitalization scheme you want for your class and ID names, although you should try to be consistent. Eventually, you may need to edit your CSS manually in code, and so you should be aware that selectors are case-sensitive: The casing you use when you create the class or ID name in the CSS needs to match what you use in the class or ID attribute.

Many designers have adopted a practice of using something called *camel casing*, where you use a lowercase letter for the first word in the class name, but capitalize the first letter of each subsequent word.

What happens if I accidentally apply the same ID to two or more elements on my page?

▼ Fortunately, Dreamweaver makes it extremely difficult to do this, as IDs do not appear in the drop-down menu on the Property Inspector if they have already been applied to another element on the page. However, no such protection exists if you edit the code directly. The exact effect of applying an ID more than once depends on the browser, and it can be unpredictable; you should always take care to avoid it.

Edit a Style in the CSS Panel

Once a style has been created, you can modify its properties at any time using the CSS panel. You can use the panel to add additional properties to the style, delete properties, or change existing properties' values.

The panel is divided into two or three sections. The top section displays either a summary of the properties of the currently selected style, or a list of all of the style rules currently applied to the document. If you are viewing the current styles, a middle section

appears that can be used to either display a description of the current style property or display the cascade of styles applied to the current selection on the page.

The lower portion is where you primarily work. Buttons along the bottom of the panel allow you to choose to view this list so that you only display those properties currently applied to the style, or all possible CSS properties, organized either alphabetically or in a categorized list.

① Click within an element on the page.

② Click Current.

③ Click Add Property.

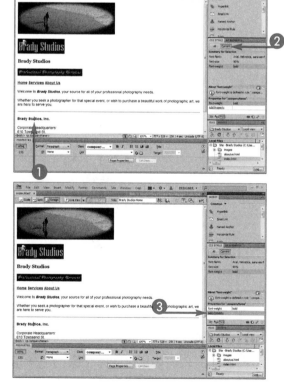

④ Click font-style.

⑤ Click the drop-down arrow.

⑥ Click italic.

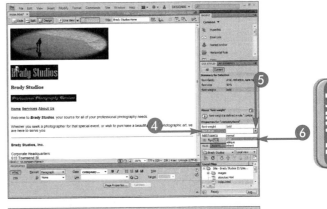

The page updates, showing the new style properties in the selected text.

Why can I see more properties in the alphabetical or categorized property list than are in the drop-down menu when I add a property?

▼ The drop-down menu that lists the CSS properties when you click Add Property only displays a subset of the possible CSS properties, representing the most popular or commonly used properties. The alphabetical and categorized lists display every possible CSS property, including some that may not be supported by all browsers.

How can I add a property that is not listed in the drop-down menu?

▼ You can click directly in the box containing the style drop-down menu and type the name of the missing style into the box. Somewhat oddly, Dreamweaver recognizes the property you added, even though it was not on the program's list, and still displays valid properties.

Can I use CSS shorthand properties such as font or border when adding properties?

▼ Yes. Most of the shorthand properties actually appear in the drop-down menu, and so you can simply select them and then type the values you want to add. You do not, however, see any prompts as you type the values, and so you should only use the shorthand properties after you become familiar with them.

Move Styles to an External Style Sheet

One of the biggest advantages of using CSS for your designs is that you can copy the styles to an external document. Then, you can apply the styles to as many other pages in your site as you want. You can then make global changes to the site's appearance by modifying this one document, rather than having to open and edit individual pages.

The external style sheet is a document with a .css filename extension. You can give it any filename you want, as long as you follow the normal Web file-naming rules, the most important of which is that the name cannot contain spaces. The file can be saved anywhere within your Web site's folder structure, although it is usually saved either in the root folder or in a folder specifically designated for styles.

Once created, the external style sheet can be linked to the documents in your site. Styles that use (X)HTML element selectors are instantly applied, and class and ID selectors become available in the drop-down menus on the Property Inspector and in the CSS panel.

① In the CSS panel, click All.

② Click the first style you want to move.

③ Press and hold the Shift key.

④ Click the last style you want to move.

⑤ Right-click any of the selected styles.

A context menu appears.

⑥ Click Move CSS Rules.

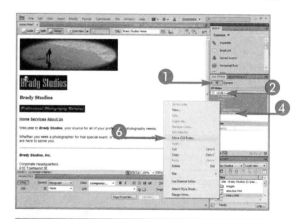

The Move to External Style Sheet dialog box appears.

⑦ Click A new style sheet option.

⑧ Click OK.

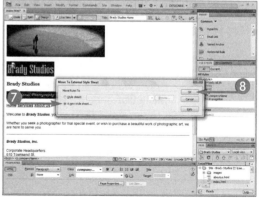

The Save Style Sheet File As dialog box appears.

9 Type a name for the style sheet.

10 Click Save.

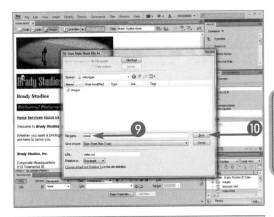

The style sheet is saved. The selected styles are moved to the external sheet.

● The styles from the linked style sheet appear in the CSS Styles panel.

Can I use more than one external style sheet per page?

▼ Yes, you can have as many style sheets per page as you want. Designers of large, complex sites often separate CSS into a series of smaller, more manageable documents, rather than having one large page with hundreds of lines of code.

If I create new styles after I create the external style sheet, will I have to keep moving them over?

▼ No. After you have created your style sheet, you can choose to have new styles added to the external style sheet by selecting the appropriate document in the New CSS Rule dialog box. In fact, Dreamweaver assumes that you want your new styles to be in the external style sheet.

If I am using the external style sheet to define styles for my site, how can I add a style that I only want on a single page?

▼ You can choose to have styles apply only to the current page by making that selection in the New CSS Rules dialog box, instead of placing it in the linked style sheet. Styles applied to the page override conflicting styles in the linked style sheet, and so this gives you the ability to have elements on a specific page differ from those on other pages.

Attach an External Style Sheet to a Page

Y ou can attach an external style sheet to a page to apply its formatting. This can be done either after content on the page has already been added, or on a new blank page. In fact, adding the style sheet to the page before you start adding content allows you to see what that content will look like as you create it.

You can either link to the external style sheet or import it. Linking is the more common method, but importing has some advantages. Imported style sheets take precedence over linked sheets, and so if you have two style sheets that you need to apply to a page but need to ensure that one overrides the other, you can link to the less important document and import the more important one. For example, you might have a style sheet that you want to apply to your site as a whole, but then have a section of your site, such as pages for a particular department, that need their own styles in addition to the site's. By linking to the site's sheet, and then importing the departments, you can maintain the most control.

Attach an External Style Sheet to a Page

① Click the Attach Style Sheet button.

The Attach External Style Sheet dialog box appears.

② Click Browse.

The Select Style Sheet File dialog box appears.

③ Select the style sheet to attach to the page.

④ Click OK.

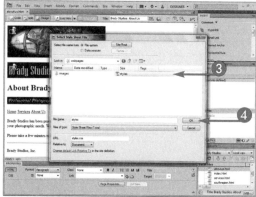

5 Click Link.

6 Click OK.

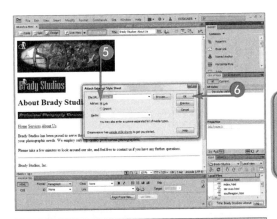

The style sheet is linked to the page and styles are applied.

● The styles from the linked style sheet appear in the CSS Styles panel.

Is there a limit as to how many style sheets I can link to a particular page?

▼ No. Some designers like to organize their style sheets into a series of small documents rather than trying to maintain a single, large sheet. You can have as many link tags as you need, or as many import statements. You can even combine the two, linking to some sheets while importing others.

If I use more than one link tag, does the order in which I list them matter?

▼ Yes. The style sheets will be applied in the order in which they appear in the (X)HTML document, which will cause the sheets that appear last to override those that appear first.

View Related Files

When you edit pages that rely on external style sheets, you may need to edit the code in those documents directly. In Dreamweaver, you can access external style sheets directly from the Related Files bar.

The Related Files bar appears just above the Document toolbar whenever a file is open that relies on external resources such as style sheets. Buttons appear for each related document. If you are viewing the original file in Design view, you can click the button for the

related file and have Dreamweaver automatically switch you to Split view, where the related file's source code is displayed in the Code view portion of the split, with the original document displaying in the Design view portion.

You can edit the source code of the related file and see the effects of those changes reflected in the original file. You can view the original file's code by clicking the Source Code button, or you can return to editing the file by switching back to Design view.

View Related Files

1 Click styles.css.

The document appears in Split view, with the source code for the related file appearing.

2 Edit a property's value.

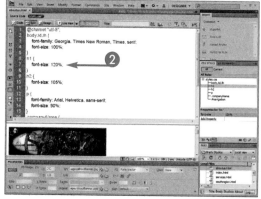

③ Click in the Design view window.

The page updates to show the changes.

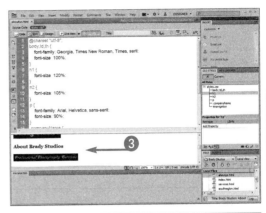

④ Click Source Code.

The Code view window displays the code for the original document.

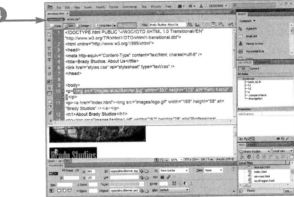

Can I use the Related Files bar to view documents other than CSS?

▼ Yes. If you have external JavaScript files, they appear on the Related Files bar as well. If you use a server-side processing language such as PHP or ColdFusion and are using included files, they appear on the bar.

How does Dreamweaver determine the order in which it lists related files?

▼ The related files appear in the order in which the links to those files appear in the source code. External CSS and JavaScript files are most often referenced using the (X)HTML `<link>` tag, and so the order in which the `<link>` tags appear in the document set the order in which the files are listed on the Related Files bar.

If I have more related files than will fit on the bar, is there some other way to access them?

▼ Yes. You can click View, and then click Related Files to see a list of the related documents. You can click any of them to see their code. You can also navigate using the arrows that appear at either end of the Related Files bar to scroll through the list files.

PART II

Format Hyperlinks

CSS provides for a set of pseudo-classes to allow you to apply formatting to links when they are first encountered, have been visited, and are being selected. A pseudo-class is merely a special CSS selector that is applied by the browser in certain conditions.

Most modern browsers support five pseudo-classes for links. The first, link, is used to control the regular appearance of the link. Visited allows you to apply styles to links to sites the user has visited. You can apply styles when the user moves his mouse over a link with the hover pseudo-class, and when the user

selects the link using his Tab key with focus. The final pseudo-class, active, appears on most browsers when the user actually clicks the link.

You do not need to provide style rules for all five pseudo-classes. However, CSS requires that the pseudo-classes exist in a specific order in the style sheet in order for them to work properly: link, visited, hover, focus, active. Because Dreamweaver writes rules into the style sheet in the order in which you create the rules, you need to be sure that you create them in that order.

Format Hyperlinks

① Click the New CSS Rule button.

The New CSS Rule dialog box appears.

② Click Compound (based on your selection).

③ Select a:link from the drop-down menu.

④ Click OK.

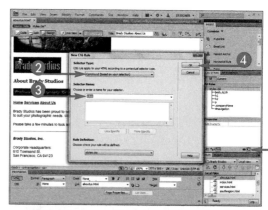

The CSS Rule Definition dialog box appears.

⑤ Select none.

⑥ Select a color.

⑦ Click OK.

The link style is created.

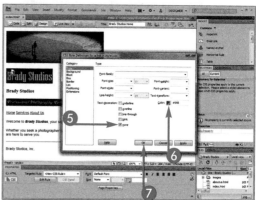

8 Repeat steps **1** to **7** to create styles for the other link states.

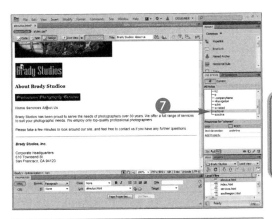

The links are formatted.

How do I remove the underline from links?

▼ The CSS `text-decoration` property controls the underlining of links. While there are a lot of possible values for text-decoration, the only two that are commonly used are `underline` and `none`. Because links are underlined by default, setting the property to `none` removes the underline. A common technique is to remove the underline for the `link` and `visited` pseudo-classes, and then apply it again with `hover` and `focus`. You can do this by setting `text-decoration` to `none` on the first two, and then specifically setting it to `underline` for the others.

Is there any reason that I shouldn't remove the underline?

▼ Be aware that a link's underline is often the only visual clue to the user that a link exists. Too many designers mistakenly believe that making text bold or a different color will distinguish it as a link, but the only visual indicator the average user looks for is the underline; so, unless it is clear from the context, you should leave the underline in place. The reverse is also true: you should never underline any text on a page that is not a link.

Format Lists

You can have an enormous amount of control over the appearance of your lists by using CSS to format them. Because lists are becoming more common on sites, you should familiarize yourself with the formatting options that are available.

Many designers use unordered or bulleted lists for the logical structure, but would prefer to remove the bullet or replace it with their own graphic. You can remove the bullet by setting the `list-style-type` property to `none`, or replace it with your own image by providing the path to the image in the `list-style-image` property. For numbered lists, you can modify the `list-style-type` property to change the numbering system to upper- or lowercase alphabetic characters or upper- or lowercase Roman numerals.

You can use Dreamweaver's CSS panel to easily adjust any of these settings as needed while you design your page.

Format Lists

① Click the New CSS Rule button.

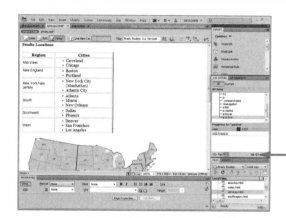

The New CSS Rule dialog box appears.

② Select Tag (redefines an HTML element).

③ Select ul from the tag drop-down menu.

④ Click OK.

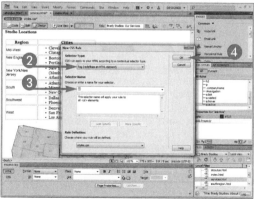

The CSS Rule Definition dialog box appears.

5 Click List.

6 Select none from the List Style drop-down menu.

7 Click OK.

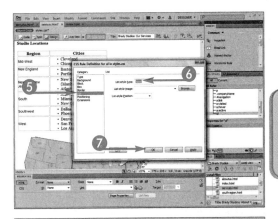

The style is created and the bullets are removed from the list.

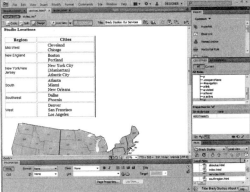

How can I prevent the list items from being indented?

▼ The CSS specification says that list items should be indented, but it is unfortunately silent on which CSS property should create the indentation. Therefore, some browsers use the left margin, while others use left padding. To be safe and certain that your list will look the same across all browsers, you should set both `margin-left` and `padding-left` to 0. Note that you need to set this property on the list itself — the `<ul>` tag — and not the list items.

I have a list nested within another list. When I applied an image as the bullets on the outer list, it applied to the inner list as well. How can I get the inner list to maintain its normal bullets?

▼ You can use a contextual selector to target a style on the inner list and apply the default bullet. The inner list's `<ul>` tag is nested within the outer list's `<li>` tag, and so creating a contextual selector that uses `ul li ul` and applying `circle` as the `list-style-type` will work. Remember that the contextual selector should be read right to left, and so `ul li ul` says an unordered list that is inside a list item of another unordered list should be styled.

Insert Background Images

Prior to the advent of CSS, you could only display an image as the background of the page as a whole, a table, or a table cell. Those background images were inserted in the top-left corner of the page or table, and would tile both horizontally and vertically on the page.

With CSS, you can still insert images as the background of those three elements, but now you can apply them to any other element on the page as well. In addition, you can now control the placement of the image

within the element, and set it to tile in both directions, only vertically, only horizontally, or not at all.

Any content in the element is rendered on top of the background image, and so care needs to be taken to ensure that text is readable across the image. If you are using a dark background image and thus light-colored text, you should also set the background color of the element to a dark shade similar to the image. That way, if there is an error loading the image, the light-colored text will still be readable.

Insert Background Images

1 Click the New CSS Rule button.

The New CSS Rule dialog box appears.

2 Click Tag (redefines an HTML element).

3 Select body.

4 Click OK.

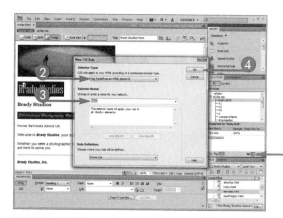

The CSS Rule Definition dialog box appears.

5 Click Background.

6 Type the path to your image.

Note: You can also click Browse and use the file system to select the image.

7 Select a color that matches the overall shade of the image.

⑧ Select repeat-x.

⑨ Select left.

⑩ Select top.

⑪ Click OK.

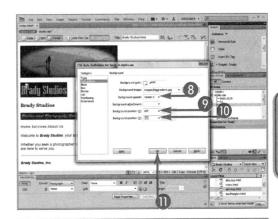

The style is created and the background image displays.

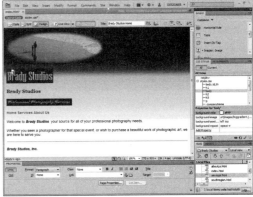

How can I insert two images into the background of the same element?

▼ Technically, you cannot, as CSS only allows one image to be used as a background for a single element. To get around this limitation, you can add an additional nested element. For example, you might nest a `<div>` directly inside another `<div>`, so that you can apply one image to the outer `<div>` and another to the inner one. You can see an example of this technique in Chapter 8.

Can I stretch my background image?

▼ No. CSS does not provide any means by which the background image can be manipulated. You cannot specify a size for the image, or change anything on it. If you need the image to be a different size, you can open the file in Adobe Photoshop, Adobe Fireworks, or another image editor and make the changes there.

Where do I specify the alternate text for the background image?

▼ Alternate text is designed to provide a description of the image for screen readers. Background images are, by definition, not an important part of the content of the page. If they were, they would be included using the `<img>` tag. Therefore, screen readers ignore background images, and no alternate text is required.

Create an HTML E-mail Message with Inline CSS

The majority of the time, you want to rely on styles that are either embedded in the head of your pages or in external style sheets. There is, however, another option when working with styles: you can add styles directly to individual (X)HTML tags, creating *inline styles.* One of the most important concepts behind the development of CSS was the idea of allowing designers to separate the content of their page from its presentation. Inline styles work counter to that principle: By adding style instructions directly to individual tags, you can once more mix the content and the presentation.

However, inline styles are still necessary if you want to create an e-mail message that relies on (X)HTML formatting. Unfortunately, while most modern e-mail programs allow you to use (X)HTML to structure the message and link to images, and they allow you to use CSS, they completely ignore the head section of the document and only read the body. As both embedded style sheets and links to external sheets are included in the head section, many e-mail programs do not correctly display CSS unless you use inline styles.

① Click an element you want to style.

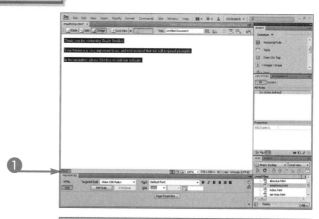

② Click CSS on the Property Inspector.

③ Click <New Inline Style>.

④ Click Edit Rule.

The CSS Rule Definition dialog box appears.

⑤ Edit the properties you want to apply.

⑥ Click OK.

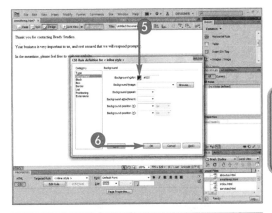

An inline style is added to the page.

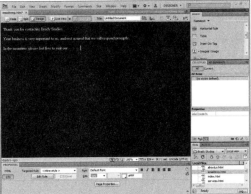

After I have created the message, how do I send it?

▼ The precise steps for sending an HTML-based e-mail depend on the program you use for e-mail, and so you should check the inline help file in your e-mail client.

Most allow you some method of copying and pasting code into a special message window, and so in Dreamweaver you can switch to Code view, click Edit, and then click Select All to select the code. Click Edit, click Copy to copy the code, and then follow the instructions in your e-mail program to paste the code into a message window.

Can I include images in my e-mail message?

▼ Yes. However, you need to be sure that you always use absolute paths for your images. Recall that absolute paths begin with http:// and include the domain name and full path to the image. You can use relative links in Web pages for images because the browser knows which server the page came from and can request images back to the same server. The e-mail client did not get the page from a Web server at all, and so it must have the absolute path to make the request.

Insert div Elements

I n the early days of the Web, the only way to create layouts for pages was to use tables. Unfortunately, this resulted in pages that contained much more code than they needed to convey their content, and that were hard to maintain and difficult for disabled users. It also created designs that were impossible to share across pages. Today, you can use CSS to create flexible, usable, and accessible layouts with much less code that are easier to maintain and very easy to reuse across pages.

In order to lay out your page, you need to ensure that each section of the page is enclosed in an element to

which you can apply the CSS layout properties. The most commonly used element for this purpose is div. The div was introduced to allow designers to have an element that could be used for styling that did not start with its own default styles. It is particularly useful when you have a series of other elements that need to be grouped together, such as a heading and its supporting paragraphs.

When you insert a div into a page, you can assign it an ID or class. Then, you can apply CSS to control its appearance.

Insert div Elements

① Click-and-drag to select a group of elements on the page.

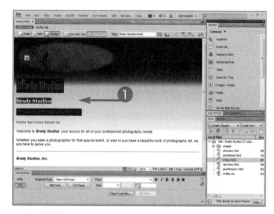

② Click Insert Div Tag.

The Insert Div Tag dialog box appears.

③ Select Wrap Around Selection from the Insert drop-down menu.

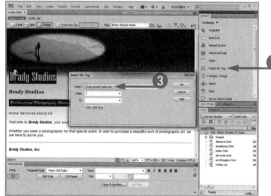

④ Type a name for the ID for this
element.

⑤ Click OK.

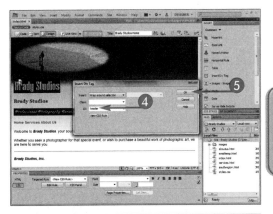

The `div` is inserted around the
elements.

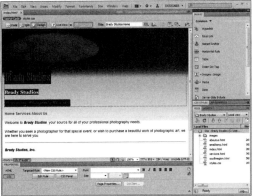

How many `divs` can I have on a single page?

▼ There is no limit to the number of `divs`
you can place on a single page. Most
pages that rely on CSS for layout contain
many `divs` per page. You want at least
one `div` for each section on your page. In
fact, the name `div` is derived from
division, implying that its purpose in the
code is to create sections on the page.

Can I place `divs` inside other `divs`?

▼ Yes. This again is a very common
technique. You can have sections that
contain subsections by nesting `divs` inside
other `divs`. Many designers begin their
work on a page by wrapping the entire
contents of the page inside a `div`, and
then nesting `divs` inside that `div` as
needed. In theory, there is no limit to the
number of nesting levels that you can have
when using `divs`.

Add Borders to Elements

You can add a border around any element using CSS. Borders can be used to separate content, draw the user's eye to a particularly important topic, or simply create visual effects on the page.

Borders are made up of three parts. You specify the width of the border, using any of the CSS measurement units, although border widths are almost always given in pixels. You set the color of the border to any color you want, using either named colors or hexadecimal. You also set the style of the

border, using one of ten keywords: none, hidden, dotted, dashed, solid, double, groove, ridge, inset, and outset.

You should always be sure to specify a width, style, and color for your borders. Most browsers default the color to black, the style to solid, and the width to 1 pixel if any of those properties are omitted, but this cannot be assured. The exception to the rule is when you are trying to turn off existing borders; in that case you can simply set the style to none and ignore the width and color.

Add Borders to Elements

① Click in an element to which you want to add a border.

② Click the New CSS Rule button on the CSS panel.

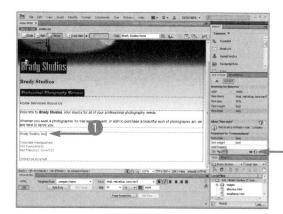

The New CSS Rule dialog box appears.

③ Ensure that the Selector is set to the correct element, class, or ID.

● If necessary, click the Less Specific or More Specific buttons to change the selected rule.

④ Click OK.

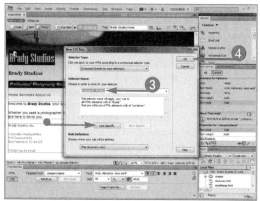

The CSS Rule Definition dialog box appears.

⑤ Click Border.

⑥ Select a style.

⑦ Set a width.

⑧ Select a color.

⑨ Click OK.

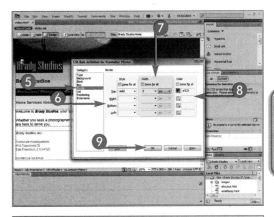

The border is applied to the element.

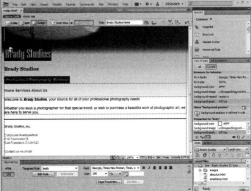

Can I use different settings on each of the four sides of a box?

▼ Yes. If you uncheck the Same for all option in the CSS Rule Definition dialog box, you can set the style, width, and color of each side independently. You can experiment with different combinations of colors and border styles to find the design that works best for you.

When would I need to set the border to none?

▼ Borders for most elements are set to none by default. The one exception is with images. Unfortunately, a border automatically appears around an image when you make it into a hyperlink, but you can override this by setting the CSS border to none. Remember that you do not need to specify a width or color in this case.

You may also choose to set the border to none in situations where you need to override a border being applied from some other style sheet. For instance, you may have an external style sheet adding a border, but then want an individual page to not use the border, and so you could set border to none in an embedded style sheet on the page.

Control Padding

The CSS *box model* defines a series of properties that can be used to define the space in which each element appears. The box model is made up of four parts. The innermost is the *content*, or the actual element. Surrounding the content is an area of *padding*. Outside of the padding is the *border*, which is in turn surrounded by a *margin*.

The padding of an element is the space between the content and the border. To create more space between the border and the content, you would add padding. Padding can be set in a number of units, although pixels, percentages, and ems are most frequently used. When you enter the values in Dreamweaver, you can either select the desired unit from a drop-down menu or type it yourself. You can also set padding to 0, removing it altogether and forcing the content to touch the border, if one is showing, or possibly an adjacent element.

You can set equal padding on all four sides of the content, or control padding on each side. If you choose the latter, you do not need to use the same units of measurement for each side.

① Click All.

② Click an existing selector.

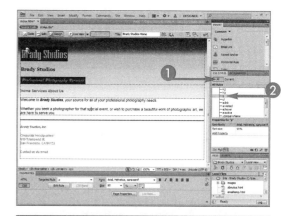

③ Click Add Property.

④ Click padding-top.

5 Type a number for the amount of padding.

6 Select a unit.

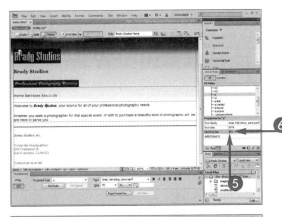

7 Repeat steps **3** to **6** to add padding to any other sides of the box.

The padding is added to the box.

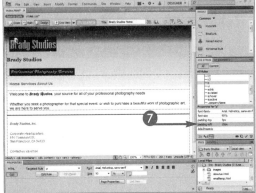

Why would I want to use ems for padding?

▼ One em is equal to the height of the current font. Therefore, if you set your font size to 12 pixels, 1 em equals 12 pixels. If the font size of the current selector is 100 percent, then 1 em is equal to whatever the browser calculates as the size based on the size of that element's parent element.

Setting both the padding and font size in ems allows the padding to resize proportionally to the font size. As text size increases, so does the padding. This ensures that your layout will hold together for users who need larger text, such as visually impaired users who use the browser's capability to resize text to make it larger and thus more readable.

Control Margins

Yyou can further control the whitespace on your page through the `margin` property in CSS. The area between elements on the page is the margin. Margins visually separate one element from another. They exist outside of the borders of elements, and so you can use margins to control the space between elements with borders.

Perhaps the most confusing aspect of margins for beginners is that adjacent vertical margins on the page collapse into each other. For example, the space between a heading and the paragraph immediately below it is simultaneously the bottom margin of the heading and the top margin of the paragraph. Merely reducing the heading's bottom margin does not cause the elements to move closer to one another, as the top margin of the paragraph continues to force space to be between the elements. It is therefore necessary to adjust both margins.

Just as with padding, you can set the margin using any supported unit of measurement. You can set the margin of an element to be the same on all four sides, or control each side individually.

Control Margins

① Click p.

② Click Add Property.

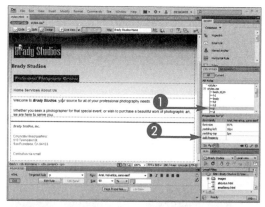

③ Click margin-top.

④ Type a number for the amount of margin.

⑤ Select a unit.

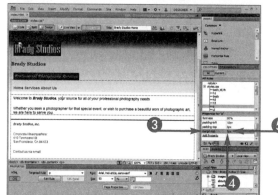

6 Click Add Property.

7 Click margin-bottom.

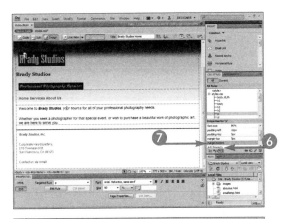

8 Type **0**.

The margin is set, moving the paragraphs closer together.

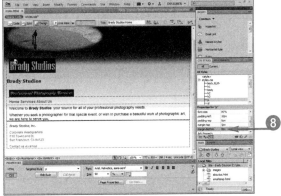

Why does it not appear to work when I apply margins to images?

▼ Elements on the page are classified as either block or inline. Block elements such as paragraphs, headings, and tables create their own space on the page, whereas inline elements do not. CSS uses a slightly different box model for inline elements than it does for block elements. The most important difference between the two models is that the block box model supports margins while the inline does not. Because images and hyperlinks are inline, it is possible to set padding and border properties for them, but not margins.

Can I set the margin of an element to zero?

▼ Yes. In fact, zeroing out a margin is a common technique to overcome the fact that vertically adjacent margins collapse. By setting one of the two collapsed margins to zero, you can more easily control the spacing between elements, as it is now possible to work with only the remaining margin.

Are negative margins allowed?

▼ Yes. However, you should be aware that CSS does allow elements to overlap, and so setting an element's margin to a negative value may cause it to overlap other elements on the page. While this can be a desired effect, it should be thoroughly tested in multiple browsers to be sure that portions of the page do not become unreadable or unusable.

Set Element Widths

You can control the width of any block element on the page. By default, the width of a block element is equal to 100 percent of the width of the nearest parent element, which also has a specified width. If you have not set any other widths on the page, the elements default to being 100 percent of the width of the body, which means that they stretch across the width of the browser window.

The width property of an element sets the width of the content, and so the total width of the block is the sum of the width property, the left and right padding, and the left and right borders. Note that the left and right margins are not included in the width calculation, although it is necessary to account for margins when placing elements next to one another. As with other size-based properties, any valid unit of measurement is allowed, although widths, like padding and margins, are most often set in pixels, percentages, or ems. Negative values for width are not allowed.

Set Element Widths

① Click the New CSS Rule button.

The New CSS Rule dialog box appears.

② Select ID (applies to only one HTML element).

③ Type #container.

④ Click OK.

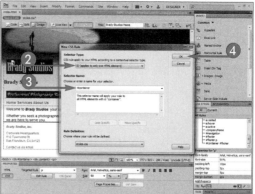

The CSS Rule Definition dialog box appears.

5 Click Box.

6 Type a width.

7 Select a unit.

8 Click OK.

The style is created and the margins are applied to the specified element.

Can I set the width of the body of the document?

▼ No. The body's width is always equal to the width of the browser window. You should keep in mind that there is no way to detect the width, and while there are JavaScript implementations that let you reset the browser window's width, these are considered to be intrusive and most browsers allow the user to disable them. If you want the content of your page to be a set width, you need to add another container element — usually a `div` — just inside the body. You can then give that container a width, and place all of the other content within it.

Can I set the width of an image to resize it?

▼ The CSS specification does allow for this, but it is not a recommended practice. The browser is generally not very good at resizing images, and so it is much better to resize the image in an image-editing program such as Adobe Photoshop CS4 or Adobe Fireworks CS4. Note that you should always specify the image's correct width in the image tag itself to ensure that the browser correctly draws the page.

Float Elements

All block elements on the page exist within the page flow. Normally, the flow is simply a vertical stack of the elements. You can, however, change this flow to create multicolumn layouts using the *float* or *positioning* properties in CSS.

Floating elements has recently become one of the more common methods of controlling page layout. You can set the `float` property to `left` or `right`. Left allows the selected element to float to the left of any element that appears after it, in effect causing the next element to move into the space to the right of the selected element. A float set to right has the opposite effect, causing elements that follow the floated element to move to the selected element's left.

In order to allow a float, the elements in question must have specified widths, and the total sum of the widths must be less than or equal to the width of the elements' parent. If the widths are too large to allow the float, then it simply does not occur and the elements continue to stack vertically.

Float Elements

① Click the New CSS Rule button.

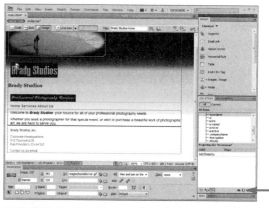

The New CSS Rule dialog box appears.

② Select ID (applies to only one HTML element).

③ Type an ID for the element you want to float.

④ Click OK.

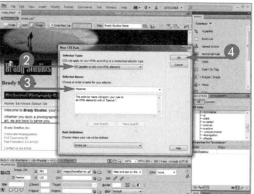

The CSS Rule Definition dialog box appears.

5 Click Box.

6 Select a width.

7 Select left.

8 Click OK.

9 Repeat steps **1** to **7** for each additional element.

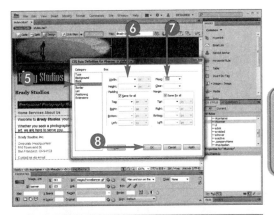

The elements float next to one another, creating a multicolumn layout.

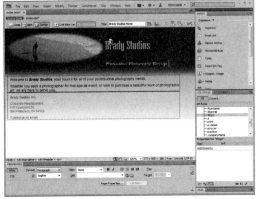

I have heard that floating is not well supported on browsers and should be avoided. Is this true?

▼ Full browser support for the `float` property was slow to develop, particularly on Microsoft Internet Explorer. Because this is the most commonly used browser, many designers have avoided properties that it does not support. However, floating-related bugs have been fixed as of version 7. Because Microsoft has been pushing version 7 through its Automatic Updates feature, and version 7 is the only version supported on Windows Vista, usage of older versions of Internet Explorer is steadily dropping. While you should continue to be aware of the issues around float in older versions of Internet Explorer, float remains the best way to lay out pages in CSS. Mozilla Firefox, Apple Safari, and the Opera browser do not have issues around floats.

Can I have two elements on the same line where one is left aligned and the other is right aligned?

▼ Yes, through a technique referred to as *opposing floats*. All you need to do is to set the first element to `float:left`, and the second to `float:right`. The interaction between the two will result in the desired effect.

Clear Floats

W hen you apply a float to an element, any element that follows it floats if possible. Therefore, using floats can often create layout problems when elements that you do not want to float, such as footers, attempt to do so.

You can control this behavior and prevent undesired floats by using the *clear* property. An element with a clear property does not attempt to float, and prevents elements that appear after it from floating. You can set clear to both, which blocks both left and right floats; left, which prevents a left float but still allows for right floats; and right, which blocks right floats while allowing left floats.

Many designers add an additional element to their page that will not contain any other content in order to insert a clear property. Some use a line break — the br tag — for this purpose, reasoning that the element was designed to create breaks in the flow of the page. Others prefer the div tag, while still others avoid the additional element altogether and simply apply the clear property to whichever element is next on the page.

Clear Floats

① Click the New CSS Rule button.

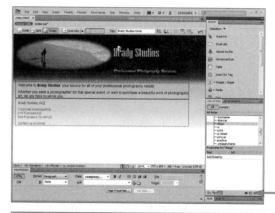

The New CSS Rule dialog box appears.

② Select Class (can apply to any HTML element).

③ Type **.clearFloat** as the class name.

④ Click OK.

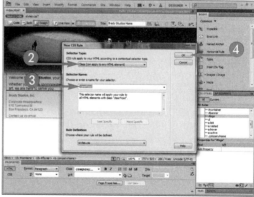

The CSS Rule Definition dialog box appears.

⑤ Click Box.

⑥ Select both from the Clear drop-down menu.

⑦ Click OK.

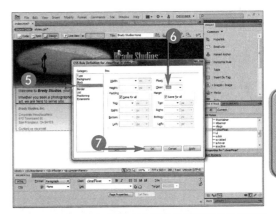

The style is created.

⑧ Click within the content of the element you want to clear.

⑨ Use the Tag Selector to select the tag for the element.

⑩ Select clearFloat from the Class drop-down menu.

The class is applied to the element and the float is cleared.

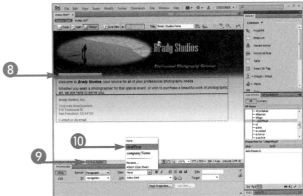

If I have floated elements whose width equals the width of the parent, is it still necessary to clear the float?

▼ It would depend on how the widths are specified. If you have a container element with a width in pixels, and it includes two floated elements with pixel-based widths, then it should not be necessary to clear the floats. However, if you use percentages or ems for the widths of any or all of the elements, then you cannot be sure that they will always be the same relative sizes, and so you should be sure to clear the float to prevent elements that follow from floating.

I have added all of the widths of the floating elements, and it is less than the width of the container, but I still do not see the float. Why is this?

▼ Most often, this issue results from a miscalculation of the element widths. The value of the width property is only the content, whereas the browser adds that width, along with the left and right padding, border, and margins, to determine if there is sufficient space to allow elements to float. Many designers forget to double the padding, border, and margin values to account for both the left and right margins, border and padding, while still others forget to include the one or all of them altogether.

Apply Absolute Positioning

You can also create multicolumn layouts using the CSS `position` property. This powerful property allows you to remove elements from the normal flow of the page and position them yourself. The two most commonly used position values are `relative` and `absolute`.

An element that is using absolute positioning can be placed in a specific location on the page. The exact positioning of the element is controlled by the top, left, right, and bottom properties, and at least one of

these must always be present when using absolute positioning. The positioned element is placed on the page based on these values, and so if you specify a top of 50 pixels, the element's top edge is 50 pixels from the top of the browser window.

Absolutely positioned elements are removed from the flow of the page, and so other elements become unaware of the positioned element, and it is unaware of other elements. Therefore, it can be common for elements to begin to overlap as they do not know that the other element is there.

① Click the New CSS Rule button.

The New CSS Rule dialog box appears.

② Select ID (applies to only one HTML element).

③ Type the name of the ID you want to use.

④ Click OK.

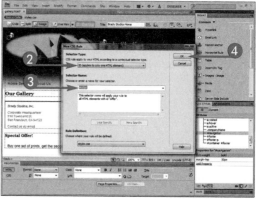

The CSS Rule Definition dialog box appears.

5 Click Positioning.

6 Select absolute.

7 Type values for Top and Left.

8 Click OK.

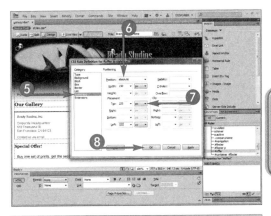

The style is created.

9 Click the element you want to position.

10 Right-click the element's tag in the Tag Chooser.

11 Click Set ID.

12 Click the ID you created in step 3.

The ID is applied to the element, and it is positioned on the page.

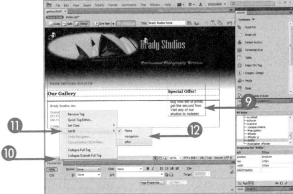

I created a page that uses absolute positioning, but when I view it on a different computer, the page is a mess, with elements overlapping each other. How can I fix this?

▼ While absolute positioning is a very useful tool at times, it should be used with caution and only on select elements on the page. Absolutely positioned elements are unaware of the elements around them, and so they overlap on smaller resolutions or when the browser is resized. They can also create problems when content is added or removed from the element, as the other elements on the page do not adjust their locations to compensate for the changes in the size of the positioned element. Therefore, absolutely positioned elements should be used sparingly on the page. There are very few examples of sites that properly function when they are laid out using only absolute positioning.

Draw an Absolutely Positioned Element

You can draw an element that you want to absolutely position on the page and have Dreamweaver automatically create the corresponding CSS for you. The AP Element tool creates a `div` in your code and automatically generates an ID.

You can resize the element by simply dragging the corner handles. You can reposition it by dragging it to a new location on the page. In either of these cases, Dreamweaver adjusts the CSS code as needed. AP

Elements appear in Design view with a thin border to allow you to see them while you work, but this border does not appear in the browser. When it is selected, the AP Element appears with a thicker, blue border.

You can use the AP Elements panel to show and hide the element, which can be useful when you are intentionally overlapping elements and need to see the ones further down in the stacking order. You can further control this stacking order by adjusting the z-index of the element. Elements with higher z-index numbers appear on top of those with lower numbers.

Draw an Absolutely Positioned Element

1. Click Common on the Insert bar.
2. Click Layout.
3. Click Draw AP Div.
4. Click-and-drag in the Design window.

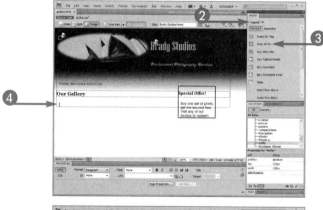

The AP Element is drawn.

5. Click within the element and type to add content.

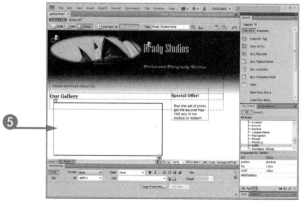

6 Click the border of the element.

The element is selected.

7 Drag the element by the handle in the top-left corner.

The element repositions on the screen. **7**

8 Click Window.

9 Click AP Elements.

The AP Elements panel appears.

10 Click under the eye icon.

The element is hidden.

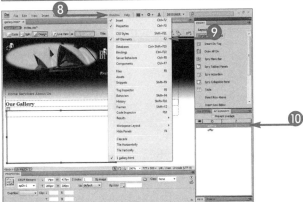

This seems to allow me to create layouts like I can in page design programs such as Adobe InDesign. Is it really that easy?

▼ Yes and no. On the one hand, you can use AP Elements to create pages using the same kinds of techniques as you do in InDesign and other page-layout programs. However, you should keep in mind that the Web is not print, but is instead a completely different medium, and so the techniques you would use for print rarely apply well to the Web. Pages that rely entirely on AP Elements frequently break as the size of the content in them changes.

This appears to be similar to the layers feature I remember from earlier versions of Dreamweaver. Is this the case?

▼ It is not just a similar feature; it is the exact same feature. The term *layers* was adopted in early versions of Dreamweaver because that was the term used by an early version of the Netscape browser that introduced absolute positioning. Dreamweaver continued to use the term long after other programs, including Netscape, abandoned it. The feature was renamed in Dreamweaver CS3 to be more descriptive and prevent confusion with the completely different layers concept from Photoshop.

Apply Relative Positioning

A second and more flexible option for positioning is to set the property to `relative`. Relative positioning allows you to move an element based on its nonpositioned location on the page, and so it is possible to use the property to move an element up or left by a set number of pixels.

You can use relative positioning in conjunction with absolute positioning to better control the layout. When you set top, left, right, or bottom coordinates for an absolutely positioned element, you are positioning it based on its nearest positioned parent.

In most cases, this is the body, and so the element is positioned based on the browser window. However, if you place an absolutely positioned element inside an element with relative positioning set — even if the parent is not itself going to be moved on the page — the AP Element positions itself according to the edges of the parent, rather than the browser window. For example, an AP Element with a top and left of 10 pixels, each placed within a relatively positioned container, appears 10 pixels from the top-left corner of the parent element, instead of the browser window.

Apply Relative Positioning

① Click inside an AP Element.

② Use the Tag Chooser to select the `div`.

③ Click Insert Div Tag on the Insert panel.

The Insert Div Tag dialog box appears.

④ Select Wrap Around Selection from the Insert drop-down menu.

⑤ Type an ID name.

⑥ Click OK.

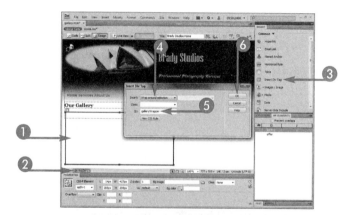

⑦ Double-click CSS Styles.

⑧ Click the New CSS Rule button.

⑨ Select ID (applies to only one HTML element).

⑩ If necessary, type the name of the ID you created in step 5.

⑪ Click OK.

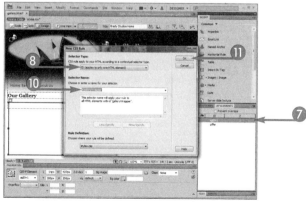

12 Click Positioning.

13 Select relative from the Position drop-down menu.

14 Click OK.

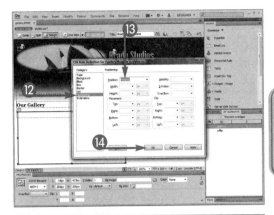

The AP Element repositions to be relative to the new `div` instead of the body.

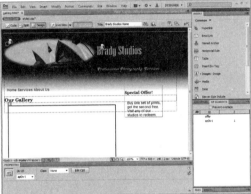

Can I actually position elements on the page using relative positioning?

▼ Yes. Relative positioning removes the element from the flow of the page, but other elements on the page continue to be laid out as if the positioned element was in its original location.

For example, if you have a heading and a paragraph, and you apply relative positioning to the paragraph with a top of 30 pixels, the paragraph shifts down by that amount, but the heading remains in place. The paragraph also overlaps anything that comes after it.

Therefore, relative positioning is rarely used for laying out elements as it leaves gaps on the page where the element used to be. Instead, it is almost always used, as shown in this example, as a way of better controlling AP Elements.

Find CSS Rules Using the Code Navigator

You can simplify the process of finding which CSS rules are applying to an element by using the Code navigator. This feature displays a tooltip next to the currently selected item that displays all of the CSS rules that are affecting the element's display.

Due to the complexities of the CSS cascade, it can be very difficult at times to be sure what rules may be applying to an element. You usually end up with a combination of element selectors, classes, IDs, and inherited properties, all combining to create the

rendering you see on screen. The Code navigator can make determining these styles much easier.

Perhaps the nicest feature of the Code navigator is that it is not only for reference. When you mouse over an element and determine which CSS rule you need to edit, you can click directly on it in the navigator window. Dreamweaver then switches to Split view and displays the appropriate CSS rule. This way, you do not have to manually wade through multiple CSS files or use trial and error to guess which property needs to be changed.

Find CSS Rules Using the Code Navigator

① Alt-click an element on the page.

The Code navigator appears.

② Click a rule.

Note: On a Mac, Option-click the element.

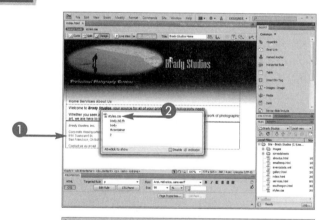

Split view opens and the code navigates to the selected rule.

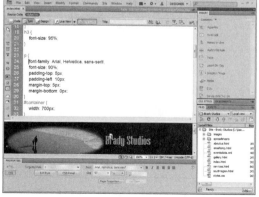

③ Click another element on the page.

The Code navigator icon appears.

④ Click the Code navigator icon.

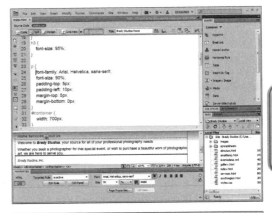

PART II

The Code navigator appears.

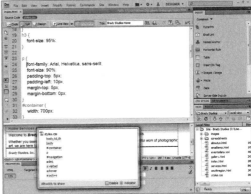

Is there a way to prevent the Code navigator icon from appearing whenever I select something?

▼ Yes. You can open the Code navigator window, where you will notice an option to disable the icon in the bottom-right corner of the navigator. Simply check this option, and you will no longer see the icon.

Is there another way I can view the Code navigator?

▼ There are actually six ways to view the Code navigator. You can Alt-click (Command-Option-click) an element in Design view or Code view or click the Code navigator icon, if it has not been disabled. You can also right-click an element and click Code Navigator from the right-click menu. You can click View, and then click Code Navigator from the menus to open it, or use the keyboard shortcut Control+Alt+N.

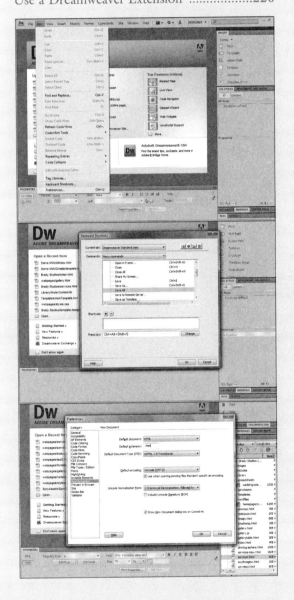

Create a Template

Almost every Web site has certain components that are used across multiple pages. These components might include something as simple as a company logo, or more complex like a navigation bar, or they might possibly constitute the overall layout and structure of the pages as a whole. While CSS has simplified the process of unifying the layout of the pages, the need to share content across a site still exists.

You can greatly reduce the time needed to update and maintain a site and ensure uniformity across multiple pages by using a Dreamweaver template.

Templates are special files created in Dreamweaver that are designed to allow you to share their components. Once you have created the template, you can create new pages based on the template. These new documents automatically contain all of the content from the template.

More importantly, Dreamweaver maintains a connection between the pages created based on templates and the actual templates. This way, if you change something on the template, Dreamweaver automatically updates every page that was based on it.

Create a Template

1 Open an existing Web page.

2 Click Common on the Insert panel.

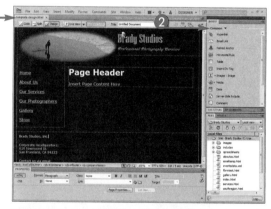

3 Click Templates.

4 Click Make Template.

The Save As Template dialog box appears.

5 Type a name for the template.

6 Click Save.

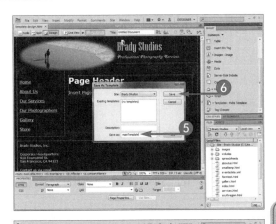

The Update Links dialog box appears.

7 Click Yes.

● The template is created and saved with a .dwt extension.

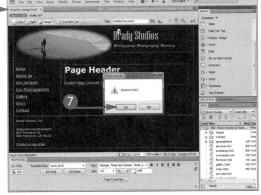

The Save As Template dialog box did not allow me to specify a location for the template. Where are the files saved?

▼ Template files must be saved in a folder called Templates, which must be in the root folder of your Web site. If this directory does not exist, as when you create your first template, Dreamweaver creates it for you. After completing the steps in this example, you should see a Templates folder in your Files panel.

Why does the template have a different filename extension?

▼ Templates are not regular Web pages, and so they do not take an .html or .htm extension. Instead, they use a .dwt extension, which stands for Dreamweaver Template. Dreamweaver recognizes files of this type as template files, as does Adobe Contribute. Contribute is covered in Chapter 14.

When I attempt to save a template, I get an error message saying that I must first create a site. Why does this happen?

▼ Dreamweaver can only use templates when you are working in a site, and so you have to define a site before you can create and use templates. This requirement is due mostly to the fact that Dreamweaver needs to create the Templates folder in the root of the site, which it obviously cannot do if there is no site defined. The process of creating a site in Dreamweaver is covered in Chapter 2.

PART III

Add Editable Regions to a Template

Whentem you create a site using templates, you are trying to create pages that will contain similar components such as navigation bars. You want to ensure that the contents of these components cannot be accidentally changed on a page-by-page basis, as this would defeat the purpose of the template.

On most sites, there will be much more of the page that you do not want to be changeable from page to page than there will be changeable areas, and so Dreamweaver takes the approach of locking down everything and then allowing you to unlock those portions of the page that you want to become editable. You can create these editable regions on any portion of the document, and you can have as many editable regions as you want.

When you create an editable region, you need to give it some kind of logical name so that you or other designers who may work on the pages will be able to understand the purpose of the region. Editable regions can contain placeholder text or be empty.

Add Editable Regions to a Template

1 Select an area on the page that you want to be editable.

● You may want to use the Tag Chooser to select the entire element instead of just its contents.

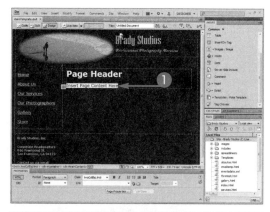

2 Click the arrow next to Templates: Make Template.

3 Click Editable Region.

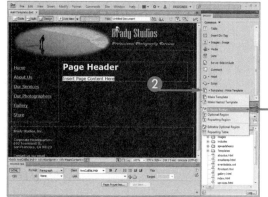

The New Editable Region dialog box appears.

4 Type a descriptive name for the region.

5 Click OK.

The editable region is created.

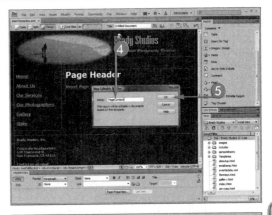

6 Repeat steps **2** to **5** to create additional editable regions.

The regions are added to the page.

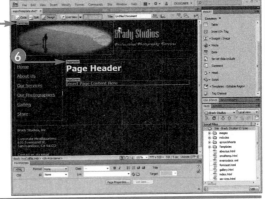

Do I have to create editable regions in order to use the template?

▼ Yes, you must create at least one editable region, or pages you create from the template will be nothing more than exact copies of one another. Dreamweaver warns you if you attempt to create a page from a template that does not contain any editable regions.

When I attempt to save my template page, I get a message that says that I have placed a region within a block tag, and that this might cause problems. Why is this happening and how can I avoid it?

▼ If you simply select the visible text in Design view, Dreamweaver selects the contents of the tag in the Code view, but does not include the actual tag. For example, if you have a header on the page and you select the header text, the actual (X)HTML header tags are not selected. Therefore, when you add the editable region, it is added inside the header tags.

When should I place a region in a block and when I should I avoid it?

▼ This can be a desired behavior. If you plan to have others edit your page content, placing a region inside a tag like this ensures that the tag is always present; so, for example, a headline would always have to be a heading 1. However, it can also limit you, because headers cannot be inside other headers. The message is therefore merely a warning. You can safely ignore it if you want only the contents selected, or change the editable region to include the tag.

Create a Web Page Based on a Template

You need to create pages based on your templates in order to start building your Web site. Once you create the file from the template, you can add or modify the content in any of its editable regions.

Editable regions on the page are shown with a blue border and a small tab showing the name of the region. If content was left inside the region as placeholder text or images when it was created on the

template, it appears on the page and needs to be deleted or replaced with the actual content.

You can create pages from templates by using the New Document dialog box, as shown in this example.

You cannot make any changes to any portions of the page outside of editable regions. If you discover something outside of a region that you need to change, you need to open the template document and alter it directly.

1 Click File.

2 Click New.

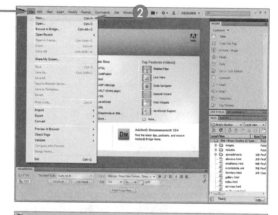

The New Document dialog box appears.

③ Click Page from Template.

④ Click the current site.

⑤ Click the template.

⑥ Click Create.

The page is created from the template.

Is there another way to create a template?

▼ Yes. You can go to the Assets panel, click the Templates button, and then right-click the template and select New from Template.

Does Dreamweaver add additional code to my page when I use a template?

▼ Yes. Dreamweaver identifies the various template regions through special code that it adds to your page. However, this code is enclosed within HTML comment tags, and so Web browsers ignore the additional code; as a result, it does not affect the final display of your page.

Can I format page elements with CSS if I use a template?

▼ Yes. In fact, you can even format portions of the page not included within editable regions if you use an external style sheet. This is possible because the CSS in the external document is not locked as part of the template. Therefore, when you make changes to your CSS, all of the relevant portions of the page, whether contained within editable regions or not, will be updated.

You cannot, however, apply class- or ID-based styles to elements outside of editable regions, as this does require changes to your underlying HTML and will thus be blocked.

Update a Template

Y ou can open and change the template document at any time in your design process. When you save the document, any changes you make to the template are applied to any pages that are created based on the template.

The locking from editable regions only applies to pages created from the template, and so you are free to make any changes you want on the page. This might include updating a company address or copyright notice, or possibly a complete redesign of the site.

As soon as you save the changes to the template, Dreamweaver displays a dialog box that lists all of the pages created based on the template. While it is not possible to manually exclude documents from the update, you should check the list and make sure that it does not include any pages that you do not want to update. Once the update is complete, you are given a report on which documents were updated and have the opportunity to save this information in case there were any errors.

Update a Template

① Click Assets.

② Click the Templates button.

③ Double-click the template you want to open.

④ Make any necessary changes.

⑤ Click File.

⑥ Click Save.

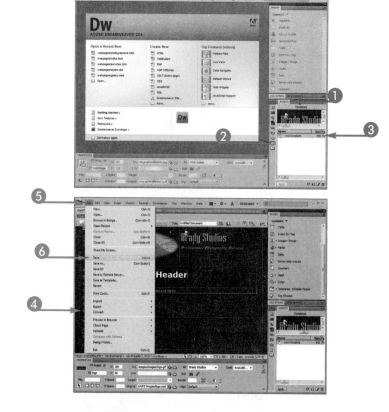

The Update Template Files dialog box appears.

7 Click Update.

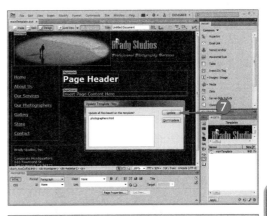

The Update Pages dialog box appears.

8 Click Close.

The template is updated.

Is it possible to create a page based on a template that does not automatically update?

▼ Although this is rarely done, it is possible. If you create a page from a template by clicking File, and then New, you can check the Do not update check box in the New Page dialog box, which creates the new page from the template but does not link it back to the original; as a result, it will not be updated based on changes to the template.

When Dreamweaver updates my pages, is it necessary for me to save the changes?

▼ It depends. If the pages being updated are not currently open in Dreamweaver, then the changes are applied automatically and you do not need to do anything. However, if the documents are currently open in the program when you update the template, then Dreamweaver applies the changes to the pages but marks the pages as unsaved, and so it will be necessary for you to save them. You can always tell if an open document contains unsaved changes, as the document's tab displays an asterisk. If you have multiple open documents with unsaved changes, you can click File and then click Save All to save the changes in one step.

Add a Repeating Region to a Template

There will be times when you need to create a template that will be used as the basis of a document that may contain varying amounts of information. For example, if you have a series of product pages, you can create a template on which you can base all of them. However, if each product listing contains a table of the product's features, how can you know how many rows to include in the table on the template? Most likely, you would only want the individual rows, or possibly only select cells within the table to be editable, and not the actual table.

You can solve this potential issue by inserting only a single row for the table into the template, but then designating that row as a repeat region. When you create a page based on this template, you have the opportunity to add as many additional rows to the table as you need for that particular page. You should note that a repeat region is not actually an editable region, and so it must contain at least one editable region in order for the document to be usable.

① Click Table.

The Table dialog box appears.

② Set the rows to 2, the columns to 3, and set the width to 100 percent.

③ Click Top.

④ Click OK.

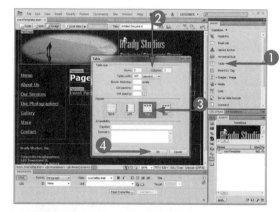

The table is inserted.

⑤ Add header data to the table.

⑥ Add an editable region to each of the cells in the second row.

⑦ Click <tr>.

The row is selected.

8 Click Templates.

9 Click Repeating Region.

The New Repeating Region dialog box appears.

10 Type a name for the region.

11 Click OK.

The region is added to the page.

12 Save the page.

13 In the Update Template dialog box, click Update.

14 In the Update Progress dialog box, click Close.

The template is updated.

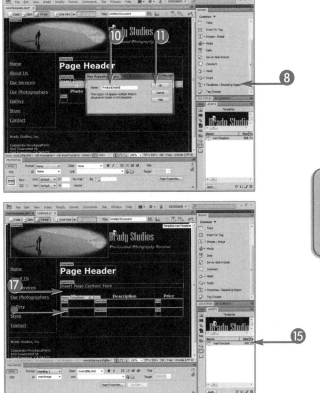

15 Right-click the template.

16 Click New from Template.

The new page is created.

17 Click the Add button.

● A new row is added to the table.

Can I only use repeat regions on tables?

▼ No. Repeat regions can be used around any element. Certainly, their most common use is on tables, but they can also be useful on lists or any other page component that might need them. You would not usually need a repeat region on a set of paragraphs, however, as you should be able to freely add paragraphs to the page without the need for the repeat region. They are only particularly useful for elements that are made up of a set of nested HTML tags, such as tables and lists.

How can I sort a table that relies on a repeat region?

▼ You cannot use Dreamweaver's Sort Table command, as there may be rows in the table that are not included in the repeat regions. However, you will note that Dreamweaver provides two small arrow icons at the top of the table, which allow you to shift rows up and down as needed; so, while automatic sort is not supported, you can do it manually.

Add an Optional Region to a Template

You can maximize the flexibility of your template documents by setting some components in optional regions. Doing so allows you to show or hide these page components on each document created from the template.

Product pages provide a good example. Some products may need detailed descriptions with data tables outlining features, while others may be simpler and not require a table. Rather than needing two templates — one with the table and another without — you can simply set the table in an optional region.

You can designate whether or not the optional region appears on the page by default. Then, using the Modify Template command, you can turn it on and off on each page.

Optional regions are not actually editable, and so like repeat regions, they must contain editable regions if you want to be able to edit their contents. Optional regions can contain any content or other template features such as repeat regions. It is therefore possible to have a template that contains a data table only when needed, but that data table, if used, can contain an indeterminate number of rows.

Add an Optional Region to a Template

1 Click Table.

2 Click Templates.

3 Click Optional Region.

The New Optional Region dialog box appears.

4 Type a name for the region.

5 Click OK.

The optional region is added.

6 Save the page.

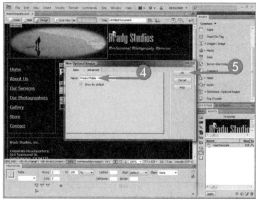

The Update Template Files dialog box appears.

⑦ Click Update.

⑧ Click Close.

⑨ Right-click the template.

⑩ Click New from Template.

A new page is created.

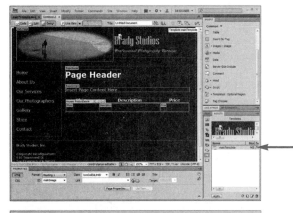

⑪ Click Modify.

⑫ Click Template.

The Template Properties dialog box appears.

⑬ Click the optional region.

⑭ Click Show ProductTable.

The check box is unchecked.

⑮ Click OK.

The optional region is removed from the page.

How can I tell the difference between an optional region, a repeat region, and an editable region when I am looking at my page in Design view?

▼ Each template region is outlined with a tab in the top-right corner denoting its purpose. Editable regions have tabs that display the region name. Repeat regions show the text *Repeat:* followed by the region's name. Optional regions display the word *If* with the name of the region. The tab and outline of the editable region is a darker blue than that of the optional and repeat regions.

If I have an optional region hidden, how can my content providers know that it exists?

▼ Dreamweaver does not have any obvious display of hidden optional regions. You need to provide some kind of instruction to your content providers, possibly through placeholder text in another region, that the optional region exists and that it can be displayed by clicking Modify, and then clicking Template Properties. Many designers prefer to have optional regions shown by default for this reason.

Make Attributes Editable

You can maximize your control over template-based pages by adding editable attributes to otherwise uneditable page elements. In particular, it can be helpful to make ID and class attributes editable on elements that may serve as containers for editable regions.

For example, a common technique in creating slight variations to the styling of a page without having to rely on embedded style sheets is to add an ID attribute to the body of each document. Then, you can use CSS contextual selectors to target styles that the document uses with that ID. However, in a normal template, the body tag is not editable, and so it is impossible to modify the ID on each page. By making the attribute editable, you can maintain the control over the page that a template provides while still giving yourself the flexibility to create page-specific styles.

Another common situation that requires editable attributes is the use of JavaScript effects on your page. While the JavaScript code will likely be contained in the document's head section, you may need to add a reference or trigger to a specific element. If that element is not within an editable region, you need to make the attribute required by the script editable.

Make Attributes Editable

1 Click Modify.

2 Click Templates.

3 Click Make Attribute Editable.

The Editable Tag Attributes dialog box appears.

4 Click Add.

A dialog box appears.

5 Type the name of the attribute you want to add.

6 Click OK.

7 Type a label.

8 Click OK.

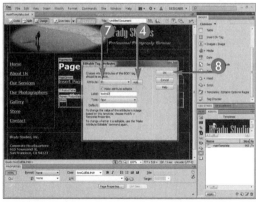

140

⑨ Click File.

⑩ Click Save.

The Update Template Pages dialog box appears.

⑪ Click Update.

The Template Progress dialog box appears.

⑫ Click Close.

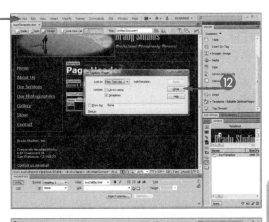

⑬ Right-click the template.

⑭ Click New from Template.

⑮ Click Modify.

⑯ Click Template Properties.

The Template Properties dialog box appears.

⑰ Click bodyID.

⑱ Type a value for the attribute.

⑲ Click OK.

The attribute's value is edited.

Can more than one attribute be editable on a single element?

▼ Yes. It is possible to make the ID attribute of the body editable to facilitate styling, while also making the `onload` attribute of the same tag editable for scripting. You may also find times when you need to add both `onmouseover` and `onmouseout` events to a single element.

How can I add JavaScript to the head of a document created from a template?

▼ While nothing in the body of a document is editable by default, Dreamweaver does automatically create two editable regions on the page. One is within the document's title, allowing you to make each document's title unique, while the other exists within the head of the document for adding scripts or style sheets. You can switch to Code view and add your code between the following tags:

```
<!-- TemplateBeginEditable
name="head" -->

<!-- TemplateEndEditable -->
```

PART III

Create a Library Item

While templates are useful for creating the overall layout of your page, you may find that you need to share individual page components across multiple documents. For example, most likely every page in your site, whether based on a template or not, will need a common footer with your company name and address and a copyright notice.

You may not need to edit your company name or address often, if ever, but a copyright notice should be kept up-to-date with the current year. If you manually type the notice on every page, you will have to

manually edit each page every year, which can be tedious on small sites and impractical on large ones.

The biggest advantage to templates is that you can edit the content in one place — the template document — and then let Dreamweaver update the pages automatically. Library items share the same feature. You can add a page component such as a footer to the library, and then use that library item on any number of documents. When you edit the main library item, every page that contains an instance of that item is updated for you.

Create a Library Item

1 Select content on the page.

2 Click Assets.

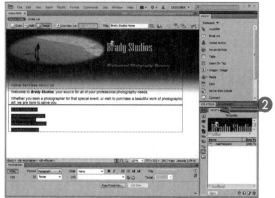

③ Click the Library button.

④ Click the New Item button.

Note: If you receive a warning about the selection's appearance changing, click OK.

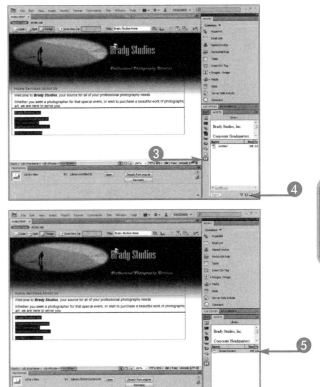

⑤ Type a name for the item.

The library item is created.

Templates and library items seem very similar. What is the difference?

▼ Templates are designed to contain the overall content and structure of the page. Library items, on the other hand, are designed to contain a single page component, such as a navigation bar, header, or footer.

When I insert a library item, I get a message warning me that my styles might be lost. Why is this, and how can I prevent it?

▼ Dreamweaver is only saving the specific snippet of code you selected as the library item. Styles are applied to it from the head section of the document or possibly from an external document. In this case, Dreamweaver is merely reminding you that the specific CSS code to style the item is not included with the actual library item. Therefore, if you insert the item into a page that does not apply the same styles as the one from which you created it, it may appear differently. It will almost certainly appear differently in the Assets panel, as the panel does not read styles at all, and so you will see an unstyled version in the panel.

Insert a Library Item onto a Page

Once you have created a library item, you can insert it onto any page or pages in your site by simply dragging it from the Assets panel and dropping it in the location on the page where you want it to appear.

When you insert a library item, you will notice that it appears to have a light yellow background. This is simply Dreamweaver's way of reminding you that the component is a library item, and the background color will not appear on the page in the browser.

When you select an inserted library item on the page, you see that the Property Inspector gives you the option of editing the library item or of detaching the item. If you choose to detach the item, it will no longer be updated when the library item is changed. This can be helpful for maintaining the appearance of archived pages that should not be kept up-to-date with the rest of the site. Should you accidentally detach an item, you can simply delete it from the page and then reinsert the library item.

Insert a Library Item onto a Page

① Click Assets.

② Click the Library button.

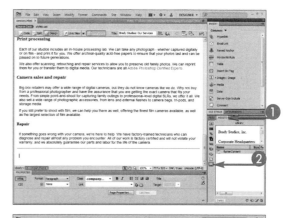

③ Press and hold your mouse down on the library item.

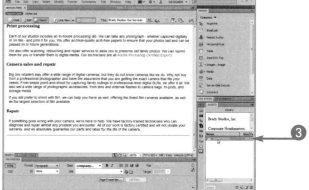

④ Drag the item to the page.

⑤ Release your mouse.

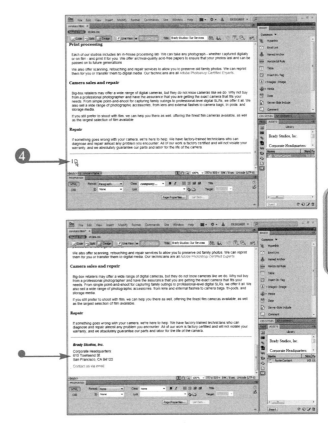

● The library item is inserted.

Can library items be used on templates?

▼ Absolutely. While it may not make sense to do so in a site with a single template, sites that use more than one template for different site sections will find that those templates will all need to share common components such as footers. By placing the component in a library item, and then adding the item to the template, you can have a cascading update effect, where if you update the library item, Dreamweaver automatically updates the templates, which in turn force an update on the pages created from the templates.

Does Dreamweaver use special code for the library item?

▼ As with templates, Dreamweaver inserts library items by surrounding them with special markup. This added code is hidden from browsers due to its being included within HTML comment tags. You can switch to Code view to see the comment that allows Dreamweaver to keep track of the library item.

Update a Library Item

Once you have inserted library items onto the page, you can update them when changes become necessary. Just as with templates, Dreamweaver automatically updates the pages on which the library item has been placed.

You can edit a library item by selecting it on the page and clicking Edit, or by double-clicking the item in the Assets panel. It then opens in a separate document, and you can make any necessary changes.

Keep in mind that the library item does not contain the necessary references to the CSS code, and so it will appear in its completely unstyled state. You can completely ignore this styling, or rather lack of styling, as the item will appear as you intended once you insert it onto a page with the proper CSS reference.

As soon as you save the library item, Dreamweaver updates the pages upon which it is based. The program uses the exact same interface for this update as it does for template updates, and so you will first be given a list of the pages to be updated, and then a report dialog box that indicates that the updating is complete.

1 Double-click the library item.

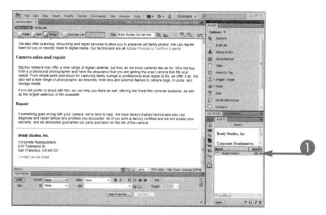

The item opens in its own window.

2 Make a change to the content.

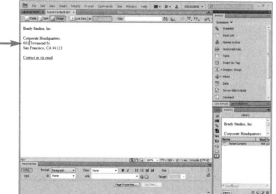

3 Click File.

4 Click Save.

The Update Library Items dialog box appears.

5 Click Update.

The Update Complete dialog box appears.

6 Click Close.

The library item is saved, and the pages upon which the item was inserted are updated.

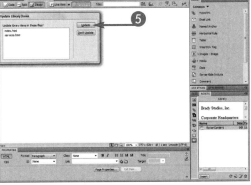

Where are library items stored?

▼ All library items are stored in a Library folder, which must be in your site root. Dreamweaver creates this folder if it does not exist when you first save a library item.

Can my library item contain links?

▼ Yes. Any page content can be a library item. However, you need to be aware that any links internal to your site must have their path set relative to the Library folder, not relative to the page or pages that will end up containing the item. To avoid possible confusion, you should always use the Browser button or the point-to-file icon on the Property Inspector, and not type it in directly for fear of getting the path wrong and causing the link to break.

Why is the document that was updated marked as unsaved?

▼ Dreamweaver updates pages that contain library items in the same way it updates pages based on templates. Therefore, if the document being updated is open, Dreamweaver makes the changes but then you must save it.

Use Snippets

Dreamweaver contains a collection of pre-built, reusable blocks of code called *snippets*. These code blocks can be reused on pages to reduce development time.

You can use any of the snippets that come with Dreamweaver or create your own. Over time, you can build a collection of snippets that contain blocks of code that you use across the various sites you develop.

Snippets differ from library items in two key respects. First, they are not site specific. You can only access a library item within the site in which you create it,

because library item files are stored within the site. Snippets, on the other hand, are stored within the Dreamweaver configuration folder, and so they are accessible within any site. Second, snippets do not have the automatic update feature of library items, and so if you change the contents of a snippet, pages that use it will not be updated.

Some designers place a *site designed by* notice on pages they create. Because this would need to be used on many sites, and would not likely need to be updated often, it would make sense to use a snippet for this instead of a library item.

Use Snippets

① Click Window.

② Click Snippets.

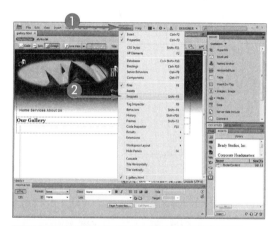

The Snippets panel opens.

③ Select a block of content on the page.

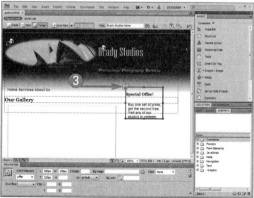

④ Click the New Snippet button.

The Snippet dialog box appears.

⑤ Type a name for the snippet.

⑥ Click OK.

The snippet is saved.

⑦ Open another document.

⑧ Drag the new snippet to the page.

The snippet is added to the document.

Why does my snippet appear different when I place it on a new page?

▼ Like library items, the final display of snippets will most likely be controlled through CSS. The snippet only contains the basic (X)HTML markup that surrounded the text, and not any CSS. Therefore, the contents of the snippet may change from one page to the next, depending on the CSS controlling that page.

While this may appear to be a problem when you first use snippets, you will find that it is actually an advantage. By using CSS that is not contained within the actual snippet to format it, you are free to use the same content from one site, or even one page, to the next and rest assured that you can tailor the display of the content to match the current site or page.

What is the preview type?

▼ The Snippet panel can preview the snippets by either displaying their (X)HTML code or by displaying them as they might appear in Design view. The Snippet dialog box allows you to choose which of these methods will be used, but it does not affect the actual use of the snippet.

Add a Behavior

You can add basic interactivity to your Web pages by inserting JavaScript code. JavaScript was originally developed by the Netscape Corporation, but is now an open scripting language that can be freely used by anyone and is supported in every major browser.

While you can write JavaScript yourself, Dreamweaver provides two methods by which you can implement JavaScript in your pages without writing code. The first is through behaviors, which exist as prebuilt blocks of JavaScript with specific functionality. The second, Spry, is discussed in the next chapter.

Behaviors free you from needing to learn how JavaScript works or from writing and debugging your own code. Dreamweaver includes 26 behaviors, ranging from simple effects such as generating pop-up windows to more complex effects like creating page transitions.

One of the more common JavaScript behaviors is creating an image roll-over effect, where users can move their mouse over an image and have either that or another image on the page change. This can require complicated code if you write it yourself, but with a Dreamweaver behavior, you can do it without writing any code at all.

Add a Behavior

① Click an image on the page.

② Type an ID for the image.

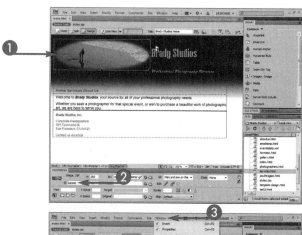

③ Click Window.

④ Click Behaviors.

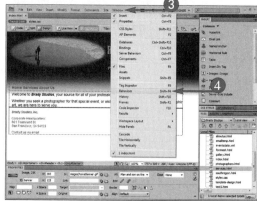

The Tag Inspector panel opens, displaying the Behaviors.

⑤ Click the Add button.

⑥ Click Swap Image.

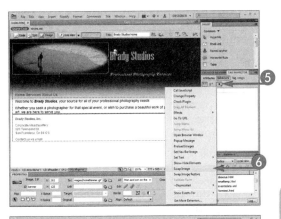

The Swap Image dialog box appears.

⑦ Select the ID of the image you created in step 2.

⑧ Click Browse.

The Select Image Source dialog box appears.

⑨ Select the new image.

⑩ Click OK.

⑪ Click OK.

The behavior is added and displays in the panel.

How can I test to see if my behavior worked?

▼ Behaviors, and in fact any JavaScript, do not run in Design view. In order to preview the effect, you either need to preview the page in a Web browser, or else use Dreamweaver's Live view, which is discussed later in this chapter.

What do the Preload images and Restore images onMouseOut options do?

▼ The Preload images option adds some additional JavaScript to ensure that the browser requests the second image when the page first loads. If you deselect this option, the browser will wait until the user actually moves his mouse over the image and triggers the behavior before it attempts to download the image.

The Restore image onMouseOut option adds the necessary code to your page to have the image revert to the original when the user moves his mouse away from the triggering image. As this is almost always the desired behavior, you should leave it checked.

Modify a Behavior

Once applied, you can modify a behavior that you place on a page. You can modify behaviors as often as you need to make sure that they do what you want.

Behaviors can be modified by double-clicking them in the Behaviors panel. The dialog box that you saw when you originally added the behavior appears again with the last settings you applied, and you can then change the settings as needed.

If you do not see your behavior listed in the panel, you most likely have the wrong element selected on the page. Behaviors are always applied on a specific element, and so you need to reselect the element to which you applied the behavior in order to see it listed and be able to edit it.

As when you inserted the behavior, you can only preview it using the Preview in Browser feature or Dreamweaver's Live view. Live view is discussed later in this chapter.

Modify a Behavior

① Click the image to which you added a behavior.

② Double-click the behavior.

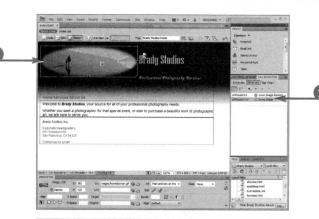

The Swap Image dialog box appears.

③ Change any desired settings.

For example, you might select a different image for the Set Source To setting.

④ Click OK.

The behavior is updated with the new settings.

Change an Event

Every behavior is made of two parts: the actual behavior, and a trigger or event for the behavior. JavaScript is known as an *event-driven language*, which simply means that your users need to do something on the page, such as moving their mouse over an image, before the code will execute.

Each behavior in Dreamweaver has a predefined action. For example, the Swap Image behavior's default action is onMouseOver, and so it is activated when the mouse is moved over the image. However, you can change the default to another action if you would prefer your page to behave differently.

The possible actions available depend on the type of behavior and the element on the page being used to trigger the behavior. Most elements on the page that are clickable support onMouseOver, onMouseOut, and onClick events. Behaviors applied to the actual document, on the other hand, can only use onLoad and onUnload actions. These limitations are part of the JavaScript language, and are not limitations in Dreamweaver. When you insert a behavior, if you do not see the events you expect, you should double-check to be sure that it was added to the correct element on the page.

Change an Event

1 Click the drop-down menu next to the current event.

2 Select a new event.

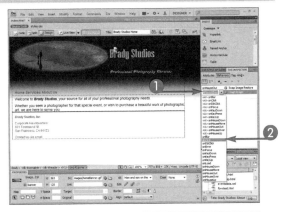

● The event is changed.

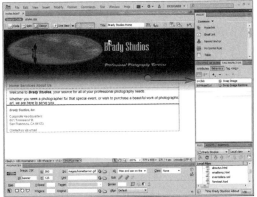

Open a New Browser Window

Normally, when you click a hyperlink, the target page opens in the same browser window as the page that contained the link. While this may be the desired behavior for most links, there will be times when you want links to open a separate, new browser window. For example, if you have a page that displays small thumbnail images, you may want them to serve as links to bigger versions of the images, which you will want to open in another window.

You can add an Open New Browser Window behavior to add this functionality to the page. This behavior

allows you to set the page that should open in the window, as well as a set of attributes of the window. You can set the width and height of the new window, and control whether or not it contains standard browser features such as scroll bars, address bars, and toolbars. Note that you must check each of these items to turn them on — they are disabled by default. Be aware that if the new content contains its own links or links to another Web site, you should always add these functions.

Open a New Browser Window

① Click a link on the page.

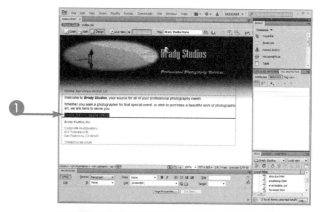

② Click the Add button.

③ Click Open Browser Window.

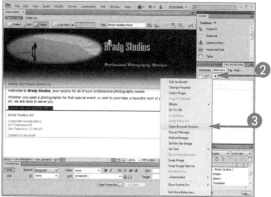

154

④ Type the address to the page you are targeting.

⑤ Select any additional browser features you want to add.

⑥ Click OK.

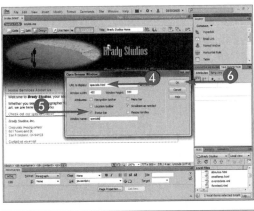

● The behavior is added.

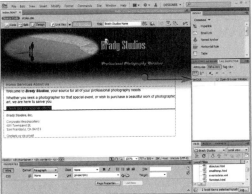

Why would I need to name the new window?

▼ The window name in the New Browser Window dialog box is optional, but if you have more than one link on a page that will contain this action, you need to decide whether you want each link to open in the same new window, where each set of new content replaces the last, or open in individual new windows. If you add the same name in each link, they will all use the same new window. If you either leave the name blank or enter unique names, they will open in individual windows.

Does this behavior always need to be added to hyperlinks?

▼ Technically, yes, as some older browsers only support clicking hyperlinks. If you should add it to an element that is not already a link, you can set the event to <A> onClick, in which case, Dreamweaver adds a hyperlink around the text and applies the behavior to the link.

If you do want to add the link yourself, you should type **javascript:void();** in the link box, as this code informs the browser that the action for the link will be handled by the script.

Preview a Page Using Live View

Prior versions of Dreamweaver forced you to preview your pages in a Web browser in order to see what they might look like. Many page elements, such as borderless tables, and all behaviors do not display properly in Design view.

Dreamweaver now supports a new method of viewing pages, called Live view. Unlike Design view, Live view uses an actual browser-rendering engine. Features such as JavaScript behaviors will work in Live view just

as they do in a browser, allowing you to interact with these features while remaining in Dreamweaver.

You can switch to Live view at any time by clicking its button on the document toolbar. Dreamweaver switches to Split view, showing the code in one half of the document, and the Live view version in the other. Live view is not editable, however, and so you will need to either make modifications in the code or else switch back to Design view to edit your page.

Preview a Page Using Live View

① Click Live view.

Live view opens, and the page displays as it will in a browser.

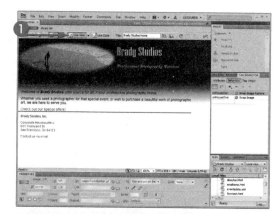

② Mouse over an image that has a swap image behavior attached.

The image changes.

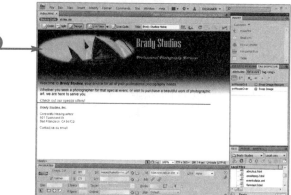

③ Move your mouse away from the image.

The image reverts to the original.

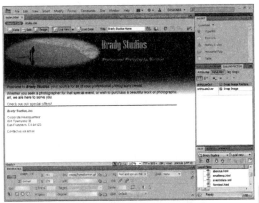

④ Click Live view.

Dreamweaver exits Live view.

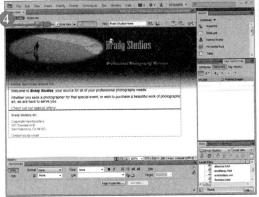

Does using Live view mean that I do not need to preview pages in an actual browser?

▼ No. Dreamweaver uses the open source WebKit engine for its Live view preview, but this is not the same rendering engine used by many other browsers. Therefore, Live view is not a suitable substitute for actually previewing the page in a browser, as the display may be different. Live view is intended to give designers a way to test JavaScript and server-side code functionality directly within Dreamweaver, but it should not be considered a substitute for previewing in multiple browsers to ensure that your page, and in particular your CSS, will correctly render in them.

Understanding the Spry Framework

In a traditional HTML document, no part of the page can be changed without having the browser make a new request back to the Web server and receiving either a new page or an updated version of the same page. This meant that an entire page had to be refreshed to change even a small portion of the content. All of that changed with the introduction of Ajax.

Ajax

Ajax originally stood for Asynchronous JavaScript and XML, although most users today no longer treat it as an acronym.

Ajax relies on four languages working together in the browser to enhance the overall user experience. The first two are contained in the original acronym: JavaScript and XML. JavaScript is responsible for all of the interactivity and behaviors in the browser; it serves as a sort of director and engineer for everything that Ajax does. XML stands for Extensible Markup Language. It was developed by the World Wide Web Consortium (W3C) — the organization responsible for developing and maintaining Web technologies such as (X)HTML — as a way to allow developers to describe data in a simple, open, text-based markup language.

Ajax's other two components are ones with which you are becoming familiar: (X)HTML and CSS. Much of what Ajax accomplishes is done by using JavaScript to manipulate (X)HTML and CSS documents, often tying into XML data to populate the page.

Ajax Libraries

A common misconception about Ajax is that it is somehow a single language or technology that can be learned in a traditional manner. In fact, it is really almost nothing more than a concept: How can you use JavaScript, XML, CSS, and (X)HTML together to achieve a better user interface and better Web experience for your users?

While it is possible to write your own code in some combination of the Ajax languages, few designers either want or need to. Instead, a series of Ajax libraries have been developed over the years to facilitate development. These libraries usually consist of a series of prebuilt JavaScript documents that can be called by designers, freeing them from having to learn, write, and debug the JavaScript, which is by far the most complex area of Ajax.

Several extremely popular Ajax libraries exist today. JSON, which is short for JavaScript Object Notation, is useful for those who want to focus heavily on the data-exchange side of things. Microsoft has developed an Ajax library for use within its .NET platform.

Spry

In 2006, Adobe announced the development of its own Ajax library, called the Spry Framework. Unlike most other libraries, which tend to focus on the XML side of Ajax and rely on getting and using data from servers, Spry focuses much more heavily on the design side of the equation. While there are several Spry components that can be used for data, which is explored later in this chapter, most of the Spry Framework's components are used for manipulating (X)HTML and CSS to achieve effects that were previously beyond the scope of most designers' skill sets.

Spry Components

The Spry Framework contains three basic sets of components. The Web page widgets can be used to create simple drop-down menus, collapsible page regions, and other page elements. The effects components allow you to achieve visual effects such as having areas of the page slide or fade in and out. Finally, the data components allow you to read XML or (X)HTML data and display it dynamically.

Spry Versions
As of this writing, the most recent version of Spry is 1.6.1, although it is constantly under development and may be several subversions beyond that by now. You can view the documentation and download the latest version of the Spry Framework from Adobe's Spry Web site at labs.adobe.com/technologies/spry.

Spry 1.6.1 adds many new features to the framework, including the ability to use (X)HTML files as a data source and many new form field widgets. These are discussed in the upcoming sections in this chapter.

Spry and Dreamweaver
Dreamweaver CS3 included an earlier version of Spry, 1.4, when it was released. In addition to the JavaScript files that are necessary to actually implement the framework, Dreamweaver also included a Spry toolbar in the Insert bar that allowed developers to easily use Spry effects on their pages without writing any code.

Dreamweaver CS4 includes the Spry 1.6.1 framework, and like its predecessor, includes a Spry section on the now-renamed Insert panel. This new version of the program has added tools for inserting and working with the new additions to Spry.

Spry and Web Standards
Spry ties its effects to specific Web page elements by inserting nonstandard attributes. At first, this was seen as a stumbling block to its adoption, as many designers today focus heavily on creating only standards-based pages. This is in fact the approach taken throughout this book.

While Spry still technically relies on these special attributes, a compromise approach has now been found that allows designers to extract all of the JavaScript and attributes out of the document and place them in an external file. This way, you can have the best of both worlds: Spry-based pages that validate under Web standards.

Accessibility and Degrading Spry
Two of the biggest issues facing many Ajax developers are accessibility and graceful degrading. Accessibility ensures that users who suffer from disabilities and thus must interact with Web sites using alternate devices such as screen readers will still be able to understand the site. Because screen readers and other assistive technologies tend to ignore JavaScript, many Ajax-driven pages quickly become inaccessible.

Another related issue is how the page responds if JavaScript is disabled on a user's browser. While rare, there are users who choose to disable JavaScript for various reasons, but many Ajax sites partially or completely break when JavaScript is turned off. Screen readers ignore JavaScript, and so pages that cannot be successfully used without JavaScript are generally not accessible either.

Fortunately, Spry 1.6.1 has introduced several techniques to solve both of these problems. Its (X)HTML data set, which is examined later, is an example of a Spry component that degrades gracefully. The Spry Web page widgets are all built using standards-based (X)HTML that displays their content with JavaScript disabled and exposes the content for screen readers and assistive devices.

Add a Menu Bar Widget

Web designers have long struggled with finding a way to implement drop-down menu systems on their pages that are easy to insert, easy to maintain, and easy to design. Unfortunately, few menu systems available for download off the Web meet all three requirements, and fewer still follow Web standards and are accessible and degradable.

Fortunately, you can insert a menu bar that meets all of the above requirements through the Spry menu bar widget. The menu bar can be inserted either horizontally or vertically. It includes a simple set of

properties, available on Dreamweaver's Property Inspector, for adding and deleting items on the menu. The menu exists in the code as a series of unordered lists, and so it remains fully functional and is fully accessible if JavaScript is disabled. Its appearance is managed entirely through CSS, and is fully customizable.

As with any JavaScript-driven page component, you cannot preview Spry effects in Design view. You need to use either the Preview in Browser feature or the Live view functionality to see the Spry menu in action.

Add a Menu Bar Widget

① Click in the page at the point at which you want your menu to appear.

② Click Common.

③ Click Spry.

④ Click Spry Menu Bar.

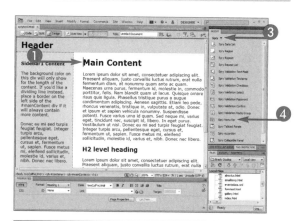

The Spry Menu Bar dialog box appears.

⑤ Click Horizontal or Vertical.

⑥ Click OK.

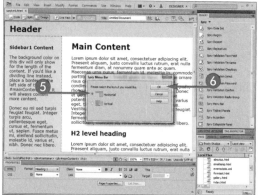

The menu bar is inserted.

7 Click Spry Menu Bar: MenuBar1.

The Property Inspector updates.

8 Change the names of the menu items.

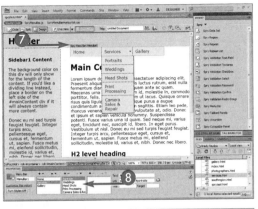

9 Click Live View.

Live view displays.

10 Mouse over the menu.

The drop-down menu appears.

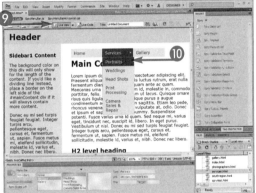

Do I have to use the Property Inspector to change the menu's properties?

▼ No. When you select the menu, you can click Turn Styles Off from the Property Inspector. This disables the CSS on the page and displays the menu as a series of unordered lists. These can then be directly manipulated in Design view, and so you can add, change, and delete items just as you would on any other list.

When I save the page after inserting the menu bar, Dreamweaver asks if I want to save several other files. What are these?

▼ All Spry components rely on a set of external files. At a minimum, there will be one JavaScript file and one CSS file per component, but several require more than that. The menu bar component, for example, adds a set of GIF images that it uses for the arrows pointing to the submenus. The dialog box you are seeing is merely Dreamweaver asking for permission to copy these files into your site. The files are placed in a folder called SpryAssets in the root directory of your Web site.

Insert a Tabbed Panels Widget

You can present more content in less space using the Spry tabbed panels widget. This widget uses a series of `div` elements stacked on top of one another, with a set of links along the top to navigate between the tabs.

You can place any content you want into the panels just as you would add content to the regular page. When you insert the panels, you see a small blue bar appear along the top-left corner; clicking this bar

allows you to activate the Property Inspector and use it to add more tabs or rearrange existing ones.

You can open the other tabs and add content to them by clicking the small eye icon that appears when you mouse over the tab on the page. By default, each tab only appears as large as its content, and so if you add a lot of content to one tab and only a small amount to another, you will not have a lot of empty space on the tab with less content.

Insert a Tabbed Panels Widget

① Click the page at the point at which you want to insert the panels.

② Click Spry Tabbed Panels.

The tabbed panel widget is inserted.

③ Select the text Content 1.

④ Press Delete.

⑤ Insert new content into the panel.

⑥ Select the text Tab 1.

⑦ Type a new title for the tab.

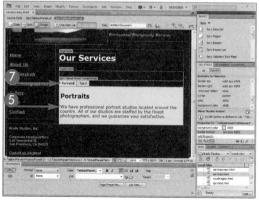

⑧ Mouse over Tab 2.

⑨ Click the eye icon.

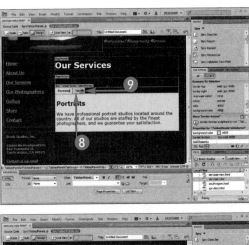

Tab 2 appears.

⑩ Insert your new content.

⑪ Type a new title on the tab.

The tabbed panels are updated with the new content and tab names.

Is there a limit to how many panels I can have?

▼ No. You can add as many tabbed panels as you need. If you add more panels than will fit in a single row, the tabs automatically wrap to additional rows. In fact, this occurs automatically in the browser, and so users with wider screens will see fewer rows of tabs than those on smaller screens.

Will search engines find content that I place in the panels?

▼ Yes. Like screen readers, search engines ignore JavaScript, and so they read your page as if the tabbed panel effect was not there. If you disable JavaScript in your browser and view the page, you will simply see a series of consecutive blocks of content. Because all of this content exists directly in the (X)HTML of the page, it can all be read by search engines, screen readers, or users with JavaScript disabled, and so using the tabbed panels can be seen as a way of enhancing your sighted users' experience without harming anyone else's.

Add an Accordion Widget

You can display stacked content through the tabbed panels widget or an accordion widget. Both use essentially the same underlying (X)HTML. The key difference between the accordion widget and the tabbed panels widget is the navigation between the panels. Whereas the tabbed panels widget inserts a set of tabs along the top of the widget for navigation, the accordion widget displays its content in a series of collapsing panels. When a page containing the accordion first loads, the top panel is expanded, displaying its content, and the rest appears as a series of bars along the bottom. Clicking

any of these bars causes that panel to expand and whichever other panel is open to collapse.

While the accordion widget can be used to display blocks of content similar to the tabbed panels, it is often used as a navigation bar. This allows you to group your navigation into a series of logical sections, with subsection links appearing as your user expands and collapses the accordion.

As with tabbed panels, any content can be placed within the accordion. You can switch between the accordion tabs in Design view by clicking the eye icon.

Add an Accordion Widget

1 Click in the page.

2 Click Spry Accordion.

The accordion is added to the page.

3 Select the text Content 1.

4 Press Delete.

5 Insert new content into the panel.

6 Select the text Label 1.

7 Type a new title for the label.

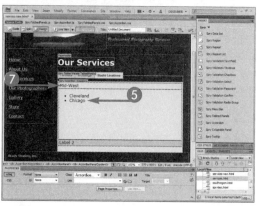

⑧ Mouse over Label 2.

⑨ Click the eye icon.

Label 2 appears.

⑩ Insert your new content.

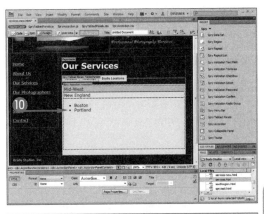

⑪ Click Spry Accordion: Accordion1.

The Property Inspector displays the accordion properties.

⑫ Click the Add button.

A new panel is added.

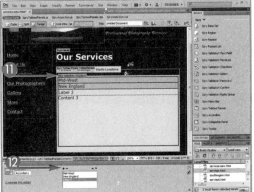

Will users have a hard time understanding how to use the accordion?

▼ While Web sites have employed accordion-style navigation in the past, it is still fairly rare to encounter sites that use accordions for their main content. If you do display content in the accordion, be sure that the labels you use on the accordion panels make it clear that they contain content, as many users may be unfamiliar with how accordions should work and may not understand that content exists in the panels. Careful usability testing should be carried out on the accordion, as with any other aspect of your page, to be sure that users are not missing out on content because they fail to understand its presentation.

Is there a way to control which panel is open by default?

▼ The top panel in the accordion is always open by default. Through code, it is possible to set another panel to be open first, but this is not supported through the Dreamweaver visual interface. The same applies to setting the accordion to be either entirely collapsed or entirely expanded by default: Both are only possible through manipulating code.

Insert a Collapsible Panel Widget

Often, you may want to place content on your page that might be considered extra content: information that is not vital to understanding the site, but nonetheless worth presenting. In this case, you can add the content in a Spry collapsible panel widget. For example, you will most likely want to place the address of your company or organization on the site. Many sites today like to place a map to the site as well, but of course a map can take up a lot of space. Placing it in a collapsible

panel effectively hides it when the page initially loads, but those who want to see it can do so by expanding the panel.

In a way, the collapsible panel is a special implementation of the Spry accordion, but, by definition, it only contains a single panel of information. When clicked, the panel expands with an animated effect, pushing down the page content that appears below it. You should test this effect to be sure that the act of pushing content down does not negatively impact other aspects of your page design.

Insert a Collapsible Panel Widget

1 Click in the page.

2 Click Spry Collapsible Panel.

The panel is added to the page.

3 Select the text Content.

4 Press Delete.

5 Insert new content into the panel.

6 Select the text Tab.

7 Type a new title for the label.

The panel is created.

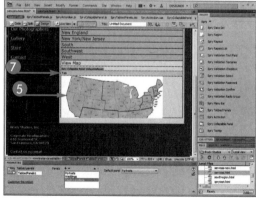

Add a Spry Tooltip

Computer users have become accustomed to seeing tooltip displays that further explain tasks in desktop applications. For example, Microsoft Word displays additional information when you mouse over some text that it recognizes as an address.

(X)HTML supports the addition of small tooltips over sections of content through its `title` attribute, but browsers can at times be inconsistent in how the `title` attribute is supported. More important, however, is that the `title` attribute's tooltip is

generated by the operating system, and so you as a developer have no control over its appearance.

The Spry tooltip widget gives you a consistent display across all browsers and allows you to control the details of its appearance by simply modifying its CSS. The tooltip can be added to any text, although you should probably limit it to text that the user is likely going to want to mouse over; otherwise, he will never know that the tooltip exists.

You are not limited to text in the tooltip; you can insert images or anything else you want in the tooltip's content section.

Add a Spry Tooltip

① Click Spry Tooltip.

The tooltip is inserted.

② Replace the text, *Tooltip trigger goes here*, with your own text.

③ Replace the text, *Tooltip content goes here*, with your own text.

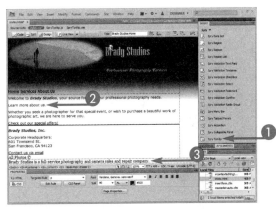

④ Click Live View.

⑤ Mouse over the tooltip trigger text.

The tooltip appears.

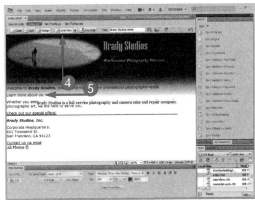

Add a Spry Data Set

Spry also includes a set of components that allow you to use external data. These allow you to load data from external sources — either XML or (X)HTML — into pages.

XML is a data definition language. While a full discussion of XML is beyond the scope of this book, you should know that XML files are simple text files that describe their content through a markup language that looks very much like (X)HTML. In fact, both (X)HTML and XML are derived from the same parent language.

To load data into your page, you first need to create a Spry Data Set. You can use the Spry Data Set wizard to specify the location of the data. The data file can be any valid XML file or an (X)HTML file that contains some kind of structured data, such as that in a table. You can then choose which data on the page you want to display. The wizard then allows you to quickly add the data to your page using one of four preset layouts. You can also choose to have it simply create the connection, and then design the layout portion yourself.

Add a Spry Data Set

1 Click Spry Data Set.

The Spry Data Set Wizard opens.

2 Ensure that Select Data Type is set to HTML.

3 Type a name for the data set.

4 Click Browse.

5 Select the file you want to use for the data.

6 Click the yellow arrow.

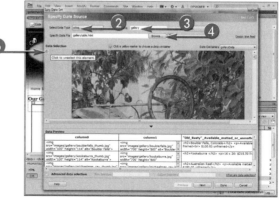

7 Click Next.

8 Click Next.

9 Select a layout option.

10 Click Set Up.

The Spry Data Set Insert Master/Detail Layout dialog box appears.

11 Add rows you want to display in the Master Columns section or remove rows you do not want to show in the Details columns.

12 Remove rows you do not want to display in the Detail Columns section.

13 Click OK.

14 Click Done.

The data region and display are added.

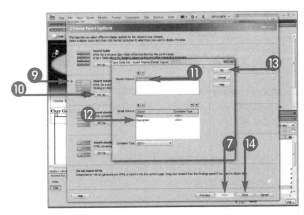

15 Click Live View.

Live view displays the page with the external data.

When I attempt to add an (X)HTML file as a data region, I get a message saying that no selectable elements were found. What am I doing wrong?

▼ In order to identify the region of the page you want to use for your data, that region must have an ID attribute. You may need to go back to the original page and add an ID on the parent element, such as `table`, of the region you will use for data.

Can the data and the display exist on the same page?

▼ Yes. You can use a table on the page that you plan to use for display. Spry automatically includes code to hide the table, so that your users will only see the Spry region, but users who disable JavaScript will see the original table instead. An implementation of this is shown in Chapter 20.

I understand how to create an (X)HTML table to use for data. Where might XML data be coming from?

▼ Many resources use XML today. RSS, a popular format for syndicating Web site content, is a form of XML. Most database systems have the ability to export to XML, as do programs like Microsoft Word and Microsoft Excel.

Change Styles for Spry Widgets

You can alter the appearance of the Spry widgets so that they match the overall look and feel of your site. All of the Spry widgets use CSS for their formatting.

When you open a page that contains a Spry widget, the CSS documents that control the widget — which were automatically added to your site when you first saved the page after inserting the widget — appear on the Related Documents bar. You can simply click one of these documents to view the CSS and then make whatever changes are necessary.

Many of the widgets rely on roll-over effects that are not visible in Design view, but Live view allows you to interact with them as if you were in a browser. You can also use Dreamweaver's Live code option to see the (X)HTML that is being rendered by the JavaScript. This can help you to determine which styles need to be edited. When using Live code, you can freeze the code so that it remains in its current state as you edit the CSS.

① Click Live View.

Live view displays.

② Click Live Code.

Live code displays.

③ Move your mouse over the widget to activate it.

The Live code displays the new (X)HTML.

④ Press F6.

The code is frozen.

⑤ Click a class selector.

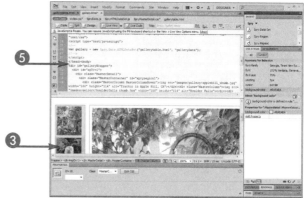

6 Click the property you want to change.

7 Type a new value.

8 Press F6.

The code is unfrozen.

9 Move your mouse over the widget to activate it.

The widget's styles are changed.

When I attempt to change something in Live code, I get a message that it is read-only. Why is this and how can I use it to edit?

▼ Live code view is not intended as a place where you can edit your source code. Rather, it was designed to make it easier to see code that is being generated by JavaScript so that it can be edited elsewhere. Because the generated code does not exist in the page until the JavaScript activates it, editing the code could cause the script to stop functioning, which is why Live code is read-only. Changing the styles on the Spry widgets presented a challenge in the past because you had to dig into the code and guess which style might be applying at any given time; Live code was designed to simplify this by showing you the styles. As is shown in the task steps, you can edit the styles using the CSS panel, but you cannot edit the source code directly.

Use the JavaScript Extractor

More and more Web designers are realizing the advantages to creating pages that adhere to the published standards of the World Wide Web Consortium (W3C). Dreamweaver has, for the last several versions, been focused on creating standards-based pages. Unfortunately, however, Spry uses nonstandards-based (X)HTML attributes as a key part of its implementation.

You can resolve this issue and use Spry while maintaining a standards-based design approach by using the JavaScript Extractor. This feature scans through an (X)HTML page and removes any Spry attributes as well as any JavaScript that is enclosed in embedded `script` tags, copies them into an external file, and then links that file back to the page. The Extractor removes any JavaScript in the document, regardless of whether it was added by Spry, by Dreamweaver Behaviors, or by you coding it manually.

You can maintain control over your page when using the Extractor. It first presents you with a dialog box listing all of the changes it is going to make and then allows you to deselect any changes and thus prevent those blocks of code from being extracted.

Use the JavaScript Extractor

① Click Commands.

② Click Externalize JavaScript.

The Externalize JavaScript dialog box appears.

③ Click Externalize JavaScript and attach unobtrusively.

④ Select or deselect any scripts to be extracted.

A warning dialog box appears.

⑤ Click Yes.

⑥ Click OK.

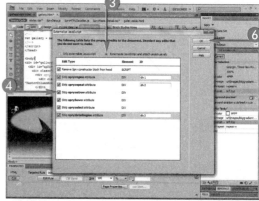

A summary dialog box appears.

7 Click OK.

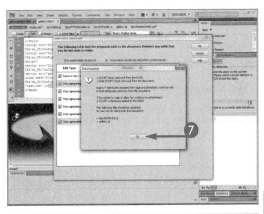

● The JavaScript code is removed and placed in an external file.

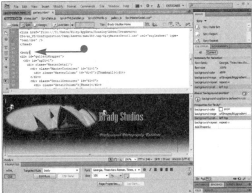

Why are some of the blocks of code on my page unchecked?

▼ JavaScript that is located directly in the body of a document may not be able to be extracted and continue to run properly. Therefore, Dreamweaver identifies those blocks of code, but does not attempt to extract them automatically. You need to analyze them and determine whether or not they can be extracted.

Can I continue to edit my behaviors after I extract the code?

▼ While the behaviors could be edited directly in the JavaScript code, you cannot edit them in the Behaviors panel. This includes Spry effects, as they are added through the Behaviors panel, but does not include other Spry widgets, which continue to be editable after extraction.

Can I undo these changes?

▼ You can undo the extraction at any time until you close the current document by clicking Edit, and then clicking Undo. You cannot close the document, reopen it, and then undo the extraction of the JavaScript.

Edit Source Code

While Dreamweaver provides a powerful visual editing environment, you will often need to directly edit the underlying code on a page. You can do so in either Code view or Split view.

Most Web pages are written in (X)HTML, a fairly simple, text-based markup language that describes the structure and, to an extent, presentation of a document to a program such as a Web browser so that it can be properly displayed. In addition to (X)HTML, Web pages frequently also contain code for CSS and JavaScript, and possibly other programming languages such as ColdFusion.

You can edit any text-based language in Dreamweaver. When editing code, you get helpful code hinting that prompts you for the correct language constructs when you are editing in any of the languages directly supported by Dreamweaver. You can use these code hints to complete much of the code for you, thus reducing the amount you have to type, saving you time and reducing the chances for errors. Code view also uses different colors for different code features, allowing you to more easily view the code.

Edit Source Code

1 Click Code.

Code view appears.

2 Type <.

Code hints of (X)HTML elements appear.

3 Select the element you want to insert.

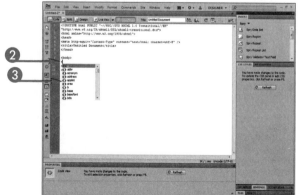

4 Press Enter.

The element is inserted.

5 Type >.

6 Type the text to be contained in the element.

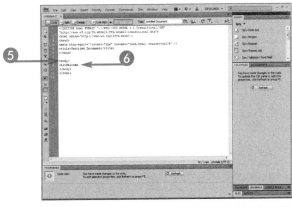

7 Type </.

The closing tag is inserted.

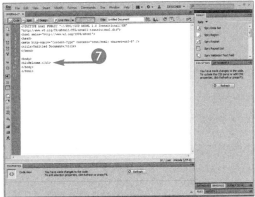

Is it possible to see two different sections of my code at the same time?

▼ Yes. When you are in Code view, you can click View, and then click Split Code. This takes you to Split view, but instead of seeing Code view on one side and Design on the other, you see Code view on both sides. You can scroll each view individually so that you can edit two different sections of your page at once or reference one area of the page while you edit another.

Can I print my code?

▼ Yes. When in Code view, click File, and then click Print Code. You are given a standard print dialog box from which you can select your printer and other options. If you are using a color printer, the code prints in color, and so you are able to use the same colors to differentiate your code as you do on screen.

Use the Code View Toolbar

You can access additional coding functionality while in Code view using the Code view toolbar. This toolbar appears by default down the left edge of the screen.

The toolbar is divided into six sections. The first allows you to open a new document and access the code navigator. In the second section, you can expand or collapse blocks of code, which is useful to hide large sections of code to make editing other portions easier. The third section contains tools to select the parent tag of the currently selected tag, which can help

troubleshoot problems if you are missing a closing tag, and it lets you balance curly braces, which are commonly used in programming languages such as JavaScript. The fourth section allows you to turn line numbering on and off and control whether Dreamweaver highlights invalid code and provides syntax errors. You can add or remove comments to your code, wrap a tag around a selection, access snippets, and move CSS from the fifth section, while the sixth section gives you tools to control code formatting.

Use the Code View Toolbar

① Click the Line Numbers button.

Line numbering is disabled.

② Select a block of code.

③ Click the Apply Comment button.

④ Click Apply HTML Comment.

The code is commented.

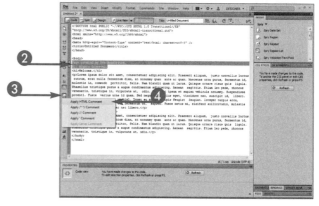

5 Select another block of code.

6 Click the Collapse icon.

The code collapses.

7 Click the Expand icon.

The code is shown.

Can I customize the toolbar?

▼ Unfortunately, Dreamweaver does not provide anything within its interface to customize which buttons appear on a toolbar. Customizing the toolbar is not impossible, but it requires editing one of Dreamweaver's configuration files, which is written in a markup language called XML.

Can I move the toolbar to another place on the screen?

▼ No. You cannot undock the toolbar nor position it elsewhere on the screen. You can turn it off by clicking View, then Toolbars, then Coding, and turn it back on using the same menu command.

Edit a Tag in Design View

Y ou can edit tags to an extent in Design view, which frees you from having to switch between the views as often. The Tag Chooser provides a Quick Tag Editor from which you can add or modify attributes of any element.

You can also indirectly work with code from Design view using the Tag Inspector panel. This panel is where you go to work with behaviors, but it has a second set of functions under its Attributes tab. While Dreamweaver's various Design view tools provide much of the functionality needed to insert objects into

the page, there are many less-known and less-used attributes that can be applied to tags. When you encounter one of these, it can be helpful to be able to set its value in the Tag Inspector, rather than having to go to Code view.

The Tag Inspector can be accessed through the Window menu. It remembers the tab you set when you last used it, and so the behaviors may appear first, but you can click Attributes to access those functions. You can view the attributes either grouped by categories or in an alphabetical list.

① Click Split.

Split view appears.

② Click an element on the page in the Design view.

③ Right-click its tag in the Tag Chooser.

④ Click Quick Tag Editor.

⑤ Type an attribute and its value.

The attribute and its value are added to the code.

6 Click another element on the page.

7 Click Window.

8 Click Tag Inspector.

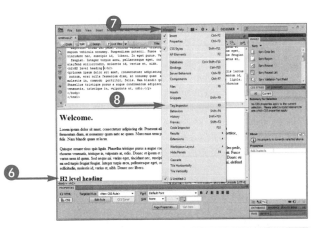

9 Click Attributes.

10 Click the attribute you want to add.

11 Type a value.

12 Press Enter.

The attribute and its value are added to the code.

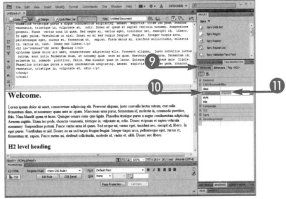

Can I add new tags to my page through the Quick Tag Editor or Tag Inspector?

▼ No. The Design view tools are only for modifying attributes of existing elements. You can only add or edit attributes to existing tags. If you want to add new tags to the document, you should either use the appropriate item from the Insert panel or switch to Code view and add the element there.

Can I not just use the Property Inspector to do the same things as the Tag Inspector?

▼ Sometimes. The Property Inspector does present many of the attributes of the current selection. However, there are a few important differences. The Property Inspector does not always use the exact (X)HTML attribute name, whereas the Tag Inspector does. For example, the Property Inspector has settings of W and H on tables, while the Tag Inspector would provide for Width and Height — the actual attribute names.

The Property Inspector also only lists the most commonly used attributes for tags, whereas the Tag Inspector lists every attribute. Again using a table as an example, you cannot add or modify the summary from the Property Inspector, but you can from the Tag Inspector.

Find and Replace Text

You can search for text within files in your site. You can also replace instances of text with updated text. Both functions are provided through the Find and Replace dialog box, which can be accessed by clicking Edit, and then clicking Find and Replace.

The first choice you have to make in using Find and Replace is to determine what documents you want to search. You can look in text selected in the document, the current document, all open documents, a folder, selected files in the site, or the entire local site. Next,

you can choose whether to search text, meaning that you are looking through the visible text on the page or the source code, where it searches the underlying (X)HTML. You can also work with an advanced text search to find instances inside or outside of certain tags, or search for instances of specific tags.

You can also restrict the search to be case-sensitive, to pay attention to whitespace, match whole words, or use regular expressions. If you create a fairly complex search, you can save it to reuse later.

Find and Replace Text

① Click Edit.

② Click Find and Replace.

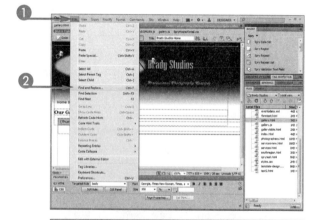

The Find and Replace dialog box appears.

③ Click Current Document.

④ Click Source Code.

5 Type the value from an existing `alt` attribute.

6 Type a new value.

7 Click Replace All.

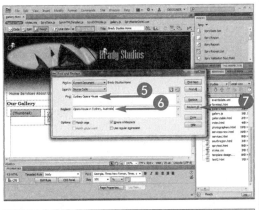

● The text is replaced, and the Results panel opens to show the items replaced.

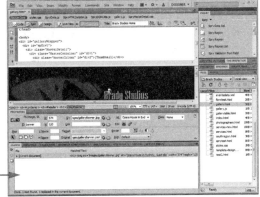

What is a regular expression?

▼ Regular expressions are a method by which you can match patterns in text. They allow you to express in code the pattern that you need to match.

For example, a United States Zip code can be expressed as a series of five digits, followed by a dash, followed by four digits. An e-mail address is one or more characters followed by the @ symbol, followed by one or more characters, a dot, and two or more characters.

How do I use regular expressions?

▼ Most programming languages and many applications, including Dreamweaver and most databases, allow you to search based on regular expressions. Both of the above examples would be difficult to express programmatically, and would require different approaches depending on the language you were using. Regular expressions provide a concise, standard way to look for those strings. Using regular expressions, you can express almost any pattern you need.

An excellent resource for prebuilt regular expressions that you can copy and paste into Dreamweaver can be found at www.regexlib.com.

Look Up Information in the Reference Panel

You can look up information you need on (X)HTML, CSS, JavaScript, and several other programming languages in Dreamweaver's Reference panel. In fact, the panel contains the complete text of 13 different reference books. The Reference panel can be accessed by clicking Window, clicking Results, and then clicking Reference. The panel opens by default along the bottom of the screen.

When the panel opens, you can choose from one of a number of reference books. If you select the (X)HTML Reference, you can then select a tag from a drop-down menu, and then view a description of the tag that includes usage examples, or select any of the tag's supported attributes to view its description and examples. The other reference books are arranged along similar lines.

When viewing the details of the reference, you can right-click the sample code and click Copy. Then, you can go into the code in your page and paste the sample so that you can modify it for your use instead of having to type it from scratch.

Look Up Information in the Reference Panel

① Click Window.

② Click Results.

③ Click Reference.

The Reference panel appears.

④ Click the tag you want to look up.

● The description of the tag appears.

Insert a Special Character

While most of the contents of your pages will be made up of normal text, you may encounter situations where you need a special character, such as a copyright symbol. You can insert these characters through either Design view or Code view.

You can insert special characters in Design view by clicking the Text category of the Insert bar. The last button on the bar provides a drop-down menu of the common characters you might insert, as well as access to a dialog box from which you can select other characters.

You can also type the special characters into Code view. In order to do this, you need to know the proper entity for the character you need. Entities are special codes in (X)HTML that allow you to insert nonstandard characters. All entities begin with an ampersand (&) and end with a semicolon (;). In between is a code for the character. For example, the entity for the copyright symbol is ©. Fortunately, the code hinting in Code view is helpful here, as you see a list of the entities whenever you type an ampersand and can then simply select the one you need.

Insert a Special Character

1. Click Text.
2. Click Other Characters.
3. Click Copyright.

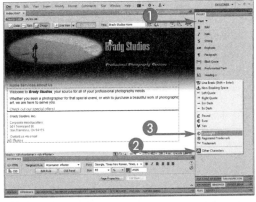

● The copyright symbol is inserted.

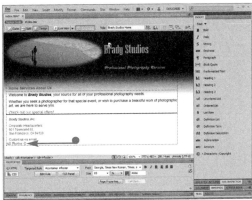

Manage Files in the Files Panel

As your Web site becomes bigger and more complex, you will need to have a plan in place to deal with your files. While you could simply place all of your Web pages, images, CSS documents, and other site files in the root folder, this will make your site unmanageable fairly quickly, and so it is best to organize them logically.

While it is ideal to plan out the organization before you start working on the site, you will probably need to create new folders, move files into folders, and sometimes even rename files as you work. You can do all of these file-management tasks directly in Dreamweaver's Files panel.

If you rename a file directly through Windows Explorer or some other operating system tool, any links to that file are broken and have to be fixed manually. However, if you rename or move a file in Dreamweaver, the program automatically fixes any links to that file, and so it is always recommended that you use the Files panel for this work, rather than doing it outside of Dreamweaver.

Manage Files in the Files Panel

1 Right-click a file.

2 Click Edit.

3 Click Rename.

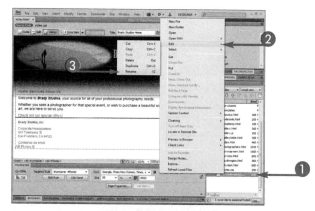

4 Type a new name for the file.

Note: Be sure that you do not change the filename extension.

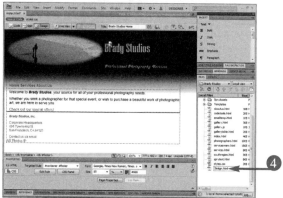

The Update Files dialog box appears.

⑤ Click Update.

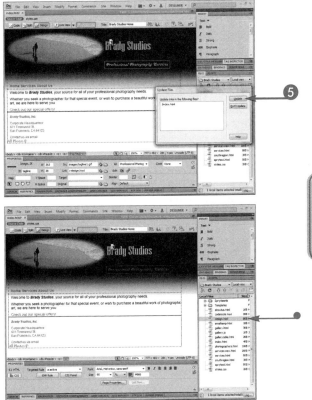

● The filename is changed.

Do I need to do anything to save the changes to the files that contained links to the one I renamed?

▼ If the files with the links are closed when you rename them, then Dreamweaver automatically saves the changes without any further action from you. However, if any of the files are open when Dreamweaver performs the update, then you need to manually save the file. You can tell that it has been updated but not saved because an asterisk appears on the document tab.

Can I delete a file out of the panel, and if so, what happens to links to that file?

▼ Yes, you can delete a file by right-clicking, choosing Edit, and then clicking Delete. You can also simply select the file and press the Delete key on your keyboard. If you delete a page that was linked from other pages, Dreamweaver warns you that those other pages contain links, but it does not automatically update them. Instead, you need to open each of those documents and delete the link. You can also click Site, and then click Change Links Sitewide to have Dreamweaver change any link to the deleted page into a link to a different page.

Buy a Domain Name

You can purchase your own domain name to use for your site. A domain name is the recognizable identifier for your site, and will become an important part of your overall brand.

In order to get a domain name, you need to search for one that is still available and then purchase it for a small yearly fee from a company called a domain registrar. There are thousands of domain registrars in existence, and so you need to do some comparison shopping in order to find the best price.

You can get a domain name that ends in .com, .net, or .org, regardless of how you plan to use it or what kind of organization you have. There are several other choices available, but they are not as popular or well recognized, and so this may limit the visibility of your site. Unfortunately, you may find it very difficult to find a domain name ending in one of those extensions — in particular .com — that is still available, and so you may have to get creative with your naming.

Buy a Domain Name

1 Open your Web browser.

2 Browse to www.networksolutions.com.

Note: *Network Solutions is merely one of the more popular registrars. It may pay to shop around before you purchase.*

3 Type a domain name you would like to purchase.

4 Click Search.

The next page opens, either informing you that the name is available or prompting you to search again.

5 When you have found a name that is available, click Add Domain(s) to Order.

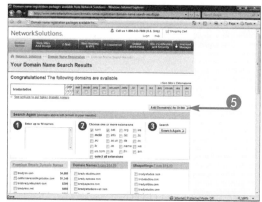

The next page opens, offering domains.

6 Click No thanks.

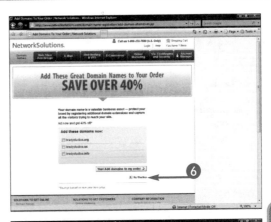

7 Complete the remainder of the steps for the checkout process.

Your domain name is now purchased.

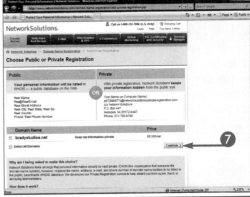

I see a lot of other domains that end in .edu, .gov, and .mil. I also see a lot with two-letter endings such as .us or .uk. What are these?

▼ When the domain name system was developed, six top-level domains were created. Three were designed to be open to anyone: .com, .net, and .org. The other three were reserved, and so only nonprofit educational institutions can use .edu, only governmental entities within the United States can use .gov, and only branches of the U.S. military can use .mil.

The two-letter top-level domains are country codes; so, for instance, www.amazon.co.uk is the British version of Amazon. Most countries restrict the use of these endings to their citizens, although a few — such as the Island of Tuvalu, which uses .tv — have made them available to anyone. You can view a complete list of the country codes at www.iana.org/domains/root/db.

What happens if I do not continue to pay for my domain?

▼ The precise policies for nonpayment vary from one registrar to the next, but at a certain point they will release the domain name if you do not pay, and so there is a chance at that point that someone else could purchase your domain from you. Most registrars today allow you to make a one-time payment for domains for as many as ten years, so that you will not have to worry about it every year.

Sign Up for a Web-Hosting Account

I n order for others to view your Web site, you need to transfer the files from your local computer to a Web server. If you work for a large company, you may already have access to a server that the company owns, but if you work for a smaller company or are building a personal site, you probably want to use a Web-hosting company.

Web Hosts

Web hosts are companies that rent space on their servers. Using a Web host offers many advantages: You do not need to install, configure, or maintain the server operating system or deal with security on it; you do not need to worry about maintaining the Web server software; and you do not need to deal with hardware issues. With a Web host, you can worry about the design and implementation of your site, and let others worry about the technical details of running a server.

Shopping for a Host

There are literally millions of Web hosts available — a Google search for Web hosting in January 2008 returned 428 million results. Therefore, you want to spend some time comparison shopping. Hosts have widely varying fees for their services, from free to thousands of dollars per month. They also offer a wide range of services for these fees, and so you need to investigate which ones offer the services you want for the price you can afford.

Shared versus Dedicated Hosting

Most Web hosts offer a service called *shared hosting*, where your site is on a server with many other sites. If one or more of those sites begins to use too much bandwidth or server resources, the performance of your site might suffer. Most good hosts monitor this and may move sites that cause problems to less-busy servers, but it is a reactionary measure that can only be taken after the problem arises.

Dedicated hosting, offered by many higher-end hosts, allows you to rent an entire server for your site, so that yours will be the only one running on the computer. This is, for obvious reasons, a much more expensive alternative, but if the performance of your site is of paramount concern, or if you think your site might become one that needs more resources, you should consider this option.

Domain Hosting

Free Web hosts generally require that you use their domain name, but most other hosts offer domain hosting, where you can purchase a domain name and use it for your site. Some hosts even offer multiple domain hosting, allowing you to purchase several domains and host them all, either as a single site that has many domains pointing to it, or as separate sites.

Services Offered by Hosts

All hosts should offer a certain amount of disk space, a maximum allowed amount of monthly bandwidth, and some sort of control panel interface to allow you to administer your site. Usually, the hard drive space and bandwidth are more than sufficient for most sites, although hosts generally offer à la carte options for both additional space and bandwidth should you need them.

Hosts generally offer e-mail services as well, allowing you to use e-mail accounts attached to your domain name. They may also offer server-side scripting features, such as support for PHP, ASP, ASP.NET, and ColdFusion, as well as space on database servers.

All hosts should offer some sort of backup system to protect against data loss on their side, and many make the Web server logs for your site available, either as a raw data file that you need to analyze yourself or through a graphical interface on the control panel.

As with most things, the more services you opt for, the higher the cost of the package.

Hosting Reviews

With the overwhelming number of available Web hosts, it is impossible for a single person to effectively compare all of the options. You should first seek out trusted friends, coworkers, or affiliated businesses to get personal recommendations on hosting.

You can also visit one of several online forums in which users share their views — good and bad — on Web hosts. The forums at www.whrforums.com are a fantastic resource for this information. *Web Host Magazine* offers a categorized search process that allows you to find hosts based on the services it offers on its Web site at www.webhostmagazine.com, and FindMyHost.com offers a search feature, reviews, and a guarantee to assist you in

dealing with problems with any host that they recommend.

Tech Support

All Web hosts should offer technical support, although the level and quality of support you get may vary greatly from one host to the next. In general, only expensive plans include live phone support. Many hosts now offer a support chat feature that allows you to discuss issues with a technician in real time, and most rely on a support ticket system to handle non-emergency issues. The quality of tech support is the most-often cited reason for people to choose to stay with, or leave, a host.

Signing Up with a Host

Once you have found the host you want to use, you can sign up through its Web site. Most ask for basic contact and billing information. Many offer monthly or yearly billing, with a discount for longer terms. Once it receives your information, you should receive an e-mail with details of how to log into the control panel and set up other details of your site, and with the login information so that you can upload your files. Keep this e-mail, as you may need to refer to it later should you forget your login information or need to contact your host.

Once the registration process is complete, you should be able to upload your files immediately. If you are using domain hosting, there may be a delay before the name servers on the Internet recognize the new location of your site, but many hosts provide a temporary address to allow you to access the site in the meantime.

Set Up a Connection to a Web Host

Before others can view your files online, you need to upload the files to your hosting company. You can transfer files to your host using a technology called File Transfer Protocol, or FTP.

Dreamweaver includes a built-in FTP client. In order to use it to transfer your files, you need to set up your connection information in the site definition. When you signed up with your Web host, you should have received an e-mail with the necessary information. It should include at least the address to the FTP server, your username, and your password. You can enter this

information into Dreamweaver and then save it so that you do not need to keep remembering or inputting it.

If you connect to your host from work or some other location with a firewall, you may need to enter additional settings so that Dreamweaver can still communicate with the server. You need to get this information from your IT department.

In certain situations, you may be able to connect directly with your Web server over the local network. In this case, you can simply enter the network path into the Site Definition dialog box to enable Dreamweaver to transfer the files.

Set Up a Connection to a Web Host

1 Double-click the site name.

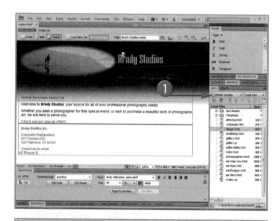

The Site Definition dialog box appears.

2 Click Remote Info.

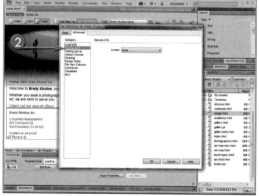

3 Select FTP.

4 Type the FTP address.

5 Type your username and password.

6 Click Test.

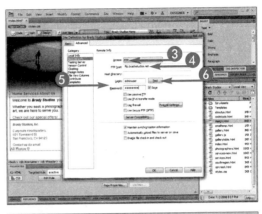

Dreamweaver attempts to connect to the server and returns a message that it either succeeded or failed.

7 Click OK.

The connection is set up in Dreamweaver.

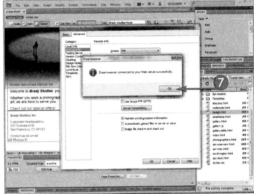

When do I use the Host Directory, Passive FTP, or IPv6 settings?

▼ The Host Directory field is used by some Web hosts to help organize files. If your host provides a path for a host directory, type it here; if not, leave it blank. Passive FTP is used by some servers, and so if you test the connection and it fails, you might try checking this box and then testing again. The same applies for IPv6 transfer mode — it is a specific setting that you can use when your host instructs you to, but you should not use it unless you need it.

What is Secure FTP?

▼ Secure FTP transfers files using encryption. In a normal FTP transaction, everything is sent in plain text and could in theory be intercepted. Secure FTP must be set up and enabled on the server before you can use it.

What are synchronization and check in/check out?

▼ The settings at the bottom of the dialog box are optional. Maintain synchronization information is a setting to help you work with synchronizing files, which is discussed later in this chapter. You can have files transferred automatically when you save by selecting that option, and check in and check out is discussed in Chapter 14.

Upload Files

You can upload your files to your Web server directly from the Files panel. In its normal state, the Files panel provides a Put button that uploads the file to the server.

You can also expand the Files panel so that it displays in full screen. When you connect to the server in this expanded mode, you can view the files and folders on your local computer side-by-side with the server files. You can drag local files to the server to upload, and drag files from the server to download.

You need to be sure that the file and folder structure on the server exactly matches that on the client. You can add or delete folders on the server and move, rename, or delete files just as you would on your local computer.

Dreamweaver transfers files to and from the server in the background. Therefore, if you have large files that you need to upload or download, you can continue to work in the program while they are copied. You cannot do any other interaction with the server while the files transfer, but you can return to Design or Code view and continue editing files.

Upload Files

1 Click a file.

2 Click the Put button.

The file is uploaded to the server.

3 Click the Expand button to show local and remote sites.

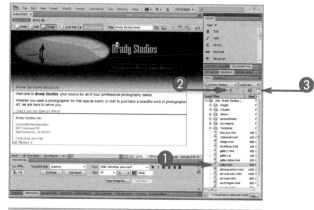

4 Click the Connect to Remote Host button.

A connection to the server is made.

5 Drag a file from the local files to the server.

The Dependent Files dialog box appears.

6 Click Yes.

The file is uploaded, along with any images, style sheets, or JavaScript files it uses.

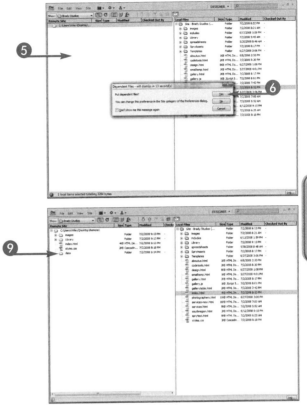

7 Right-click the server files.

8 Click New Folder.

9 Name the folder.

The folder is created on the server.

Do I have to save files before I upload them?

▼ Yes. You can only copy the most recently saved version of a file to the server. If you have a file open with unsaved changes, Dreamweaver prompts you to save the file before it uploads it.

Is there an easy way to transfer all of the files from my site at once?

▼ Yes. You can upload your entire site by clicking the site root folder and clicking the Put button, or by dragging the site root folder to the server. Dreamweaver asks if you are sure you want to upload the entire site, and then proceeds to upload all of the files. Be aware that for very large sites, this may take some time.

Synchronize Local and Remote Files

Y ou need to maintain two copies of your Web site: your local copy on your computer that you use for editing, and the remote copy on the server that your visitors see. You also need to make sure that these copies are the same. You can upload files as you edit them to transfer newer copies to the server, but there may be times when your local computer ends up containing older versions of files, such as when you edit and upload files from another computer.

You can ensure that your local and remote copies are the same by using the Synchronize Files command in

Dreamweaver. The program looks at the Last Modified dates on files on both the server and your computer, and then copies any older files from one computer to the other to ensure that both have the latest editions of all of the files.

Before it synchronizes, Dreamweaver displays a list of the files it plans to act on. Therefore, you can choose to not synchronize certain files, delete files you no longer need, or compare the contents to make sure that you are actually getting the latest version.

Synchronize Local and Remote Files

① Click the Synchronize button.

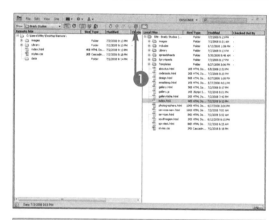

The Synchronize Files dialog box appears.

② Select Entire site.

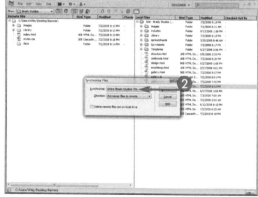

3 Select Get and Put newer files.

4 Click Preview.

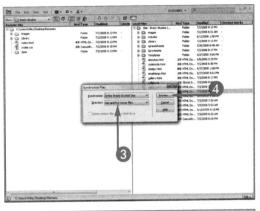

The Synchronize dialog box appears.

5 Click OK.

Dreamweaver performs the synchronization.

It appears that Dreamweaver copied a file to the server, even though it said that the last modified date on the server file was later than the local file. Why is this?

▼ Your Web host is most likely in a different time zone, and so while Dreamweaver does not display this, it is aware of the time difference and compensates for it.

How can I compare the contents of the files?

▼ When you select the Compare button in the Synchronize dialog box, Dreamweaver opens the files in a comparison application. Dreamweaver does not do this comparison for you, but rather simply opens the files in another program. You need to purchase a third-party application to do the actual comparison, and you need to configure the application in Dreamweaver's Preferences so that the program knows where the comparison application is.

Cloak Files

You can prevent certain files from being uploaded to the server during a site-wide upload or during synchronization by using the Cloak feature. Cloaking a file type or folder tells Dreamweaver that you do not want that file transferred to the remote server.

You do not need to transfer template files with a .dwt extension or library items that have an .lbi extension to the server. You may also have original source files for certain assets in your site. For example, if you are using the Photoshop Smart Objects feature to insert

Photoshop PSD files into your site, you need to upload the resulting JPEG or GIF file, but would probably not want to upload the original PSD file. If your site contains Adobe PDF documents, you need to upload them but not the original files from which they were created.

You can cloak an entire directory, individual files, or files by type. You can cloak a directory or file by right-clicking it in the Files panel. You can cloak by file type by going into the Site Definition dialog box and entering the extensions you want to cloak.

Cloak Files

1 Right-click a file in the Files panel.

2 Select Cloaking.

3 Select Cloak.

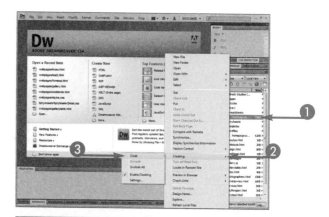

The file is cloaked.

4 Right-click a file in the Files panel.

5 Select Cloaking.

6 Click Settings.

The Site Definition dialog box appears.

⑦ Click Cloaking.

⑧ Click the Cloak files ending with check box.

⑨ Type **.doc**.

⑩ Click OK.

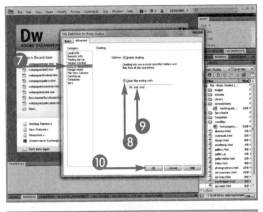

● Microsoft Word documents in the site are now cloaked.

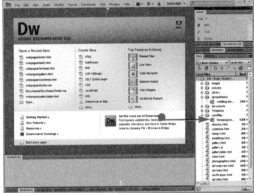

How can I tell if a file is cloaked?

▼ Files and folders that you cloak individually appear in the Files panel with a red slash through their icon. Files that are cloaked based on their file extension appear as normal in the Files panel, and you just need to remember that they are cloaked.

Will I receive any warning or notification that cloaked files will not be uploaded or synchronized?

▼ No. Once a file is cloaked, the rest of the processes performed on it by Dreamweaver are transparent. The program does not inform you every time it attempts to perform an action from which cloaked files are excluded.

Back Up a Dreamweaver Site

You should perform regular backups of your site files in case something happens to your local computer. However, backing up your site files does not back up the site settings, and so if you needed to rebuild your computer, you would have to manually re-create your site in Dreamweaver.

You can export your site in the Manage Sites dialog box. Exporting your site creates a special STE file that contains all of the site settings. Then you can import the site back into Dreamweaver and have it be automatically set up.

If you export a site that contains remote server information, Dreamweaver asks if you want to include the FTP information, including your password, in the STE file. If you are backing up the site, then you should include this information but be sure to keep the STE file in a secure location; if you are exporting the site so that you can share the basic settings with another user who will have his own FTP credentials, then you should exclude them. You can save the STE file anywhere on your computer, but be sure to include it in any backups.

Back up a Dreamweaver Site

① Click Site.

② Click Manage Sites.

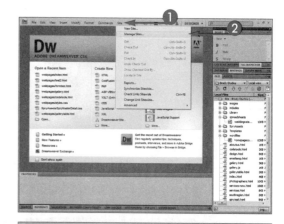

The Manage Sites dialog box appears.

③ Click the site that will be backed up.

④ Click Export.

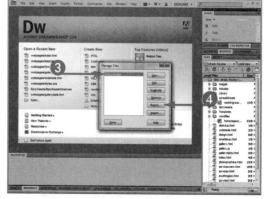

The Exporting Site dialog box appears.

Note: If you have not set up FTP information, this dialog box does not appear.

5 Click Back up my settings (includes login, password, and local paths).

6 Click OK.

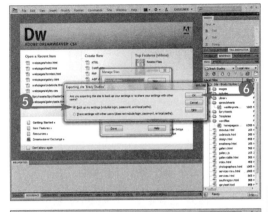

The Export Site dialog box appears.

7 Click Save.

The STE file is created.

Is it possible to back up all of my sites at once?

▼ Yes. You can select as many sites as you want to export. You can press and hold the Ctrl (Command) key while selecting sites to choose noncontiguous sites, or press and hold the Shift key while selecting to choose contiguous sites.

Can I view or modify the information in the STE file?

▼ The STE file is actually an XML file that Dreamweaver can read to reconfigure a lost site. You can open the file in an XML editor or in Dreamweaver if you would like to view the settings. While you can change settings in the file, you should be very cautious, as an incorrect setting can cause the site import to fail, forcing you to manually re-create the site. If you exported a site with FTP information, the password will be encrypted, so that it is not possible to read or edit the password within the STE file.

Validate Your Code

Y ou can validate the (X)HTML code in your pages. Validating your code ensures that you are using the proper tags. In order to make the development of Web pages as easy as possible and to easily facilitate backward compatibility, browsers are designed to simply ignore bad or questionable code. This means that you can add any markup to your document that you want to, whether or not it is valid, and the browser does not return an error. When it encounters an element, attribute, or attribute value that it does not recognize, it simply ignores it and goes on processing the page as if the offending code

did not exist. Although beginners, who often become frustrated at the appearance of constant error messages, may find this lack of errors refreshing, experienced programmers know that troubleshooting errors is far easier than troubleshooting unexpected behavior.

Therefore, you should always ensure that your markup validates as proper (X)HTML. You can validate your pages directly within Dreamweaver. If there are problems in the code, Dreamweaver lets you know exactly where the problem is to make it easier to fix.

Validate Your Code

① Click Window.

② Select Results.

③ Click Validation.

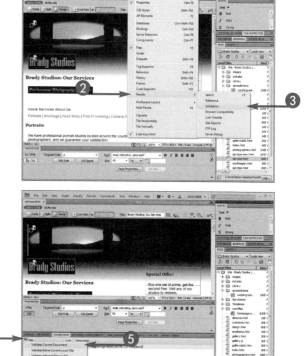

The Validation panel opens.

④ Click the Validate button.

⑤ Click Validate Current Document.

The validation runs, and returns either a message that there are no errors or a list of errors.

Check Browser Compatibility

You can increase the chances that your pages will work properly in all browsers by checking for browser compatibility. Dreamweaver scans your document for known browser issues and helps you solve them.

Today, most browser compatibility issues revolve around incorrect or incomplete support for CSS. Designers have spent the last several years identifying these issues and developing workarounds. However, the browser market is constantly changing, and so Adobe decided that it would be better to not embed browser compatibility solutions into Dreamweaver; instead, it created a Web site, known

as the Adobe CSS Advisor, where the community could help post and maintain common solutions to these problems. When Dreamweaver detects a potential browser compatibility issue, it lets you know what the problem is and provides a link to the appropriate section of the CSS Advisor site where you can research an appropriate solution.

You can configure the browsers that you want to scan against. The most recent versions of the major browsers are automatically checked, but you may choose to not bother looking for compatibility issues for older, discontinued browsers such as Internet Explorer 5 for the Macintosh.

Check Browser Compatibility

1 Click Browser Compatibility.

2 Click the Check Browser Compatibility button.

3 Click Check Browser Compatibility.

The report runs, returning a list of potential problems, if any.

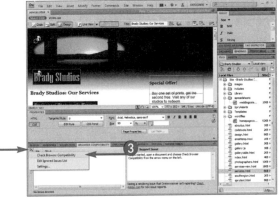

Lock Files with a Check-Out System

If you work on a site that is developed by a team of designers, you can run into problems when more than one designer attempts to edit a page at the same time. For example, say a coworker downloads the latest version of a file from the server and begins editing it. Later, you need to work on the same file, and so you go and download what you believe is the latest version. However, you are unaware that your coworker is already editing the page. In this case, one of the two of you — whoever finishes their edits and reuploads the page last — will overwrite the other's work.

You can avoid this problem by requiring that all designers involved with the site check files in and out as they work. In the scenario above, your coworker would have checked the file out when he downloaded it, and you would have then been informed that he had the file checked out and was working on it when you tried to download it. When he finishes and uploads the file to the server, it is checked back in and you are then able to work on it.

Lock Files with a Check-Out System

1. Click Site in the menu bar.
2. Click Manage Sites.

The Manage Sites dialog box appears.

3. Click your site.
4. Click Edit.

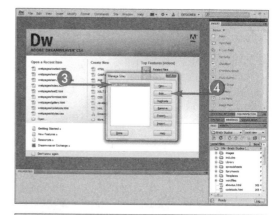

The Site Definition dialog box appears.

5. Click Remote Info.

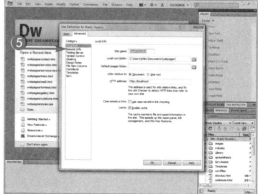

6 Click the Enable file check in and check out option.

7 Type your name.

8 Type your e-mail address.

9 Click OK to close the dialog box.

10 Click Done in the Manage Sites dialog box.

Check in is enabled on the site.

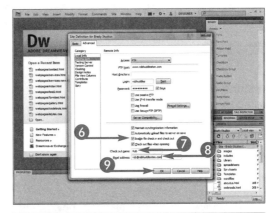

11 Right-click a file.

12 Click Check Out.

The file is checked out.

How does Dreamweaver know a file is checked out?

▼ Dreamweaver places a special file on the server to designate that another file is locked. This file has the same name as the locked file, but it has an added .lck extension. So long as the LCK file is on the server, Dreamweaver designates that the related file is locked.

You cannot see these LCK files when you view your remote files in the Files panel. However, if you use another program to log into the server using FTP, you can see them.

Can I open a locked file?

▼ Yes, but it opens as a read-only copy. This means that while you can make changes to the file, you cannot save those changes under the same filename as the original. Keep in mind, however, that if the file is locked, it is most likely being worked on by someone else, and so the read-only copy you see does not have the latest changes.

How can I find out who checked out a file?

▼ When you set up the check-in system, you are asked for your name and e-mail address. This information displays in the Files panel for anyone looking at the site, so that they can contact you if they need the file.

Add and Use Design Notes

One of the biggest challenges faced by designers working in teams, particularly those who work in different physical locations, is communication. When you open a file that has been changed by someone else, you want to know what changes he has made.

You can improve the communication with others in your team by using Design Notes. These are special messages that you can associate with a file, and they automatically appear whenever the file is opened. These notes can contain information about who last modified the file, what changes he made and why, or anything else you feel is relevant.

You can enable Design Notes on a site by checking the option in the Site Definition dialog box. You can also instruct Dreamweaver to upload the notes when the file is uploaded so that if another designer downloads the file, he can still see the notes.

Once enabled, you can add Design Notes to any page in the site. You have the option of setting a revision status on the document and embedding the current date, and you can choose whether or not you want the notes to appear when the file is opened.

① Right-click a file.

② Click Design Notes.

③ Set the status.

④ Click the Insert Date button.

⑤ Type a note.

⑥ Check the Show when file is opened option.

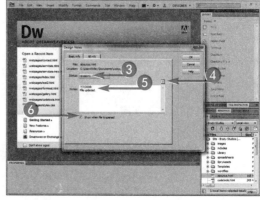

7 Click All info.

8 Click the Add button.

9 Type **Author.**

10 Type your name in the Value field.

11 Click OK.

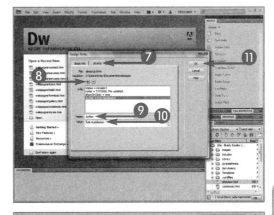

The Design Note is added to the file.

12 Double-click the file.

The file opens and the Design Note displays.

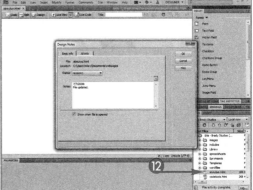

Where are Design Notes stored?

▼ Dreamweaver creates a folder called _notes in the root of your site to store Design Note information. You cannot see this file in Dreamweaver's Files panel; instead, you need to open the root folder in another program such as Windows Explorer. The Design Notes are files with the name of the page followed by .mno; so, for instance, the notes for services.html would be services.html.mno. This is an XML file that contains the note information.

I do not have Design Notes enabled, but I am still seeing the _notes folder. Why is this?

▼ Dreamweaver uses the _notes folder for other purposes beyond Design Notes, and so you may see the folder even if you do not use notes. Dreamweaver stores information here relating to its integration with Flash and Fireworks, and stores the file column layout for the Files panel in a file it may create here. Therefore, you should not delete this folder even if you do not use Design Notes.

Set Up an Adobe Contribute CS4 Site

Large Web sites may have designers creating the look and feel of the site, developers doing back-end programming, and content providers who are responsible for updating the actual content in the site. Often, these content providers have little or no (X)HTML or CSS knowledge, and need something less complicated than Dreamweaver to use to update.

Adobe Contribute CS4 is designed for this purpose. As the site designer, you can create Dreamweaver templates to manage the layout of the site and the content such as navigation bars that will be shared across all pages. Then, the content providers can install Contribute and open pages created from the templates. Contribute follows the rules imposed by the template, and so users can only change content in editable regions.

In order to use Contribute, you must enable it in your Dreamweaver site. You provide basic contact information, and can then launch Contribute to set up the rest of the information needed to administer the site.

Set Up an Adobe Contribute CS4 Site

① Click Site in the menu bar.

② Click Manage Sites.

The Manage Sites dialog box appears.

③ Click the site.

④ Click Edit.

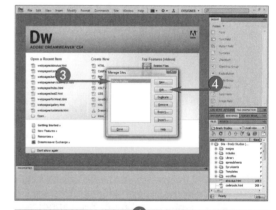

The Site Definition dialog box appears.

⑤ Click Contribute.

⑥ Click the Enable Contribute compatibility option.

A pop-up window appears.

⑦ Click OK.

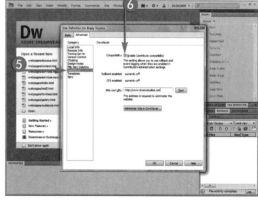

8 Click Test.

A dialog box appears, telling you that Dreamweaver is connecting to the remote server.

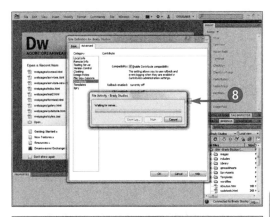

9 When Dreamweaver is connected, click OK.

The site is configured to use Contribute.

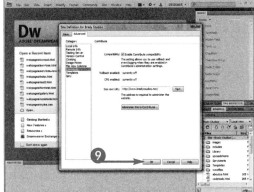

How do I get Contribute?

▼ Contribute is a stand-alone application sold by Adobe. If you purchased the Creative Suite 4 Web Standard, Web Premium, or Master Collection edition, you already have a copy of Contribute. If you purchased one of the other editions of Creative Suite, or purchased Dreamweaver alone, you need to buy Contribute. Also, each of your content providers need their own copy of the product. You can find out more about Contribute from the Adobe Web site at www.adobe.com/products/contribute.

How do I use Contribute to edit the site?

▼ Once the site is configured in Dreamweaver, you open Contribute. You are prompted to enter basic connection information, including your name, e-mail, and a password. The program then connects to the server and accesses the site.

Editing in Contribute is similar to using a word processor such as Microsoft Word. It is designed with nontechnical users in mind, and so the interface is intentionally left simple.

Set Up a Page for InContext Editing

You can allow authorized users to edit pages in your site directly in their Web browser using InContext Editing. InContext Editing is a new approach to allowing content providers to work on pages. It is in many ways very similar to Contribute, but whereas Contribute is a stand-alone application, InContext Editing allows users to work on pages directly in their Web browsers.

You need to set up the page for InContext Editing by adding special tags to the document to designate editable and repeating regions. These can be added from the InContext Editing category of the Insert

panel. When you add an Editable Region to the page, you can designate what kinds of changes can be made by the user.

You can also add a repeating region, which functions much like the repeat region in templates. With a repeat region, your users can add new copies of the region and reorder the existing copies.

Once you have created the necessary regions on the page, you can upload it to your Web server and then use the InContext Editing site to make changes. Editing the page is discussed next.

Set Up a Page for InContext Editing

① Click File in the menu bar.

② Click New.

   The New Document dialog box appears.

③ Click a desired layout.

④ Click Create.

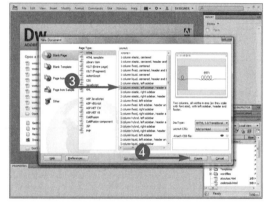

⑤ Select the main heading on the page.

⑥ Click Common.

⑦ Click InContext Editing.

⑧ Click Create Editable Region.

   The Create Editable Region dialog box appears.

⑨ Click OK.

The region is added to the page.

10 Click the formatting options that will be allowed.

11 Save the page.

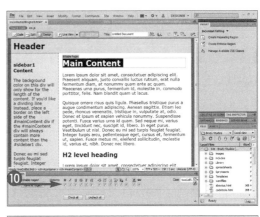

12 Click the Put button.

The page is uploaded.

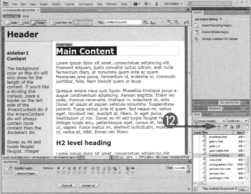

What is the Manage Available CSS Classes option?

▼ This option allows you to associate an external style sheet that is already linked to the page with InContext Editing, so that your users can apply class selectors to elements within editable regions.

What are the files that are being copied when I save the document?

▼ These files work together to provide the editing functionality in the browser. You need to be sure to upload these files to the server, or you will not be able to edit pages in InContext Editing.

Can I use a regular Dreamweaver template with ICE?

▼ You can use a template to create a file that will be editable in InContext Editing, but template editable and repeat regions and InContext Editing editable and repeat regions are different. Therefore, you need to create InContext Editing regions within the existing template regions in order for the system to work.

Do I need to include editable regions within repeat regions?

▼ Yes. Just like with template repeat regions, InContext Editing repeat regions are not themselves editable. You need to be sure to include at least one editable region in the repeat region.

Modify a Page in InContext Editing

You can edit pages using InContent Editing by logging onto the InContent Editing Web site. InContent Editing is an online hosting service from Adobe that provides an editing environment for Web pages.

The first step in editing a page in InContext Editing is to visit http://incontextediting.adobe.com and set up an account. Then, you can visit the page you wish to

edit in a browser and use the Control-E keyboard shortcut to log into the page in InContext Editing.

When you provide your username and password, you are shown the page within the InContext Editing context. You can click in editable regions and make whatever changes are allowed. If formatting was enabled in Dreamweaver, you can format the text as well. You can click in a repeat region to add or remove instances of the region and reorder them.

① Open a Web browser.

② Type the address of the page you want to edit.

The page opens in the browser.

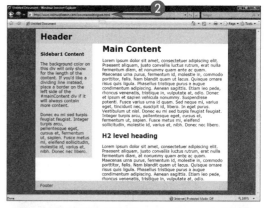

③ Press Ctrl+E.

The InContext Editing Sign in screen appears.

④ Type your e-mail address.

⑤ Type your password.

⑥ Click Sign In.

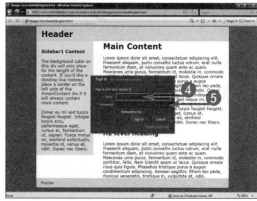

The page opens in InContext Editing.

7 Click Edit.

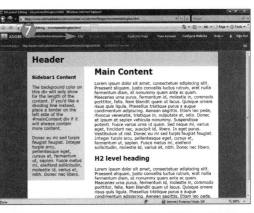

InContext Editing switches to editing mode.

8 Click in an editable region.

9 Modify the contents.

10 Click Save.

The page changes are saved.

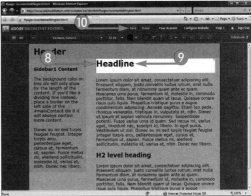

What browsers can I use with InContext Editing?

▼ InContext Editing supports Internet Explorer 6 and 7, Safari 3, and Firefox 3. You cannot use the service if you do not have one of these browsers. In addition, you need to have Flash Player 9 installed on your computer and JavaScript enabled.

Can I use InContext Editing if my site is an intranet site behind a firewall?

▼ No. InContext Editing needs to have FTP access to your site as well as direct Web browser access. Therefore, it cannot be used for intranet sites that reside behind a firewall.

When I attempt to save my changes, I am being prompted to enter some information. Why is this?

▼ InContext Editing needs to be able to connect to your Web server so that it can upload the changed files. Therefore, the first time you try to use the service, you will be prompted to enter information about your Web server and your hosting account. This is the same information that you enter when you upload your site from within Dreamweaver.

Create a Subversion Account

Whenever groups of people attempt to edit the same set of files, conflicts can occur when one designer needs to work on files being edited by another. Dreamweaver's locking feature has long existed in the program to assist with this, but professional developers often rely on an open-source server technology known as Subversion. Within Dreamweaver, you can manage your page versions through Subversion.

You can use a free hosting provider to manage the technical details of Subversion, freeing you to simply use its features. One such host is CVSDude, which also

offers commercial packages with more features. Once you have signed up for an account, you can follow a series of simple onscreen instructions to finish the setup process.

To begin using Subversion, you need to add a module, which is a repository for your Subversion data. The site then provides you with a complete path to the module.

If you are working in a team, you can configure individual user accounts for each team member so that you can track who made what changes to the site files.

Create a Subversion Account

① Open your Web browser.

② Type **cvsdude.com/product.pl**.

③ Press Enter.

The CVSDude site loads.

④ Click Sign Up.

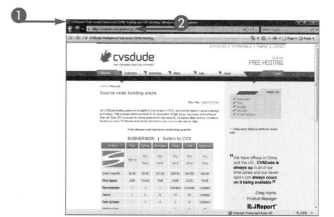

The Sign Up page appears.

⑤ Enter the required information.

⑥ Click Create Account.

The account is created.

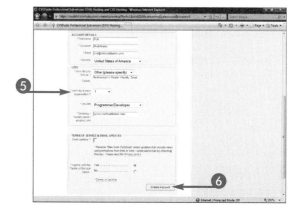

⑦ Click Settings.

⑧ Click Modules, and then click Add.

⑨ Type a name for the module.

Note: The name cannot contain spaces.

⑩ Click Add new.

The module is created.

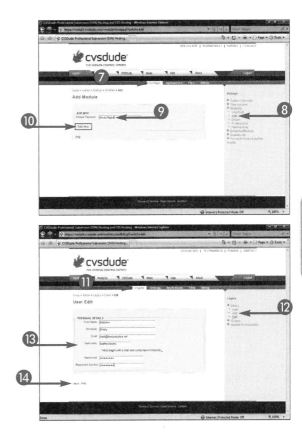

⑪ Click Logins.

⑫ Click Users, and then click Add.

⑬ Enter the user information.

⑭ Click save.

The user account is created.

Is it possible to run my own copy of Subversion?

▼ Yes, you can download and install Subversion from subversion.tigris.org. It is free and open source. However, it can be fairly difficult to install, configure, and manage, and so it is only recommended for larger organizations. Many companies find that the cost of using a commercial account on a site such as CVSDude is less expensive than paying an employee to manage his own installation of Subversion.

What kind of support is there?

▼ CVSDude offers e-mail support for specific issues and hosts an active user forum on its site for more immediate needs. There is also a detailed PDF document on getting started on your account available on its site. Because Subversion is very widely used, you will also find many other resources online for using the tool.

Can I manage users based on groups?

▼ CVSDude allows you to manage access permissions for the site either through individual accounts or by groups. If you have many users, you can add an account for each, assign them to groups, and then control access to modules based on the groups. The free account to CVSDude only allows for a single-user account.

Integrate Subversion with Dreamweaver

Subversion differs from file locking in that it allows you to edit the same document at the same time as another user. When you upload the document to the Subversion repository, it checks to see if your copy of the document conflicts with the most recent version of the file. If it does not, it attempts to merge your changes with the current version.

This way, if you are editing contents near the top of a document, and another user has been editing towards the bottom, you could both be working on the file. When your co-worker finished, they would have uploaded it to the server; when you finish, you upload

the file and Subversion is able to determine that you edited a different part of the document and so simply merges your changes into the existing file. If, however, you edited the same portion of the file as your co-worker, then Subversion would inform you that a conflict exists. You could then discuss the changes with your co-worker and resolve the conflicts in the edits.

You can set up Dreamweaver to connect to a Subversion server. Then you can use the Site panel to upload files to Subversion.

Integrate Subversion with Dreamweaver

① Click Site in the menu bar.

② Click Manage Sites.

   The Manage Sites dialog box appears.

③ Click your site.

④ Click Edit.

   The Site Definition dialog box appears.

⑤ Click Version Control.

⑥ Select Subversion.

⑦ Type the server address and the module name in the Repository path.

⑧ Type your username and password.

⑨ Click Test.

   Dreamweaver connects to the server and displays a success message.

⑩ Click OK.

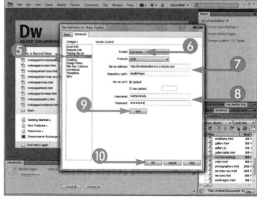

⑪ Click the Expand button.

The Site panel expands.

⑫ Click the Repository Files button.

The files in the repository display.

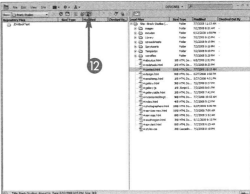

PART III

Are using Subversion and locking files mutually exclusive?

▼ No. Subversion was developed as an alternative to locking. The biggest problem with locking files is that it can reduce the effectiveness of a team of developers, as one user has to wait for another to finish editing a file even if he is not working on the same part of that file.

However, the theory behind Subversion allowing you to simultaneously edit files is based on the idea that you are working on text-based files that are easy to compare. Binary-based files such as images and media are not quite so simple, and so Subversion still allows for locking in those cases.

Where can I learn more about Subversion?

▼ The official homepage of the Subversion project at subversion.tigris.org contains a Frequently Asked Questions (FAQ) page and a link to the Subversion Book, a free online book with all of the information you need to fully implement Subversion in your projects.

Edit Preferences

You can customize the settings and control much of the behavior within Dreamweaver by editing the preferences. Most of the preferences can be found in the Preferences dialog box.

The Preferences dialog box is divided into 19 categories: General, Accessibility, AP Elements, Code Coloring, Code Format, Code Hints, Code Rewriting, Copy/Paste, CSS Styles, File Compare, File Types/Editors, Fonts, Highlighting, Invisible Elements, New Document, Preview in Browser, Site, Status Bar, and Validator. Most of the time, when Dreamweaver is defaulting to something that you do not like, you will find a setting in one of these categories to control it.

If you are working on an existing site that uses .htm as the default extension, you will find a setting in the New Document category that allows you to tell Dreamweaver to use .htm instead of .html for new documents. You can control which invisible elements — helper icons that appear in Design view to designate page elements that would not otherwise be visible — you see in the Invisible Elements category, and you can set the size and font that you use in Code view by selecting the Fonts category.

Edit Preferences

1. Click Edit.

2. Click Preferences.

The Preferences dialog box appears.

3. Click New Document.

4. Change the default extension to .htm.

5. Click OK.

The preferences are changed.

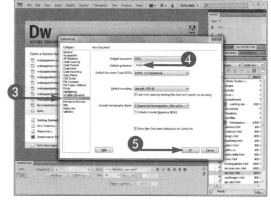

Edit Keyboard Shortcuts

Y ou can increase your efficiency when using a program by learning and using keyboard shortcuts. You will find that many shortcuts that have become standard across most programs work in Dreamweaver; so, for example, Control+S is Save, Control+C is Copy, Control+X is Cut, and Control+V is Paste.

By default, many commands do not have a keyboard shortcut assigned to them. You can modify the settings in Dreamweaver and add your own shortcuts to any commands. You can also assign shortcuts to Snippets.

In order to edit the keyboard shortcuts, you must create a copy of the current shortcut list. This can be done in the Keyboard Shortcuts dialog box, which is the same dialog box you use to edit the shortcuts.

When you create your own shortcuts, you may often discover that the command you want to use is already assigned to another command. For example, many designers find it useful to have a keyboard shortcut to insert an (X)HTML comment. Because the comment code contains dashes, Control+- would make sense; however, this shortcut is already assigned to the Zoom Out command. In cases such as this, you are given the option of overriding the existing command.

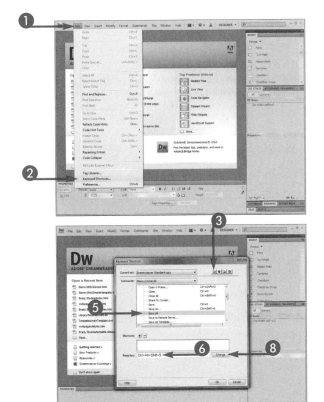

Edit Keyboard Shortcuts

1 Click Edit.

2 Click Keyboard Shortcuts.

The Keyboard Shortcuts dialog box appears.

3 Click the Duplicate Set button.

A dialog box appears asking for the name of the set.

4 Click OK.

5 Select a command.

6 Click in the Press key box.

7 Type the command you want to use.

Note: *You need to press the actual keyboard combination you want to use for the command.*

8 Click Change.

The shortcut is assigned.

Install a Dreamweaver Extension

You can expand on the functionality of Dreamweaver by installing extensions. Extensions are add-ons to the core functionality of the Dreamweaver product. While Adobe creates and distributes some extensions, most are created by independent third-party developers. Some are free, while others may be commercial products that you have to purchase.

One company that has developed an entire business model around Dreamweaver extensions is called WebAssist. While most of its extensions are for purchase — and in fact several cost more than Dreamweaver itself — it also offers a variety of free extensions. One of the newer of these is the PalettePicker, which extends the functionality of Dreamweaver's fairly limited color picker. The PalettePicker uses Adobe Kuler, an online service where designers can create and share color schemes. The extension allows you to access Kuler schemes directly within Dreamweaver, and select from those schemes when you need to choose a color, either from the Property Inspector or from the CSS panel.

Once you have downloaded the extension, you can install it by simply double-clicking the MXP file that you download from the WebAssist site. Then, you simply need to close and reopen Dreamweaver.

① Open a Web browser.

② Go to www.webassist.com/professional/products/productdetails.asp?PID=147.

The Web page loads.

③ Click get it now.

④ Click proceed to checkout.

⑤ Click submit order.

⑥ Click go to download center.

Note: *Be sure to write down or copy the serial number shown in the download center to your Clipboard.*

⑦ Click PalettePicker.

⑧ Click Open.

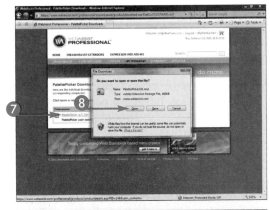

The extension downloads, and the Extension Manager opens.

⑨ Click Accept on the license screen.

The extension is installed.

Note: *You need to close and reopen Dreamweaver before you can use an extension.*

What are some other places to find Dreamweaver extensions?

▼ You can go to the Adobe Exchange Web site at www.adobe.com/exchange. Any extension created by Adobe is available here, as are many extensions created by third-party companies.

In addition to WebAssist, other leading Dreamweaver extension developers are Project Seven at www.projectseven.com, and Kaosweaver at www.kaosweaver.com. Like WebAssist, both offer a variety of free and for-purchase extensions. You can also search for Dreamweaver extensions in a search engine to see a list of other sites with available extensions.

How can I remove an extension I no longer want to use?

▼ You can control all of your extensions in the Adobe Extension Manager, which is a separate application available on the Start menu or Dock. This program lists all of the extensions by product, and gives you the opportunity to enable, disable, or uninstall extensions as well as manually install new ones.

Use a Dreamweaver Extension

Once installed, a Dreamweaver extension functions as if it were a part of the core program, and so you can use it as you would any other part of the application. Some extensions add new panels to the program. Others may add new icons or even new categories to the Insert panel. There are extensions that add new features to the Behaviors or Server Behaviors panels, and still others that simply add new commands to existing menus.

One example is the PalettePicker extension from WebAssist, which works like a panel. As with any other

panel, it is available from the Window menu. Once opened, you can use a drop-down menu at the top of the panel to select which set of Kuler schemes you want to use. You can select Most Popular, Highest Rated, or Random. You can also search for specific schemes by the designer's e-mail address, a tag in the scheme, one of the specific colors, or by title. You can also view all schemes. Once you find a scheme you like, you can use any of the normal color controls in the program to select a swatch from the scheme.

Use a Dreamweaver Extension

① Click Window.

② Click PalettePicker.

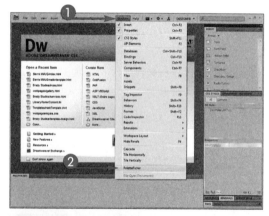

The PalettePicker panel opens, along with the activation window.

③ Type the serial number you received from WebAssist.

④ Click activate.

⑤ Click Close.

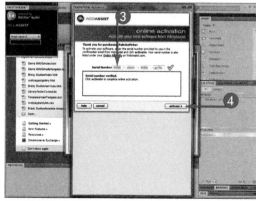

6 Click Most popular.

The most popular Kuler schemes appear.

7 Click an element on the page.

8 Click Add Property.

9 Click color.

10 Click the color picker.

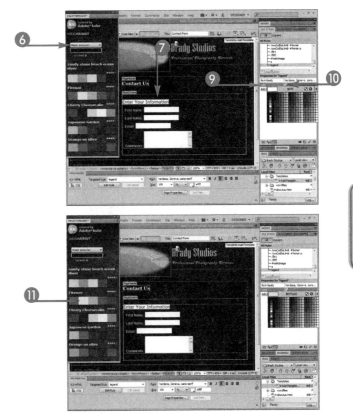

11 Click a color from the PalettePicker panel.

The selected color is applied from the extension.

Can I create my own swatches?

▼ You can create your own swatches in Adobe Kuler, but not the PalettePicker panel. However, the panel does provide a direct link to Kuler — you can click the Powered by Adobe Kuler button at the top of the panel to be taken to the Kuler Web site at kuler.adobe.com.

Once in Kuler, you can click Create to start building a scheme. You can create a scheme based on a specific color by clicking in the color wheel and choosing whether you want Analogous, Monochromatic, Triad, Complementary, Compound, or Shades for the scheme.

I have a really great image that I am using. Can I base a color scheme on this image?

▼ You can also click From an Image to upload an image into Kuler. Once uploaded, the Web site analyzes the image for the five most prominent colors in the image and creates a scheme based on them.

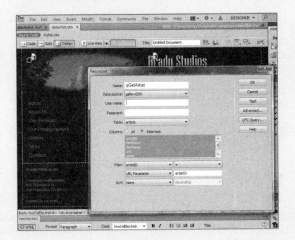

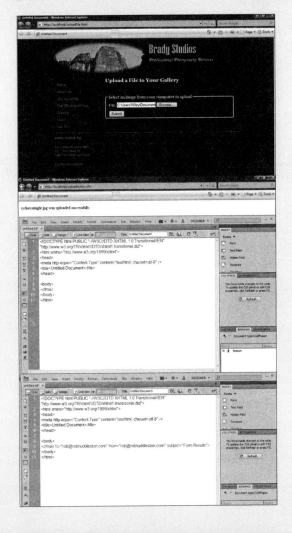

Introducing Dynamic Sites

Today, few Web sites can rely on static information, with content hard-coded into the (X)HTML document. Instead, they need to be able to respond to changes such as new members joining a site or customers adding items to shopping carts. Dynamic sites typically either retrieve information from or write data to databases, although they may also be used to send or receive e-mail, gather information from other sites, or perform any number of other tasks.

Plain (X)HTML does not provide the capabilities to offer dynamic content. Other programming languages, however, offer the ability to generate (X)HTML documents at the moment a user requests them. Many such programming languages exist, but three are fully supported by Dreamweaver.

Dreamweaver Server-side Language Support

For the last several versions, Dreamweaver has offered developers the ability to create dynamic Web sites using a variety of languages. While you can use Code view to manually type code for any language, Dreamweaver also includes a set of Server Behaviors for three of the most popular languages through which it can create code for you.

Adobe ColdFusion

The original server-scripting language, ColdFusion is currently in version 8, released in the fall of 2007. The biggest advantage of ColdFusion is that it is designed as a rapid-development language. Many processes that require complex code in other languages are implied in ColdFusion. It relies on a tag-based markup language and looks and acts very similar to (X)HTML, so it also has one of the lowest learning curves.

ColdFusion also enjoys close integration with other Adobe technologies. For example, it features the capability to generate PDF documents dynamically; it can create Adobe Flash-based forms; and version 8 introduced image manipulation. The language is built on Java, and has access to server-side Java code so that advanced developers can further expand its capabilities. It can also communicate with almost any relational database.

Microsoft Active Server Pages

Now popularly referred to as Active Server Pages (ASP) Classic, this older server-scripting technology from Microsoft is still in widespread use, despite having been officially discontinued by Microsoft in 2002. ASP is tightly bundled with the Microsoft Web server,

Internet Information Services, and thus installs automatically on Windows servers. It can also access other Windows services such as user account control.

ASP pages can technically be written either in JScript, the Microsoft implementation of JavaScript, or VBScript, a scripting version of its Visual Basic programming language; however, almost all are written in VBScript. Like ColdFusion, ASP is database agnostic, but most ASP pages use the Microsoft SQL Server as the database backend.

Besides being discontinued, ASP's other main disadvantage is the fact that it only works in Windows environments without a significant additional cost.

PHP Hypertext Preprocessor

Most developers who are looking for an open-source alternative to Web development languages turn to PHP Hypertext Preprocessor (PHP). Originally developed as an alternative to Perl, another older language, PHP now enjoys an extremely active and robust development community and is used on tens of thousands of sites around the Internet.

PHP uses a fairly simple yet robust scripting language. While the language itself can function with any relational database, it is most often implemented with MySQL, the open-source, enterprise-grade database system. Dreamweaver only supports creating PHP sites with MySQL. PHP has many functions developed specifically with MySQL in mind, making the transition easier.

PHP can be run on any platform, using almost any Web server. Many PHP applications run on the free Apache Web server, and many of those are installed on open source, Unix-based operating systems, although PHP, Apache, and MySQL all run on Windows.

Web Servers

Whenever you type a Web address into your browser's Address bar, the browser requests the document from a Web server, which is a software application designed to listen for and respond to such requests. With static pages, however, the server merely sends the document back to the browser without looking at it, and it is up to the browser to read the document, interpret the (X)HTML, and make additional requests for images, CSS, JavaScript, or other external resources. Because most of the work is done by the browser in this scenario, it is possible to open static Web pages without using a server at all. This is in fact how you have been testing pages up to this point.

Dynamic pages, on the other hand, must be processed by the server first. Browsers cannot read ColdFusion, ASP, or PHP code. In these cases, the Web server still passes off the request, but this time it sends it to the application server first. In the case of ColdFusion and PHP, the application server is a separate piece of software, usually residing on the same computer as the Web server. ASP is integrated directly into the Microsoft Web server, so it technically functions slightly differently, but the concept is the same.

In order to properly view a dynamic page, it cannot be opened directly by the browser, but must instead be requested by a Web server. In order to test dynamic pages, you need to install and run a Web server on your computer.

While dozens of servers actually exist, two completely dominate the market. One is the Apache HTTP Server from the Apache Software Foundation, while the other is the Microsoft Internet Information Server.

Apache

The Apache HTTP Server is an open-source Web server distributed by the nonprofit Apache Software Foundation. While the Foundation uses Native American symbolism in its marketing, the name of the software is actually a play on words: It was created by piecing together several existing components, and was thus literally *a patchy* server.

The Apache server can be downloaded and installed on almost any operating system, including Windows, Mac OS X, and most versions of Unix and Linux. In fact, it comes pre-installed on Macintosh computers. It is in widespread use, so while the foundation does not offer any official technical support, many resources exist both online and in print to help users.

The biggest downside to Apache is that it does not offer a traditional graphical interface for management and configuration. Instead, you have to edit text files to change its settings.

Internet Information Services

Microsoft Internet Information Services (IIS) is the other most widely used Web server. It comes preinstalled in Windows server environments, and is available to be installed on Windows XP and Vista. However, it does not run at all on any other operating system.

Because it is a Windows component, IIS may seem very easy to set up and configure even for the novice, as its Windows interface will be familiar to most users of the operating system. While understanding basic settings is fine for testing purposes, you should keep in mind that fully configuring — and securing — a Web server, regardless of whether you run IIS or Apache, is a full-time job requiring specific training.

Download the Apache Web Server

I f you choose to use the Apache Web server, you first need to download it from the Apache Web site. As an open source project, the Web server is free to download and use for any purpose. In fact, you can even download the raw source code for the server, but it does provide a precompiled installer similar to what you are used to from other programs.

As of this writing, the latest stable release of Apache is 2.2.9, but this is likely to change. When you visit the Web site to download the server, you see links to the latest stable release, as well as past versions and new,

still-in-development versions. You want to get whatever version is being offered as the latest stable release.

You can download the server from a mirror site, which is simply another Web site that offers the downloads, thus allowing the main Apache site to keep its costs down. You should pick whichever mirror site is physically closest to you, although any will work. You want to download the Windows binary version, which has the installer, rather than the source code.

Download the Apache Web Server

① Browse to www.apache.org.

The main Apache Web site opens.

② Click HTTP Server.

The new page appears.

③ Click Download.

Note: *The text of the heading might be slightly different if a newer version is available.*

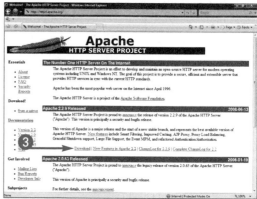

226

The File Download dialog box appears.

4 Click Save.

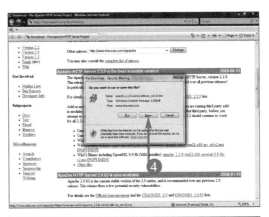

The Save As dialog box appears.

5 Click Save.

The software downloads.

Which version do I need to download if I am running a Macintosh?

▼ Because Mac OS X runs on Unix, you would want to download one of the Unix versions. However, on most computers this is unnecessary as Apache comes preinstalled — although not enabled — on Mac OS X.

Which versions of Windows can I use to run Apache?

▼ Apache runs on almost every version of Windows: 95, 98, Me, NT4, 2000, XP, Vista, and Server 2003. If you are setting up a computer to run as an actual production Web server — one to which outside users will connect to access pages — you should use one of the server-based versions, such as 2000 or 2003. For your development computer, you can use whichever version you already run.

Do I need any other software in order to run Apache?

▼ No, Apache is a stand-alone application that does not require any additional components. It does require that you have Service Pack 1 installed if you use XP, and the very old versions of Windows, such as 95, 98, and Me, require that you download a component in order to run the MSI installer; but once installed, it runs by itself.

Install the Apache Server

While the actual process of installing Apache is very straightforward — it uses an installer wizard that guides you through the steps — there are several important configuration issues you should address. You need to provide administrative information such as the domain name of the Web site and a contact e-mail address, both of which display in default error messages. You can also choose to install Apache completely, or perform a custom installation to choose which components you want to have available.

You can also decide whether or not you want to run Apache as a service, and control how it starts. If you run it as a service, it is configured to run silently in the background, which simply means that you do not have a visual indicator that it is running while working. You can have the server start automatically when you start Windows or you can set it so that you have to manually start the server when you want to use it. Most of the time, it makes the most sense to have it run as a service and start automatically, although you can choose either of the other options if you prefer more control.

① Double-click the installer.

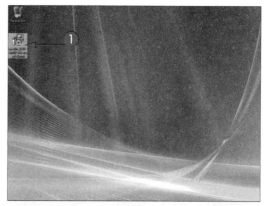

The Installer launches and the Welcome screen appears.

② Click Next.

③ Click I accept the terms in the license agreement.

④ Click Next.

⑤ Click Next.

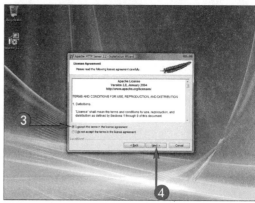

6 Type a name for your network.

7 Type a name for your server.

8 Type an administrative e-mail address.

9 Click Next.

10 Click Typical.

11 Click Next.

12 Click Install.

The installation begins.

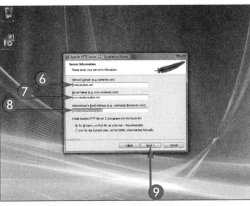

13 Click Finish.

Apache is installed.

Does it matter what I enter for the domain and name of my server?

▼ If you are creating a testing computer for your own use, then you can enter anything you want into either of these fields. The same applies to the e-mail address: for testing purposes, it is not necessary to be accurate.

On the other hand, if you are setting up a production server, then you need to be sure this information is correct. It will appear in error messages and will thus be confusing if it is wrong.

How can I tell if Apache is running?

▼ The easiest way to tell if the server is running is to open your Web browser and go to http://localhost. If a page appears with information about Apache, then the server is running. If you receive a Page not found error, then you need to be sure that the server installed correctly and that it has been started.

How can I start and stop Apache?

▼ Click Start, click All Programs, and then click Apache. There you find a set of applets that start or stop the server. You can also click Start, click Control Panel, click Administrative Tools, and click Services and start or stop the server there.

Install Internet Information Services

Internet Information Services, or IIS, is considered a Windows component. Therefore, you do not need to download it, as it is included as part of the operating system. However, it is only installed by default on the server versions such as NT4, 2000 Server, or 2003. If you are running 2000 Professional, XP Professional, or any variety of Vista, you need to install it.

To install IIS, you need to go into the Programs and Features Control Panel applet. In versions prior to Vista, this was called Add/Remove Programs. Once in the applet, click Windows Components. Place a check mark next to Internet Information Services and then follow a simple wizard to install the server.

Once installed, IIS runs as a service in Windows and automatically starts when you boot your computer. It can be stopped and started from the Services applet in the Administrative Tools section of the Control panel. Oddly, you will not see a service listed as IIS or Internet Information Services, but instead you will need to start or stop the World Wide Web Publishing service to control IIS.

Install Internet Information Services

① Click Start.

② Click Control Panel.

The Control Panel displays.

③ Double-click Programs and Features.

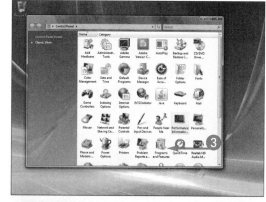

④ Click Turn Windows features on or off.

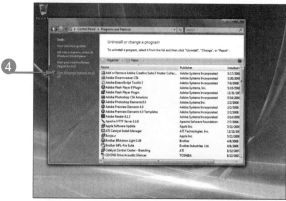

The Windows Features dialog box appears.

⑤ Click the check box next to Internet Information Services.

⑥ Click OK.

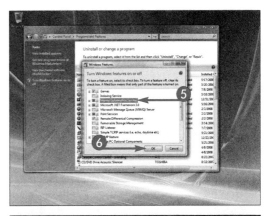

IIS is installed. Once complete, the installer window and the Windows Features dialog box automatically close.

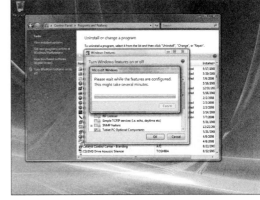

How can I tell if IIS is running?

▼ The easiest way to test your installation of IIS is to open a Web browser and go to http://localhost. If a page appears with information about IIS, then everything is working correctly.

Can I run both IIS and Apache at the same time on the same computer?

▼ While it is technically possible to run both together, they will not both function properly. They will each be trying to duplicate the functionality of the other, so while it may appear that both are working correctly, only one will. Some developers like to have both available for testing purposes, but you only need one to create your site, so you should determine which you are most comfortable with and use it exclusively by either disabling or uninstalling the other.

Can I use IIS on Windows 95, 98, or XP Home?

▼ No. IIS only works on the server-based versions of Windows or on the desktop versions that are actually built on the server model, such as 2000 Professional, XP Professional, and Vista. Microsoft used to offer a limited version of IIS, called the Personal Web Server or PWS, for Windows 98 and Me users, but has since stopped distributing. Because of its limited networking capabilities, neither PWS nor IIS runs on XP Home.

Download PHP

PHP, like the Apache server, is open source and can be downloaded and used without charge. You can download the raw source code for PHP, but this should only be attempted by experienced developers. Instead, you can download either a ZIP archive that contains all of the files you need, but requires that you manually copy them to specific locations on your computer and then manually configure your Web server to work with PHP, or a Windows installer that handles all of the details for you. While some developers like the fine-tuned

control offered by the ZIP method, it is fastest and easiest to use the Windows installer.

You should download the latest stable release of PHP. At the time of this writing, that is version 5.2.6; however, a later version, possibly including PHP 6, may be available when you visit the site.

If you are using a Macintosh running OS X or later, PHP should already be installed on your system. Therefore, you do not need to do anything to get started developing sites in PHP on the Mac.

Download PHP

① Browse to www.php.net/downloads.php.

② Click PHP 5.2.6 Installer.

Note: *The version number may be different.*

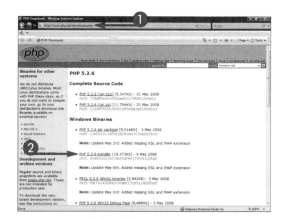

The Get Download site loads.

③ Click a mirror site close to you.

The File Download dialog box appears.

④ Click Save.

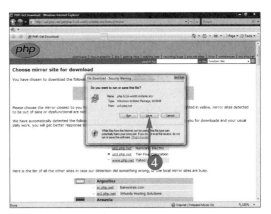

The Save As dialog box appears.

⑤ Choose a location to save the file.

⑥ Click Save.

The file downloads.

Does the mirror site I select really matter?

▼ Only to a point. Mirror sites that are closer to you may download the file faster than those far away, particularly if they are on a different continent, but there are many other factors that may affect your download speed, including your connection speed and the number of other users currently attempting to download from the same server. Most likely, you will not see any noticeable difference between downloading from one mirror or another.

Are there important differences between the versions of PHP?

▼ The various subreleases of PHP 5 do not have significant differences, so while the text discusses PHP 5.2.6, everything will work the same if you have a slightly later or earlier release.

PHP 6, on the other hand, will offer many very big differences; however, it is supposed to be backward-compatible. In any event, Dreamweaver will be writing the same PHP code for you, regardless of the version of PHP you have.

Install PHP

Once you have downloaded PHP, you can install it by following the steps outlined in the installation wizard. You need to be sure that either Apache or IIS is installed and running on your computer before you begin the installation.

As with other software installers, PHP begins by asking you to read and agree to the end-user license agreement. It then asks you to confirm the directory into which you want to have it installed and the Web server you are using.

A default installation of PHP installs only the minimum files needed to run it. In order to communicate with a database, you must install the appropriate database modules. You can do this in the installer on the Choose Items to Install page by expanding Extensions and then selecting the appropriate modules. Most likely, you will want to use either the MySQL or MySQLi extensions, as you must use MySQL with PHP in order to do development through Dreamweaver's Server Behaviors. Once you have completed these steps, the actual installation should be fairly quick.

Install PHP

① Double-click the file you downloaded from the PHP Web site.

The Windows security warning appears.

② Click Run.

The installer welcome screen appears.

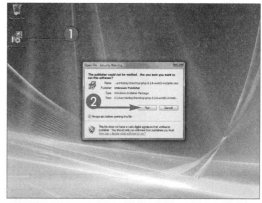

③ Click Next to proceed.

④ In the End-User License Agreement, click the I accept the terms in the license agreement check box.

⑤ Click Next to proceed.

⑥ In the Destination Folder screen, click Next to proceed.

⑦ In the Web Server Setup screen, select the proper version of your Web server. If you are using a recent version of Apache, you select Apache 2.2.x Module; if you use IIS, you want the IIS ISAPI Module.

⑧ Click Next to proceed.

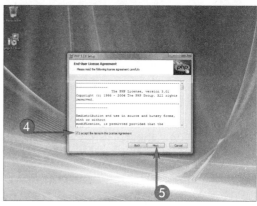

The Choose Items to Install screen opens.

9 Click the Add button.

10 Click MySQL.

11 Click Will be installed on local hard drive.

12 Click Next to proceed.

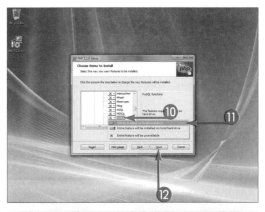

The Ready to Install PHP screen appears.

13 Click Install.

PHP installs. When complete, a message appears.

14 Click Finish.

If I realize later that I need an additional module, how can I install it?

▼ You can run the installer again. If PHP detects that the same version is already installed, it will run in Repair mode. You can tell it that you want to change your installation and then select the modules you want to install.

You can also manually install modules by downloading the files from pecl.php.net/packages.php or pear.php.net and then following the instructions provided in the PHP documentation online to install the module and configure PHP to use it. Note that many of the modules are packaged as TAR files, so you need a special application such as GZip or WinRAR to extract them.

Test Your PHP Installation

Before you begin creating Web sites using PHP, you want to test your installation to be sure it was successful. Otherwise, you might waste time attempting to troubleshoot an error on a page that is actually the result of PHP not working.

You can test your installation by simply creating a PHP page and then opening that page in your browser. You can use a special function in PHP to generate a page that contains detailed information about your installation of PHP, including the version you installed and any configured modules.

The test page, along with any other PHP document you want to create, must be saved in the root directory of the Web server. If you use Apache and performed a default installation on Windows, the root folder is located at c:/program files/apache software foundation/apache 2.2/htdocs. If you use IIS, the root folder is at c:/inetpub/wwwroot. The Web server does not normally have access to any files outside of this Web root, so you need to be sure that you store all of your site's files here.

Test Your PHP Installation

① Click File in the menu bar.

② Click New.

The New Document dialog box appears.

③ Click PHP.

④ Click <none>.

⑤ Click Create.

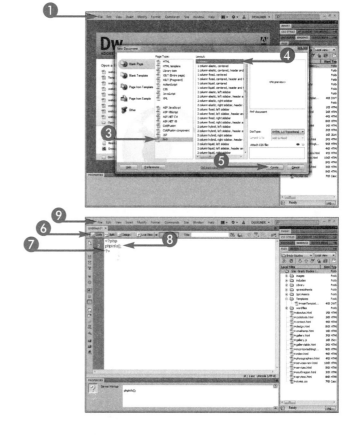

A new page is created.

⑥ Click Code.

Code view displays.

⑦ Delete all of the existing code.

⑧ Type <?php phpinfo(); ?>.

⑨ Click File in the menu bar.

⑩ Click Save As.

The Save As dialog box appears.

⓫ Navigate to the root directory of your Web server.

⓬ Type **phpinfo.**

⓭ Click Save.

⓮ Open a Web browser.

⓯ Type **http://localhost/phpinfo.php**.

The test page appears, displaying information about PHP.

How do I find the server's root directory?

▼ If you did not perform a standard installation of the Web server and the root directory is not at one of the locations mentioned on the opposite page, you can use the operating system's Search feature to find it. If you are using Apache, search for htdocs; with IIS, search for wwwroot.

What do the `<?php` and `?>` signify?

▼ PHP relies on its code being embedded directly within an (X)HTML document. As such, PHP pages contain a mix of (X)HTML and PHP code, so the PHP application needs to know which parts should be processed as PHP and which should be ignored and sent straight back to the browser as (X)HTML. You designate the blocks of code that contain PHP by enclosing them within the PHP delimiters. The opening delimiter is `<?php`, and the closing is `?>`, so any code within these delimiters is read and processed as PHP, while code outside of them is treated as (X)HTML.

Download ColdFusion

Adobe ColdFusion is a commercial product with a Standard Edition that retails for about $1,300 and an Enterprise Edition for around $7,500. However, you can develop and test applications in ColdFusion using the Developer Edition, which can be downloaded for free from the Adobe Web site.

The Developer Edition of ColdFusion includes all of the features of the Enterprise Edition, but is limited to access from only two other computers. It is designed so that developers can create ColdFusion applications without needing to purchase a license. You need to

deploy your application to a server that is running one of the two commercial editions of ColdFusion, but you can find third-party hosting companies that offer ColdFusion hosting. With some comparison shopping, you can find ColdFusion hosting plans for the same cost as, and in some cases less than, that for other technologies such as PHP.

ColdFusion runs with almost any operating system, as it is available for Windows, Macintosh, and several varieties of Unix. The installation package is a very large file, so it may take some time to download over slower Internet connections.

Download ColdFusion

① Browse to www.adobe.com/products/coldfusion.

② Click Download the free Developer Edition.

A login page appears.

Note: You must log in or create a free account before you can download trials from the Adobe Web site.

③ Select the version for your operating system.

④ Click Download.

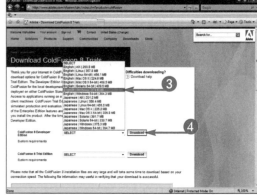

The File Download dialog box appears.

5 Click Save.

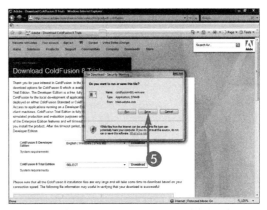

The Save As dialog box appears.

6 Click Save.

The download begins. A message appears when the download is complete.

What is the difference between the 30-day trial and the Developer Edition?

▼ The 30-day trial is a fully functional copy of ColdFusion Enterprise. If you do not purchase a serial number within the 30 days, it automatically becomes the Developer Edition.

The most important limitation of the Developer Edition is that it cannot be accessed by more than two remote computers. ColdFusion has several language functions that create documents on the server, usually as PDFs. Documents created from the Developer Edition are watermarked, whereas those created from the purchased versions or the trial version are not.

Where can I find out more about ColdFusion?

▼ In addition to the official support offered by Adobe to those who purchase its products, ColdFusion has a very active developer community online. You can use a search engine such as Google to find answers to specific issues. You can also join the weekly ColdFusion Meetup, an online meeting of ColdFusion developers, at www.coldfusionmeetup.com. You may also have a local ColdFusion user group in your area. You can find a list of user groups at http://groups.adobe.com.

Install ColdFusion

Once downloaded, ColdFusion can be installed by using the Install wizard. It takes you through a series of steps to install the program and get it set up. Once completed, you can begin using ColdFusion immediately.

ColdFusion can be run with a Web server such as Apache or IIS, but the Developer Edition can also be run with its own stand-alone server. If you are going to use Apache or IIS, you need to be sure that the server is installed and running before you install ColdFusion. You can also install the database connectors, search services, and documentation for ColdFusion.

Your ColdFusion server is configured through an Administrator, which requires a password that you set during installation. In order to communicate with the server, Dreamweaver uses a technology called Remote Development Services (RDS). You can choose to enable RDS on your server when you install, and provide a password to limit access.

Once complete, ColdFusion launches your Web browser and completes a few additional configuration steps. This does not require your input, and generally only takes a few minutes. When installation succeeds, you are taken to the login page for the Administrator.

Install ColdFusion

① Double-click the file you downloaded from the Adobe Web site.

② In the Open File dialog box, click Run.

③ Complete the initial screens, clicking Next or OK to move through each Installation Wizard screen.

④ In the License Agreement screen, select the Accept the license agreement option and then click Next to proceed.

⑤ In the Install Type screen, select the Developer Edition check box and then click Next to proceed.

The Installer Configuration screen appears.

⑥ Select the Server configuration option.

⑦ Click Next to proceed.

⑧ In the Subcomponent Installation screen, select the desired components check boxes and then click Next to proceed.

⑨ In the Select Installation Directory screen, click Next to proceed.

⑩ In the License Agreement screen, select the Accept the license agreement option and then click Next to proceed.

⑪ In the Adobe LiveCycle Data Services ES Installation, complete the series of screens and then click Next to proceed.

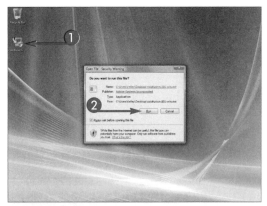

The Configure Web Servers/Websites screen appears.

⑫ Click the All IIS websites option.

Note: If you do not want to use IIS or Apache, click Built-in web server.

⑬ Click Next twice to continue to the Administrator Password screen.

⑭ Type an administrator password twice and then click Next to proceed.

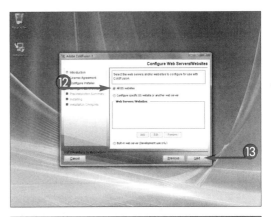

⑮ In the Enable RDS screen, click the Enable RDS option.

⑯ Type an RDS password twice.

⑰ Click Next to proceed.

⑱ In the Pre-installation Summary screen, click Install.

The application installs. Once complete, a message displays.

⑲ Click Close.

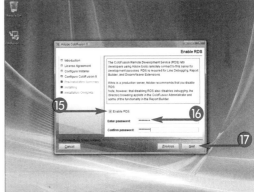

What are ports used for?

▼ To access Web pages, you type an address to a Web server, such as www.wiley.com. However, that server may be able to process requests from many different applications in addition to Web browsers, such as FTP clients or e-mail. Therefore, it can be helpful to think of the server as an apartment building. To send mail to someone in an apartment, you not only need their street address, but you also need their apartment number. The equivalent of apartment numbers for servers is called a port.

How do I access my pages if I use stand-alone Web server?

▼ By default, Web servers listen on port 80. However, the stand-alone version of ColdFusion, in order to not conflict with a Web server on the same computer, uses port 8500. You specify the port number by typing the server address, a colon, and then the number. Therefore, in order to access pages using this configuration, you need to type **http://localhost:8500**.

Install the ColdFusion Extension for Dreamweaver

Dreamweaver does not come with the necessary configuration files to enable it to provide code hints and other functionality to help you write applications using ColdFusion 8. While it may seem odd that Adobe would release a version of its Web editor without including an update for its own Web application server, it was done to allow it to more easily keep Dreamweaver up-to-date with future releases of ColdFusion, because the two applications are released on different schedules.

You can install a free extension for Dreamweaver that allows it to provide code-hinting for ColdFusion 8

tags. The extension can be downloaded from the ColdFusion Web site. It is an MXP file, so when you download and run it, the Adobe Extension Manager launches and installs the extension. The extension is not specific to any particular operating system.

The extension does not add any additional functionality to the Server Behaviors within Dreamweaver that allow you to create ColdFusion applications with little or no code. However, you will want them installed when you begin building more complicated ColdFusion applications where you write most of the code yourself.

Install the ColdFusion Extension for Dreamweaver

① Browse to http://www.adobe.com/support/coldfusion/downloads.html.

② Click Download ColdFusion 8 Update for Dreamweaver.

The File Download dialog box appears.

③ Click Open.

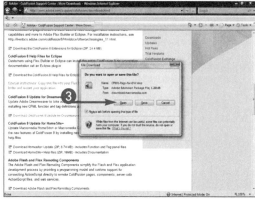

The Extension is downloaded. When it completes, the Adobe Extension Manager opens and presents a license agreement.

4 Click Accept.

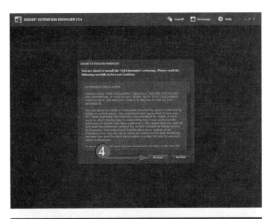

The extension is installed. When complete, a message appears.

5 Click OK.

Note: *If a message appears warning that you have a newer copy of certain files, click Yes to All to replace them with those from the extension.*

Do I need to have Dreamweaver open to install the extension?

▼ No, the Adobe Extension Manager is a separate application that manages extensions for all of the Adobe products. In fact, if you do have Dreamweaver open when you install the extension, you need to close and reopen it in order for the extension to take effect.

What new features do I get with the extension?

▼ You do not see any visual change to the application once the extension is installed. There are no new panels or menu commands. Instead, you are able to go into Code view and see the new tags and functions that are a part of ColdFusion 8, such as `<cfimage>`, appear in the code hinting as you type. The extension also updates the Dreamweaver help files with information about ColdFusion 8 and its features.

Set Up a Dynamic Site

When you have a Web server and an application server installed and configured, you are ready to start building dynamic Web sites. However, before you can begin using Dreamweaver's server behaviors and other dynamic features, you will need to reconfigure your Dreamweaver site by letting Dreamweaver know which server language you plan to use and where it can find the files.

When you create a static Web site, you can place your site's files anywhere on the hard drive, and you can test them by opening them directly from the local file system. Dynamic sites, however, must be processed by a Web server. Therefore, you have to store your Web site's files in the server's root folder, and you must browse to your files by using the http://localhost address in your browser.

You need to edit the Site Definition in Dreamweaver. You can click the Testing Server category to enter the necessary information. You need to select the proper development language. Then, you can tell Dreamweaver where the files reside on your computer, and the URL it should use when you preview the pages.

❶ Click Site.

❷ Click Manage Sites.

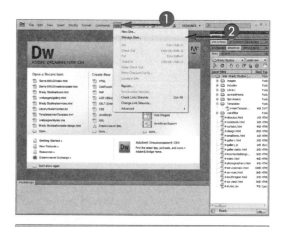

The Manage Sites dialog box appears.

❸ Click Edit.

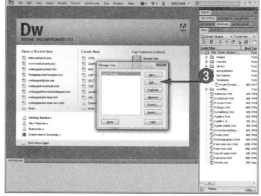

The Site Definition dialog box appears.

④ Click Testing Server.

⑤ Select the server model you will use.

⑥ Select Local/Network.

⑦ Type the path to the folder that contains your site's files.

⑧ Click OK.

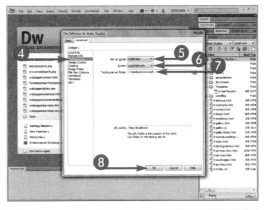

The Manage Sites dialog box reappears.

⑨ Click Done.

The site is configured to use the server model.

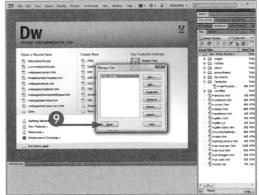

Can I use Dreamweaver to develop ASP.NET or JSP pages? I had heard that I cannot, but I see them listed in the server models.

▼ Older versions of Dreamweaver included support for ASP.NET and JSP development. Dreamweaver CS4 dropped that support for server behaviors and other Design-view functionality. However, they are still listed as options under Server Model because Code view still supports code hinting for them, so you can still use Dreamweaver to write the code for ASP.NET and JSP pages and you can still preview pages you create using those models. You cannot, however, use the Server Behaviors that are discussed in Chapter 19.

I am using ColdFusion. When I view the Administrator, it says its address is 127.0.0.1, not localhost. What is the difference?

▼ When you view Web pages, you most likely rely on domain names such as wiley.com. This system was created to mask the actual addresses used by servers, called Internet Protocol or IP addresses, which are made up of 4 numbers, each between 0 and 255, separated by periods. Just as localhost is a special reserved domain name for referencing a Web server on the same computer as the browser, 127.0.0.1 is the special IP address. The two are equivalent and can be used interchangeably.

Add a Form to a Page

You can collect data from your users by adding forms to your pages. (X)HTML provides for a host of form controls to accept different types of data, all of which can be added to pages through Dreamweaver. Which controls you use depend on the needs of your site, but regardless of what kind of information you need to collect or what you plan to do with it, you always begin by adding a form, which serves as a container for the rest of the form controls.

The form tag takes two required attributes or parameters. Both of these can be configured on the Property Inspector. The easier attribute to understand

is `action`, which is simply the path to the page on the server that processes the form — that is, the page to which you need to send the data. The second attribute, `method`, instructs the browser as to how it should send the data: `get` and `post`. When using `get`, the data from the form is sent as part of the URL, visible in the browser. The `post` parameter, on the other hand, sends the data in the background of the page request. While `get` is the default method in (X)HTML, it is recommended that you always use `post`.

Add a Form to a Page

① Click in the page in Design view.

② Click Common.

③ Click Forms.

④ Click Form.

● The form is inserted, and appears as a red dotted line in Design view.

Add a Fieldset and Legend

You can make your forms look more organized and easier to read by grouping form controls with `fieldsets`. When you add a `fieldset` to your form, the browser draws a border around the elements. Some browsers slightly vary the color of the opposite edges of the border, creating a raised effect.

Simply using the `fieldset` to wrap form fields assists in both usability and accessibility, but you should also provide a `legend`. The `legend` appears near the top-left corner of the `fieldset`, bisecting

the border. This unique display of the `legend` — by default, no other element exists in the border of another element — is part of why using `fieldsets` and `legends` can greatly enhance the overall appearance of the form. Dreamweaver automatically prompts you to add the legend when you insert a `fieldset`.

It is legal in (X)HTML to nest `fieldsets`. For example, you can have a user data `fieldset`, and within that, add a personal information set with name, address, and phone fields and a site data set with username and password fields.

Add a Fieldset and Legend

① Click within the form.

② Click Fieldset.

● The Fieldset dialog box appears.

③ Type a legend.

④ Click OK.

● The fieldset and legend are inserted into the document. Design view only displays the legend.

Add a Text Field

The most common form control by far is the single-line text field. Search engines use it to provide entry for search terms; registration systems use it for names, addresses, and credit card numbers; login systems rely on it for usernames.

When you insert a text field, Dreamweaver presents a dialog box with accessibility attributes. You need to provide an ID for the field. This uniquely identifies the field within the form, and is used by the server-side script to which you submit the form to identify the

data from the field. The ID may consist only of letters, numbers, dashes, and underscores. The ID should begin with a letter and not a number.

You can input a label in this dialog box to provide visible text next to the field to identify the field. You can either have the label wrap around the text field or be attached to it through a special `for` attribute; both give you the same visual result. You can choose whether to place the label to the left or the right of the field.

Add a Text Field

1 Click within the form.

2 Click Text Field.

The Input Tag Accessibility Attributes dialog box appears.

3 Type an ID for the field.

4 Type a label for the field.

5 Select Attach label tag using the `for` attribute.

6 Ensure that the Before form item option is selected.

7 Click OK.

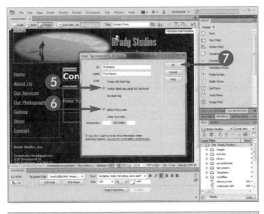

● The field is inserted into the document.

What is the difference between wrapping with the label tag and attaching using `for` attribute?

▼ The (X)HTML label tag is used to identify the text that describes the field in the form. You can either wrap both the field and the label within the tag, which would result in code like this:

```
<label>First Name:<input type="text"
name="firstname" id="firstname" /></label>
```

Or, you can keep the label separate and provide the association using the label's `for` attribute, whose value will match the ID of the field:

```
<label for="firstname ">First name:</label>
```
```
<input type="text" name="firstname"
id="firstname" />
```

Either is legal. The second option, using the `for` attribute, provides more flexibility because other page content can be placed between the label and the field.

Are there any other advantages of using either technique?

▼ Browsers also allow users to click the label or the field to begin inserting data, but unfortunately this feature only works with Internet Explorer if you use the `for` attribute method.

Insert a Text Area

Single-line text fields are fine for most text input, but there will be times when you need to encourage or allow your user to input large blocks of text. For example, social networking sites such as MySpace.com and online dating sites such as Match.com have a field when you register in which you can write a short biography of yourself. E-commerce sites may provide a space in which customers can write a message to be printed on a greeting card for gifts. Online classified advertising sites like Craigslist.org must provide a space for the text of the ad.

You can provide for these scenarios by inserting a text field through the use of the `textarea`. Like the text field, you are prompted to add the accessibility attributes, such as `ID` and `label`, when you insert a `textarea`.

You can control the size of the `textarea` by setting the width in characters and a height as a number of lines using the Property Inspector once the `textarea` has been inserted. You can also enter default text that will appear when the form first loads.

① Click within the form.

② Click Textarea.

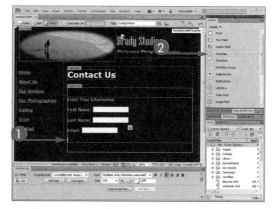

The Input Tag Accessibility Attributes dialog box appears.

③ Type an ID.

④ Type a label.

⑤ Click OK.

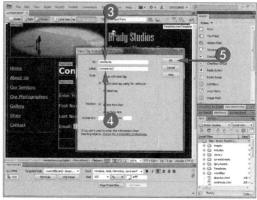

The field is inserted.

6 Click in the text field.

7 Change the character width.

8 Change the number of lines.

● The text field resizes.

Can I add formatting controls to the textarea?

▼ (X)HTML does not have a control for a rich text form field that provides a toolbar to allow the user to set the font and typeface properties such as bold, italic, and size. However, several implementations of rich text editors exist, and most are free to use. One popular rich text editor is FCKEditor.

What are the capabilities of the FCKEditor and where can I get it?

▼ One of the most robust and popular rich text editors is the FCKEditor. It can be downloaded free of charge from www.fckeditor.net. Implemented through a combination of (X)HTML and JavaScript, it includes a full feature set that allows you to set which tools appear. It then takes the formatted text and translates it to (X)HTML for submission to the server. For example, if the user selects some text and clicks the Bold button, the editor wraps the text with a `strong` element. The editor even allows users to create hyperlinks within their text block. FCKEditor is also highly customizable, allowing you to choose which buttons appear on its toolbars.

Add Check Boxes and Radio Buttons

Y ou can provide a list of options from which your user can select a value by using check boxes, radio buttons, and select lists. Check boxes and radio buttons are useful when you have a fairly limited set of choices or when you need to present additional information about each choice. They differ in that check boxes allow the user to select none or more of the choices, while radio buttons restrict the user to a single choice.

You can insert individual check boxes or radio buttons from the Insert panel. However, you need to ensure that each of the check boxes or radio buttons within a

group have the exact same name, which you need to set for each control individually on the Property Inspector.

Instead, you can use the Checkbox Group and Radio Button Group features. These present you with a single dialog box in which you can enter the name you want to use for all of the controls in the group, and then add labels and values for each control. You can choose to lay out the controls using either line breaks or a table.

① Click Checkbox Group.

The Checkbox Group dialog box appears.

② Type a name for the group.

③ Click the text Checkbox.

④ Type a label for the first item.

⑤ Press Tab.

⑥ Type a value.

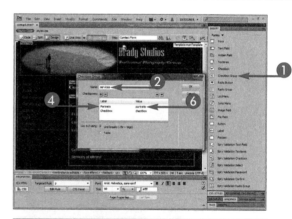

⑦ Repeat steps **3** to **6** for the next item.

⑧ Click the Add button to add another item.

⑨ Click OK.

The check box group is inserted.

⑩ Click Radio Group.

The Radio Group dialog box appears.

⑪ Type a name for the group.

⑫ Click the text Radio and type a label for the first item.

⑬ Press Tab and type a value.

⑭ Repeat steps **12** and **13** for an additional item.

⑮ Click OK.

● The radio group is inserted.

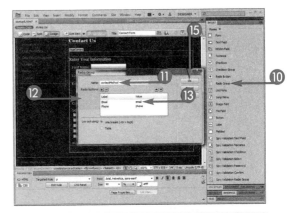

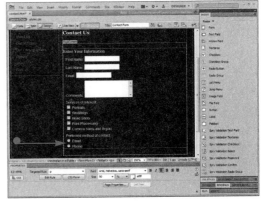

Can I preselect one of the items in the check box or radio group?

▼ You can preselect a check box or radio button by clicking the control you want to preselect and then clicking Checked on the Property Inspector. You can preselect as many check boxes in a group as you want, but only one radio button can be preselected. Note that if you do preselect a radio button, it will not be possible for your user to submit the form with none of the radio buttons selected, as he will only be able to change your initial selection rather than deselect the entire list.

What is Checked Value?

▼ Unlike text fields, where the user supplies the value by typing something in the field, check boxes and radio buttons need to have their value coded into the (X)HTML. This value is what will be submitted to the server.

Build a Drop-Down List or Menu

If you have a lot of options from which you would like your user to choose, such as a list of the states in the United States or countries in the world, you can use a drop-down list instead of check boxes or radio buttons. You can use the List/Menu button on the Insert panel to add a drop-down list to your page. You are presented with the same accessibility options as you see when you insert text fields and text areas. Once you have inserted the drop-down list, you can click it and click the List Values button on the Property Inspector to add items

to the list. You want to provide a label, which is the text that appears in the list, and a value, which will be sent to the server when this item is selected, for each item in the list.

You can change the type from Menu to List on the Property Inspector. Menus only allow for a single selection; lists allow for multiple items to be selected. If you choose List, you can set the number of lines that will be visible onscreen; the browser will automatically add a scroll bar to display additional items.

Build a Drop-down List or Menu

1 Click List/Menu.

The Input Tag Accessibility Attributes dialog box appears.

2 Type an ID.

3 Type a label.

4 Click OK.

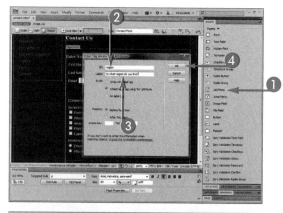

The list is inserted into the page.

5 Click the list.

6 Click List Values.

The List Values dialog box appears.

7 Type a label for an item.

8 Type a value.

9 Repeat steps **7** and **8** for additional items.

10 Click OK.

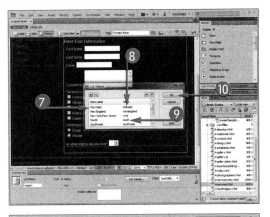

● The list is updated.

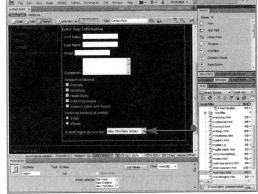

How can I select more than one option in a list?

▼ If the type is set to list, you can choose multiple adjacent options by pressing and holding the Shift key, or you can press and hold the Control key in Windows or the Command key in the Mac OS to select more than one nonadjacent item.

How can I test the list?

▼ Design view does not provide a list with which you can interact. Whichever item in the list is the longest is the only one displayed in Design view. In order to see that the list works, you need to either use Live view or preview the page in a browser.

Will users know how to select more than one item?

▼ You can assume users will not know how to do this, so it is a good idea to add some helper text near the field to explain its use. For example, to choose more than one item, press and hold the Ctrl key (Windows) or Cmd key (Macintosh). Many designers simply place this instruction next to the field in question. Do not worry about making the distinction between holding the Shift key and holding the Ctrl key. As the latter works in all situations, it is simpler to just give your users the single option.

Add a Password Field

Many Web sites need to be able to identify the user. Whether it is a social-networking site that allows pages to be personalized for individuals or intranet sites that simply require users to be securely logged in before they can access information, you are likely to encounter many cases where you want your user to enter a username and password.

In most cases, the username is entered through a text field. The password, however, is always entered through a field that masks the input. You can insert a

normal text field and change the type to Password to insert a password field. Nothing more is required of you: The browser automatically replaces the text being inserted into the field with a bullet or asterisk.

You should note that the password field is only being masked by the browser, and is not at all secure. You need to secure the transmission of the data to the server, as otherwise, the password, along with all of the other data from the form, is sent in plain text and can be easily intercepted and read.

Add a Password Field

① Click Text Field.

The Input Tag Accessibility Attributes dialog box appears.

② Type an ID.

③ Type a label.

④ Click OK.

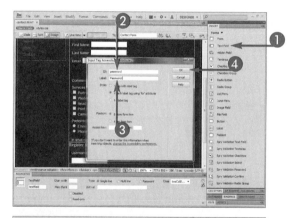

The text field is inserted.

⑤ Click the text field.

⑥ Click Password.

The field is converted to a password field.

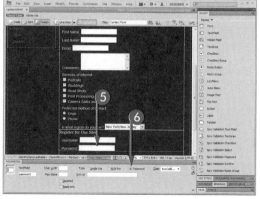

Add a Hidden Field

Most form controls are, by definition, designed to allow your users to input the data they want to send. However, there may be times on a form that you need to embed data to be sent that should not be editable by, or even visible to, users.

A good example of the use of hidden fields can be found on Google. When you search for a term in Google, you see that the Address bar on the results page looks something like this:

www.google.com/search?q=dreamweaver&hl=en&btnG=Search+Google.

In this case, www.google.com/search is the form's `action`; q=dreamweaver is the data from the text field; and btnG=Search+Google is the Search button. However, note that a third option exists from the form: hl=en, which represents the user's preference for the language in which the page should be displayed, and is embedded on the pages in a hidden field named hl.

Hidden fields can be added to the page from the Insert panel. You see an icon in Design view indicating the presence of the field. You can click this icon and use the Property Inspector to give the field a name and value.

Add a Hidden Field

1 Click Hidden Field.

The field is added to the page and an icon appears to represent it.

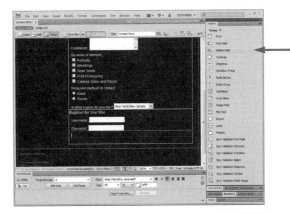

2 Click the icon.

3 Type a name.

4 Type a value.

The properties of the field are set.

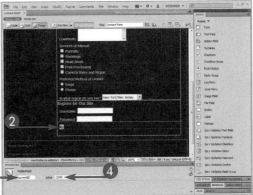

Add a Submit Button

You can allow your user to send the form data to your server script with a Submit button. Buttons can be added through the Insert panel.

As with other visual controls, you need to provide an ID for the button, but in general you want to leave the Label field blank and click No label tag in the Accessibility Attributes dialog box. Browsers vary on the default text they use for buttons. You can overcome this and ensure consistency by providing a

value on the Property Inspector. For example, you can have the button on a contact form say Contact Us rather than Submit.

Multiple Submit buttons are allowed on forms, but obviously only one may ever be clicked. A simple online calculator needs at a minimum four buttons, one for each of the basic mathematical operations. In this case, you need to provide a unique name for each, and use your server-processing script to determine which button was clicked and then perform the necessary processing.

Add a Submit Button

1. Click Button.

The Input Tag Accessibility Attributes dialog box appears.

2. Type an ID.

3. Click No label tag.

4. Click OK.

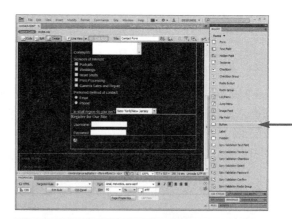

● The button is inserted.

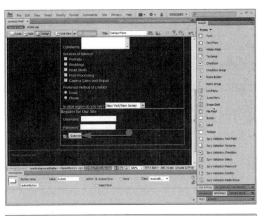

5️⃣ Click the button.

6️⃣ Type a new value.

7️⃣ Press Enter.

The button is added to the form.

Should I always include a Reset button?

▼ Except in very rare cases, a Reset button is more likely to confuse your users than it is to help. How often have you filled out a long form and then decided that you did not want to send it and so pressed Reset? Very few users do this intentionally; however, it can be common for users to accidentally click the Reset button instead of the Submit button, so it is best to leave the Reset button off your form entirely.

How can I make sure that my users can press Enter instead of needing to click the button?

▼ As long as your form has only a single button, the browser automatically submits the form when the user is in any of the fields within the form. If you have more than one button, then pressing Enter does not work, as there is no reliable way for the browser to know which button should be activated.

What is the button type?

▼ Setting the type to button creates a generic button with no automatic behavior. You then need to write JavaScript code to instruct a generic button as to its function.

Make an Image into a Button

You can use an image for the Submit button if you want. You can click the Image Field button to have the browser place an image on the page in place of the normal gray button with text. You can select any image you want as the button's source, and then provide the normal accessibility options for the form field. As with Submit buttons, you need to provide an ID but will most likely set No label tag.

The main disadvantage is that, without JavaScript, there is no way to get an image button to do

anything other than submit the form. A somewhat strange side effect of using image buttons is that the browser automatically transmits the x and y coordinates of the spot on the image that was actually clicked. In theory, this data, sent as `field_name.x` and `field_name.y` variables (where `field_name` is the `name` or ID you set for the field) could allow the developer to respond differently depending on the area of the button that was clicked. The origin point of the coordinates is the top-left corner of the image.

Make an Image into a Button

① Click Image Field.

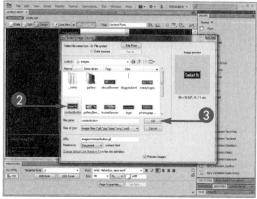

The Select Image Source dialog box appears.

② Select an image.

③ Click OK.

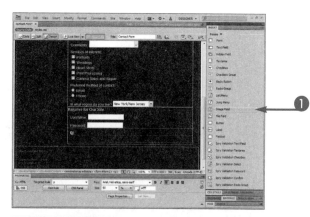

The Input Tag Accessibility Attributes dialog box appears.

④ Type an ID.

⑤ Click No label tag.

⑥ Click OK.

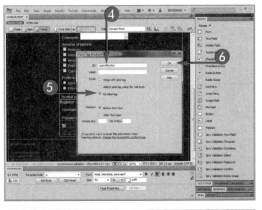

● The image is inserted.

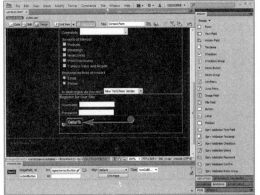

Do I still need to provide alternate text for this image?

▼ You should provide alternate text for any image on your page other than those being used as background images through CSS, and so you should also include it for images being used as buttons. You can click the image on the page and use the Property Inspector to set the alternate text. Any images that contain text should have their alternate text set to match the text on the image.

How will my users know that the image is a button?

▼ Many designers are tempted to try new and unusual things on their pages to make them stand out from others. While this is fine, it should only be done to a point. In the case of using images as buttons, it is absolutely vital that the image still look mostly buttonlike. If the image you are using for the button does not look like something that should be clicked, then your users are likely to become frustrated and may potentially leave the site for one that does not confuse them.

Add a Validation Text Field

Data being submitted from a form should always be validated. Validation ensures that the user entered the data as you expected: that they provided data for any fields that must contain data and that the data they entered is appropriate. You can validate your forms either at the browser through JavaScript — in which case the validation occurs before the data is actually sent to the server — or on the server after submission. Both techniques have advantages and disadvantages, and so many developers prefer to err on the side of caution and validate both locally and server side.

In the past, creating local validation required a thorough knowledge of JavaScript. Using the Spry framework, however, allows you to add validation to your form without touching JavaScript code at all.

Spry provides a wide variety of validation fields. The most basic of them is a text field. The Spry validation text field allows you to require that data be entered into the field. You can require that the field contain certain kinds of data, such as an e-mail address or credit card number, set minimum and maximum values for the data, and set minimum and maximum numbers of characters.

① Click Spry Validation Text Field.

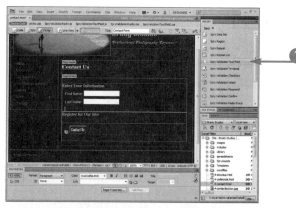

The Input Tag Accessibility Attributes dialog box appears.

② Type an ID.

③ Type a label.

④ Click OK.

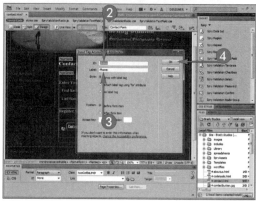

● The field is inserted.

5 Click the Type drop-down menu.

6 Select Phone Number.

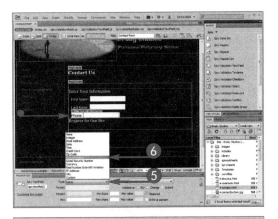

7 Select the current field name.

8 Type a new name.

The field is inserted and its properties set.

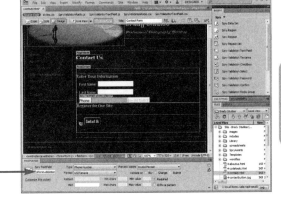

What are the Validate At settings?

▼ When using Spry for validation, you can control what user action will trigger the validation. For instance, setting the Validate At setting to Blur will cause the validation to be triggered as soon as the user moves his cursor out of the field, either by clicking away or pressing the tab key. Change triggers the validation as soon as the data in the field changes, so for text fields it will trigger as soon as the user starts typing. Submit, the default setting, only causes the validation to trigger when the user clicks the form's Submit button.

How can I let my user know what kind of data I am going to require?

▼ You can use the Hint field to provide text that will appear in the field by default, but that will disappear as soon as the user clicks or moves into the field. However, the hint can only display as much text as will appear in the field, so you should also provide clear text directly on the form, above, below, or next to the field, that explains what information will be required. Users should never have to guess what you need in the fields.

Format Spry Validation Messages

When Spry validation is triggered, messages appear next to the fields that contain errors, and the fields' background color changes. By default, the background color turns pink, and the text is formatted in red with a red border. Many of the validation widgets also contain different messages for different errors. For example, the Text Validation widget normally displays a message when the form is submitted while the field is blank, but if you set it to expect a format such as Phone Number, an additional message is available to display if the data is not in that format.

You can change the wording of the validation error messages by controlling the field's Preview state from the Property Inspector. When you select a state, Design view changes to show the display of that state, allowing you to modify the text of the error directly onscreen. You can format the appearance of the errors through the CSS panel while in a Preview state. You can test the final appearance of the fields by previewing the page in a browser or by using Live mode and intentionally submitting the form while violating your rules.

Format Spry Validation Messages

1 Click the blue Spry TextField tab.

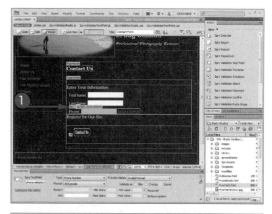

The Property Inspector updates.

2 Click the Preview states drop-down menu.

3 Select Required.

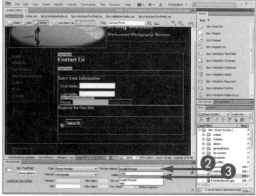

Design view shows the required error.

④ Click in the error message.

⑤ Delete the current text.

⑥ Type a new error message.

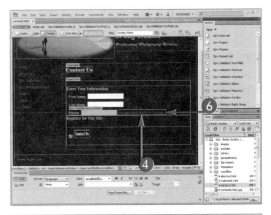

⑦ Click CSS Styles.

⑧ Click Current.

⑨ Click border.

⑩ Click the Delete CSS Property button.

The border is removed and the message is formatted.

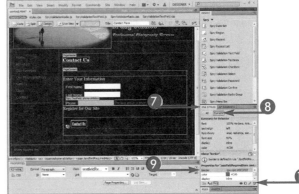

Are the styles created by Spry added to my site's style sheet?

▼ No, adding a Spry widget does not modify your site's style sheet. Instead, Spry creates a style sheet for each of the validation fields that you add; so, for example, adding a Spry TextField to the page adds a document called SpryValidationTextField.css to your site. As with the JavaScript files used by Spry, the CSS files are stored in a SpryAssets folder in your site. Should you need to access these files directly, you can click their name in the Related Files bar.

When does the Valid state appear?

▼ If you rely on Submit for your validation trigger, your user will not see the Valid state. Validating on Submit means that the validation only occurs when the user clicks the Submit button, and because the browser is attempting to navigate away from the page, it does not show the state. However, if you validate using the Blur trigger, you will see the Valid state as soon as you move your cursor out of a field that contains the correct data, and if you use Change, you will see it appear as soon as the correct data is entered.

Add a Validation TextArea Field

When you need to collect larger amounts of text from your users, you can use a text area. Spry includes a widget that allows you more control over the data being input into a text area.

You can set the text area as being required so that it cannot be left blank. As with text fields, text areas include an Initial preview state, a Required state, and a Valid state; can be validated on blur, change, or submit; and can include a hint. However, unlike text fields, text areas cannot be set to expect a certain

format. Instead, you can set a minimum and maximum number of characters that you will allow to be entered into the field. When the maximum is reached, you can choose to block additional characters rather than displaying an error.

You can also choose to display a counter next to the field. This counter can be set to either begin by showing the maximum number of allowed characters and then counting down as each character is entered, or begin at zero and count up to the maximum.

Add a Validation TextArea Field

① Click Spry Validation Textarea.

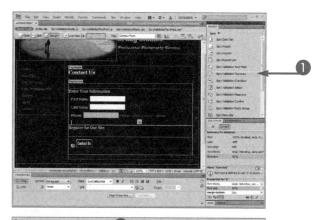

The Input Tag Accessibility Attributes dialog box appears.

② Type an ID.

③ Type a label.

④ Click OK.

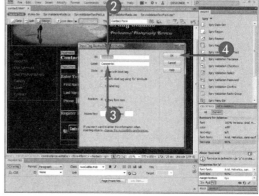

The field is inserted.

5 Type a number for minimum characters.

6 Type a number for maximum characters.

7 Click Chars count.

8 Click Live View.

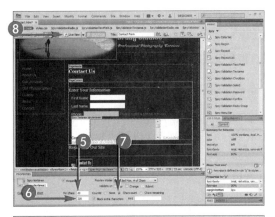

Live view displays.

9 Click in the field.

10 Type some text.

The character count updates.

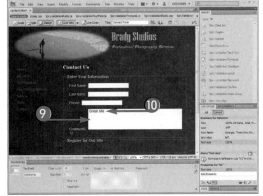

Can I convert existing fields to Spry validation fields?

▼ Yes, regular fields can be converted to Spry fields. While it is much easier to create form fields that need to be validated as Spry fields from the beginning, you can convert an existing form to one that uses Spry by simply clicking in the existing field and then clicking the corresponding Spry field type. For example, if you have a normal text field and you want to convert it to a Spry TextField, you can click the existing field, and then click Spry Validation Text Field on the Insert panel. Dreamweaver simply replaces the existing field with the new Spry field.

How can I access the normal settings for the text area so that I can change its size or other (X)HTML properties?

▼ You can click directly in the field in Design view to get the Property Inspector to display the normal (X)HTML settings for any field. If you need to switch back to editing the Spry properties, you can click the light-blue tab that appears just above the field in Design view.

Is it important that I rename the Spry fields?

▼ It can help to rename the Spry fields so that you can more easily find the fields if you ever need to update the code. The names of the form fields themselves, however, are far more important as they will be used by your server-side script. Only Spry's JavaScript ever uses the Spry field names.

Insert a Spry Validation Checkbox and Radio Group

You can use the Spry Validation Checkbox feature to insert (X)HTML check boxes with validation. If you are using a single check box, such as on a form where you enable the user to select whether or not he agrees to your terms of service by checking the box, you can use the Spry validation to require that he check the box. If you have multiple check boxes, you can control the minimum and maximum number of boxes that your user may select.

Spry provides a Radio Group validation widget as well. This inserts a group of radio buttons, but allows you to use Spry to set a value for the radio group if no selection is made or if an invalid selection is made.

The key difference between check boxes and radio buttons lies in the number of possible selections.

Insert a Spry Validation Checkbox and Radio Group

① Click Spry Validation Checkbox.

The Input Tag Accessibility Attributes dialog box appears.

② Type an ID.

③ Type a label.

④ Click OK.

The check box is inserted.

⑤ Add additional check boxes.

Note: See Chapter 17 for details on how to insert check boxes.

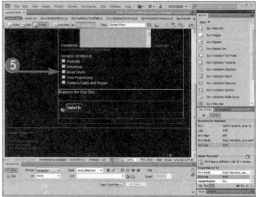

6 Click Spry Validation Radio Group.

The Spry Validation Radio Group dialog box appears.

7 Type a name for the group.

8 Type a label.

9 Press Tab and type a value.

10 Repeat steps **8** to **10** for additional radio buttons.

11 Click OK.

● The radio group is inserted.

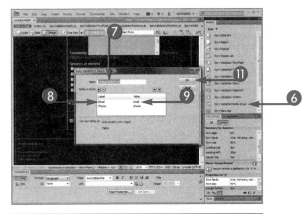

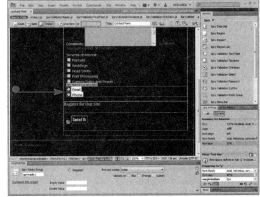

How do you specify when validation occurs?

▼ You can set the point at which validation occurs by selecting the Validation Checkbox widget in the Document window. The point of *validation* occurs when the user clicks outside the widget after making a selection, or when the user tries to submit the form. To perform this task, click Window and then Properties. Select the option that indicates when you want validation to occur. You can select all of the options (Blur, Change, and Submit), or Submit only.

How can I specify a minimum and maximum selection range?

▼ If you insert multiple check boxes on your page, you can specify a minimum and maximum selection range by following these steps. Select a Validation Checkbox widget in the Document window. Click Window and then Properties. In the Property inspector, select the Enforce Range option. Enter a minimum or maximum number (or both) of check boxes that you want the user to select.

Add a Validation Drop-down Menu

The Spry Validation Select feature allows you to insert a select or drop-down menu with associated validation. This menu is structured exactly as a normal select menu. You can choose whether to have it appear as a drop-down menu, thus allowing only a single selection, or as a list that allows multiple selections.

The validation controls allow you to set whether or not an option must be selected from the menu, as well as to set an invalid value. If you use the list as a drop-down menu, your user must have something

selected, and so the option to require a selection is moot. However, if you have as an initial value in the field with some generic phrase such as Select an option, and you want to be sure that the user changes the list to another option, you can use the invalid value setting.

If you allow multiple selections, then you may want to apply the setting to not allow a blank value. If the list still contains an initial, generic setting, then applying the invalid value setting as well ensures that the user chooses at least one option other than your default.

Add a Validation Drop-down Menu

1. Click Spry Validation Select.

   The Input Tag Accessibility Attributes dialog box appears.

2. Type an ID.

3. Type a label.

4. Click OK.

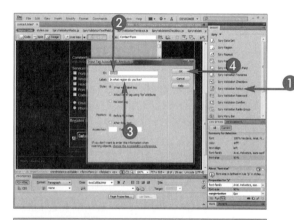

The field is inserted.

5. Click in the field.

6. Click List Values.

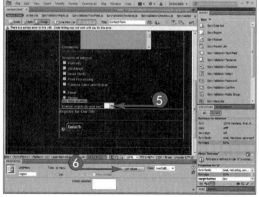

The List Values dialog box appears.

7 Click under the Item Label and type **Please select a region.**

8 Press Tab and type 0 to set the value.

9 Press Tab and type a label.

10 Press Tab and type a value.

11 Repeat steps **9** and **10** for additional options.

12 Click OK.

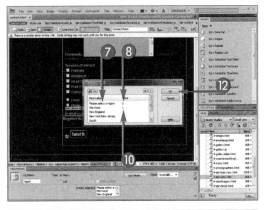

The field is updated.

13 Click the Spry Select tab.

14 Click Invalid value.

15 Type **0.**

The Spry options are configured.

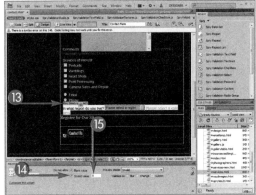

I used the Invalid value option and set the value, but when I test the page, I am able to submit the form without triggering the validation error. What did I do wrong?

▼ You need to be sure that the Initial value setting on the Property Inspector matches the value of the default item, not the label. In the example, you typed **Please select an option** as the label and **0** as the value, and so the setting in Spry is for an invalid value of 0, not Please select an option.

If I use a text string for my options, will the invalid value match be case-sensitive?

▼ No, the matching of a text string for the invalid value is not case-sensitive.

Include a Validation Password Field

Many sites allow users to create login credentials such as a username and password. Increasingly, sites are trying to improve their security by requiring that users select a strong password. The Spry Validation Password widget allows you to insert a password field on your page that can require that your user create a password that is more than a simple string of letters.

Hackers must correctly guess a user's password in order to log in as the user. The longer a password is, the harder it is to guess. Also, passwords that contain characters other than letters are more difficult to hack, as each additional possible character in the password greatly expands the number of possible combinations. For example, there are 26^5 possible combinations for a 5-letter password that contains only alphabetic characters, or 11,881,376 combinations. Expanding the password to 8 characters increases the possibilities to 26^8, or 208,827,064,576. If you add in uppercase letters, numbers, and other so-called special characters, such as the dollar sign or @ symbol, to an 8-character password, you have 2,478,758,911,082,496 possible combinations — almost 12,000 times more.

Include a Validation Password Field

1 Click Spry Validation Password.

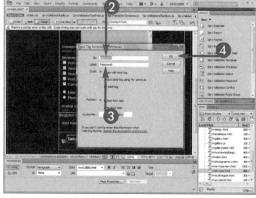

The Input Tag Accessibility Attributes dialog box appears.

2 Type an ID.

3 Type a label.

4 Click OK.

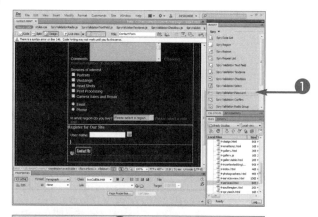

The field is inserted.

⑤ Use the Property Inspector to set the desired password parameters.

⑥ Click Preview states and select an option.

⑦ Click Required.

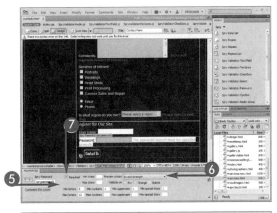

⑧ Type a new error message.

The parameters for the field are set.

Are strong passwords more difficult to remember?

▼ Depending on the password, they might be. The strongest password would be a completely random set of upper- and lowercase letters, numbers, and special characters, such as dh$F23G@&hY. Obviously, however, this would be close to impossible to remember. So a more common approach is to replace certain memorable letters with numbers or special characters, such as using the @ symbol in place of an *a* or a *zero* instead of an *O*. This way, the password can still somewhat resemble a word. For example, the word password could be written as P@ssw0Rd.

Can I limit the number of times a user enters an incorrect password?

▼ The Spry password widget is only able to verify the strength of the password, and is most often going to be used on forms where a user creates a password, not on a login form. The actual process of checking to make sure that the correct username and password are entered and thus logging the user in must be handled by a script on the server, and so it is beyond the scope of what Spry, or JavaScript in general, is designed to do.

Add a Validation Confirm Field

When allowing users to create an account in a system, you want to have a password field, probably using a Spry Validation Password field, for them to create their password. Then, you usually want to have the user type the password a second time. Because users cannot see the password as they enter it, they do not know whether they made a mistake. Having the user retype the password in another field helps them to feel confident that the password they created is what they thought it was.

The Spry Validation Confirm field allows you to provide this second field. It associates itself with another field in the form and checks its contents against that other field. By default, the confirm field looks for a password field and associates itself with it; if there are two or more password fields, it most likely picks the one closest in the code to the confirm field. If no password field exists, it associates itself with one of the text fields on the page. Either way, you have the ability to change this association.

Add a Validation Confirm Field

① Click Spry Validation Confirm.

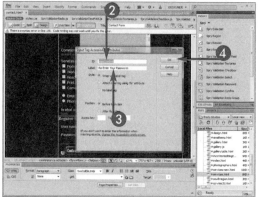

The Input Tag Accessibility Attributes dialog box appears.

② Type an ID.

③ Type a label.

④ Click OK.

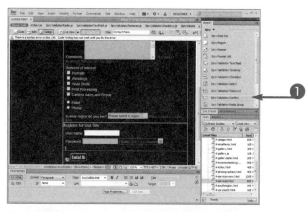

The field is inserted.

⑤ Click the Validate against drop-down menu.

⑥ Ensure that the password field is selected.

⑦ Click Preview states.

⑧ Select Invalid.

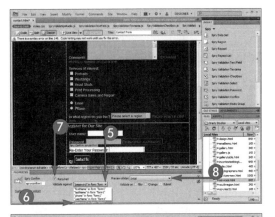

⑨ Type a new error message.

The field is inserted and configured.

What are all of these `<span>` tags that are being added to my page as I use Spry?

▼ Forms that use Spry rely on normal (X)HTML form fields. In order for the Spry code to associate with the form fields, each field is wrapped within a `<span>` tag that essentially defines the Spry region. Within that `<span>` is the form field's label and the actual field. Any error messages associated with the field are in individual `<span>` tags following the field, but still contained within the `<span>` tags for the Spry region. The Spry JavaScript changes the display property of the messages' `<span>` tags from none to inline when the error is triggered.

Why would I have a confirm field on the page that is not required? It seems that I would always want my user to fill in this field.

▼ Most of the time, a confirm field is required, which is why it is set to required by default. However, if the field against which the confirm field is being compared is not required, then it would not make sense that the confirm field itself would be required. For example, some sites might have a section on a form for a user to create a username and password, and thus include a confirm field, but they may make this entire registration section optional. In that case, neither the password field nor the confirm field would be required.

Introducing Databases

A database, in the simplest terms, is a structured collection of information or records. Computer databases can be used to store massive amounts of information in a format that makes it easy to sort and find specific data points.

Database History

Databases represented some of the earliest applications of computers. In the years immediately following World War II, several early computers were built in part to track the large numbers of veterans and active-duty military personnel created by the war.

The term *database* was coined in 1963 at a symposium on data storage techniques. It was originally spelled as two words, but was merged into a single word in Europe during the 1970s.

In 1970, E.F. Codd proposed a new model of data storage in databases. He believed that more efficient data storage would be possible if databases were created as a series of related tables. However, it would be almost a decade before commercially viable relational databases came onto the market with the introduction of Oracle and DB2. Today, almost every major database system on the market follows the relational database model.

Also in the 1970s, a group of developers at IBM developed the Structured Query Language (SQL). SQL allows developers to write code to execute commands against a database. SQL is discussed in more detail later in this chapter.

Database Management Systems

A computer program that stores data is technically called a Database Management System, or DBMS. There are many hundreds of DBMSs available today, and Web developers mostly rely on one of four systems for their work.

Microsoft SQL Server

Microsoft SQL Server is the primary DBMS from Microsoft. It is an enterprise-grade server system, meaning that it is designed to be used in very large organizations and to store potentially huge amounts of data. It is extremely robust and scalable, but at the same time, it is fairly difficult to learn to use. Managing an SQL Server system can be a full-time job, and specialized experts are often hired for that purpose.

SQL Server DE

The full version of SQL Server requires a high-end computer running one of Microsoft's server operating systems, and costs several thousand dollars. However, Microsoft does offer a smaller version, called SQL Server DE, available for developers. This version cannot handle the amounts of data or concurrent users that the full version does, but the basic structure is the same so that you can use it to develop your database systems and Web pages based on those systems, and be confident that they will still work when transferred to the full version of SQL Server later.

MySQL

MySQL is an open-source database system developed by MySQL AB, a division of Sun Microsystems. MySQL is designed to be a competitor to Microsoft SQL Server, and thus has many of the same features. Unlike SQL Server, however, MySQL runs on almost any operating system, including Mac OS, most flavors of Unix, and any version of Windows. A free developer edition of MySQL is available.

Oracle

Oracle databases are considered the top end on the database spectrum. They tend to be extremely robust and scalable, offering developers almost unlimited data storage and manipulation possibilities. However, they also tend to be extremely complex, and can be very difficult to configure. Like their competitors in MySQL and Microsoft, Oracle offers a free developer edition of its databases with data storage and access limitations.

Microsoft Access

Microsoft Access is the company's end-user relational database system. In comparison to systems like SQL Server, MySQL, or Oracle, Access is very easy to use. However, it was designed to be used by individuals on their desktop, and to store limited amounts of data. Many Web developers use Access to do their initial design and testing for their applications' databases, but it is not stable or robust enough to serve as the back-end database for Web sites that receive a lot of traffic; as a result, it is recommended that sites initially developed with Access switch to one of the other systems when they are deployed to the production Web server.

Databases and the Web

Web sites can interact with databases through a variety of technologies depending on the server-scripting language being used.

Open Database Connectivity

Open Database Connectivity (ODBC) was developed by Microsoft in the early 1990s to provide a method by which applications could communicate with database systems. Today, ODBC is an open standard and is available to almost any database system.

ODBC relies on a special driver to provide communication between the database and other systems. This allows for a level of abstraction between the application and the database. The application can simply contain SQL queries that it passes to the driver, which translates the query into code that can be read

by the database. The database in turn sends the data retrieved by the query back to the driver, which then translates it and returns it to the application.

Web applications that use ODBC are generally unaware of the specific database application being used, which is referred to as being *database agnostic*. This allows developers to create an application with one database system and then later switch to a different system, often without having to change any code at all. Web applications written in PHP, ASP, and ASP.NET can use ODBC to connect to a variety of databases.

Java Database Connectivity

Java Database Connectivity (JDBC) is an implementation of ODBC written in Java. It functions in essentially the same way as ODBC, but provides some Java-specific functionality. Like ODBC, JDBC allows for a level of abstraction between the application and the database. ColdFusion uses JDBC to connect to databases.

Microsoft Data Access Components

Microsoft Data Access Components (MDAC) provides a framework that allows applications a variety of methods to connect to databases. ODBC is one component, but it also includes the ActiveX Data Objects (ADO) and Object Linking and Embedding Database (OLE DB), each of which can connect to databases directly. ASP and ASP.NET applications can use either ODBC directly or the MDAC to connect to databases.

PHP MySQL

While PHP can use ODBC to connect to Microsoft SQL Server, Microsoft Access, or Oracle, it includes the ability to directly connect to a MySQL database. While this has the advantage of removing much of the abstraction and additional overhead required when using ODBC, JDBC, or MDAC, it also means that PHP applications must be written with a specific database in mind.

Download MySQL

In order to begin developing data-driven Web applications, you need a database. You may already have Microsoft Access installed on your computer. Access works for initial development and testing, but should not be used for your final, live Web site.

You can download and install MySQL for free from http://dev.mysql.com/downloads/mysql/5.0.html#downloads. The Community Edition of the database is fully functional. You can download the server for almost any major operating system.

As of this writing, MySQL is in version 5. You want to be sure that you download the latest stable release. New minor releases of the database are issued on a fairly regular basis. Windows users can download either an essentials version, which contains all of the components of the database server in an installer, or a ZIP archive that you unzip and install yourself.

You should save the downloaded file to your hard drive before you install it, rather than running the installer directly from the browser. This saves you from having to download it again if a problem occurs during installation.

Download MySQL

① Browse to http://dev.mysql.com/downloads/mysql/5.0.html#downloads.

The MySQL Downloads page appears.

② Click to select your operating system.

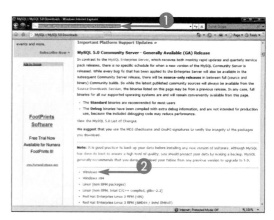

The page displays the options for the operating system.

③ Click Pick a mirror.

A page displays a listing of download mirror sites.

④ Click HTTP.

The File Download dialog box appears.

⑤ Click Save.

The file location screen appears.

⑥ Click Save.

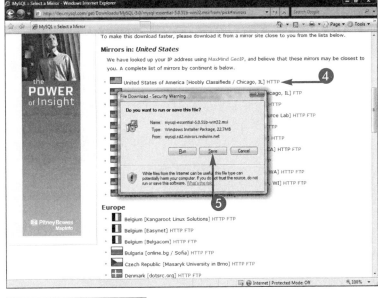

The software downloads.

A confirmation dialog box appears when the download is complete.

What is the difference between the Community Edition and the Enterprise Edition?

▼ As with other open-source projects, MySQL is available for free. However, you can purchase a license for the Enterprise Edition if you want. The Enterprise Edition is the exact same core software application as the free Community Edition. What you pay for is not the actual software, but rather support from the company. You also receive regularly scheduled updates when you pay for the Enterprise Edition (the Community Edition is updated on an unpredictable schedule), as well as better tools to administer and monitor the server.

If I use the Community Edition, where can I get support if I need it?

▼ MySQL is one of the most widely used database systems in the world, so while you do not receive official support from MySQL AB when you use the free version, you will find no shortage of resources available to you on the Web. Usually, a Google search for the problem you are having turns up plenty of results. You can also search message boards and discussion lists on MySQL to find additional help.

Install MySQL

O nce downloaded, you can install MySQL by simply double-clicking the installer file. Like other programs, MySQL uses a wizard to step you through the installation process.

Most of the default settings presented in the wizard suffice for beginning users, and even for more advanced users who simply need the database for development purposes. After the installation completes, the wizard steps you through the process of initially configuring your database. Because MySQL

is based on a Unix model, the account that is given unfettered access to the database is called root, instead of administrator. You need to set a password for the root account. For local development computers, this password can be anything; for servers deployed in production environments, you need to be sure that this is a very strong password to reduce the chance of your database becoming compromised. You can also decide whether to have MySQL run as a Windows service, meaning that it is always available, or if you want to start and stop it manually.

Install MySQL

① Double-click the file you downloaded from the MySQL Web site.

The Open File – Security Warning dialog box appears.

② Click Run.

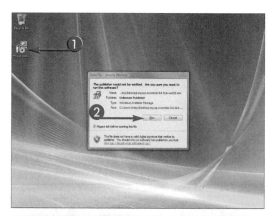

The Setup Wizard welcome screen appears.

③ Click Next.

The Setup Type screen appears.

④ Click Typical.

⑤ Click Next.

A settings summary appears.

⑥ Click Install.

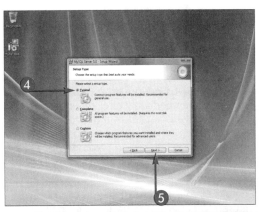

The database installs, and a message appears that the setup is complete.

⑦ Click the Configure Server now check box.

⑧ Click Finish.

The Configuration Wizard starts.

Note: The Configuration Wizard is discussed in the next section.

Can I install MySQL on a Mac?

▼ Yes, MySQL can run on a Mac. You can download the installer for the Mac from the same Web site from which you can download the Windows version. Once downloaded, you can double-click the file to launch the installer. As with the Windows version, the Mac installer runs through a wizard that takes you step-by-step through the installation process. Once complete, you can start the server by opening a terminal window and changing to the MySQL bin directory by typing **cd /usr/local/mysql/bin**. Then, you type **mysql_safe &**. A message appears, indicating that the server has started.

Can I download the MySQL manual, or must I only use it online?

▼ You can download a copy of the complete MySQL manual from dev.mysql.com/doc. The download consists of a ZIP archive file that contains a complete copy of the manual in both HTML and PDF formats.

You can also download a CHM file, which is a Windows Help file. This opens in a normal Help window that you may be familiar with from other applications.

Configure MySQL

The MySQL Configuration Wizard — which begins immediately after the installation if you check the box to start it in the final installation screen — steps you through the process of setting up your MySQL server. If you do not tell it to start automatically, you can access it from your Windows Start menu.

The details of your server installation can be configured to better suit your needs in the wizard. You can choose to use a set of default parameters, or completely customize the installation. The default parameters are generally best for most beginners. You use the wizard to set up the password for the root account and to choose whether to have MySQL running all of the time as a service or to have it only run when you specifically start it. You can also choose to enable an anonymous account that will allow anyone to access the database without providing a username and password. You should never enable this account except on computers where you can control who gains access, as it presents a major security risk.

Configure MySQL

Note: If the Configuration Wizard is already open because you are continuing from the previous section, go to step 6.

① Click Start.

② Click All Programs.

③ Click MySQL.

④ Click the folder that contains your version of MySQL.

⑤ Click MySQL Server Instance Config Wizard.

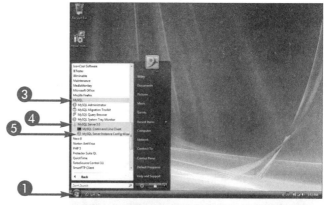

The Configuration Wizard opens.

⑥ Click Next.

The Windows Options screen appears.

⑦ Click the Install as Windows Service check box.

⑧ Click Next.

The Security Settings dialog box appears.

9 Type a new password for root in both the New Root Password and Confirm fields.

Note: *Because you are configuring the server for the first time, you leave Current password blank.*

10 Click Next.

A Ready to Execute screen appears.

11 Click Execute.

The server is configured.

A confirmation dialog box appears when the configuration is complete.

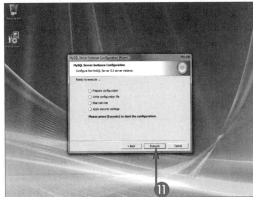

Do I need accounts other than the root?

▼ If you work on a development computer on which you are the only user, then you can use the root for accessing the MySQL server. However, if your computer is in a production environment — that is, it can be accessed from the Internet at large — then you need to create an account specifically for your PHP applications. When you create this account, you need to be sure that you can keep it from being compromised.

Download the MySQL GUI Tools

By itself, MySQL does not provide a graphic user interface (GUI) with which to interact with the database. Instead, you must use a DOS-based command line.

Because most computer users today are unfamiliar with DOS and uncomfortable using a command-line interface, many graphical interfaces have been developed for the database. MySQL AB, the company that produces the server, has created a suite of tools for it. These include MySQL Administrator, MySQL Query Browser, and several others.

You can configure your database server, manage user accounts, create databases, and add tables to

databases in MySQL Administrator. You can use MySQL Query Browser to interact with the database. They can be used to administer both the local database server on your development computer as well as a remote database on your Web server or Web hosting account.

Both tools are available at dev.mysql.com/downloads/gui-tools/5.0.html. They are packaged together as a bundle, and are available for Windows, Mac, and Linux. Like the database server, the tools are available at no charge.

Download the MySQL GUI Tools

① Browse to http://dev.mysql.com/downloads/gui-tools/5.0.html.

The Web page loads.

② Click No thanks, just take me to the downloads!

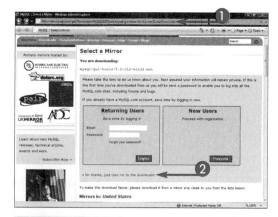

③ Click HTTP.

The download dialog box appears.

④ Click Save.

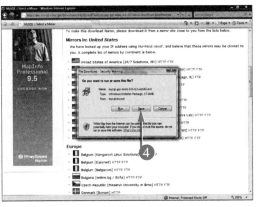

The file downloads.

A message appears when the download is complete.

What is the MySQL Migration Toolkit?

▼ The third tool included with Windows versions of the MySQL GUI Tools is the MySQL Migration Toolkit. This is a wizard-based application that simplifies the process of converting databases that were created in other formats to MySQL. The toolkit can convert databases from Microsoft Access, Microsoft SQL Server, MaxDB, Oracle, or Sybase to a MySQL database. As of this writing, it is only available for Windows, although the Web site says that a version for other operating systems will be available in the future.

Is there any difference between using the HTTP or FTP mirrors?

▼ HTTP is the Hypertext Transfer Protocol, which is how Web pages are transmitted from servers to browsers. FTP is the File Transfer Protocol. FTP is an older technology, predating the Web, and it has been used for decades to transfer large files between computers. Most likely, you will use FTP to upload your site to your Web server.

When downloading from a MySQL mirror, there is generally no difference between the two. Often, the HTTP mirrors are faster, but as the GUI toolkit is a fairly small download, you will not likely notice the difference.

Install the MySQL GUI Tools

Once downloaded, you can install the MySQL GUI Tools onto your computer. You can do this by simply double-clicking the file you downloaded from the Web site and following the installation wizard's instructions.

By default, the tools are installed in Windows in the Start menu in the same folder as the MySQL database server, which will most likely be simply called MySQL. You do not need to restart your computer after installing the tools.

After installing the tools, you may want to keep a copy of the installer program on your computer. If you run it on a computer that already has the tools installed, it allows you to modify the installation or repair it if the tools have stopped working for some reason. If you do not keep the installer program, and a problem develops after a newer version of the tools is released, you may have to uninstall your version and reinstall the new version. While upgrading to a newer version may have its benefits, it is more time-consuming than repairing an existing install.

Install the MySQL GUI Tools

① Double-click the file you installed in the last section.

The Open File – Security Warning dialog box appears.

② Click Run.

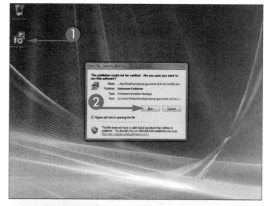

The first screen of the setup wizard appears.

③ Click Next.

The License Agreement screen appears.

④ Click the I accept the terms in the license agreement option.

⑤ Click Next.

The Destination Folder screen appears.

6 Click Next.

7 In the Setup Type screen, click Next.

The Ready to Install screen appears.

8 Click Install.

The tools install.

When complete, a confirmation message appears.

Is there any official support offered for the GUI Tools?

▼ No, MySQL AB does not offer any official support for the GUI Tools. Customers who have purchased a license for the Enterprise Edition can receive support on the tools, but those using the free Community Edition do not receive any support.

That said, the tools are very widely used, and so you should have no trouble finding support for them online. You can use a search engine like Google to search on specific keywords to solve problems, or you can join an online discussion group about MySQL, which is likely to include other users of the tools.

If I work at a company that does not allow me to download and install software, are there other alternatives to managing my databases?

▼ Yes. Another very popular solution to administering a MySQL database is phpMyAdmin. This is a Web-based application, written in PHP, that provides essentially the same features as MySQL Administrator and MySQL Query Browser. It can be downloaded from www.phpmyadmin.net. You need to install it on a Web server that is running PHP (your company's IT staff may be able to assist you with this). Because it is designed to be a Web-based tool, phpMyAdmin is specifically tailored to remote administration of a MySQL database.

Create a Database

I n order to start using MySQL, you first need to create a database, and then create tables within it. The program you have downloaded and installed is not a database, but rather a database server. The database server is the application that manages your databases, which are the actual data stores in which your data resides. Your MySQL database server can contain any number of databases.

You can add databases through MySQL Administrator in the Catalogs section. You must add a new schema for each database you want to add. A schema is the

definition of the data structure, but MySQL uses the term to refer to the databases created within it.

Your schema should be given a clear, descriptive name without spaces. If you are developing your site on a different computer than your Web server, you should check the names already in use on the server. Schema names must be unique on a server, and you do not want to have to recode your Web pages to change the name later, so be sure that the name you use from the beginning works.

Create a Database

① Click Start.

② Click All Programs.

③ Click MySQL.

④ Click MySQL Administrator.

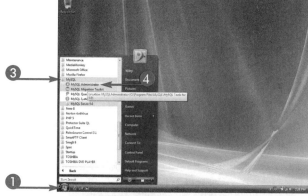

The MySQL Administrator Logon screen appears.

⑤ Type **localhost.**

⑥ Type **root.**

⑦ Type your password.

⑧ Click OK.

MySQL Administrator opens.

9 Click Catalogs.

10 Right-click in the schemata area.

11 Click Create New Schema.

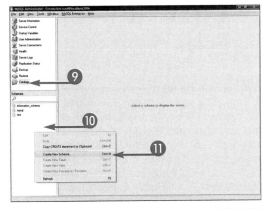

The Create New Schema window appears.

12 Type a name for the schema.

13 Click OK.

The schema is created.

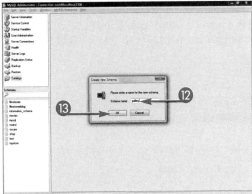

Do I need to set up any user accounts?

▼ For local development purposes, you can use the default root account for MySQL as long as only you have access to your computer. However, you should not have your actual Web site connect to your database using the root account. Instead, you should create another user account specifically for your Web application. This account should only have the absolute minimum security privileges needed to perform the actions required by the Web site. You can create the user account through MySQL Administrator.

How do I use MySQL Administrator to work with a remote database?

▼ You can log onto a remote MySQL server by opening MySQL Administrator and then providing the required login information for your remote host. You need to know the address of the MySQL server, the port number, and your username and password. If you are using a Web-hosting company, it should be able to provide you with the server address; you can assume that the port is 3306 unless it tells you otherwise.

Create a
Table

Y ou can create tables in your database in MySQL Administrator. Tables make up the core of your database; they are where your data is actually stored. Relational databases are made up of a series of tables. Each table should be single-purpose, storing data only on a single topic. For example, you would not store information about your customers in the same table as information about your products. Instead, you would need a customers table and a separate products table.

Tables are made up of rows of fields. Each field represents a distinct piece of your data, and so your

customer table will likely have a field for the customer's first name, another for his last name, another for his address, and so forth. Each field needs to store a specific kind of data, called its *data type*. MySQL supports many different data types. The most common are the variable-length character field, the fixed-length character field, integers, floating-point or decimal numbers, dates and times, and Boolean or true-false. When you create your table, you specify the data type for each field, and from then on, that field can only contain information that matches that type.

Create a Table

① Click your schema.

② Click Create Table.

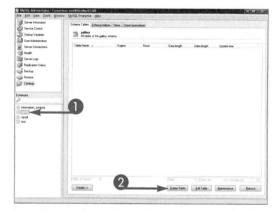

MySQL Table Editor opens.

③ Type a name for the table.

Note: The table name cannot contain spaces.

④ Double-click in the first row under Column Name.

⑤ Type a name for the first column.

Note: The column or field name cannot contain spaces.

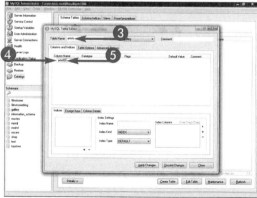

6 Double-click the second column name field.

7 Type a name for the column.

8 Press Tab.

9 Type an appropriate data type.

10 Repeat steps **6** to **9** for each additional field.

11 Click Apply Changes.

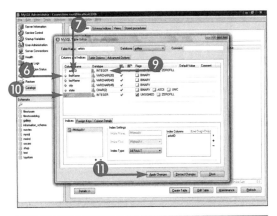

The Confirm Table Edit dialog box appears.

12 Click Execute.

The table is created.

What is a primary key?

▼ A primary key is a special field in your database that is used to uniquely identify each record. For example, while it is possible to have many customers named Malcolm Reynolds in your table, you will only have one customer number 10. Primary keys must contain data for each record — they can never be left blank — and that data must be unique for each record. You can create the primary key data yourself, or you can have the database do it for you through its auto-increment feature, which sets the first record to 1, the second to 2, and so forth.

What is a foreign key, and when will I use it?

▼ Relational databases relate the data in each table to other tables through primary key and foreign key relationships. Say customer Inara Serra, whose customer ID — the primary key — is 42, purchases a product that has a product ID of 50. You would likely have a table that stores order information. That table would have its own primary key, but would also contain fields to store the primary keys from the customer and product tables. So order number 745 would record that customer 42 purchased product 50. The customer ID field and product ID field in the orders table are the foreign keys.

Understanding the Structured Query Language

I n the 1970s, Donald Chamberlin and Raymond Boyce at IBM, working off of E.F. Codd's relational model, created the Structured English Query Language. They designed it to allow developers to work with relational databases through a powerful language that nonetheless relied on a fairly clear syntax. The language was originally referred to as SEQEL, but due to a trademark dispute, was later shortened to SQL. In addition, English has been dropped from its name.

Standardization

In 1986, the American National Standards Institute (ANSI) released an open, standardized version of SQL. Later versions of the language have been released by the International Organization for Standardization (ISO). Any relational database also supports some form of SQL; however, many database systems rely on nonstandard versions of the language, and so you need to be aware that SQL statements may require slight modifications when moving from one database system to another.

Pronunciation

According to ANSI, the language should officially be read as an acronym and pronounced *es cue el*. However, many database professionals read it more as a word, pronouncing it *see-quel*.

Syntax

SQL is designed to be fairly easy to learn and use. It is comprised of a series of command words or phrases, all in simple English. For example, if you want to add data to a table, you use the INSERT INTO command.

Whitespace

Officially, SQL is whitespace insensitive, and so you can add whitespace to your SQL statements to ensure readability without impacting their execution. However, some implementations of SQL may not adhere to the whitespace insensitivity, and so you need to familiarize yourself with the application or programming language in which you are using SQL.

Case

SQL is also officially case-insensitive, but as with whitespace, there may be implementations of the language that do not adhere to this. Traditionally, SQL command words are written in all uppercase letters, while database object references, such as table and field names, are written in the same case as they are defined in the actual database.

Language Subsets

SQL is divided into three sublanguages: the Data Definition Language (DDL), the Data Manipulation Language (DML), and the Data Control Language (DCL).

Data Definition Language

The DDL is the subset of SQL that allows you to create, alter, and delete the actual tables. It is made up of four basic commands. CREATE TABLE allows you to create a table in the database. A CREATE TABLE statement gives the table name and then a list of its fields, their data types, and any other settings for the field, such as whether it can be left blank. You also define the primary key in the CREATE TABLE statement.

```
CREATE TABLE customers (customerid
INT AUTO-INCREMENT, firstname
VARCHAR(30) NOT NULL, lastname
VARCHAR(40) NOT NULL, address
VARCHAR(40), city VARCHAR(30), state
CHAR(2), zip CHAR(5), dateregistered
DATETIME, PRIMARY KEY (customerid))
```

DROP deletes a table from the database. You need to be aware that no database operations can be undone, so use this with caution. TRUNCATE deletes the data from a table while leaving the actual table in place. ALTER allows you to modify the table's settings, such as if you need to add an additional field.

If you use MySQL Administrator, you probably do not need to use any of the statements in the DDL, as all of its operations can be handled in the GUI. However, you should still be aware of its commands.

Data Manipulation Language

By far the most commonly used subset of SQL is the DML. These commands allow you to interact with your data.

The SELECT statement allows you to retrieve data from a table. SELECT statements contain a list of the fields being retrieved, and are followed by a FROM statement that lists the table or tables that contain the data. You can optionally add a WHERE clause to filter the records, and an ORDER BY clause to sort them. For example, to retrieve the first and last names of your customers who live in California, sorted by last name, you might write the following:

```
SELECT firstname, lastname FROM
customers WHERE state = 'CA' ORDER
BY lastname
```

The DML also contains an INSERT INTO command to add new data to the table, an UPDATE command to alter the existing data in the table, and a DELETE command to remove data.

Most databases support the use of functions within queries as well. Functions within SELECT statements can be used to manipulate the appearance of the data as it is returned. For example, MySQL supports a CONCAT function that combines several fields into one, as follows:

```
SELECT CONCAT(firstname, ' ',
lastname) FROM customers
```

You can also perform mathematical calculations on the data through functions such as SUM or AVE, or return the number of records in a table with COUNT.

```
SELECT COUNT(*) FROM customers
```

In the example above, the asterisk is used as a wildcard; it is telling the database to count any field.

In the MySQL GUI tools, you can write DML statements and view their results in MySQL Query Browser. You can also use Dreamweaver to create DML statements in your Web pages and use those pages to view the results. This technique is covered in the following sections.

Data Control Language

The DCL is the subset of SQL that allows you to create and manage user accounts. It contains a GRANT statement to authorize users to access the data, and a REVOKE statement to remove that authorization. As with the DDL, you are unlikely to use the DCL directly, as its commands can be executed through the MySQL Administrator interface in the User Administration section.

```
GRANT SELECT ON customers TO
web_user
```

Add Data to a Table

Before you can start building Web pages that retrieve data, you need to add some data to your table. While it is possible to create a set of Web pages to allow you to add data (which is covered in Chapter 21), you generally want to begin with some data in your table before you get to building Web pages.

Data can be added to tables in MySQL by using MySQL Query Browser to execute INSERT INTO statements. Query Browser can be accessed through MySQL Administrator by clicking Tools, and then

clicking MySQL Query Browser, or directly through the Windows Start menu. Before you can start executing queries, you need to tell the server which database you will use. You can do this by typing a USE statement, which is simply USE *databasename*.

The SQL INSERT INTO statement takes a table name, followed by a list of fields in parentheses. That is in turn followed by a VALUES command, which then takes a list of the data you will be inserting. The data list needs to match the field list.

Add Data to a Table

① Click Tools.

② Click MySQL Query Browser.

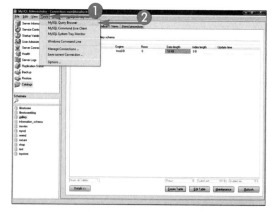

MySQL Query Browser opens.

③ Type **USE gallery;**.

④ Click Execute.

The database is selected.

5 Type **INSERT INTO artists (firstName, lastName, city, state, artID) VALUES ('River', 'Tam', 'Miranda', 'CA', 1).**

6 Click Execute.

The data is inserted.

7 Repeat steps **5** and **6** to add additional records.

Do I always need to use quotation marks around my data?

▼ That depends on the data type of the field. Fields that store text information, or those that have data types such as CHAR and VARCHAR, require that their data be enclosed in single quotation marks. Fields with numeric data types, such as INT or FLOAT, require that their data not be within quotes.

Note that there are times when certain kinds of numbers are actually stored as text, such as Social Security numbers or ZIP codes. These are stored as text because you do not use them in mathematical calculations. As such, those values would need to be quoted as well.

If the primary key field is always required, why is a value for it not included in the example?

▼ The table in the example is using MySQL's auto increment feature for the customerid field, which is the table's primary key. The auto increment automatically adds the next highest integer to the field when a new record is added, and so you do not need to provide that. In fact, if you attempt to provide data for it, the database throws an error.

Create a ColdFusion Data Source for MySQL

ColdFusion uses Java Database Connectivity (JDBC) to connect to databases. This allows you to create your pages without referencing a specific database in a specific location. That way, you can develop your pages against a local database, and then upload the pages to a Web server. As long as the server has a database with the same table structure, and as long as a JDBC data source with the same name exists on both your local computer and the server, you do not need to change anything on the individual pages.

You can create a data source for ColdFusion using ColdFusion Administrator. This is an application that is installed when you install the ColdFusion server. When you log into the Administrator, you can go to the Data Sources page.

Each data source needs to have a name that is unique on that server. Each ColdFusion document you create that interacts with the database has a reference to this data source name, so to avoid having to change your pages later, you should check with your Web host or server administrator to be sure that the name you choose will continue to work when you upload your files.

Create a ColdFusion Data Source for MySQL

① Browse to http://localhost/cfide/administrator.

ColdFusion Administrator opens.

② Type your password.

③ Click Login.

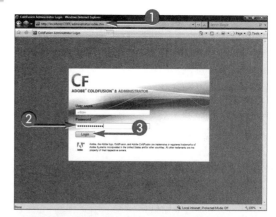

You are logged in.

④ Click Data Sources.

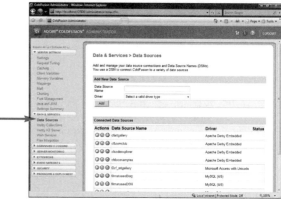

The Data Sources page loads.

⑤ Type a data source name.

⑥ Select MySQL (4/5).

⑦ Click Add.

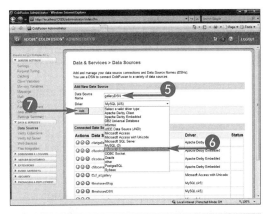

The MySQL page loads.

⑧ Type a database name.

⑨ Type **localhost.**

⑩ Type **root.**

⑪ Type your password.

⑫ Click Submit.

The data source is created.

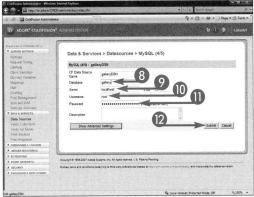

PART IV

What options are available under the Advanced Settings?

▼ When you set up the data source, you can click Show Advanced Settings for additional options. Most of the settings are advanced network settings that you only need if you are specifically directed by a network administrator. More important are the settings in the lower section, under Allowed SQL. You can use these settings to restrict the SQL statements that this data source is allowed to execute. A common security threat to Web pages is through something called an *SQL injection attack*, where a malicious user attempts to send his own SQL statements — often DELETE statements — through your forms. By restricting a connection to, for example, only SELECT statements, you can prevent this sort of attack.

View Database Information in Dreamweaver

You can view pertinent information about your database in Dreamweaver, saving you from having to continue to return to MySQL Administrator or Query Browser to figure out the names of tables or fields. This information appears in Dreamweaver in its Databases panel.

In order to display database information, Dreamweaver needs to connect to ColdFusion Administrator. To do so, Dreamweaver relies on Remote Development Services (RDS). RDS is a technology built into ColdFusion that allows other applications such as Dreamweaver access to

information such as the configured data sources. You need to know the RDS password, which is initially configured during the ColdFusion installation but can be changed in ColdFusion Administrator.

Once Dreamweaver connects through RDS, the Databases panel updates to display the data sources. You can click the plus sign next to each data source to expand it to view its tables, and then expand each table to view its fields and their data types. You can also view the data in the table. You cannot, however, make any changes to either the data or the database structure; the Databases panel provides a read-only interface.

View Database Information in Dreamweaver

① Click Window.

② Click Databases.

The Databases panel opens.

③ Click RDS login.

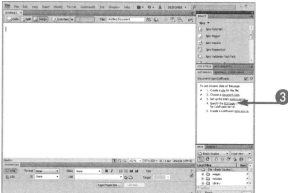

The RDS Login dialog box appears.

4 Type your RDS username.

*Note: If you have not created a specific RDS
      account, the username is admin.*

5 Type your password.

6 Click OK.

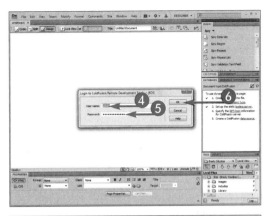

The Databases panel updates to
display the data sources.

7 Click the plus sign next to the data
source.

8 Click the plus sign next to Tables.

9 Click the plus sign next to a table.

The field information displays.

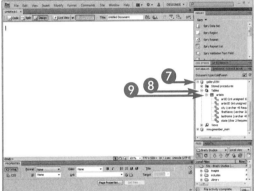

How can I view the data in a table?

▼ You can right-click the table name in the
Databases panel and select View Data. A
dialog box appears, displaying the first 25
records in the table. Buttons at the bottom
of the dialog box allow you to move
forward to see the next 25 records, or
backward to see the previous 25.

What do the symbols next to each field represent?

▼ You can determine the field's data type by
both the identifier next to the field name
and the icon to the left of the field. A field
with a text data type, such as CHAR or
VARCHAR, displays a small page icon. A
datetime field displays with a clock, while
numeric data types display with a Roman
numeral.

Create a Recordset with the Bindings Panel

I n order to display data on a Web page, you need to create a query to retrieve the information. This query is part of the ColdFusion page you are creating. Dreamweaver refers to a query as a recordset. Queries can be built in Design view without having to work with code through the Recordset builder.

You can create simple, one-table queries using the Simple mode of the Recordset builder. You can give the recordset a name, select the data source you want to use, select the table from which you want to retrieve the data, select the fields you want, and provide a single filter to limit the returned data and a single sort field. Dreamweaver adds the necessary ColdFusion code to your page so that you can use the data.

The Recordset builder also has an Advanced mode that can be used to build more complex queries that retrieve data from multiple tables, use multiple filters, or require multiple sort fields. Unfortunately, using the Advanced mode does require a certain amount of familiarity with SQL, whereas using Simple mode completely hides the SQL from you.

1 Click Bindings.

2 Click the plus sign.

3 Click Recordset (Query).

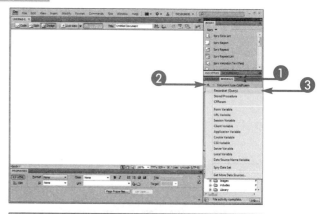

The Recordset dialog box appears.

4 Type a name for the recordset.

5 Select the data source.

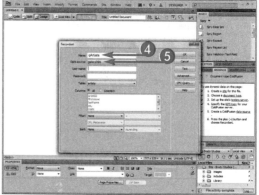

6 Select a table.

7 Click Selected.

8 Click a field.

To select multiple fields, you can press and hold the Control key while you click additional fields.

9 Click OK.

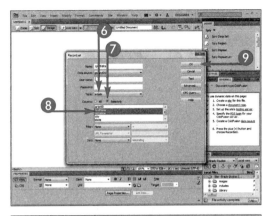

● The recordset is created.

The Bindings panel updates to display the fields returned by the query.

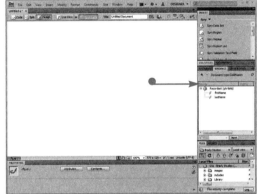

What code is written to my page by the recordset?

▼ ColdFusion uses a `<cfquery>` tag to create queries. The code from the example would look like this:

```
<cfquery name=
"qGallery"
datasource=
"galleryDB">

SELECT photoID,
photoName,
dateTaken,
description FROM
gallery

</cfquery>
```

Does it matter where my cursor is on the page when I create the recordset?

▼ No. Dreamweaver always adds the `<cfquery>` to the top of the page, before any (X)HTML code, when you use the Recordset builder. This way, the query's results are always available to all of the other code on the page.

Why do I need to name my recordset?

▼ ColdFusion uses the recordset's name to reference the data returned by it on the rest of the page. Therefore, you should make sure that your recordset's name logically describes the query. It is common, although not required, for ColdFusion recordsets to begin with the letter *q*.

Display Data on a Page

Y ou can display the data retrieved by a recordset on a Web page. If you want to use a table to display the records, you can use Dreamweaver's Dynamic Table feature. This frees you from having to build the table yourself. The Dynamic Table feature prompts you for the name of a recordset on the page, and then constructs an (X)HTML table from the data. The first row of the table displays the field names from the database. A second row is inserted with a cell for each field, and the necessary

ColdFusion code is added to loop over the data so that this second row is repeated, once for each record returned.

Once inserted, the dynamic table can be edited just like a normal (X)HTML table. You most likely want to designate the first row as being a table header, and you may need to edit the field names to add spaces for multiple words or to change capitalization. As this is a normal table, you can use CSS to format the table or any of the information in it.

Display Data on a Page

1 Click Common.

2 Click Data.

3 Click Dynamic Data.

4 Click Dynamic Table.

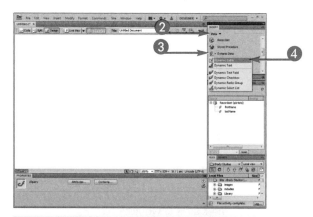

The Dynamic Table dialog box appears.

5 Select a recordset.

6 Click All records.

7 Click OK.

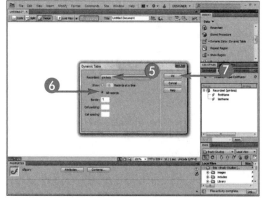

The dynamic table is inserted.

8 Fix the spacing and capitalization in the header row.

9 Click and drag to select all of the cells in the header row.

10 Click Header.

11 Click Live View.

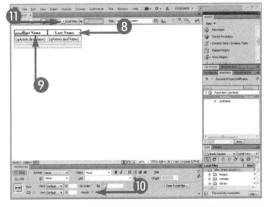

Live view displays, showing the data from the database table.

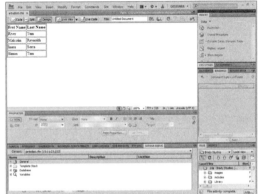

Can I combine several fields, such as a first name and last name, together into a single table cell?

▼ You cannot do this using the Dynamic Table feature, as it does not provide any ability to customize the results from the query. You must display all of the fields from the recordset, and each field must be in its own cell.

If you did want to display the first name and last name in a single cell, you could use the MySQL CONCAT function in your query so that they were being returned as a single entity; however, this would require that you write the SQL yourself. You could also construct your own table to display the data, which is covered in the next section.

How can I add a caption and summary to my table?

▼ Unfortunately, the Dynamic Table dialog box does not provide the accessibility options that are available when you insert a table normally. There is no way to insert a caption in Design view, and so you must switch to Code view and manually enter the <caption> tag. Remember that it must come immediately after the opening <table> tag, before any other code.

You can add a summary in Design view using the Tag Inspector panel, or simply enter it in Code view when you create the caption. The summary is an attribute to the <table> tag.

PART IV

Insert a Repeat Region

Because databases display records in tables, there is a certain logic behind using (X)HTML tables to display the data. However, you are not required to use a table — any (X)HTML can be used to structure the data on the page. You might also decide that while you want to use a table, you do not like the restrictions of the Dynamic Table feature and you want to construct the table elements yourself.

You can add the data from the recordset to any place on the page by simply dragging the field name from the Bindings panel to the page. The resulting dynamic text is displayed with a light-blue background, and the name of the field is surrounded by curly braces.

You can add the code needed to loop over multiple rows of data by using the Server Behaviors panel and the Repeat Region behavior. Server behaviors are similar to Behaviors, but while Behaviors are always JavaScript, Server Behaviors are written in whichever server-side language you have defined for the site. The Repeat Region server behavior loops over records from a recordset.

① Click Data.

② Click Common.

③ Click Table.

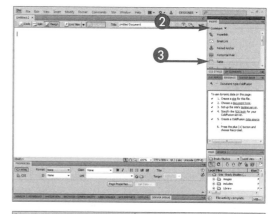

The Table dialog box appears.

④ Set rows to 2, and columns to the number of fields you plan to display.

⑤ Click Top.

⑥ Type a caption and a summary.

⑦ Click OK.

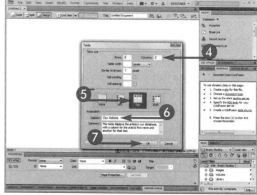

The table is inserted.

8 Create a recordset.

Note: See the section, "Create a Recordset with the Bindings Panel," for details on how to create a recordset.

9 Type appropriate headers.

10 Drag the first field to the first cell.

11 Repeat step **10** for each additional field.

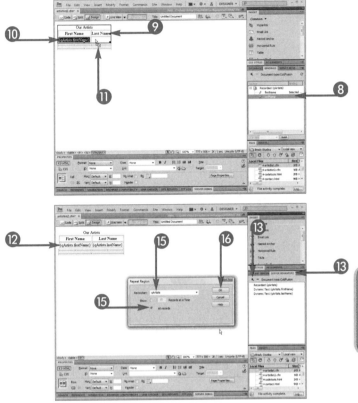

12 Select the row with the data.

13 Click Server Behaviors, and then click the plus sign.

14 Click Repeat Region.

The Repeat Region dialog box appears.

15 Select the recordset, and then click All Records.

16 Click OK.

The repeat region is added to the page.

Why would I only want to display some of the records from my query?

▼ If your query returns many records, you would most likely not want to display them all on a single page. Instead, you might only display the first ten records, and then provide navigation to the next ten. The Dynamic Table and Repeat Region dialog boxes allow you to restrict the display to only the first set of records. This is a technique called Recordset Paging, which is covered in Chapter 20.

If I want the page to display a single, specific record, can I use a Server Behavior to control which record I see?

▼ No, this is better done in the actual query. You can use the Filter feature on the query to restrict the data returned to only that which meets a criterion you specify; if you want to be guaranteed that you return exactly one record, you can filter on the table's primary key field. Then, you could construct the page as shown here, but you would not need to add a Repeat Region Server Behavior.

PART IV

Display the Number of Records in a Recordset on a Page

You can let your users know how many records are being displayed on a page. The number of records is always returned by ColdFusion with every query, and so you do not need to do anything special to add it to the page.

The Data category of Dreamweaver's Insert panel includes a Display Record Count section. Here, you have the ability to display the starting and ending record numbers — which is useful when you are paginating the results — or the total number of

records returned by the query. Displaying results across multiple pages is discussed in Chapter 20.

It is generally helpful to display this record count near the top of the page. It helps users to know how many records they are viewing. They can use this information to understand how big the page will be, which is particularly useful if they plan to print it. They may also use it for comparison purposes. For example, if they know that a search for one criterion returned 20 records, and a second returned 10, they can better judge the usefulness of those searches.

Display the Number of Records in a Recordset on a Page

① Click to the right of the table.

② Press Enter.

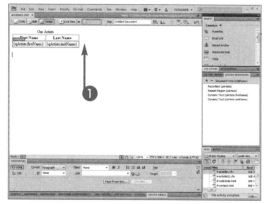

The cursor is placed on the blank line.

③ Click Common.

④ Click Data.

⑤ Click Display Record Count.

⑥ Click Total Records.

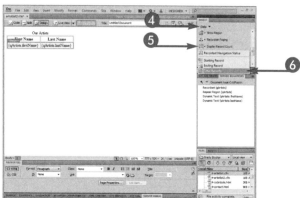

The Display Total Records dialog box appears.

7 Select a recordset.

8 Click OK.

The RecordCount dynamic text is added to the page.

9 Click Live View.

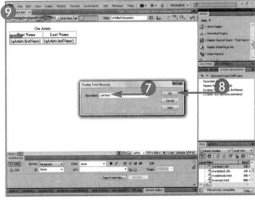

- Live view displays, showing the total number of records.

How can I help my users to navigate through the recordset results?
You can enable your users to move from one record to another record, or from one set of records to another set of records by using recordset navigation links. You can do this by adding four types of links that will enable users to view multiple recordsets, such as First, Previous, Next, and Last. A single page can contain any number of these four links, provided they all work on a single recordset. Note: You cannot add links to move through a second recordset on the same page.

How can I sort the data when it appears?
The data appears in the table in the order that it is encountered in the recordset. You cannot change the order when you display the data. To sort the data into the order you prefer, you need to specify a sort order when you create the recordset. The Recordset dialog box allows you to specify a column to sort on and whether to sort in ascending or descending order.

Create a Search Interface

Y ou can allow your users to search for records in your database by creating a form that allows users to enter their search criteria and a page to process the search by querying the database using the form's data. The search page is usually a fairly simple form, often nothing more than a single text field and a button.

The results page needs to contain a recordset. In the Recordset builder, you can add a filter. When Dreamweaver creates the SQL statement, the filter becomes the WHERE clause. You can specify where the

value for the filter is coming from; in the case of forms, it is a Form Variable, with a name equal to the name from the form field. You can test to see if the form field's data is exactly equal to a value in one of the fields from the database, or if the data begins with the form field value, ends with it, or just contains it.

The resulting recordset can be treated like any other recordset. You see the resulting fields in the Bindings panel, and can use any (X)HTML elements to display the results.

Create a Search Interface

① Create a form.

Note: *For details on how to create a form, see Chapter 17.*

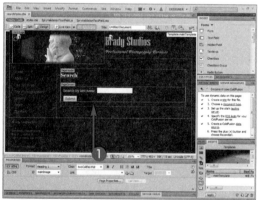

② Create a new document.

Note: *For details on creating new documents, see Chapter 2.*

Note: *Be sure to select a file type that uses your selected server model.*

③ Click Bindings.

④ Click the Add button.

⑤ Click Recordset (Query).

The Recordset dialog box appears.

6 Type a name for the query.

7 Select a data source and a table.

8 Select the fields to include.

9 Select Form Variable and type the matching form field's name.

10 Click OK.

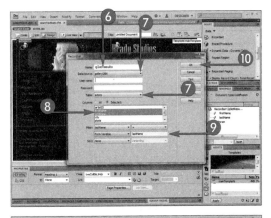

The recordset is added to the page.

11 Type a heading for the page.

12 Add a dynamic table to display the results.

Note: *Details on adding a dynamic table can be found in Chapter 19.*

The search results page is created.

When I try to view the results page in Live view, I get an error. How can I test it to be sure it is working?

▼ The results page cannot be viewed directly in the browser, as it expects a value to come from the search page. Instead, you need to view the search page, type in a value, and click the Submit button. This should correctly display the results page.

Note that you cannot test these pages in Live view, as the links and buttons do not work in it. Instead, you need to preview the search page in an actual Web browser.

How can I allow my user to search on multiple criteria?

▼ If your form contains more than one field, you can use a combination of any or all of them in your results criteria. Unfortunately, the Simple mode of the Recordset builder only allows you to work with a single filter, and so you need to switch to Advanced mode. You also need to write the WHERE clause of your query yourself, and so you need to be somewhat comfortable with SQL.

Create a Master Detail Page Set

Many Web sites display a list of items in their database and allow users to click an item to be taken to another page that displays details of the item. For example, if you search for a term on Amazon.com, a list of books that match the term appear. You can click one of the books to be taken to a page with the details of it. This is known as a data drill-down interface or a master detail page set.

You can have Dreamweaver do a lot of the work in creating this kind of interface on your site by using the Master Detail Page Set Wizard. You are prompted to create a recordset, which needs to include all of the fields you will use on both the master page, which will be the list, and the detail page. Then, you have the opportunity to choose which fields you want to display on the master page, and which fields you want to display on the detail page. You can choose which page to use as the detail page.

Create a Master Detail Page Set

① Create a new document.

Note: *For details on creating new documents, see Chapter 2.*

Note: *Be sure to select a file type that uses your selected server model.*

② Click Common.

③ Click Data.

④ Click Master Detail Page Set.

The Setup Instructions dialog box appears.

⑤ Click Recordset.

The Recordset dialog box appears.

⑥ Type a name for the recordset.

⑦ Select a data source.

⑧ Select a table.

⑨ Click OK.

The Master Detail Page Set dialog box appears.

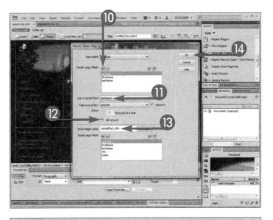

⑩ Click the Remove button to remove fields from the master page.

⑪ Select the field to use as the link.

⑫ Click All records.

⑬ Type the name of the page to use as a detail page.

⑭ Click OK.

The table is added to the master page, the detail page is opened, and the table is added to it.

Are there any layout options other than a table for the two pages' data?

▼ No, the Master Detail Page Set Wizard does not provide any layout options, and it always uses a table for the data on both pages. If you want to lay out the information using something other than a table, you should create the pages yourself. See the next section for details on how to do that.

If I notice something I want to change after I use the wizard, can I run the wizard again to change it?

▼ No. The Master Detail Page Set Wizard is a run-once wizard. However, everything that it creates is completely editable. If you need to alter the query, you can double-click Recordset on the Bindings panel to open the Recordset builder, although you should be aware that editing the recordset on one page does not edit it on the other. All of the information on the page is simply text, and can be freely edited.

Manually Create a Data Drill-Down Interface

Instead of using the Master Detail Page Set Wizard, you can create the pages yourself. In order to create a data drill-down interface or master detail page set, you need to create a list or master page. This page contains a recordset that retrieves the information needed for the page, which must include the primary key.

You can then add the data to the page using any structure you want. Often, the data for the master page is displayed as either a table or an unordered list. If you are only displaying a few items, such as a

customer or product name, a list is probably better. If you are displaying more information, then a table may be easier to manage. Ultimately, the structure you choose to use is a matter of personal preference, and can change from one site to the next depending on that site's needs.

Regardless of how you choose to structure your data, you need to add a repeat region. If you are using a table, you add the region around the row of the table that displays the records; if using a list, you add it around the list item.

1 Create a new document.

Note: *For details on creating new documents, see Chapter 2.*

Note: *Be sure to select a file type that uses your selected server model.*

2 Click Bindings.

3 Click the Add button.

4 Click Recordset (Query).

The Recordset dialog box appears.

5 Type a name.

6 Select a data source.

7 Select a table.

8 Select the fields you want to display.

9 Click OK.

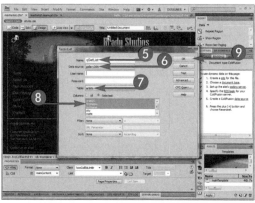

The recordset is added to the page.

⑩ Drag the fields from the Bindings panel onto the page.

⑪ Select the dynamic text.

⑫ Click Server Behaviors.

⑬ Click the Add button.

⑭ Click Repeat Region.

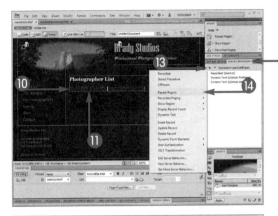

The Repeat Region dialog box appears.

⑮ Click All records.

⑯ Click OK.

The repeat region is added to the page.

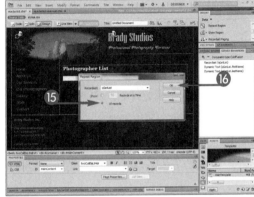

Can I accomplish these same tasks if I choose to use PHP or ASP instead of ColdFusion?

▼ Yes. Almost everything that is shown in this and the other chapters on dynamic Web sites works in the same way across all three languages supported by Dreamweaver. When you set up a site that uses PHP or ASP, you still have access to the Databases, Bindings, and Server Behaviors panels and the Data section of the Insert panel. So far, the only task that has been shown to be ColdFusion-specific is the one on setting up a data source. Creating a data source for use in ASP or a MySQL connection in PHP can be done directly from the Databases panel. The steps in this section on creating a data drill-down interface are identical across all three server languages.

PART IV

continued

Manually Create a Data Drill-Down Interface *(Continued)*

Once you have the data displayed, you need to create a hyperlink that passes that primary key value to the detail page. You can pass data through a hyperlink by adding a *query string* to the URL.

A query string is the portion of the URL that follows the actual page address. It begins with a question mark, and then contains one or more name/value pairs. The name can be any identifier that you decide on, but must contain only alphanumeric characters. The value is the data being passed, and is often

dynamic text from a recordset. Should you need to pass more than one name/value pair, you can separate each pair from the next with an ampersand (&).

The detail page needs to be set up with a recordset of its own. The important factor is that you need to add a filter, using the URL Variable setting and the name from the query string. As this contains the primary key value, you are sure to return a single record. You then display this record on the page, using any structure or formatting you need.

Manually Create a Data Drill-Down Interface *(continued)*

⑰ Select the dynamic text you want to use as the hyperlink.

⑱ Click the file folder.

The Select File dialog box appears.

⑲ Click the detail page.

⑳ Click Parameters.

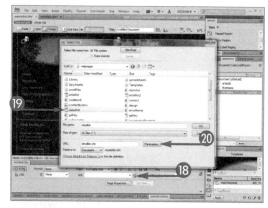

The Dynamic Data dialog box appears.

㉑ Type a name for the parameter.

㉒ Click Value.

㉓ Click the lightning bolt.

㉔ Select a field from the recordset.

㉕ Click OK.

㉖ Click OK.

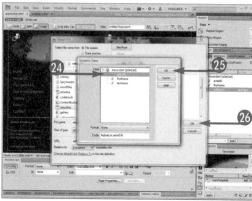

㉗ Open the detail page.

㉘ Click the Add button.

㉙ Click Recordset (Query).

The Recordset dialog box appears.

㉚ Type the information for the query.

㉛ Select URL Parameter.

㉜ Type the name from step **21**.

㉝ Click OK.

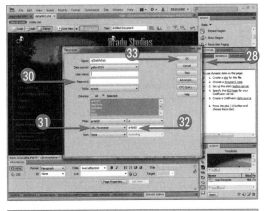

㉞ Drag the fields from the Bindings panel to the page.

The master and detail pages are created.

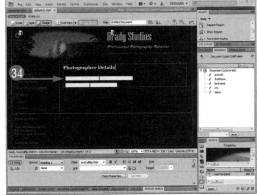

Is there a limit to how much data I can pass on a URL?

▼ Yes, but it depends on both the browser and the server, and so there is no definitive set amount. However, you can assume that the total length of the URL may be limited to as little as 1,024 characters. While that may seem like a lot, you should consider that it is the total length of the entire URL, not just the query string.

What if the data I am passing contains spaces? Does that cause problems?

▼ Yes it does, as some browsers truncate a URL at the first space. You can solve this problem by using ColdFusion's `URLEncodedFormat` function, which evaluates the data being sent and replaces spaces and other illegal characters with coded equivalents. You need to add this to the code yourself, as there is nothing in Dreamweaver's design interface to do it.

Display Results Across Multiple Pages

When you search for a relatively common term on Google, the search engine returns many hundreds of thousands, or at times millions or tens of millions, of results. Obviously, Google does want not to generate a page that attempts to display millions of results — the page would be unbelievably long and load incredibly slowly. Instead, it shows the first ten results, and then provides a set of links at the bottom of the page to move to the next ten, and then ten after that, and so forth.

This technique is called *recordset paging*. Conceptually, you need to have the query return only a limited number of records; ten is the normal number, but you can set it to anything else if you want. Then, you need to create hyperlinks that call the page you are currently viewing but pass, in a query string, variables to bring up the next set of records or the prior set. Dreamweaver's server behaviors include the necessary functionality to add recordset paging to your site.

① Click Server Behaviors.

② Double-click Repeat Region.

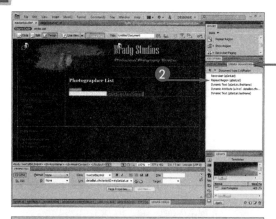

The Repeat Region dialog box appears.

③ Click Show 10 Records at a Time.

④ Click OK.

5. Click the page at the point at which you want to add the paging navigation.

6. Click the Add button.

7. Select Recordset Paging.

8. Click Move To First Page.

The Move to First Page dialog box appears.

9. Click OK.

The First link is added to the page.

10. Click to the right of the link.

11. Repeat steps **6** to **9** to add the Move to Previous Page, Move to Next Page, and Move to Last Page links.

Recordset paging is added to the page.

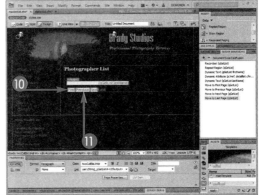

Can I create links to specific pages within the recordset like Google does?

▼ If you use ASP, then yes, this is fairly simple. For sites configured to use ASP, Dreamweaver includes a server behavior called *Move to Specific Record* that allows you to create this kind of navigation. Unfortunately, that server behavior does not exist in the ColdFusion or PHP models. This is not a limitation of either of those languages, however, and so it would be possible for you to create the code yourself to set up that navigation.

Can I use images in addition to, or in place of, the text links?

▼ Yes. Once they are placed on the page, the text links of First, Previous, Next, and Last are simple links like any others on the page. You can change the text to other wording if you would like, you can replace the text with an image, or you could add an image in addition to the text. You need to be careful when you do this to make sure that you do not delete or alter the server-side code that surrounds the link.

Show and Hide Content Based on a Recordset

You can have the server-side processing selectively display or hide content on a page based on whether or not a recordset returns results, or based on your current location within the recordset. Both of these functions are available through the Show Region set of server behaviors.

When you create a search interface, you have a results page designed to display records returned by the query. However, it is entirely possible that your user will enter a search term that does not match anything in the database table. In this case, you want to display a customized message to your user informing him that the search returned no results, and you want to hide whatever portions of the page exist to display the records, such as the table header row. To do this, you can wrap the error message in the Show If Recordset Is Empty server behavior and wrap the results display content in the Show If Recordset Is Not Empty behavior. Once added, these server behaviors display in Design view with a thin border around the region and a light-blue tab in the top-left corner.

Show and Hide Content Based on a Recordset

① Select a region on the page.

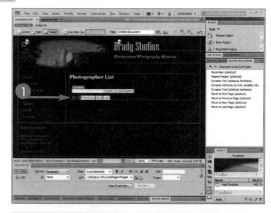

② Click the Add button.

③ Select Show Region.

④ Click Show If Recordset Is Not Empty.

The Show If Recordset Is not Empty dialog box appears.

⑤ If necessary, select the recordset.

⑥ Click OK.

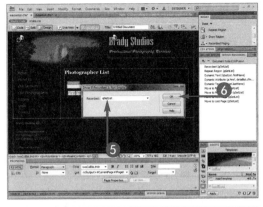

● The Show Region is added to the page.

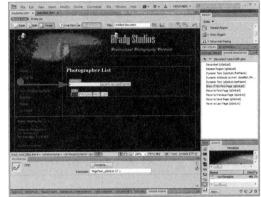

Can I apply these regions to prevent the First link from appearing on the first page when using recordset paging?

▼ When you use recordset paging, you can use the Show If Not First Page behavior to hide the link to the first page of results when you are on that first page. You can use the Show If Not Last Page behavior to achieve the same result on the last page of results, hiding the link to that last page. You can also use the Show If First Page region to add content to only the first page, and the Show If Last Page region to add content only to that page.

Can I add other conditional statements besides those based on the recordsets?

▼ Dreamweaver does have the ability to add the basic structure of an *if* statement through the language-specific Insert panel section. When you are working in ColdFusion, for example, you see a CFML section. Similar sections appear for PHP and ASP. All three have a button to begin an *if* block. However, you have to type most of the code yourself.

Insert Records

You can allow users of your Web site to add new data to your database tables. To do so, you need a form into which they can enter the information to be added, and the necessary server-side code to perform the interaction with the database.

You can use the Record Insertion Form Wizard to both create the form and add the server-side code. This run-once wizard allows you to specify a data source and table, and then set the columns into which you

want to add a record. You are also able to set the page to which the user will be taken once the insertion is complete; often, this is some sort of record list page so that he can see that the new record is indeed in the database.

Once you complete the wizard, you cannot bring it back. If you need to modify anything on the form, you can do so directly in Design view, but be aware that adding or removing fields or changing their names will likely cause the server-side code to stop functioning.

Insert Records

1 Create a new ColdFusion document.

Note: *Details on creating new documents can be found in Chapter 2.*

Note: *If your site has a template, you can also create a page based on that. See Chapter 9 for information on templates.*

2 Click Insert Record.

3 Click Record Insertion Form Wizard.

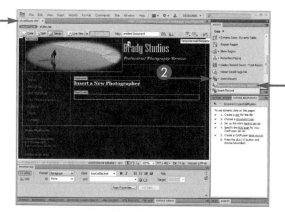

The Record Insertion Form Wizard appears.

4 Select a data source.

5 Select a table.

6 Type the page to which you want to redirect your user.

7 Click the Remove button to remove the primary key field.

8 Change any labels to be more readable.

9 Click OK.

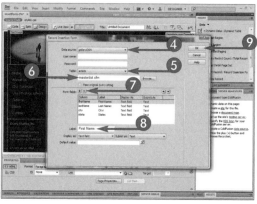

The form is created on the page.

10 Click Live View.

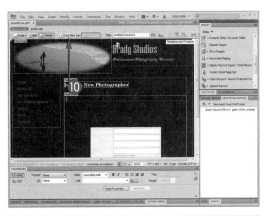

Live view displays the page.

11 Type data into the fields.

12 Click Insert record.

The results page displays.

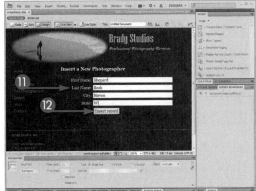

Is it possible to create the form myself so that I can have more control over its appearance?

▼ Yes. You can create the form yourself and then use the Insert Record server behavior. This server behavior modifies your form to be self-posting; that is, it changes the form's action attribute to reference the same page that the form is on. It adds a block of code at the top of the form that first checks to be sure that the form should be processed, and then adds the code required to insert the record into the table, using an SQL INSERT INTO statement.

Can I add form validation to make sure that fields are not left blank?

▼ Yes. The easiest and most feature-rich method is to use Spry. Once the form is created, you can click each field, and then click the related Spry Validation field type, which converts the field to a Spry field. This works whether you use the wizard or create the form yourself. More details on using Spry Validation fields are in Chapter 18. In a live Web site environment, you should also add server-side form validation, but this requires that you write your own code.

Update Existing Records

You can allow your users to update or modify the records that currently exist within the database. This system generally begins with a list page that displays the existing records. Users click the record they want to update and are taken to a page that displays a form. The form is prepopulated with the existing data, which users can then change as needed. When they click the form's button, server-side code updates the record and then redirects them to a page, often the list page on which they began the process.

You need to create the list page yourself, and include a link to the form page that passes the record's primary key in a query string. Details on how to do this are in Chapter 20.

On the page on which you present the form, you need to create a recordset. You can then use the Record Update Form Wizard to generate the form, which is prefilled with the data from the recordset, and the server-side code necessary to perform the database operations. The wizard also allows you to specify a page to which the user will be taken.

Update Existing Records

① Open a page that contains a list of records.

② Within the repeat region, type **Update**.

③ Click the file folder.

The Create Hyperlink dialog box appears.

④ Click once on the form page.

⑤ Create a parameter for the primary key.

Note: Details on this procedure are in Chapter 20.

⑥ Click OK three times.

⑦ Open the page on which you will place the form.

Note: This is the same page that you selected in step 4.

⑧ Click Bindings.

⑨ Click the Add button.

⑩ Click Recordset (Query).

The Recordset dialog box appears.

⑪ Fill out the dialog box as shown.

Note: Details on creating a recordset are in Chapter 19.

⑫ Click OK.

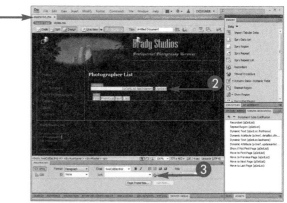

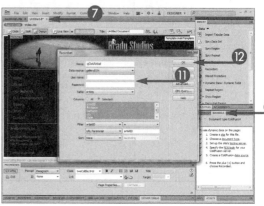

⓭ Click Update Record.

⓮ Click Record Update Form Wizard.

The Record Update Form Wizard opens.

⓯ Select a datasource.

⓰ Select a table.

⓱ Type the path to the list page.

⓲ Click the Remove button to remove the primary key column.

⓳ Fix any labels as needed.

⓴ Click OK.

● The form and necessary server-side code are added to the page.

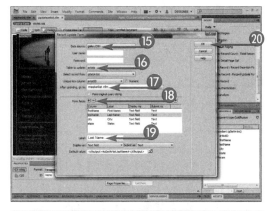

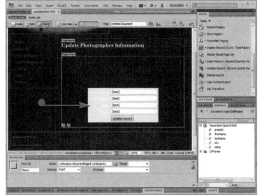

Is it possible to create my own form as I did for inserting records?

▼ Yes. Just as when inserting records, you can create your own form and then use the Update Record server behavior to add the necessary server-side code. You need to be sure that the update form is pre-populated with the data from the database. You can populate a text field or text area by simply dragging the appropriate record from the Bindings panel. You can preselect a value in a drop-down menu or precheck a check box or radio button by clicking Dynamic on the Property Inspector.

If a user updates a record and changes the data so that it is wrong, can I undo the update?

▼ No. Databases do not support undoing operations. Once a record has been updated, the change is permanent and can only be undone by manually updating the record again.

You need to consider security when creating update forms: You should only allow users who can be trusted to accurately update records, although you may want to allow users to change their own records at any time.

Delete Records

In certain situations, you may want to provide users with the ability to delete records from the database. This should always be done with caution, as deleted records are deleted permanently.

Unlike the wizards that Dreamweaver provides for inserting and updating records, there is no Record Deletion Form Wizard. Instead, you need to create the page to display the record to be deleted yourself. The process is very similar to that used for updating records: You present the user with a list of the current records and have him click an item to go to a page

that displays the record to be deleted. Most likely, this is not in a form, but rather simply displays the record. While the record is not displayed in a form, you want to have a small form on the page that contains a button that the user can click to execute the deletion.

You can use the Delete Record server behavior to have Dreamweaver add the code needed for performing the deletion to the page. This allows you to specify the form being used and the primary key column from the recordset.

Delete Records

① Open a page that contains a list of records.

② Within the repeat region, type **Delete.**

③ Click the file folder.

The Create Hyperlink dialog box appears.

④ Click once on the form page.

⑤ Click parameters.

⑥ Create a parameter for the primary key.

Note: Details on this procedure are in Chapter 20.

⑦ Click OK three times.

⑧ Open the page on which you will place the delete confirmation.

Note: This is same page that you selected in step 4.

⑨ Click Bindings.

⑩ Click the Add button.

⑪ Click Recordset (Query).

The Recordset dialog box appears.

⑫ Fill out the dialog box.

Note: Details on creating a recordset are in Chapter 19.

⑬ Click OK.

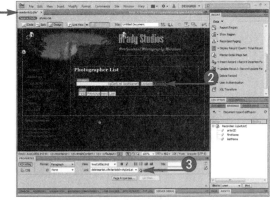

⑭ Drag the fields from the Bindings panel onto the page.

⑮ Add a form.

⑯ Within the form, add a Submit button.

Note: *Details on creating forms and adding buttons can be found in Chapter 17.*

Note: *You do not need to set the form's action attribute.*

⑰ Click Delete Record.

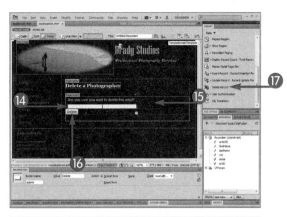

The Delete Record dialog box appears.

⑱ Select a data source.

⑲ Select a table.

⑳ Type the path to the list file.

㉑ Click OK.

The necessary server-side code is added to the page.

A coworker said that I should never delete records from my database. Is this true?

▼ Many database developers believe this, and it is not without merit. There are many reasons why you might need to keep data around. For example, it would be reasonable to expect that you would not delete customers from a database; even if the customer was angry and said that he was not going to use your business anymore, you would most likely want to keep his records in place. If you discontinue a product, you would need to keep it in the database so that you can continue to keep track of orders for it before it was discontinued.

That said, there are rarely true absolutes. Many, if not most, database systems benefit from maintaining records, but many others have legitimate reasons to have records deleted at times. It simply needs to be evaluated on a case-by-case basis.

Include External Files

Since the early days of the Web, designers have struggled to find ways to share content such as navigation bars and footers across multiple pages. Dreamweaver templates offer one solution to the problem, but server-side scripting languages offer another in their ability to include external files.

Most dynamic pages are constructed by combining a series of smaller files into one. The navigation bar is often a completely independent file, as are sidebar content, footers, and possibly even the main content of the page. Each of these components is then

included in the primary page. When this page is requested by the browser, the scripting language pulls the contents of the included pages into the main page, thereby dynamically creating a single document that can be sent to the browser.

Included pages can contain any content. They can be purely static (X)HTML, as is often the case with navigation bars and footers, or they can themselves contain scripting code to dynamically generate their content. Included pages can even include other pages, although care should be taken that this does not become overly complex.

Include External Files

① Open a new, blank document.

Note: *Details on creating new documents are in Chapter 2.*

② Create a series of links to serve as navigation.

Note: *Details on creating hyperlinks are in Chapter 5.*

③ Click Code.

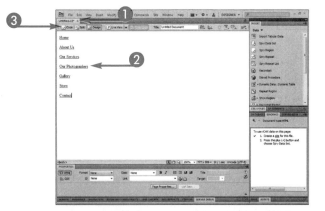

Code view displays.

④ Delete the <html> tag, the opening and closing <head> tags, everything in the <head>, and the opening <body> tag.

⑤ Delete the closing <body> and <html> tags.

⑥ Save the document.

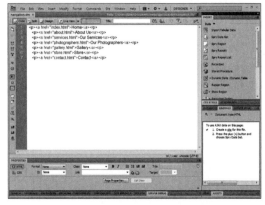

7 Open a document in which you want to include the navigation.

8 Click Common.

9 Click CFML.

10 Click cfinclude.

The Tag Editor dialog box appears.

11 Type the filename of the document you saved in step **6**.

12 Click OK.

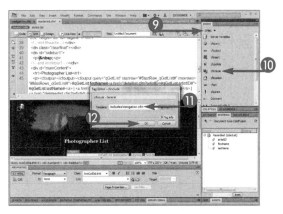

● The file is included.

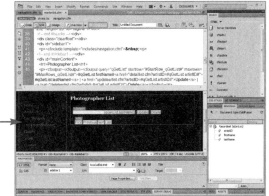

Is there anything special I need to do when I edit the included file?	**What file extension do I need to use on included files?**	**Can I use included files in PHP and ASP pages as well?**
▼ No, you can simply make your edits and save the file. Unlike with templates, where Dreamweaver needs to go in and edit the files that use the template, no other pages are actually being changed when you edit an included file — the changed version is simply included the next time this document is requested from the browser.	▼ Normally, an included file is never requested directly, and so the file extension is irrelevant. Many developers prefer to use one extension throughout their site, and so ColdFusion included files often use .cfm, but .htm or .html work as well. Some prefer to use .inc to designate the file as an included file.	▼ Yes. While the example here uses ColdFusion, both PHP and ASP support included files as well. PHP developers can click Include in the PHP section of the Insert panel; ASP developers click Include in the ASP section. In both cases, you are taken to Split mode and need to type the path to the file manually.

Use a Design-time Style Sheet

Included files are not complete (X)HTML documents. Because they eventually become part of a larger document, they do not contain all of the necessary (X)HTML structure tags, and in particular, they do not contain a head section. Without the head, there is no way to include a link to a style sheet. Therefore, when you work with a site that is made up of included files, it can become difficult to see how the site works visually.

You can use Design-time Style Sheets to work around this problem. With a Design-time Style Sheet, Dreamweaver can act as though a valid link to a style sheet exists on the page. That way, you can see your page in Design view as it should appear in a browser, and you can use the CSS panel to edit the styles as normal.

Dreamweaver applies a Design-time Style Sheet to the page without modifying the underlying (X)HTML, and so you do not need to remove the link to the style sheet when you are done editing it. It remembers the link, however, and so when you reopen the document in the future, you will not need to reattach the style sheet.

Use a Design-time Style Sheet

① Click the CSS Panel's menu.

② Click Design-time.

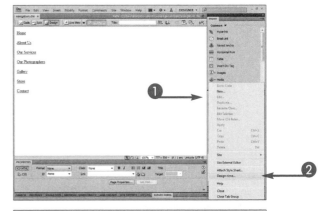

The Design-Time Style Sheets dialog box appears.

③ Click the Add button.

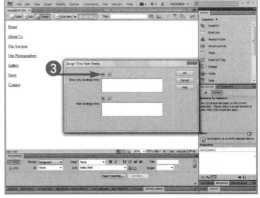

The Select File dialog box appears.

④ Double-click the style sheet.

⑤ Click OK.

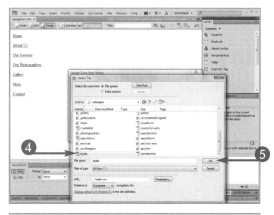

● The Design-time Style Sheet is attached to the page, and the formatting is applied.

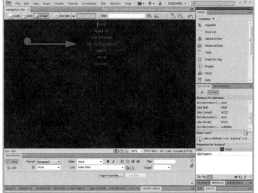

When would I need to hide a style sheet at Design-time?

▼ When browsers originally began supporting CSS, there were at times radical differences between the style properties that two browsers could display, as well as how they implemented the styles. Therefore, some designers would add different style sheets for different browsers, usually relying on JavaScript to switch between them. The ability to hide style sheets at Design-time was added to Dreamweaver to assist these developers; there is little or no reason to use it today.

If Dreamweaver is not modifying the code, how does it keep track of Design-time Style Sheets?

▼ Your Dreamweaver site folder contains a directory called _notes. Although this does not appear in the Dreamweaver Files panel, it is visible if you view the folder in Windows. The _notes folder is primarily for Design notes, but Dreamweaver also stores files in it for other purposes, such as keeping track of Design-time Style Sheets.

Dynamically Display Images

The Web is primarily a visual medium, and you will almost certainly want to add images to the display of database information. Images are not embedded directly on a Web page; rather, the page uses the (X)HTML <img> tag to link to the image file on the server. Many Web developers at first think that they need to store the actual image in a database, using the database server's binary data type. While techniques do exist to retrieve the image information from the database, you will find that it is far less work to keep the images out of the database and store

them in a folder within the Web root, in exactly the same way you store nondynamic images.

The database then contains only the filename of the image associated with the record. Web sites with complex directory structures may also decide to include the path to the image in question. When Dreamweaver constructs the <img> tag, it can use this value — the filename and, if needed, the path to the image. Thus, the browser ends up seeing a tag that instructs it to request the image from the server, just as it would any static image.

Dynamically Display Images

① Open a document that contains a recordset.

Note: *You can learn how to create a recordset in Chapter 19.*

② Click Images.

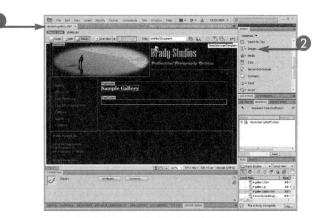

The Select Image Source dialog box appears.

③ Click Data sources.

④ Click the image field.

⑤ Click OK.

The Image Tag Accessibility dialog box appears.

⑥ Click OK.

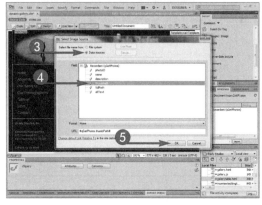

The image is inserted into the page; a dynamic image placeholder appears in its place.

7 Click Live View.

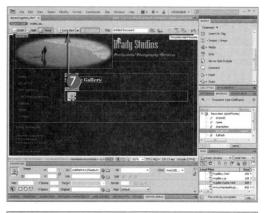

● Live view displays, showing the image.

Should I just input something generic for the alternate text for my dynamic images?

▼ No. Alternate text should be specific to each image. Ideally, you will use a field from the recordset for the alternate text. You might use a descriptive field such as a product name, or you can add a field to the database specifically to store alternate text. Unfortunately, the Image Tag Accessibility Options dialog box that appears when you insert an image does not provide an easy method by which you can select a field from the recordset. The Tag Inspector panel, however, does provide this. You can click the image, and then go to the panel and click the `alt` attribute. Click the lightning bolt and select the field from the recordset.

What can I do if the images are different sizes?

▼ Most layouts work better if all of the images being inserted dynamically are the same size, but if they are not, you can store the width and height values for the image in the database, and then use the Tag Inspector panel to set the width and height attributes from recordset values.

Store Information in a Cookie

The Web is, by design, a *stateless* environment. This simply means that Web pages are handled as independent requests by the server, and no data is shared between them. Chapter 20 shows how data can be passed between pages using forms and URL variables. While passing data using these methods is useful, it has the limitation that the data only exists for those two pages. Frequently, you need to track data across many page requests. For example, if a user logs into a site, you need a way to keep track of that user across all of the pages

protected by the login; otherwise, the user would have to continuously log in for each page.

Cookies are a common method of tracking data across multiple pages. A cookie is a small text file that the browser writes to the user's hard drive and then sends to the server along with the page request. The server can read the information on the cookie and apply it to the page.

Cookies need to be given a name and a value. The name becomes the variable by which the cookie can be read; the value is the value of that variable.

Store Information in a Cookie

① Click Common.

② Click CFML.

③ Click Advanced.

④ Click cfcookie.

The Tag Editor dialog box appears.

⑤ Type a name for the cookie.

⑥ Type a value.

⑦ Click OK.

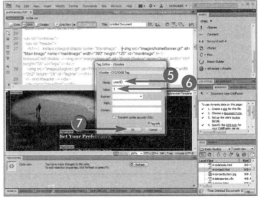

8 Click the Preview/Debug in Browser button.

9 Click Preview in IExplore.

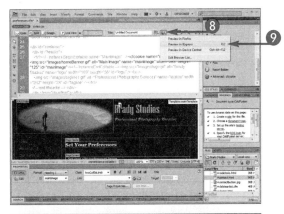

The browser opens and the page loads.

The cookie is written as soon as the page loads.

How long will the cookie be stored?

▼ If you only give the cookie a name and a value, it becomes a session cookie, which means that it is not actually written to the hard drive at all and is deleted once the browser is closed. When you create a cookie, however, you can specify an expiration date, in which case the file is written to the hard drive and stored until the date you specify. You can also set the expiration date to never so that the cookie is never deleted automatically.

What kinds of information can I keep in a cookie?

▼ In theory, you can store just about any information in the cookie, as long as it can be stored as a string of text. In practice, however, you should try to keep the information relatively short and simple. For example, if you have a user login and need to be able to retrieve that user's data across multiple pages, you could simply store his ID number — the primary key value for his record in the database — as this is all you would need in order to run a query to bring up other information for him.

Use Cookie Data on a Page

Pages can read information from a cookie to control their display. A cookie's value could be used as a filter in a query. It could be used as a variable to determine whether portions of the page, or the actual page, should display. Sometimes, a cookie's value may simply be displayed as text.

In Dreamweaver, you can use the Bindings panel to add the code needed to read a cookie. Normally, the Bindings panel is used to display fields retrieved from a recordset, but it can also be used to create other types of variables, including cookies.

Cookies are under the control of the user, as they are stored on the user's computer. It is possible to set a browser to simply reject requests to write cookies, but as a very high number of sites today require cookies in order to work, few if any users still disable cookies. However, many more users are in the habit of manually deleting cookies on a regular basis. Therefore, you should be aware that the existence of a cookie can never be assured.

Use Cookie Data on a Page

① Click Bindings.

② Click the Add button.

③ Click Cookie Variable.

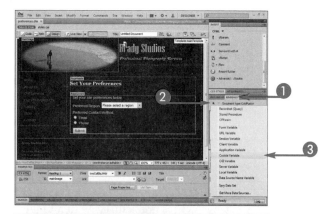

The Cookie Variable dialog box appears.

④ Type the name of the cookie.

⑤ Click OK.

The cookie appears in the Bindings panel.

6 Drag the cookie from the Bindings panel to the page.

Dynamic text representing the cookie is added to the page.

7 Click the Preview/ Debug in Browser button.

8 Click Preview in IExplore.

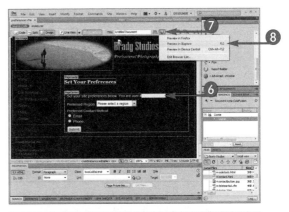

● The page displays in the browser, showing the value from the cookie.

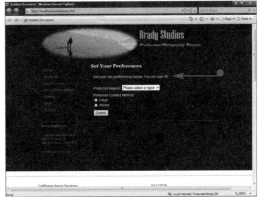

How can I set cookies in PHP or ASP?

▼ Unlike with ColdFusion, Dreamweaver does not provide a dialog box to create cookies in either PHP or ASP, and so you have to write the code yourself. You can set a cookie in PHP using the `setcookie` function:

```
setcookie("name", "value", expires);
```

In ASP, you can set the cookie using `Response.Cookies`:

```
Response.Cookies("name") = value
```

How can I read cookies in PHP or ASP?

▼ Setting cookies requires that you write code in PHP or ASP. Reading the cookie, however, is the same procedure in PHP as it is in ColdFusion, and so you can still set the cookie variable in the Bindings panel and then drag-and-drop it as dynamic text. In ASP, you can select Request variable in the Bindings panel, and then select Request.cookie.

Create an Application Component

Y ou can create and manage application-wide settings and variables through a special kind of include file, Application.cfc. This document is automatically included in every page request within the application.

Early versions of ColdFusion used Application.cfm, which was nothing more than a regular ColdFusion document that happened to contain application-wide variables and settings. In ColdFusion MX7 and ColdFusion 8, you can still use Application.cfm, but it is recommended instead that you use Application.cfc.

A ColdFusion Component (CFC) is a special type of ColdFusion document that is used to encapsulate processing code, separating it from presentational code. A CFC is made up of a series of functions, which are blocks of code that perform a specific action.

Your Application.cfc file is comprised of a series of specifically designed functions, several of which are discussed in the following sections. In addition, you can define application-wide settings and variables at the top of the page, before the functions. You need to prefix these variables and settings with this, which establishes that they apply to the current application.

Create an Application Component

① Click File.

② Click New.

The New Document dialog box appears.

③ Click ColdFusion component.

④ Click Create.

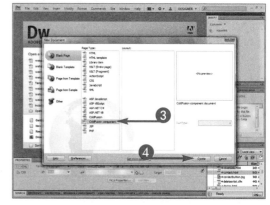

The document is created, and contains sample component code.

5 Click to the right of `<cfcomponent>`.

6 Press Enter.

7 Type **<cfset this.name = "Brady Studios">**.

8 Type **<cfset this.sessionmanagement = "yes">**.

9 Delete the sample `<cffunction>` and all of its contents.

10 Click File.

11 Click Save As.

The Save As dialog box appears.

12 Type **Application.cfc** as the filename.

Note: Be sure to save this file in the root of your Web site.

The file is saved and the application created.

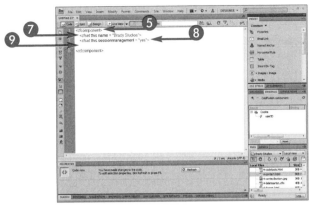

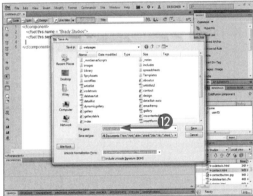

Can I use something similar in PHP or ASP?

▼ When a request is made in an ASP application, each page automatically searches for a document called global.asa and includes it. The global.asa file is similar to the older Application.cfm document in that it has no particular structure and can be used to create application-wide variables. PHP has no similar kind of document; if you want to include something in every page in a PHP application, you must do so manually.

Can I prevent pages from including Application.cfc?

▼ No. Every page within the same folder as an Application.cfc, or any subfolder of that folder, automatically includes it. If you want the component's settings to only apply to a specific set of pages, you need to place those pages, and the Application.cfc, in their own directory together. Files only look in the current directory and then up into parent folders; they do not look down into subfolders, and so an Application.cfc in a subfolder only applies to that folder and its subfolders, not to any documents in the subfolder's parent.

PART IV

Start a Session

Another option for maintaining data across pages, aside from cookies, is to use a session. Sessions serve the same basic purpose as cookies. In fact, all three server languages supported by Dreamweaver actually use cookies to track sessions. The important difference between sessions and cookies is that with cookies, you as the developer are responsible for creating the cookie, while with sessions, the server language automatically handles the cookie creation code.

In order to use sessions in ColdFusion, you must first allow sessions to be used on your server through ColdFusion Administrator. Then, you must enable sessions for the application in an Application.cfc file. (See the previous section for details on creating an Application.cfc file and an example of enabling sessions in it.)

You can create session variables by using the `onSessionStart` function in Application.cfc. This function is automatically run every time a new session begins, which in practice means each time a page is requested that is not already part of a session. You can use the ColdFusion `cfset` tag, which creates a variable, and prefix the name of the variable with session to make it a session variable.

Start a Session

① Open an Application.cfc document.

Note: *See the previous section for details on creating an Application.cfc document.*

② Click in a line above the closing `<cfcomponent>` tag.

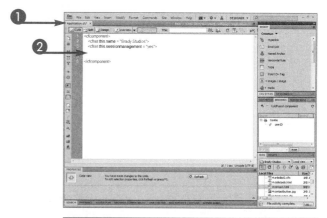

③ Type **<cffunction name="onSessionStart" returnType="void">**.

④ Press Enter.

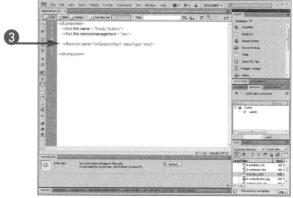

⑤ Type **<cfset session.name = "*Your Name*">**.

⑥ Type **</cffunction>**.

⑦ Press Enter.

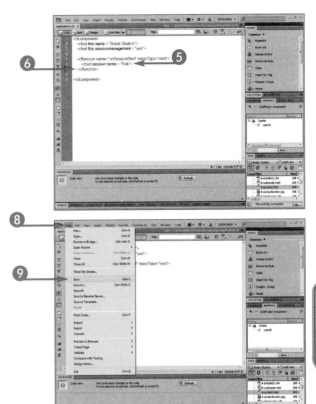

⑧ Click File.

⑨ Click Save.

The document is saved, and the application can now use sessions.

What does `returnType="void"` do?

▼ Some functions simply process code when called. Others return values to the code that called them. When a function returns a value, you add `<cfset return variable>`, where *variable* is the value being returned. In that case, the `cffunction` tag needs to specify the data type of the returned variable.

The `onSessionStart` function does not contain a return statement, and so it returns nothing. In ColdFusion, the data type for nothing is *null*.

How can I create a session in PHP or ASP?

▼ In PHP, you can simply add `session_start()` to the beginning of any page in which you want to use a session. Then, you can add variables to the session using this syntax:

`$_SESSION['name'] = 'value';`

In ASP, you can write something similar:

`session('name') = value`

In all three cases, you need to write this code yourself; there is nothing in Dreamweaver to create session code.

Use Session Variables

Once you have established a session, you can use its variables in your pages. Almost any value can be stored in a session. If you have a site where users register and then log in, you can store their first and last names in session variables, and then have instant access to those values on your pages.

Dreamweaver forces you to create the code to establish the session manually, but once the session exists, you can use its variables by adding a reference to it in the Bindings panel. Then, you can use that variable on the page by dragging it, or reference it as a filter in a recordset or anywhere else variables are allowed.

Sessions last until the user closes the browser window or until a set timeout is reached. By default, ColdFusion and ASP sessions expire after 20 minutes, and PHP sessions expire after 24 minutes. After that time, the user needs to begin the session again, even if he has left his browser window open. All three languages rely on cookies to track session information, and so the rare user who disables cookies will be unable to use the session-based pages.

Use Session Variables

① Open a document.

② Click Bindings.

③ Click the Add button.

④ Click Session Variable.

The Session Variable dialog box appears.

⑤ Type the name for a session variable.

Note: *See the previous section for details on how to create a session variable.*

⑥ Click OK.

The session variable reference is created in the Bindings panel.

7 Drag the variable to the page.

8 Click the Preview/Debug in Browser button.

9 Click Preview in IExplore.

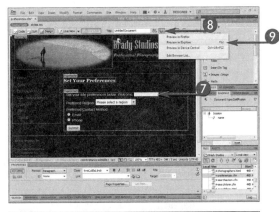

● The page opens in the browser, and the session variable is displayed.

Can I change the timeout of the session?

▼ Yes, each of the languages lets you adjust the timeout. In ColdFusion, you can set it using the `sessiontimeout` setting:

```
<cfset this.sessiontimeout = #createtimespan(0,0,40,0)#>
```

That code sets the session to timeout in 40 minutes instead of 20.

In PHP, you can adjust the setting by using the `ini_set` function to change the `session.gc_maxlifetime` setting:

```
ini_set("session.gc_maxlifetime", 2400);
```

In this case, you are setting the session to expire after 2400 seconds, or 40 minutes.

In ASP, simply change the value of the `Session.timeout` variable, in minutes:

```
Session.timeout = 40
```

Add a File Upload Field

You can allow users to upload files to your server. Many social-networking sites such as MySpace and Facebook allow users to upload their photos. A site created as a content-management solution includes the ability for its users to upload documents to share, such as Microsoft Word or Excel files or Adobe PDF documents.

You can add a field to a form that includes a text field for the path to the file, and a button that allows the user to browse for a file on his computer through the (X)HTML input tag. In Dreamweaver, you can simply click the File field button in the Form section of the Insert panel.

You cannot control the appearance of the field or the placement of text on the button. These are simply limitations of (X)HTML.

You must also add an additional attribute to the actual form in order to upload a file. The form must have its `enctype` attribute set to `multipart/form-data`. This can be done through the Dreamweaver Property Inspector. The `enctype` setting determines how the form uploads the data, and you must use this setting because the file being uploaded will most likely be binary data.

Add a File Upload Field

Create the Form page

① Open a page with a form.

Note: Form creation is covered in Chapter 17.

② Click the form.

The Property Inspector displays the form's properties.

③ Select multipart/form-data.

④ Type **uploadaction.cfm.**

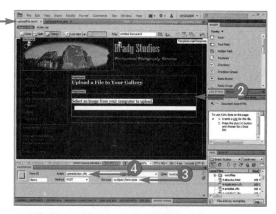

⑤ Click within the form.

⑥ Click File Field.

The Input Tag Accessibility Attributes dialog box appears.

7 Type an ID.

8 Type a name.

9 Click OK.

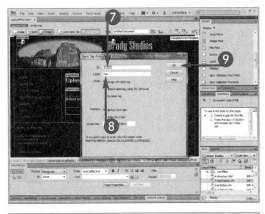

● The field and its associated button are inserted onto the page.

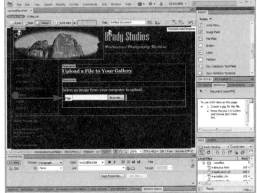

What is an enctype?

▼ The `enctype` attribute is short for *encoding type*. It defines how the browser should transmit the data to the server. The default value is `application/x-www-form-urlencoded`, which sends all of the data as plain text, avoiding characters that might cause problems on a URL, such as spaces. When sending binary data such as an uploaded file, you need to use `multipart/form-data`, which sends the text portions of the form in one part as text, and the binary data in a separate part.

When I view my page in Safari, I do not see the text field, only the button. Did I do something wrong?

▼ No, this is merely a quirk in the way that Apple has chosen to implement the file upload field. Because you cannot type anything into the field — you must use the Browse button and navigate to the file — they decided that having the field appear was meaningless. Instead, they merely show the button, and once the file has been selected, the filename appears next to it.

continued

PART IV

Add a File Upload Field *(Continued)*

When the user submits a form that contains an uploaded file, the Web server copies the file to a temporary directory and then relies on some sort of server-side code to move it to a permanent directory. Although Dreamweaver does not provide any tools in the Design environment for processing the uploaded file, the code required is fairly simple.

ColdFusion includes a `<cffile>` tag that handles the necessary operations for you. The `<cffile>` tag takes an action attribute, that when set to upload will

process an uploaded file. You simply need to include a `filefield` attribute, set to the name of the field from the form, and a destination field with a path to the permanent folder for the file.

Once uploaded, you can use the `cffile` scope to reference the file. For example, you may want to simply inform the user that the file was uploaded, and you might write: #cffile.serverfile# was uploaded, in which case #cffile.serverfile# would be replaced with the name of the file on the server. You can check the online ColdFusion documentation for more details on using the `cffile` scope.

Create the Action page

1 Create a new ColdFusion document.

Note: Creating a new document is discussed in Chapter 2.

2 Click Code to display Code view.

3 Click the end of line 8 and press Enter.

4 Type **<cffile action= "upload" filefield= "upload" destination="c:/inetpub/ wwwroot/uploads">** and press Enter.

5 Type **<cfoutput>**.

6 Type **#cffile.serverfile# was uploaded successfully.**

7 Type **</.**

The closing `<cfoutput>` tag is inserted.

8 Save the file.

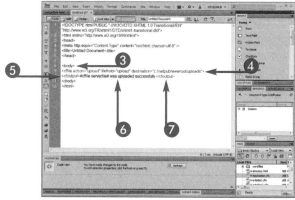

9 Open a Web browser.

10 Type **localhost/uploadfile.html.**

Note: *Use the filename for the form that contains the file field.*

The page displays.

11 Click Browse and select a file.

12 Click OK.

13 Click Submit.

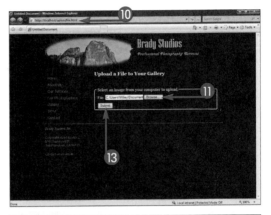

● The page created in this section displays, showing a confirmation that the file was uploaded.

What does the `<cfoutput>` tag do?

▼ ColdFusion mixes code that needs to be processed by the server and static (X)HTML in the same document. Whenever you have a block of code that you want to display on the page that ColdFusion needs to process first, you need to wrap that code in the `<cfoutput>` tag. This simply tells ColdFusion to process the code and output the results.

Why is `cffile.serverfile` enclosed in pound signs?

▼ Because the contents of `<cfoutput>` can contain both ColdFusion variables, such as `cffile.serverfile`, and static text, such as was uploaded successfully, the server needs a way to distinguish between the code that it should process and the code that it should ignore and send directly to the browser. Code that needs to be processed by the server is therefore enclosed in pound signs.

E-mail Form Results

You can have your server automatically e-mail the data from a form submission. ColdFusion includes a simple tag, `<cfmail>`, to handle sending e-mail. You need to add a series of attributes to control the behavior of the `<cfmail>` tag. If you have ever sent an e-mail through an e-mail program such as Microsoft Outlook, you know that you need to provide an address to which the mail will be sent, a subject line, and a body for the message. You also need to provide the address for yourself, the person sending the message.

Each of these is represented as an attribute of the `<cfmail>` tag. A complete tag might look like this:

```
<cfmail to="captain@serenity.com"
from="pilot@serenity.com"
subject="Reavers">
```

Following that opening tag, you can place the body of the message, either as static text or using ColdFusion variables, which need to be enclosed in pound signs. Add a closing `<cfmail>` tag and your document is complete.

E-mail Form Results

① Create a new ColdFusion document.

Note: *Creating a new document is discussed in Chapter 2.*

② Click Code.

③ Click at the end of line 8.

④ Press Enter.

⑤ Type **<cfmail.**

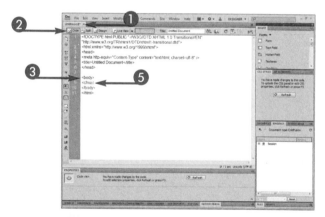

⑥ Type **to="*your_e-mail*".**

⑦ Type **from="*your_e-mail*".**

Note: *In both cases above, use your real e-mail address.*

⑧ Type **subject="Form results">** and press Enter.

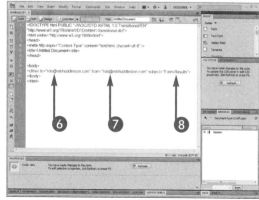

⑨ Type **The following was sent from the form:** and press Enter.

⑩ Type **#form.firstname#** and press Enter.

⑪ Repeat step **11** for each additional form field.

⑫ Type </.

The closing `<cfmail>` tag is inserted.

⑬ Save the page.

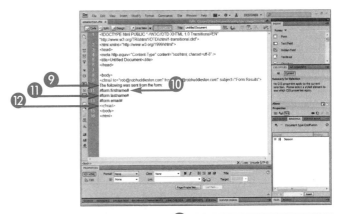

⑭ Open a page that contains a form.

Note: Creating forms is covered in Chapter 17.

⑮ Click the form.

⑯ Set the action to the page you saved in step **13**.

The form is updated and the action page can now send e-mail.

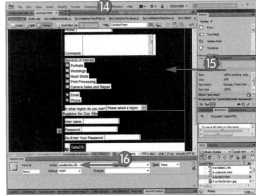

How can I test to make sure the form really works?

▼ In order to test the form, you need to upload the form to a server that is configured with a program that can send e-mail. Any third-party Web host should have this configured already, although you may need to add an additional attribute, `server`, to the `<cfmail>` tag. Check your host's help files for the proper setting.

You can also download and install a free SMTP program. SMTP stands for *simple mail transfer protocol*, and an SMTP program is one that sends mail. Details on how to set up and configure an SMTP program for local testing can be found at www.robhuddleston.com/index.cfm/2008/7/27/Setting-up-a-local-email-testing-server.

Why am I not receiving the e-mail?

▼ You may be receiving the e-mail, but not know it. Be sure to check your e-mail program's spam filter in case it is deciding that the messages coming from the form are spam, which is likely because they probably have a generic subject line, such as form results, and are from an unrecognized address.

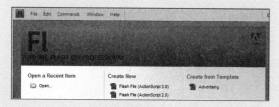

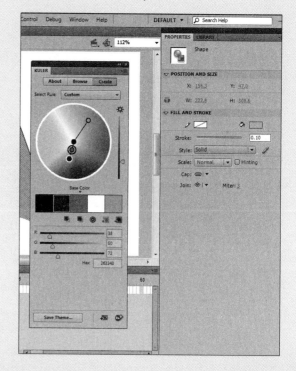

26

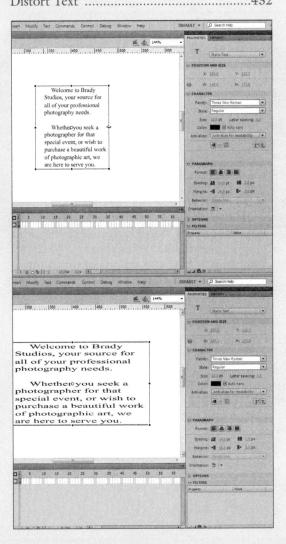

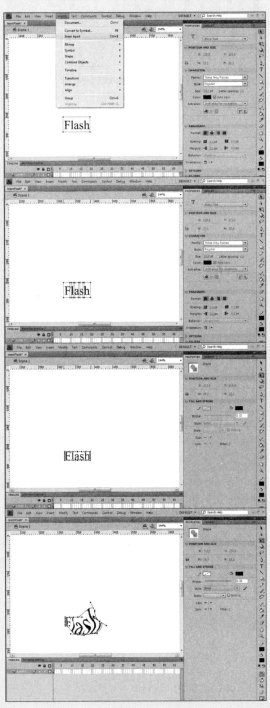

Introducing Flash

Adobe Flash is the industry-standard application for creating animation and playing video on Web sites. It is fairly easy to learn when you are first getting started, but has many powerful features that allow advanced developers to create full Web sites, interactive games, or almost anything else they need.

Flash was originally developed under the name Future Splash. At the time, it was a simple tool for creating animation. Macromedia purchased it in 1997 and changed the name to Flash. Flash was the primary motivation for Adobe to purchase Macromedia in late 2006.

The Flash Platform

Today, Adobe markets a series of products under the Flash Platform. All these products can work together to develop Flash-based applications for a variety of delivery systems. The Flash Platform's two primary applications are Flash CS4 Professional and Flash Player, but the Flash Platform also contains the Flex 3 Platform, several server-based products including the Flash Media Server, and Flash Lite.

Flash CS4 Professional

Flash CS4 Professional is the primary integrated design environment (IDE) for developing Flash movies. When you think of learning Flash or using Flash this refers to learning or using Flash Professional, and it is the application that is discussed through the remainder of this book. Unless stated otherwise, any further references in the text to Flash should be assumed to mean Flash CS4 Professional.

Flash Player

Flash Player is the free application used to view Flash movies. Regardless of the tool used to create a Flash movie, your users actually view and interact with it through Flash Player. Flash Player is the single most-installed software, with current estimates putting it on more than 98 percent of computers worldwide.

As of the release of Flash CS4 Professional, Adobe is also releasing Flash Player 10. Flash Player has enjoyed record-breaking adoption rates, with previous versions averaging 6 million downloads per day.

The Flex Platform

Flex offers a more developer-centric environment than Flash. Flex is an open-source platform that allows developers to create visual layouts in an XML-derived markup language called MXML, and to add interactivity and back-end connectivity through ActionScript 3. Regardless, Flex applications are viewed by the user through Flash Player, and unless the site specifies it, there is no real way to look at a Flash-based site and know whether it was created in Flash Professional or Flex.

Flash Media Server

Flash Media Server allows you to deploy streaming media such as video through Flash Player. Flash Media Server works as an intermediary between a Web server and the browser to deliver the content seamlessly. Any Flash video can be deployed to a Flash Media Server.

Flash Lite

Flash Lite is a version of Flash Player designed specifically for cell phones and other mobile devices. Many new cell phones allow their users to play games created in Flash and deployed to Flash Lite; some new phones even use Flash for all of the menus and other interface elements. You can test Flash applications in Flash Lite using a tool called Device Central, which is included with Flash Professional.

Vector Art

Flash uses vector art to create graphics. Traditional graphics applications and formats such as JPG and GIF are known as raster or bitmap art. These images are made up of pixels. If you think of your computer screen as a large sheet of graph paper, each square of the graph represents a pixel. By filling in each square with a color, you can create full-color images.

However, raster images are dependent on the resolution at which they were created. In order to double the size of the image, each colored pixel needs to expand to fill four squares, or pixels; quadrupling the size of the image forces each pixel to fill eight pixels, and so on. Eventually, these ever-expanding squares will be noticeable in the image, causing the file to become *pixelated*. In addition, each of these size increases has a proportional impact on file size: Doubling the pixel dimensions of an image roughly quadruples the file size. It is therefore impossible to resize a raster-based image without affecting the file size and quality.

Vector programs take a radically different approach. Rather than filling in squares, you create vector art by defining points and then having the program use mathematical algorithms to calculate a line or path between the points. The path can be either straight or curved, and the space between the points can be filled with color. In a vector image, resizing is accomplished by moving the two points either farther apart or closer together, and having the program recalculate the math. Therefore, you can freely resize vector images without impacting either the file size or the quality of the image.

Most graphics programs today lean toward being either vector based, such as Adobe Illustrator, or raster based, such as Adobe Photoshop. Both, however, contain tools to work in the other methodology: Photoshop, for example, contains a set of vector-based tools, while Illustrator contains some tools for editing raster graphics. Flash, on the other hand, is purely vector based, and you will not find any raster-manipulation tools in it. While you can import raster graphics into a Flash movie, and those graphics can be animated, you cannot edit the graphic without first converting it to vector format. The only exception is that raster graphics can be resized in Flash, but as they are raster images, they become pixelated if resized too much.

ActionScript

You can add interactive elements to your Flash movie by using ActionScript. Originally based on JavaScript, ActionScript today is an object-oriented programming language that gives you almost complete control over your movie and its assets.

When creating movies in Flash CS4, you can choose to use ActionScript 2.0 or ActionScript 3.0. Support for version 2.0 is preserved for backward-compatibility, but you will find that most of today's Flash developers have moved onto the much more powerful version 3.0. While ActionScript 3.0 does have a more difficult learning curve, that is more than made up for by the fact that it offers more features and flexibility than ActionScript 2.0. Chapter 35 provides an introduction to ActionScript 3.0.

Navigating the Flash Window

The Flash interface is designed to match that of the other CS4 products, including Dreamweaver. Once you become familiar with the interface in one program, you should be able to navigate the other programs with few problems.

Most of the screen when you first open a Flash movie is taken up by the Stage, which represents your main work area. The large white box in the center shows the visible area of your movie — the portion that will appear to your user in Flash Player — but you can also place objects on the gray area surrounding the Stage.

Wrapping around the Stage are a series of panels. As with other Adobe products, the panels contain controls that allow you to add items to your movie and manipulate them. By default, the panels are organized into three groups, all *docked*, or attached, to the sides of the screen. Panels can be undocked or regrouped as needed; see the section, "Work with Panels," for more details.

As with other programs, Flash also contains a set of menus along the top of the screen. You can also find a menu to switch between the built-in workspaces within Flash, and a search box that provides quick access to the Help files.

Ⓐ Start Screen

Provides a central location to select recently opened files, create new documents in various file types, or create documents from samples.

Ⓑ Menu Bar

Provides access to menus and commands.

Ⓒ Workspace Menu

Allows you to switch between the various workspace layouts in Flash.

Ⓓ Help box

You can search the help files by typing a keyword and pressing Enter.

Ⓔ Panels

Collapsible panels provide most of the functionality in the program.

Ⓕ Collapse to Icons

Collapses the panels to icons.

Ⓖ Tools

Provides you with the tools to create vector art and manipulate objects on the Stage.

Ⓐ Document Tab

Click a tab to switch to other open documents. Click the X to close the document.

Ⓑ Edit bar

Indicates what is currently being edited.

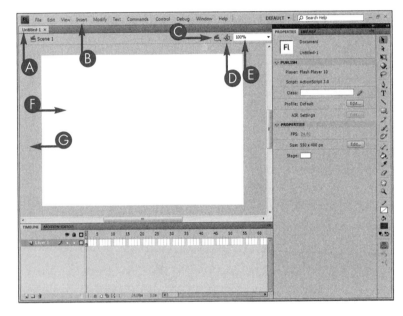

Ⓒ Edit Scene Button

You can click this button to switch between the scenes of your movie.

Ⓓ Edit Symbols Button

Allows you to switch to editing symbols.

Ⓔ Zoom Box

You can zoom in and out on your drawing by selecting a magnification here.

Ⓕ Stage

This is the main area for your movie. Anything inside the white box will appear within the Flash Player window.

Ⓖ Off-Stage Area

You can place objects here to have them *fly into* your Stage.

Create a New Flash Movie

You can create a variety of different types of files in Flash. Most of the time, you will simply create a new Flash file, using either ActionScript 3.0 or ActionScript 2.0. See Chapter 35 for more information on ActionScript and a detailed discussion of the differences between versions.

You can also create a movie to be deployed to Adobe AIR or a mobile device. Adobe AIR, which stands for the Adobe Integrated Runtime, is a technology that allows you to create applications using a variety of technologies, including but not limited to Flash, and have it run as an independent desktop application.

You can read more about AIR at www.adobe.com/products/air/.

You can create an ActionScript file, which only contains programming code instead of the normal graphical objects you place in regular Flash movies; an ActionScript Communication File, which is used to enable your movies to get and send data with external resources; a Flash JavaScript file, which enables your Flash movies to access the user's local hard drive; and a Flash project, which is nothing more than a collection of related Flash files and assets.

Create a New Flash Movie

1 Open Adobe Flash CS4 Professional.

2 Click Flash File (ActionScript 3.0).

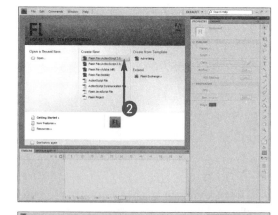

A new, blank document opens.

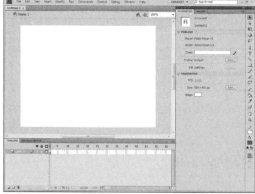

Save a Flash Movie

Y ou should get into the habit of saving your work at frequent intervals. That way, if Flash or your computer should crash, you will not lose too much of your work.

When working on Flash movies, you will end up dealing with two different file formats. The documents you create in Flash have a .fla extension, while published movies use .swf. The first, FLA, is an editable file format — you use this document to make changes to your existing files or create new

ones. The other, SWF, is not editable and is designed to be played in Flash Player. Flash Professional cannot read SWF files, and Flash Player cannot read FLA files.

When you save a file in Flash, you are creating an FLA file. You can give it any name you want. You can also save it to any folder you want on your computer. Because you do not upload the FLA file to your Web site, it does not need to reside in the same folder as your Web pages.

Save a Flash Movie

① Click File.

② Click Save As.

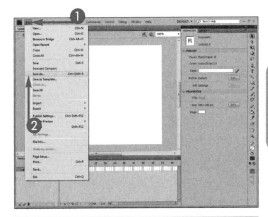

The Save As dialog box appears.

③ Select the folder into which you will save your file.

④ Type a filename.

⑤ Click Save.

The file is saved.

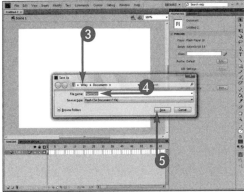

Set the Stage Size

The *Stage* in a Flash movie is the area that is visible in Flash Player. Therefore, the size of the Stage determines the size of the movie.

The default Stage size for Flash movies is 550 pixels by 400 pixels. You can use the Document Properties dialog box to change the size if you need your movie to use different dimensions. The minimum size you can set is 1x1, and the maximum is 2880x2880. You can even use decimals, and so it is possible to create a movie that is, for exapmle, 600.5x400.3.

You can also have the Document Properties dialog box set the Stage to match the printer, which uses the

maximum printable area allowed by your system's default printer. You can reset the dimensions to the default 550x400, or you can have the Stage resize to fit all of the content you currently have in your document.

Flash defaults to using pixels for measurement, as there is an assumption that the documents you produce in Flash will always be run on a computer screen. However, you can set the rulers to use inches, points, centimeters, or millimeters.

Set the Stage Size

1 Click Modify.

2 Click Document.

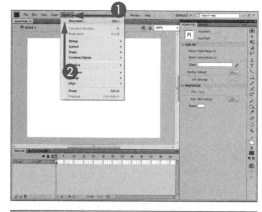

The Document Properties dialog box appears.

3 Type new dimensions for the movie.

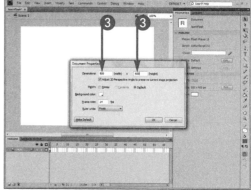

● Optionally, you can click Printer in
the Match section.

4 Click OK.

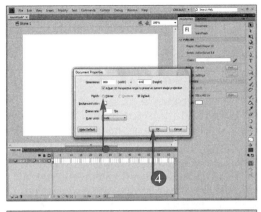

● The Stage resizes to the new
dimensions.

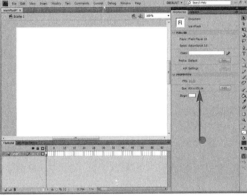

**Can I have Flash remember my new
measurements for other documents?**

▼ Yes. You can click the Make Default button
in the Document Properties dialog box to
save your new dimensions as the default.
Any Flash documents you create from then
on will use those measurements.

What is the Frame Rate setting for?

▼ The Frame Rate setting determines the
speed at which Flash plays movies and is
an important aspect of animation. Frame
rate is discussed in more detail in
Chapter 29.

Work with Panels

Y ou can access most of the features of Flash through panels along the sides of the window. Each panel provides a specific set of functions, and related panels are grouped together.

You can expand or collapse a panel by double-clicking the tab that contains the panel's name. When in a panel group, individual panels can be accessed by clicking the tabs. You can move panels to other locations on the screen or into other groups by dragging their tabs.

The set of panels that runs along the right edge of the screen can be collapsed to icons with labels so that they take up very little room, a feature that is particularly handy for designers working on small screens. The set can be further resized to show only icons. Once the panels have been collapsed to icons, you can access a panel temporarily by clicking its icon. The panel collapses again as soon as you click elsewhere on the screen. The Window menu provides a list of every panel available in Flash, and allows you to open panels that are not currently visible.

Work with Panels

① Click Window.

Flash displays a check mark next to each panel that is currently open.

② Double-click a panel's tab to expand or collapse it.

The panel expands to show its features, or collapses, depending on what you selected in step 2.

③ Click the Collapse to Icons button.

The main panel set collapses to show icons and labels.

④ Drag the left edge of the icons to the right.

The icons collapse further, hiding the labels.

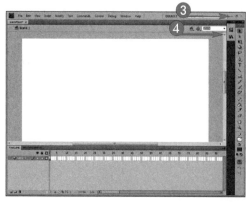

⑤ Click the Expand Panels button.

The panel set expands.

⑥ Click Window.

⑦ Click Behaviors.

The Behaviors panel opens.

⑧ Click-and-drag the Behaviors to the bottom of the Properties panel.

The panel docks at the bottom of the panel set.

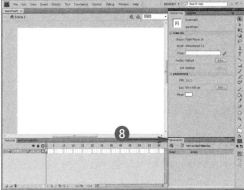

Can I quickly show or hide all of the panels at once?

▼ Yes. Simply press the F4 key on your keyboard to hide all of the panels. Pressing F4 a second time brings them all back in the positions in which they were when you closed them.

Is it possible to hide all of the panels and then have them simply appear when I need them?

▼ Yes. If you hide all of the panels using the F4 keyboard shortcut, you see a gray bar where the panels were. If you simply mouse over that bar, the panels in that area reappear, and then disappear again when you move your mouse away from them.

Can I put panels on the other side of the screen?

▼ Yes. You can drag panels to any edge of the screen. When you see a thin, blue line appear, release your mouse and the panel docks along that edge. You can also have two columns of panels along either the right or left edge, or two rows along the top or bottom.

Switch Workspaces

Flash provides a set of panel layouts called *workspaces*. You can use the workspace menu in the upper-right corner of the screen to switch between workspaces whenever you want.

Five workspaces are available by default in the program. *Essentials*, the default, displays those panels most likely to be used by the widest variety of Flash designers: the Properties and Library panels, the Tools, and the Timeline and Motion Editor panels.

Classic displays the same set of panels as Essentials, without the Library, but places the Timeline and Motion Editor along the top of the screen and the Tools along the left edge, as they were in older versions.

Debug prepares you to work with ActionScript-heavy files by hiding all of the normal panels and displaying only the Debug Console, Variables, and Output panels.

The *Design* layout places the Tools and Properties panels on the left, the Timeline along the top, and the Library, Align, Info, Transform, Color, and Swatches panels along the right edge.

The *Developer* workspace places the Properties on the right, the Project, Components, and Library panels on the left, and the Compiler Errors and Output panels at the bottom, with the Tools along the top.

Switch Workspaces

① Click Default to access the Workspace menu.

② Select Designer.

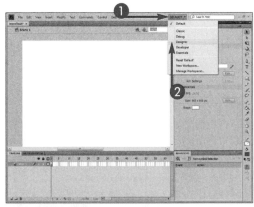

Flash rearranges the panels.

③ From the Workspace menu, click Classic.

The panels are rearranged.

④ Click-and-drag the Tools panel into the middle of the screen.

● The panel floats on the screen.

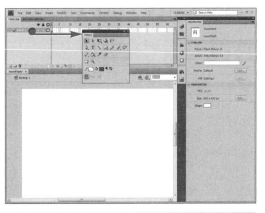

⑤ From the Workspace menu, click Reset 'Classic'.

The panel layout is restored.

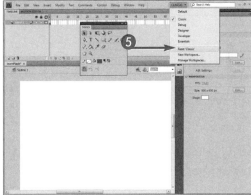

Can I create my own workspaces?

▼ Yes. You should begin by selecting the pre-installed workspace that has the panel arrangement closest to the one you want. Then, you can move panels to other locations on the screen, close those panels you are not using, or open and position additional panels. Once you have the panel arrangement you want, you can click the workspace menu, choose New Workspace, and then give it a logical name. It then appears with the other workspaces so that you can switch to it whenever you want.

Can I delete workspaces?

▼ You cannot delete any of the workspaces that are preinstalled with Flash, but you can rename or delete workspaces that you create by clicking the workspace menu and selecting Manage Workspaces. This displays a dialog box that lists all of the workspaces you have created. When you select one, you can rename or delete it.

View Rulers and Grids

You can draw with more precision by showing the rulers and grids in Flash. Neither appears in the final published movie; they are both designed to help while you create the movie.

The rulers appear along the top and left edge of the Stage. The unit of measurement displayed on the rulers is set in the Document Properties dialog box; by default, it uses pixels.

The grid displays as a light gray set of squares on the Stage. They are set to 10 pixels on a side by default.

You can edit both the color and size of the boxes in the grid by clicking View, then clicking Grid, and then clicking Edit Grid. If you have mostly gray objects on your Stage, you might want to pick a different color so that the grid stands out better. You can make the grid contain nonsquare boxes by setting the width and height to different numbers.

As you draw objects, your mouse pointer can snap to the nearest grid or ruler marker. You must turn this feature on by clicking the View menu, then clicking Snapping, and then clicking Snap to Grid.

View Rulers and Grids

① Click View.

② Click Rulers.

The rulers appear.

③ Click View.

④ Click Grid.

⑤ Click Show Grid.

The grid displays.

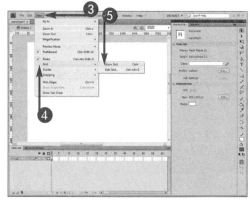

Add Guides

You can place guides on your Stage to help you align and position objects. Any number of guides can be added to a single movie. You can create either horizontal or vertical guides, and place them wherever you want.

By default, guides display as a thin, light-blue line. You can change this color by clicking View, then clicking Guides, and then clicking Edit Guides.

Once you have a guide in place, you can click-and-drag to reposition it. You can lock the guides on the Stage so that they cannot be moved by clicking View, then clicking Guides, and then clicking Lock

Guides. Locking guides is all-or-nothing: You cannot lock some guides while others remain unlocked.

As you draw and move objects on the Stage, they snap to the nearest guide. Unlike grid snapping, which is disabled by default, guide snapping is turned on by default. You can turn it off if you want by selecting View, then clicking Snapping, and then clicking Snap to Guides.

If you have placed guides on the Stage that you no longer need, you can delete them. You can click View, then click Guides, and then click Clear Guides. Individual guides cannot be deleted.

Add Guides

Note: You must have rulers turned on to add guides. See the previous section to learn how to turn on rulers.

① Press and hold your mouse button on a ruler.

② Drag to the place on the Stage where you want to position the guide.

③ Release your mouse button.

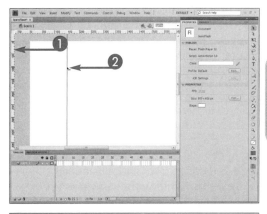

● The guide is placed.

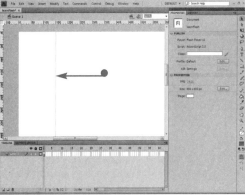

Introducing Flash Objects

Flash includes a set of powerful drawing tools that allow you to create your own art for your movies. All drawings that you create in Flash are vector based, and so they are made up of *strokes* (lines) and *fills* (the color between lines in a closed shape). When you combine strokes and fills into a shape, you create *objects*. You can use the tools on the Tools panel to create these objects.

If you have worked with other vector-based drawing applications such as Adobe Illustrator or Adobe Fireworks, the tools in Flash will be familiar. For example, Flash includes a pencil tool to draw free-form strokes and a brush tool for painting fills. You can combine objects together to create more complex artwork. After an object is drawn, you can change its color, position, or scale.

Drawing Models

Since its early days, Flash has taken a unique approach to an object that contains both a stroke and a fill. Rather than treating it as a single object, Flash has traditionally kept the stroke and fill separate. This makes it very easy to modify one without affecting the other, or even delete the fill while leaving the line in place, or vice versa. Those who are first introduced to computer drawing can find this an extremely useful and powerful feature, but those who come to Flash from other applications may find it confusing and frustrating.

Therefore, you have the choice to draw objects in one of two models. The Merge Drawing model is the default and the way that Flash has always worked: Strokes and fills are kept as separate items. When you want to move or resize both together, you need to select both.

The Object Drawing model, on the other hand, causes Flash to behave more like other applications. In this model, Flash automatically groups the stroke and the fill when you draw an object. While it is still possible to modify them separately, it takes more effort than in the Merge Drawing model. However, when using the Object Drawing model, you do not need to worry about selecting both the stroke and fill when moving or resizing objects, as they are grouped together.

You can freely switch between the models as you draw shapes, and so you can have shapes that are drawn in the Merge Drawing model in the same movie as shapes drawn with the Object Drawing model. Each time you select a tool from the Tools panel that draws an object, you can choose which model to use. Also, you can manually group shapes drawn in the Merge Drawing model so that they behave as though they were drawn as objects, and you can ungroup shapes drawn as objects so that they behave as though they were drawn in the Merge Drawing model.

Drawing Preferences

Drawing with a mouse on a computer can be difficult. Many graphic designers instead rely on a graphic tablet and pen, but even so, anyone who is not a professional artist may find it hard to draw by hand with precision. Flash can make this process easier with its drawing tools.

Flash includes a feature called Shape Recognition. While it is disabled by default, if turned on, it attempts to recognize what you draw and converts it into more precise shapes. Therefore, if you draw something fairly circular, Flash converts the shape to a smooth circle or oval. If you draw a shape with straight lines on four sides, even if they do not line up, Flash converts it to a rectangle.

You can also get Flash to automatically connect lines that end close to one another, smooth rough curves, and perform other optional functions. These settings can all be found in the Preferences dialog box by selecting Preferences under the Edit menu.

Import Graphics

In addition to drawing your own art, you can import graphics created in other programs into Flash. Imported graphics can be positioned and scaled freely on the Stage, but you should keep in mind that Flash does not contain any raster-editing tools, and so while you can draw on imported raster or bitmap shapes, you cannot manipulate their pixels directly. You can import a variety of raster formats. You can also import graphics directly from other Adobe products. Native Photoshop PSD files and native Illustrator AI files can be imported directly into Flash. These imported files maintain their layers, and Flash contains many of the same layer effects that you find in Photoshop and Illustrator.

You should consider that importing graphics increases the size of your Flash movie file. Flash does compress imported graphics, and so you do not get a one-to-one file size increase; for example, importing a 500-kilobyte file does not increase the size of the final Flash movie by 500 kilobytes. However, it still increases the file size by more than a comparable vector-based drawing would.

You can convert raster graphics to vector art, although the nature of the two formats means that your art's appearance will change. Converting raster to vector art, and importing raster art in general, is covered later in this chapter.

Reusing Artwork

You can reuse artwork in your Flash file throughout your movie. Whether the art is something that you drew yourself using the Flash tools or an imported graphic, you can convert the artwork to a symbol. When you do this, Flash needs to only keep one copy of the artwork in the file, regardless of the number of times it is actually used. Symbols are also a key to creating animation in Flash. All symbols are stored in the Flash library. Converting art to symbols and using the library are covered in Chapter 28, and animating with symbols is covered in Chapter 29.

PART V

Using the Tools Panel

Y ou can use the tools found on the Tools panel to draw, modify, and edit objects. The drawings you create in Flash are composed of strokes, the lines or borders around shapes, and fills, the colors that fill the space between lines. The Tools panel includes tools that allow you to create simple shapes such as lines, rectangles, and ovals, or more complex shapes involving layers, grouped elements, and more.

Tools Panel

Ⓐ Selection

Also referred to as the Pointer or Arrow tool, the Selection tool is used to select and move items on the Stage.

Ⓓ 3D Rotation

You can rotate three-dimensional objects with this tool.

Ⓔ Lasso

You can make freeform selections by dragging an area on the Stage.

Ⓕ Pen

The Pen tool allows you to create precise lines and curves. When you click and hold on this tool, you can access the Delete Anchor Point, Add Anchor Point, and Convert Anchor Point tools.

Ⓖ Text

Use this tool to create and edit text.

Ⓗ Line

This tool is for drawing simple, straight lines.

Ⓑ Subselection

The Subselection tool allows you to select and modify specific points along a vector path.

Ⓜ Bone

The Bone tool is used to create Inverse Kinematic animation effects. Press and hold to access the Bind tool.

Ⓞ Eyedropper

Click an object on the Stage with the Eyedropper tool to sample its color and set it as the foreground color.

Ⓒ Free Transform

Use this tool to scale, rotate, skew, and distort objects. The Gradient Transform tool, which allows you to modify gradients, can be accessed by pressing and holding your mouse down on the Free Transform tool.

Ⓘ Rectangle

The Rectangle tool is used to draw rectangles, which have both a stroke and a fill. Press and hold to access the Oval tool, the Rectangle Primitive tool, the Oval Primitive tool, and the PolyStar tool, which is used to create polygons and stars.

Ⓙ Pencil

You can draw freeform strokes with this tool.

Ⓚ Brush

Use the Brush tool to paint fills. You can press and hold to access the Spray Brush tool.

Ⓛ Deco

Fill effects can be created with the Deco tool.

Ⓝ Paint Bucket

You can paint or change fills by clicking in an enclosed area with the Paint Bucket tool. Press and hold to access the Ink Bottle tool, which is used to paint or change fills.

Ⓟ Eraser

The Eraser tool can be used to erase fills or individual segments of paths.

Using the View Tools

You can use the tools in the view section of the Tools panel to change your view of the Stage. The view tools include the Hand tool and the Zoom tool.

The Hand tool can be used to pan around on the Stage. After you select the Hand tool, you can click and drag on the Stage to pan to another area.

You can use the Zoom tool to magnify your view. Once you select it, you can click the Stage to zoom in, and press and hold the Alt or Option key on your keyboard and click to zoom out. You can also click-and-drag on the Stage to define an area; when you release your mouse, Flash zooms to a sufficient magnification to fill the screen with the selected area.

You can double-click the Zoom tool to quickly return to 100 percent magnification. You can double-click the Hand tool to quickly switch to the Fit in Window view, in which Flash determines the magnification necessary to display the Stage completely in the window.

The top-right corner of the main window also contains a drop-down menu of magnifications. You can select a setting from this menu to go to a particular magnification.

Using the Color Tools

You can use the Color tools to define stroke and fill colors that are used when you draw objects with any of the other tools. You can press and hold your mouse button on the color square next to the Pencil tool to select a stroke color, or next to the Ink Bottle tool to select a fill color. By default, a palette displays, allowing you to select from one of 228 colors. In the top-right corner of the palette, there is a white square with a red line through it: use this square to set the color to none. Next to that, you can click the small, colored circle to display another palette with a complete color spectrum. Along the bottom of the palette is a set of seven gradients.

Immediately below the fill color picker is a small icon with two overlapping squares. You can click this to reset the default colors, which are a black stroke and white fill. Finally, to the right of that button is a button that, when clicked, swaps your current fill and stroke colors with one another.

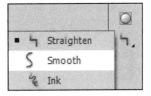

Using the Tool Options

The last section of the Tools panel is a dynamic area that presents additional options for the currently selected tool. The options that display here vary, depending on the current tool. For example, the Subselection tool has no options, and so this area is blank when it is selected, whereas selecting the Brush tool gives you an option to turn the Object Drawing model on or off, lock the fill, set the brush mode, and change the size and shape of the brush.

Draw Line Segments

Y ou can use lines to draw all sorts of objects that you use in your Flash movies and projects. Lines, called strokes in Flash, can connect other lines and shapes to create an image or new shape.

The easiest way to draw straight lines in Flash is to use the Line tool; you control where the line starts and ends. To draw a freeform line, use the Pencil tool.

The Pencil tool has three pencil modes that control how a line is drawn: Straighten, Smooth, or Ink. By selecting the Straighten mode, any line you draw on

the Stage straightens itself after you release the mouse button. By selecting the Smooth mode, your curved lines appear smooth. By selecting the Ink mode, the line you draw stays as is; no straightening or smoothing occurs.

The tool you choose to draw a line segment depends on the outcome you expect to create. You can use the Line tool for drawing objects or shapes with edges. You can use the Pencil tool to create curves. You can also draw curved lines using the Pen tool, as shown in the next section, "Draw with the Pen Tool."

Draw a straight line

① Click the Line tool.

② Position the mouse pointer over the Stage.

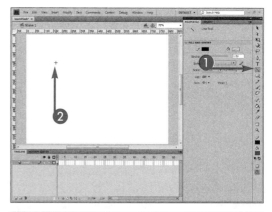

③ Click-and-drag to draw a line to the desired length.

④ Release the mouse button.

The line appears to your specifications.

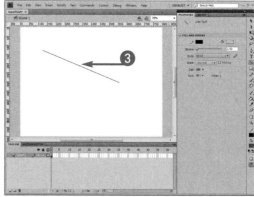

Draw a freeform line

1. Click the Pencil tool.
2. Click a pencil mode.

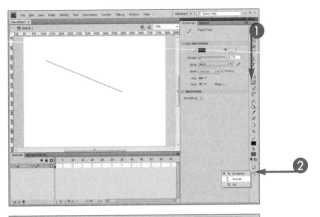

3. Click-and-drag your cursor on the Stage to draw the line.
4. Release the mouse button.

   The line appears to your specifications.

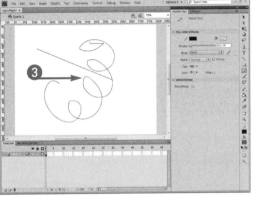

How do I control line thickness?

▼ You can set line thickness before you start drawing a line. The Property Inspector displays options for controlling line thickness, style, and color. To change the thickness, drag the Stroke height slider left or right. You can apply a new line thickness to an existing line by selecting the line with the Selection tool and then adjusting the slider.

When I draw with the Line tool, why does Flash connect the lines?

▼ You may have the Snap to Objects option selected. You can turn this option on and off by clicking the button that looks like a magnet, in the Tool Options section of the Tools panel.

How do I keep a straight line vertical or horizontal?

▼ You can press and hold the Shift key while drawing a line to constrain it. While holding the Shift key, lines you draw are perfectly horizontal, perfectly vertical, or at a 45-degree angle.

Can I use rulers, guides, and grid lines to help me to draw?

▼ Yes, Flash has several features to help you draw: rulers, gridlines, and guides. To turn the rulers on, click View and then click Rulers. Horizontal and vertical rulers appear along the top and left edges of the workspace. To place guides on the Stage, click the vertical or horizontal ruler and drag your mouse toward the Stage. To turn on the grid, click View, then click Grid, and then click Show Grid.

Draw with the Pen Tool

You can draw straight lines and smooth curves by using the Pen tool. This tool can be difficult to use at first, but becomes easier with practice. If you have experience with the Pen tool in other graphics programs such as Adobe Illustrator, you will find that the tool in Flash is very similar.

You can create curves by clicking and dragging with the Pen tool. However, unlike other drawing tools, you do not attempt to trace the path of the curve. Instead, you are defining a pair of control handles. You click at the point at which you want the curve to begin, and

then drag straight away from there in the general direction in which you want the curve to go. Then, release your mouse and move to the point where you want the curve to end. Click here and drag again, but this time drag in the opposite direction of the first drag.

Lines you create with the Pen tool are composed of points. The points appear as dots on the line segment and represent changes in the line's curve. To keep adding to the line, continue clicking away from the end of the line.

Draw with the Pen Tool

1 Click the Pen tool.

2 Position the mouse pointer over the Stage.

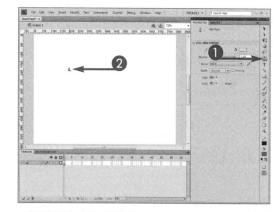

3 Click-and-drag.

● The first anchor point appears.

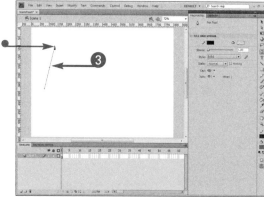

④ Stop dragging and release the mouse button.

⑤ Click and hold the mouse button as you drag from where you want the line to end.

You can rotate the control bar by dragging the mouse pointer to achieve the bend and line length you want for the curve.

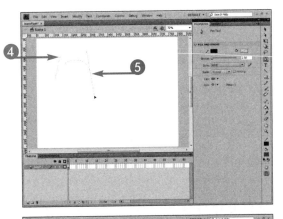

⑥ Release the mouse button.

The final curved line appears on the Stage.

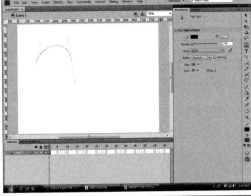

Can I draw straight lines with the Pen tool?

▼ Yes. To create a straight line with the Pen tool, you simply click where you want the line to begin. Then, move to the point where you want the line to end and click again. Note that you do not hold down the mouse button — you simply click to create a point at the beginning of the line, and click again at the end of the line.

Can I customize the Pen tool?

▼ Click Edit and then click Preferences (Mac users click Flash and then click Preferences) to open the Preferences dialog box. In the Category list box, click Drawing. The Pen tool options appear at the top of the dialog box. Click Show Pen Preview if you want to see the resulting line segment as you draw. Click Show Solid Points if you prefer to see line points as solid dots. Click Show Precise Cursors to change the tool's pointer icon to cross hairs. Click OK to exit.

How can I edit the points of a stroke?

▼ You can use the Subselection tool to make changes to strokes you have created with drawing tools. Click the Subselection tool and position the mouse pointer over an edit point, or handle, on the line or at the end of the line. Drag to reposition and reshape the line or curve.

Draw Shapes

Y
ou can use shapes to create drawings, buttons, and other graphic objects in Flash. You can create shapes using many of the tools found on the Tools panel, but for more uniform shapes, such as circles, ovals, squares, rectangles, and polygons, you can use the shape tools.

Flash offers five different shape tools: Rectangle, Oval, Rectangle Primitive, Oval Primitive, and PolyStar, all of which share space on the Tools panel. The Rectangle tool can create square or rectangular shapes, and the Oval tool can create oval or circular shapes.

Objects you draw with the Oval, Rectangle, and PolyStar tools consist of a stroke and a fill. Unless you turn on the Object Drawing model, the stroke and fill are separate objects, and so if you move the stroke, for example, the fill remains in place on the Stage.

You can use the PolyStar tool to draw multisided shapes (polygons) or stars. With any shape tool you select, the Property Inspector displays related options for fine-tuning the shape, such as controlling the corner radius and line style.

Draw Shapes

Draw a stroked shape

① Click the shape tool of your choice.

Click Rectangle Tool to draw a square or rectangle.

Click Oval Tool to draw an oval.

Click Rectangle Primitive Tool to draw a rectangle with a combined stroke and fill.

Click Oval Primitive Tool to draw an oval with a combined stroke and fill.

Click PolyStar Tool to draw a polygon.

Note: *Flash always displays the button for the last shape tool you used.*

② Click the Fill Color icon.

③ Click the No Color icon.

④ Click-and-drag to draw the shape you want.

Note: *To draw a perfect circle or square, press and hold Shift as you draw the shape.*

Flash creates the shape.

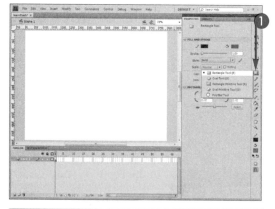

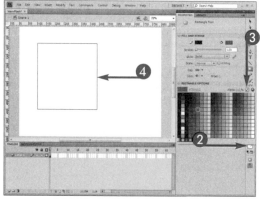

Draw a filled shape

1 Click the shape tool of your choice.

2 Click the Fill Color icon.

The Fill Color palette opens.

3 Click a fill color.

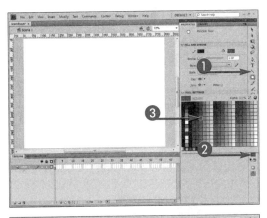

4 Click-and-drag to draw the shape.

Note: To draw a perfect circle or square, press and hold Shift as you draw the shape.

5 Release the mouse button.

Flash creates the filled shape.

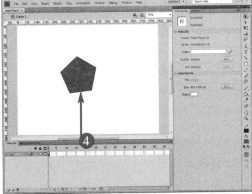

Can I automatically create a rectangle or oval of a predetermined size?

▼ Yes. You can use the Rectangle Settings or Oval Settings dialog box to create rectangles and ovals of a preset size. In the Rectangle Settings dialog box, you can also specify a corner radius. To open the Rectangle or Oval Settings dialog box, click the Rectangle or Oval tool and then Alt-click or Option-click the Stage. The Settings dialog box appears. Type the desired width, height, and, if applicable, the radius. When you click OK, Flash places the oval or rectangle at the location you clicked on the Stage.

How do I draw a rectangle with rounded corners?

▼ Click the Rectangle tool and display the Property Inspector panel. You can then type a radius setting in the Rectangle Corner Radius box or drag the slider to the setting you want. To draw regular corners again, type **0** as the radius setting.

How do I use the Oval Primitive and Rectangle Primitive tools?

▼ When you draw a rectangle with the Rectangle Primitive tool, you see small dots at each corner. Using the Selection tool, you can drag any of these dots to create a rectangle with rounded corners. The Oval Primitive tool creates an oval with similar dots; dragging them allows you to create an oval with a missing section.

PART V

Draw Objects with the Brush Tool

You can use the Brush tool to draw fills, much like a paintbrush. You can control the size and shape of the brush, as well as how the brush strokes appear on the Stage.

The Brush tool is handy when you want to draw varying sizes of freeform shapes on the Stage. You can choose a specific color to use with the Brush tool by first selecting a color for the fill.

After you select the Brush tool, several Brush tool modifiers appear in the Options tray at the bottom of

the Tools panel. You can use the Brush Shape modifiers to change the brush shape and the Brush Size modifiers to change the brush size. For example, you can use some of the brush shapes to create calligraphy effects, and you can modify the sizes to create large brush strokes or small brush strokes. With the Brush Mode modifier, you can choose to paint behind or in front of an existing shape on the Stage. Be sure to test all the Brush tool modifiers to see the interesting effects you can create.

Draw Objects with the Brush Tool

1 Click the Brush tool.

2 Click the Fill Color icon.

The Fill Color palette opens.

3 Click a fill color.

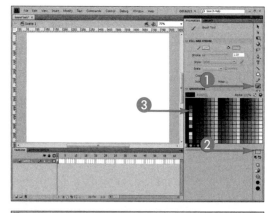

4 Select a brush size.

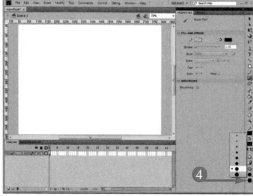

⑤ Select a brush shape.

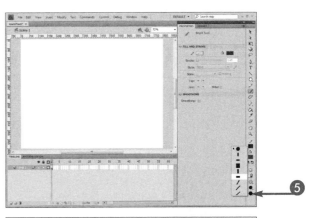

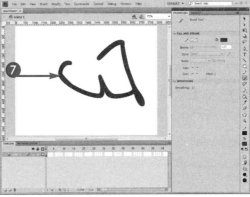

⑥ Position your mouse pointer over the Stage.

The mouse pointer takes on the brush size and shape you selected.

⑦ Click-and-drag to begin drawing.

Flash creates a brush fill as you draw.

What do the brush modes do?

▼ You find the five brush modes by clicking the Brush Mode modifier at the bottom of the Tools panel. *Paint Normal* lets you paint over anything on the Stage. *Paint Fills* paints inside fills but not on strokes. *Paint Behind* paints beneath existing objects on the Stage. *Paint Selection* paints only inside the selected area. If strokes surround an area, *Paint Inside* paints only inside the area in which the brush stroke begins.

How do I use the Brush tool with a pressure-sensitive tablet?

▼ If you use a pressure-sensitive tablet to draw, you see an extra modifier for the Brush tool at the bottom of the Tools panel. Use the Pressure modifier to activate a finer degree of sensitivity in the Brush tool when drawing. You can toggle this feature on or off.

Can I smooth and straighten objects drawn with the Brush tool?

▼ Yes. Objects you draw with the Brush tool are fills. When you use the Selection tool to select a fill, the Smooth and Straighten options become available to you on the Options tray. You can use these options to smooth and straighten fills.

Change Colors with the Paint Bucket and Ink Bottle Tools

You can use the Paint Bucket tool to fill objects that have no fill, or change the color of an existing fill. You can fill objects with a color or a gradient effect.

The Paint Bucket tool uses the current fill color. When you select a color from the palette, you can then fill the inside of any closed shape with the selected color or gradient. If you try to fill a shape that is not closed or that has gaps in the line segments comprising the shape, then you need to close the gaps before you fill

the shape. Likewise, you cannot use the Paint Bucket tool to add color to the document background. You must set a background color using the Document Properties dialog box.

You can perform similar actions on strokes with the Ink Bottle tool. You need to press and hold your mouse on the Paint Bucket tool to access the Ink Bottle tool. The Ink Bottle tool applies the current stroke color to any line segment that you click with it. It can also be used to apply the thickness of the stroke.

Change Colors with the Paint Bucket and Ink Bottle Tools

① Draw the object you want to fill.

Note: See earlier sections of this chapter to learn how to use the drawing tools.

② Click the Paint Bucket tool.

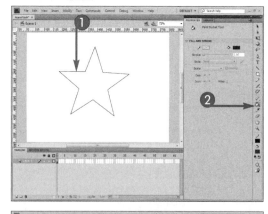

③ Click the Fill Color icon.

The Fill Color palette opens.

④ Click a fill color.

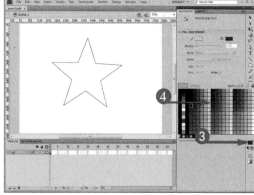

⑤ Click inside the shape you want to fill.

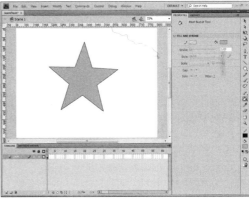

The color fills the shape.

When I select either the Paint Bucket or Ink Bottle tool, I cannot seem to display the properties for the tool in the Properties panel. Why not?

▼ If you have an object selected and then select either of those tools, the Properties panel continues to display the properties of the selected object. To force it to show you the tool properties, you can Ctrl+click any blank area of the Stage.

What does the Gap Size modifier do?

▼ When you select the Paint Bucket tool, the Gap Size modifier appears on the Options tray at the bottom of the Tools panel. Click the Gap Size icon to display a menu list of settings. Normally, the Paint Bucket tool does not fill your object if there are gaps between line segments. The Gap Size modifier determines what types of gaps Flash should close for you, thereby allowing the Paint Bucket tool to create fills. You can have Flash not close any gaps, close small gaps, close medium gaps, or close large gaps. If the gaps are extremely large, then you may have to close them manually.

Using the Object Drawing Model

You can use the Object Drawing model to create an object that automatically has its stroke and fill grouped. By default, the Merge Drawing model is in effect when you draw any element on the Stage, which means the shape or line interacts directly with other shapes and lines. For example, if you have two shapes of the same color and you overlap them on the Stage, the shapes merge and you can no longer separate the shapes.

When you draw by using the Object Drawing model, Flash groups your objects and does not merge shapes.

Each shape you draw is a separate object that you can manipulate without affecting any other object. In the Object Drawing model, as you create your shapes, Flash surrounds them with a rectangular bounding box. You can use the Selection tool to click-and-drag each object around the Stage. To draw by using the Object Drawing model, select the Object Drawing modifier before you begin drawing. You can find the Object Drawing modifier on the Options tray when you select a drawing tool, such as the Pen, Pencil, or Rectangle tool.

Using the Object Drawing model

① Click a drawing tool.

② Click the Object Drawing modifier icon.

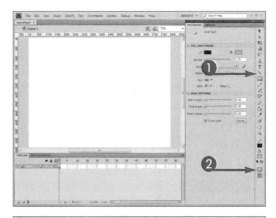

③ Draw the shape you want to create on the Stage.

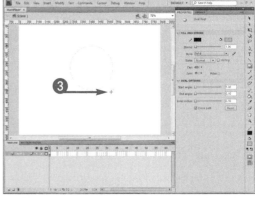

Flash groups the object and displays a bounding box around it.

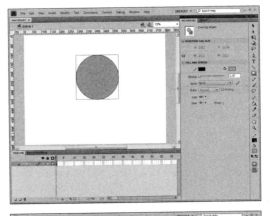

You can move the object and manipulate it without affecting any other graphics on the Stage.

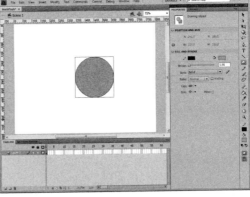

What is grouping and ungrouping?

▼ After you have drawn an object by using the Merge Drawing model, you may want to manipulate the object without worrying about whether it will merge with other objects. To manipulate the object without it merging with other objects, you must group it. Objects you draw by using the Object Drawing model are already grouped.

You can also work on multiple items at the same time by placing the objects in a group. A group enables you to treat several items as a single unit. To create a group, select the objects and then, on the main menu, click Modify, and then click Group. To ungroup objects, on the main menu, click Modify, and then click Ungroup.

How do I edit individual parts of an object drawn with the Object Drawing modifier?

▼ Click the Selection tool, and then double-click the object you want to edit, or click Edit, and then click Edit Selected. Everything on the Stage dims except for the items in the selected group. When you finish editing, double-click anywhere outside the object, or click Edit, and then click Edit All.

How can I avoid changing a group?

▼ If you have grouped objects that you do not want to change as you modify other objects on the Stage, select the objects and click Modify, then click Arrange, and then click Lock. Flash locks the objects and you cannot move or edit them. To unlock the group, click Modify, click Arrange, and then click Unlock.

Import Graphics

You can import graphics, including vector or bitmap graphics, from other sources to use in Flash. You can use imported graphics to add to an existing drawing that you create in Flash and in animations that you build for export to the Web or for other purposes. For example, you may have a product logo created in Adobe Illustrator that you want to place in a Flash document, or you might want to import a photograph in a Flash document. After you import an image, you can manipulate it with Flash commands.

If the original asset contains multiple layers or objects, such as artwork from Illustrator or Photoshop, Flash treats it as a grouped object. For example, if you import a detailed graphic, you can move and resize it as a single object rather than as separate elements.

In addition to importing graphics, you can also use the Paste command to paste graphics that you cut or copy from other programs. The Cut, Copy, and Paste commands work the same way in Flash as they do in other programs.

Import Graphics

Import a graphic file

1 Click File.

2 Click Import.

3 Click Import to Stage.

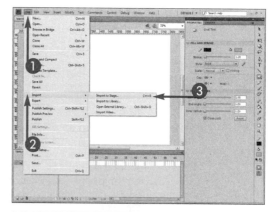

The Import dialog box appears.

4 Navigate to the folder or drive from which you want to import the image.

5 Click the file you want to import.

6 Click Open.

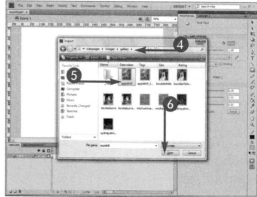

Flash imports the graphic.

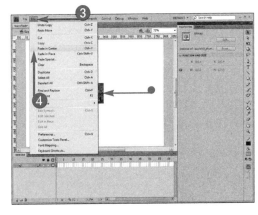

Copy and paste a graphic

1. Copy a graphic from another program.

2. Switch back to Flash.

3. Click Edit.

4. Click Paste in Center.

- Flash pastes the graphic in the center of the Stage.

Can I reuse the same graphic without re-importing each time I need to use it?

▼ Yes. You do not have to repeat the import procedure to reuse the same image. Any time you import a graphic, Flash immediately adds it to the library. You can use the graphic as often as you like. To view the library, click Window and then click Library. To learn more about using library images, see Chapter 28.

Can I import a series of images?

▼ Yes. If you want to include a series of images in sequential frames, such as an animation sequence or a slide show, you can easily import all the files at once. Flash recognizes sequentially numbered files in the Import dialog box and offers to import the entire sequence. Click Yes to import sequential files; click No to import only the selected files.

How do I remove an imported file that I no longer want to include in my movie?

▼ To remove an imported file, open the Library window and delete the file. On the main menu, click Window and then click Library. Click the imported file in the Library list and click the Delete icon. Flash removes the file. To learn more about the Flash Library feature, see Chapter 28.

Convert Bitmaps into Vector Graphics

Y ou can use the Trace Bitmap command to convert a bitmap graphic into a vector graphic. By turning a bitmap graphic into a vector graphic, you can decrease your file size and use the Flash tools to manipulate the graphic. Keep in mind, however, that you almost certainly lose some of the details of the original bitmap image.

When you apply the Trace Bitmap command, you can adjust several parameters that define the rendering of the image, including how Flash handles the color variances, the pixel size translation, and the smoothness of curves or sharpness of corners. These parameters control how closely the bitmap image matches the vector graphic image.

During conversion, Flash examines how the pixels in the bitmap relate to one another. You can specify a color threshold setting that instructs Flash on how to treat bordering pixels of the same or similar colors. A higher color threshold setting groups subtle color changes into a single vector object, thus decreasing the number of overall colors in the image. A lower setting results in more vector objects, and more colors appear in the image. For most images, the default settings work fine.

Convert Bitmaps into Vector Graphics

1 Click the Selection tool.

2 Click the bitmap image to select it.

Note: *See Chapter 25 to learn more about selecting objects.*

3 Click Modify.

4 Click Bitmap.

5 Click Trace Bitmap.

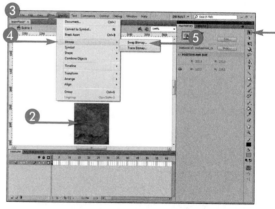

The Trace Bitmap dialog box appears.

6 Type a Color Threshold setting.

Note: *A smaller value results in many vector shapes; a larger value results in fewer vector shapes.*

7 Type a Minimum area.

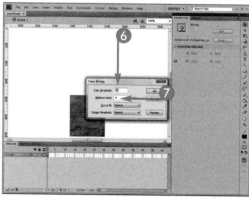

8 Select a curve fit.

9 Select a corner threshold.

10 Click OK.

Flash traces the graphic and, when finished, replaces the bitmap with vector shapes.

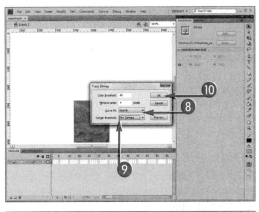

Flash converts your bitmap into a vector graphic.

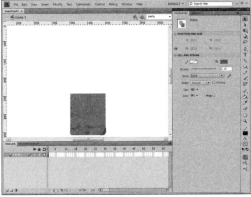

What is the color threshold?

▼ The color threshold determines the number of colors that are converted into vectors. For example, say your image is a boat on water, and the water consists of shades of blue. A high color threshold may result in a single vector object for the water — one shade of blue. A low color threshold may result in dozens of vector objects for the water — one for each shade change in the image. Flash compares the RGB color values for each neighboring pixel. If the difference between the RGB values is less than the color threshold, Flash considers the colors to be the same. You can set the color threshold value to any number between 1 and 500.

What are minimum area, curve fit, and corner threshold?

▼ *Minimum area* sets the number of neighboring pixels to consider when assigning a color to a pixel. Type a value between 1 and 1000. *Curve fit* controls how smoothly outlines are drawn. *Corner threshold* determines whether Flash should smooth edges or retain sharp edges.

Is there an ideal setting for converting a bitmap image to a vector image?

▼ To obtain the most realistic image, Adobe recommends the following settings: color threshold, 10; minimum area, 1 pixel; curve fit, Pixels; and corner threshold, Many corners. When applying the Trace Bitmap controls, you might need to experiment with the settings to get the results you want.

Select Objects with the Selection Tool

Y ou can select objects on the Flash Stage so that you can modify them. For example, you might want to change the color of the stroke outlining a fill or modify the curve of a particular line segment. Or you may want to group several strokes and fills into a single object and save the object as a symbol in your document.

You can use the Selection tool to quickly select any single object, such as a line segment or fill. To select several objects, such as several shapes or an entire

drawing, you can drag a frame, also called a *marquee*, around the items. Flash selects anything inside the marquee. Any edits you make affect all the selected items.

When selecting objects drawn in the Merge Drawing model, you can select both the fill and the stroke separately, or select either individually. If the object is drawn using the Object Drawing model, or if you use the Rectangle Primitive or Oval Primitive tool, then the stroke and fill are automatically grouped and you can only select both together.

Select Objects with the Selection Tool

Click to select objects

1 Click the Selection tool.

Note: *You can select a fill and its surrounding line border by double-clicking the fill.*

2 Position the mouse pointer over the object you want to select, and click.

Selected objects drawn using the Object Drawing model appear selected with a box around the group.

Note: *Selected objects appear highlighted with a pattern.*

Select by dragging

1 Click-and-drag a marquee around the objects you want to select.

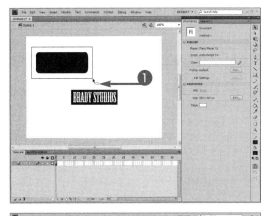

2 Release the mouse button.

● Flash selects everything inside the marquee.

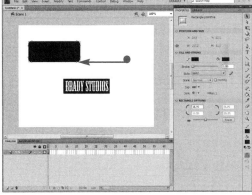

How do I select multiple objects?

▼ To modify multiple objects at the same time, you must select them all. To select multiple objects, click the Selection tool, and then hold down the Shift key as you click each object you want to select. It does not matter which layer contains the object. As you press and hold the Shift key, you can select items on multiple layers.

Is there an easy way to select or deselect everything on every layer of a scene?

▼ Yes. Click Edit, and then click Select All to select everything on every layer of a scene. To deselect everything on every layer of a scene, click Edit, and then click Deselect All.

Can I remove the highlighting from a selected object?

▼ Yes. Removing the highlighting from a selected object enables you to see what the object will look like when you complete your modifications. When you select an object, Flash highlights the object. To remove the highlighting, on the main menu click View and then click Hide Edges. To restore the highlighting, click View and then click Hide Edges again.

Select Objects with the Lasso Tool

I f you are working with several objects that have an unusual shape, or you want to only select a portion of an object, you can use the Lasso tool. The Lasso tool helps you select only what you want and nothing more.

With the Lasso tool, you can draw a freehand selection border around the objects you want to select. Using the Lasso tool with precision takes a steady hand and a bit of practice. However, it is most often used in situations where you do not need a precise shape, but

are instead trying to make a freeform or somewhat random selection shape.

If you make a mistake in your selection, you can simply try again by clicking and dragging with the Lasso tool. You can also select a portion of the shape with the Lasso tool, and then press and hold the Shift key and draw another selection to add to the first. You can even combine the Lasso and Selection tools by making a selection with one and then, while holding the Shift key, making a selection with the other.

Lasso Objects

1 Click the Lasso tool.

2 Click-and-drag the lasso around the objects until you reach the point at which you started.

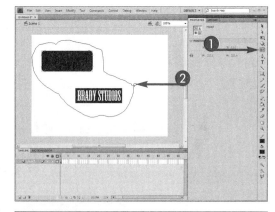

3 Release the mouse button.

● Flash highlights the selected items.

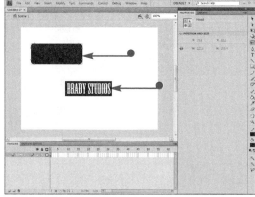

Select part of an object

① Drag the pointer to surround the part of the object you want to select.

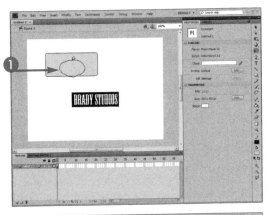

② Release the mouse button.

● Flash selects everything inside the selected area.

How do I use the Polygon Mode option?

▼ You may find it difficult to draw around objects with the Lasso tool. You can use the Lasso tool's Polygon Mode modifier to help. Click the Lasso tool, and then click the Polygon Mode modifier in the Options tray. The Polygon Mode button toggles the feature on or off. Now click your way around the object you want to select. Every click creates a line connected to the last line. When you reach the end of the area you want to select, double-click to complete the selection.

What does the Magic Wand modifier do?

▼ The Magic Wand modifier appears in the Options tray when you select the Lasso tool. You use it with the Lasso tool to help you select areas of an image. Before you can use the Magic Wand modifier on a bitmap image, it must be broken apart. To break apart a bitmap image, click Modify, and then click Break Apart.

Can I customize the Magic Wand settings?

▼ Yes, you can customize the Magic Wand Threshold and the Smoothing settings. Click the Magic Wand Setting icon in the Modifiers tray. The Magic Wand Settings dialog box appears. Use the Threshold setting to define how closely color values of adjacent pixels must match to be included in the lasso selection. Use the Smoothing setting to specify the amount of smoothing Flash should apply to the edges of the selected area.

Format Strokes

You can quickly format or change the attributes of strokes. By default, strokes are one point and solid black. You can control the thickness, style, and color of a stroke by using the formatting controls found in the Property Inspector.

You can also adjust settings for the cap and join. The Cap option determines what Flash places at the end of your stroke. Your choices are None, Round, or Square. The Join option determines how Flash joins strokes. You can select Miter, Round, or Bevel.

You can set the formatting options before you create a stroke, or you can assign formatting to an existing selected stroke. For example, you might want to change the formatting for a particular line segment in a drawing, or you might want to draw a new line that is precisely five points thick and dashed. Use the Property Inspector options to set your formatting.

You can use the options in the Property Inspector to set the formatting of strokes you draw with the Line, Pen, or Pencil tool and any outline you create with the Oval, Rectangle, or PolyStar tool.

Format Strokes

① Click the Selection tool.

② Select the line segment you want to format.

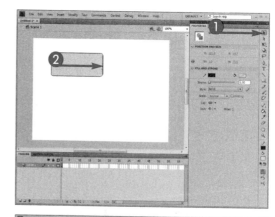

③ Drag the slider to change the stroke thickness.

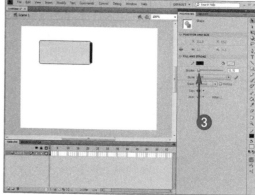

④ Click here and select a style.

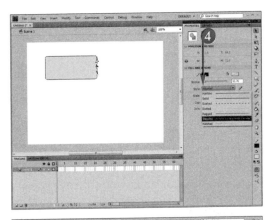

⑤ Click the Stroke color box.

The Color palette opens.

⑥ Click a color in the palette.

The stroke changes to your specifications.

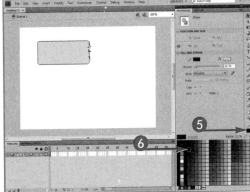

How can I set caps and joins?

▼ You can use the Property Inspector to set the Cap and Join options. When you create a stroke, the Cap option you select determines how the ends of your stroke appear on the Stage. Choosing None causes the ends of your stroke to be blunt. The stroke is square and ends where you stop dragging the tool. Choosing Round adds a round end to your stroke. Choosing Square adds a square end to your stroke.

The Join option determines what appears when two strokes intersect to form a corner. Miter creates a squared-off intersection, Round creates a rounded intersection, and Bevel creates an angled intersection.

Can I create a custom line style to use for my strokes?

▼ Yes. You can customize a stroke using the options in the Stroke Style dialog box. You display the Stroke Style dialog box by clicking Custom in the Property Inspector. This dialog box offers a variety of stroke styles ranging from dots to dashes to waves, thus allowing you to create unique or specialized stroke styles.

How do I select all the strokes on the Stage so that I can change the formatting of every stroke?

▼ Right-click (Ctrl+click) over a line segment, and then click Select All from the pop-up menu. Flash selects everything on the Stage, and any changes you make to the formatting of strokes affect all the strokes in the frame.

Edit Fills

With Flash, you can change a fill shape by adjusting the sides of the fill. A *fill* is a color or pattern that fills a closed outline or shape. Changing the fill color can change the appearance of a shape or object on the Stage. You can also change the fill color at any time.

You can easily adjust the edges of a fill to create new and unusual shapes. The fastest way to change a shape's edge is to drag it. Depending on the direction

you drag, the shape's edge may curve or straighten. If the fill shape includes a stroke, that is modified as well.

In addition to changing the fill's edges, you can also change the color using the Fill Color palette. You can assign a new color or gradient effect. You must, however, select the fill first in order to apply a new color. As long as the fill is highlighted on the Stage, you can continue trying different fill colors from the palette. Each color you select in the palette is immediately applied to the fill.

Edit Fills

Reshape a fill

① Click the Selection tool.

② Position the mouse pointer over the edge of the fill.

Note: Do not select the fill.

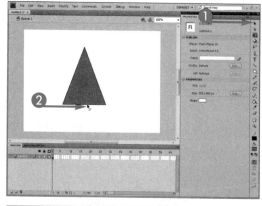

③ Drag the fill's edge in or out to reshape the fill.

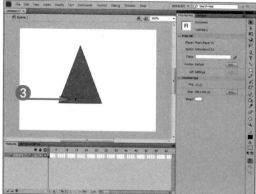

④ Release the mouse button.

● Flash reshapes the fill.

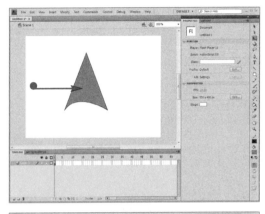

Edit the fill color

① Select the fill you want to edit.

② Click the Fill color icon.

③ Click a color.

The fill immediately shows the new color selection.

Note: To work with gradient fills, see the section, "Work with Gradients."

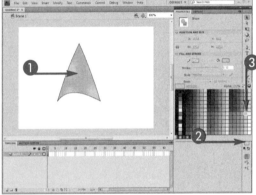

Can I adjust edit points on a fill outline?

▼ Yes. Click the Subselection tool and then click the fill shape's outline stroke. Edit points are displayed on the outline that surrounds the fill. You can then drag an edit point to change the shape of both the outline and the fill itself.

My fill object does not include strokes. Can I add an outline around the fill?

▼ Yes. Click the Ink Bottle tool and then click the edge of the object. To set stroke properties, such as line thickness, before applying the outline, open the Property Inspector and set stroke properties first.

Are there other ways to edit fill shapes?

▼ Yes. On the Modify menu on the main menu bar, you can find additional Shape commands that can help you edit fills. For example, to soften a fill's edges, click Modify, click Shape, and then click Soften Fill Edges. From the Soften Fill Edges dialog box, adjust the settings and click OK. Experiment with the settings to see what sort of effects you can create.

Use Kuler

Adobe released Kuler as a free, hosted Web application in 2008. Kuler allows designers to create color schemes through an intuitive Web site. Designers can save and share their schemes, and others can then apply the colors to their own designs, or modify colors within schemes to suit their needs.

Flash CS4 includes a panel that provides access to Kuler directly within the program. You can display the panel by clicking Window, clicking Extensions, and then clicking Kuler. Users of the online application can

rate schemes, and by default, the Kuler panel in Flash displays the highest-rated schemes, but you can also view them by other criteria, such as Most Popular, Newest, Random, Saved, and Custom. You can limit the results to time frames, including All Time, Last 7 Days, and Last 30 Days. If you know the name of a scheme, you can search for it within the panel.

You can also use the panel to create your own Kuler swatches. You can choose from several color schemes and drag on a simple color wheel to create colors.

Use Kuler

1 Click Window.

2 Click Other Panels.

3 Click kuler.

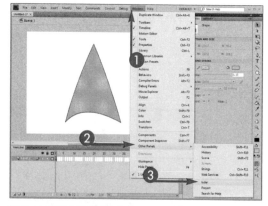

The Kuler panel opens.

4 Click Highest Rated.

5 Click Most Popular.

6 Double-click a set of swatches.

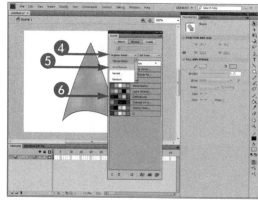

The panel switches to Create mode.

⑦ Select a color from the swatch.

⑧ Drag to modify the color.

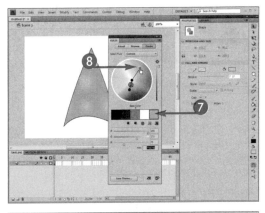

⑨ Click the Add This Theme to Swatches button.

The colors are added to the swatches.

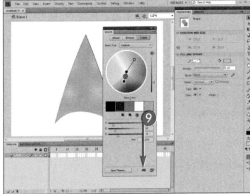

How can I access Kuler online?

▼ The Kuler Web site is at http://kuler.adobe.com. It is free to use, but if you want to upload and save color schemes, you need to sign up for a free account, which you can do directly on the site.

Can I save color schemes that I create in the panel to the Kuler Web site?

▼ Yes. At the very bottom of the panel, there is a button that allows you to upload the scheme to Kuler. You have to have already created an account through the Web site before you can upload.

How do I use the colors from the Kuler panel on my image?

▼ Once you add the theme to your swatches, the theme colors are available from any color picker in the program. For example, you can select them from the Fill color or Stroke color tools.

Can I select colors from an image?

▼ Yes. The Kuler Web site includes a utility that allows you to upload an image. The site then analyzes the image and picks the five most common colors from it to create a scheme, although you can change these colors by selecting other areas of the image.

Turn Bitmaps into Fills

You can turn a bitmap image into a fill for use with Flash drawing tools that use fills, such as the Oval, Rectangle, or Brush tools. Conventional fills include colors and gradients. You can also use a bitmap image, such as a photo, as a fill. Depending on the size of the shape, Flash may *tile*, or repeat, the image within the shape.

Bitmap images of patterns, such as pictures of grass, rocks, or bricks, make good fills that can add depth to your images. Other images, particularly those of

people or nonrepeating shapes, may work well as fills in some situations but not others. You need to experiment with the feature to determine what works best.

To prepare a bitmap image as a fill, you must import the image onto the Stage, and then use the Break Apart command, which converts the image into separate pieces. After you separate the image, you can use the Eyedropper tool to duplicate the image as a fill, or paint with the fill using the Brush tool.

Turn Bitmaps into Fills

1 Select the object you want to edit.

2 Click Modify.

3 Click Break Apart.

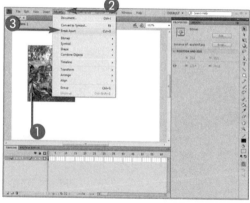

Flash breaks apart the bitmap image.

4 Select the drawing tool of your choice to create a shape to fill.

5 Draw the shape that you want to contain the bitmap fill.

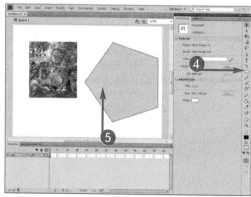

6 Click the Eyedropper tool.

7 Click the bitmap image.

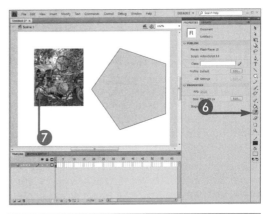

8 Click the object you want to fill.

The bitmap image appears as a fill.

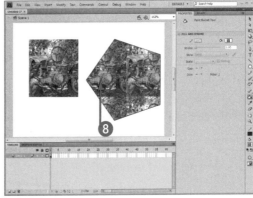

How do I use a bitmap fill with the Brush tool?

▼ Turn the bitmap into a fill using the steps in this section. Click the Brush tool, select a brush size or shape, and then draw brush strokes on the Stage. Everywhere you draw, Flash uses the bitmap image as your paint color.

How do I use a bitmap image as a tiled pattern?

▼ Click the Window menu and then click Color to open the Color panel. In the Type field, choose Bitmap. Select the image you want to use, and then click the Paint Bucket tool. You can now fill any shape with a tiled pattern of the bitmap image.

What types of edits can I perform on a bitmap fill?

▼ You can edit a bitmap fill just as you can any other fill, including rotating the image and scaling it to another size. See the section, "Edit Fills," to learn more about editing Flash fills.

How do I change the position of a bitmap fill?

▼ To change the position of a bitmap fill, use the Gradient Transform tool, which shares space with the Free Transform tool on the Tools panel. You can use the Gradient Transform tool to change the way the fill is positioned within a shape.

PART V

Edit Objects with the Free Transform Tool

You can use the Free Transform tool to alter graphics, groups, text blocks, and instances. Located on the Tools panel, the Free Transform tool includes four modifiers: Scale, Rotate and Skew, Distort, and Envelope.

You can apply the Scale modifier and the Rotate and Skew modifier to objects you create or import. For example, you can use the Scale modifier to change the size of a vector graphic you create in Flash, or you can use the Rotate and Skew modifier to rotate a photograph you import into Flash.

You use the Scale modifier to resize objects by using edit points or handles. The direction in which you drag an edit point determines whether the object grows or shrinks. For example, if you drag any corner edit point, Flash scales the object in proportion to its original size. If you drag a center edit point on any side of the selected object, the object appears to stretch or condense, depending on which way you move your mouse. When you rotate an object, you use rotation handles. You can achieve different degrees of rotation, depending on the amount and direction you drag the rotation handles.

Edit Objects with the Free Transform Tool

Rotate and skew an object

1 Click the Free Transform tool.

2 Click the object you want to edit.

A bounding box with transformation handles appears.

3 Click the Rotate and Skew modifier.

4 Drag a corner handle to rotate the object.

Flash rotates the object.

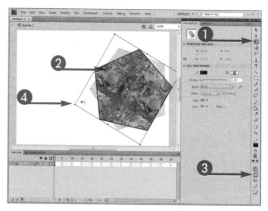

5 Position the mouse pointer over a side handle and drag the handle horizontally or vertically to skew the object.

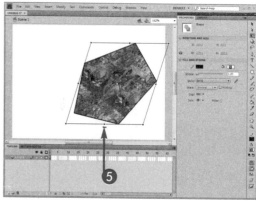

Flash skews the object.

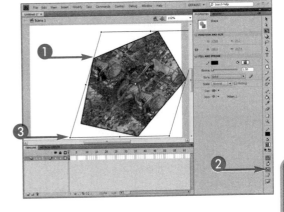

Scale an object

① Select the object you want to edit.

② Click the Scale modifier.

③ Drag a transformation handle outward to enlarge the object, or inward to reduce it.

Flash scales the object.

Can I specify the exact number of degrees I want to rotate my object and the exact percentage I want to scale my object?

▼ Yes. If you want to rotate your object 90 degrees clockwise, select the object and click Modify, click Transform, and then click Rotate 90° CW. If you want to rotate your object 90 degrees counterclockwise, select the object and click Modify, click Transform, and then click Rotate 90° CCW.

You can also select the object and click Modify, click Transform, and then click Scale and Rotate to open the Scale and Rotate dialog box. Enter the exact number of degrees you want to rotate your object in the Rotate field, or enter the percentage by which you want to scale your object in the Scale field.

What is the center point?

▼ When rotating a graphic, group, or text block, and when skewing and scaling instances, the center point is the point of origin. By default, the center point is usually located in the middle of the object. To change the center point, select the object and then click the Free Transform tool. The center point appears as a tiny circle, usually in the middle of the object. To change the center point, drag it to a new location. If you later want to return the center point to its original location, double-click it. When you skew or scale a graphic, group, or text block, the point of origin is the point opposite the point you drag.

Edit Objects with the Free Transform Tool *(Continued)*

You can use the Envelope modifier to change the shape of objects you draw in Flash. The Envelope modifier encloses the object with an envelope of edit points. You can use the edit points to change the object's shape. The Envelope modifier uses two types of edit points: regular edit points and tangent handles. Regular edit points are square, and when manipulated, can change the corners and sides of an object. Tangent handles are circles that adjust additional points along the edges of a selected object.

You can use the Distort modifier to move the corner points of an object in any direction: left, right, up, or down. Holding down the Shift key as you drag a corner handle also moves the adjacent corner proportionately on the same axis. The Distort modifier has side handles that you can move in any direction.

You can only use the Distort and Envelope modifiers to change vector graphics. You cannot use these modifiers to alter grouped objects, bitmaps, symbols, text boxes, or video objects.

After you have applied a transform, you can remove it by clicking Modify, clicking Transform, and then clicking Remove Transform.

Distort an object

① Click the Distort modifier.

② Click-and-drag the mouse pointer.

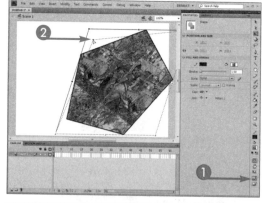

Flash distorts the object.

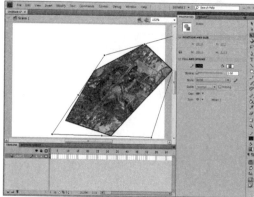

Use the Envelope modifier

1 Click the Envelope modifier.

2 Drag a handle to change the shape of your object.

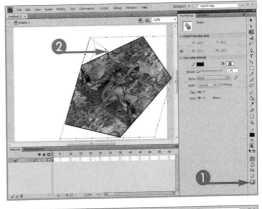

Flash changes the shape of the object.

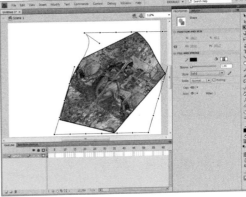

How does the Transform panel work?

▼ You can use the Transform panel to change the size, rotation, or skew of an object you have selected with the Free Transform tool. You open the Transform panel by clicking Window, and then clicking Transform. Then you enter the size change in the Size field, the degree of rotation in the Rotate field, or the degree of skew in the Skew field.

How do I set an object to a specific size?

▼ If you need your object to be a specific size, use the Property Inspector, where you can set the size of an object in the width (W) and height (H) fields. Simply type the measurement you want, and then click outside the panel to see the change.

Can I flip an object vertically and horizontally?

▼ Yes. To flip an object, select the object by using a Selection tool and then click Modify, click Transform, and then click Flip Vertical, or click Modify, click Transform, and then click Flip Horizontal. Flash flips your object.

Can I use the menu to access transform options?

▼ Yes, you can select an object, click Modify, and then click Transform, to access the Free Transform, Distort, Envelope, Scale, Rotate and Skew, and Scale and Rotate features.

Use the Eraser Tool

You can use the Eraser tool to erase objects and mistakes in drawings, or to draw new shapes within an object. The Eraser tool does not draw or paint; it eliminates drawings or parts of drawings from the Stage.

The Eraser tool has several modifiers that you can use to control how the tool works. You can use the Eraser Shape modifier to specify the size and shape of the Eraser tool. For example, perhaps you need to erase a small portion of a line at the edge of a drawing. Such a task requires a small eraser. A large eraser may erase parts of your drawing that you do not want to erase. With the Faucet modifier, you can limit what you erase to a specific stroke or a fill.

You can use the Eraser tool to erase both strokes and fills. You cannot erase grouped objects, symbols, or text blocks unless you first apply the Break Apart command.

If you want to erase everything on the Stage, double-click the Eraser tool. If you accidentally erase part of the drawing, you can apply the Undo command to reverse the action.

Use the Eraser Tool

Erase a stroke or fill

① Click the Eraser tool.

② Click the Faucet modifier.

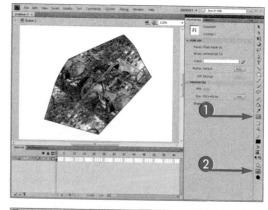

③ Click the item you want to erase, either the stroke or the fill.

Flash erases the stroke or the fill, whichever you chose.

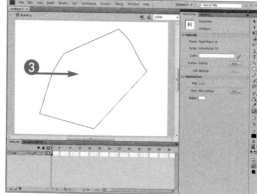

Erase an area

① Click the Faucet modifier to turn it off.

② Select an eraser shape.

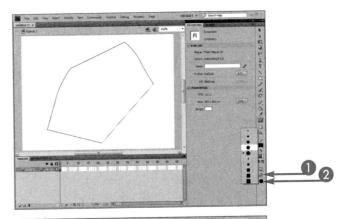
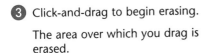

③ Click-and-drag to begin erasing.

The area over which you drag is erased.

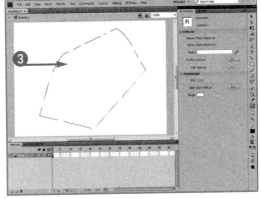

How does the Eraser tool differ from a white fill?

▼ When you use the Eraser tool, you literally erase strokes and fills from the Stage. If you set the color of your Stage to white and then paint with the Brush tool using the white fill color, you are not erasing but rather adding an object to the Stage. Even though you cannot see the object because you have painted it white and it blends with the Stage background color, the object is still there, and you can select and manipulate it. When you erase something from the Stage, Flash removes it.

What do the Eraser modes do?

▼ The Eraser tool has five modes: Erase Normal, Erase Fills, Erase Lines, Erase Selected Fills, and Erase Inside. Click the Eraser Mode button in the Options tray at the bottom of the Drawing toolbar to view the five modes. Erase Normal lets you erase anything on the Stage. Erase Fills erases inside fill areas but not strokes. Erase Lines erases only strokes. Erase Selected Fills erases only the selected fill. If you choose Erase Selected Fills and begin erasing from an empty area, Flash does not erase anything. If strokes surround an area, Erase Inside erases only inside the area in which the brush stroke begins.

Work with Gradients

You can use gradients to add interest, depth, and dimension to your Flash drawings. A *gradient* is a band of blended colors or shades of color. In Flash, you can use a gradient as a stroke or fill for any graphic.

By default, the Stroke and Fill Color palettes offer several gradients that you can use. You can choose from three vertical color bars, called *linear gradients*, and four circular gradients, called *radial gradients*. If you do not like the default choices, you can create your own linear and radial gradients.

You can save time if you plan which colors you want to use in a gradient and decide which type of gradient you want to apply. For example, if you want to create an illusion of depth and apply it to an interactive button you have created, experiment with a radial gradient. You can use a linear gradient to create the illusion of a gradually fading color.

This example shows you how to assign a default gradient from the Fill Color palette, as well as how to create a new gradient. You can apply the steps in the example to any gradient.

Work with Gradients

Assign a gradient

① Click the Fill color icon.

The Color palette opens.

② Click a gradient.

Gradients appear at the bottom of the palette.

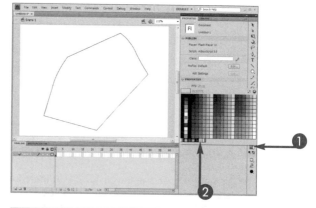

③ Click the Paint Bucket tool.

④ Click inside the shape you want to fill.

The gradient fills the shape.

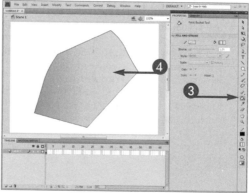

Create a new gradient

1 Click Window.

2 Click Color.

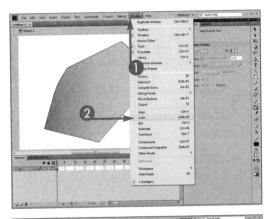

The Color panel opens.

3 Select Linear or Radial.

The gradient changes accordingly.

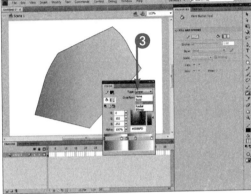

What exactly is a gradient?

▼ The term *gradient* refers to an effect in which two or more colors graduate in color intensity from one color to another. For example, a two-color gradient might show the color red blending into yellow from left to right. The middle area of the gradient shows the subtle blending of the two colors. You can create linear gradients in Flash that blend colors from left to right. You can use gradients to create a three-dimensional appearance. You can also create a radial gradient that intensifies color from the middle to the outer edges or from the outer edges to the middle.

Can I use a gradient as a Brush color?

▼ Yes. You can assign a gradient as the color you use with the Brush tool. You can choose a gradient from the Fill Color palette before you begin using the Brush tool, or you can use the Paint Bucket tool to fill the graphic after you draw the graphic.

Can I use a gradient as a stroke color?

▼ Yes. You can assign a gradient as the stroke color you use with the Line, Pen, Oval, Rectangle, or PolyStar tool. You can choose a gradient from the Stroke Color palette before you begin using a tool, or you can use the Property Inspector to change a stroke.

PART V

continued

Work with
Gradients *(Continued)*

Using the features on the Color panel, you can create your own unique gradient. You might like a certain color combination and arrangement for your gradient, or you may need to match the colors of existing objects on a Web page. After you create a custom gradient, you can save it and access it again throughout your project or in future projects.

You can change the properties of a gradient by adjusting different colors and adding color stops to create several color bandwidths. Color stops are the tiny icons beneath the gradient bar in the Color panel. By dragging a stop on the gradient bar, you can create different shades of color, resulting in a gradient.

To get a feel for how customizing works, start with one color and adjust the marker left and right across the color bar in the Color panel. After you create a gradient, you can save it as a swatch in the Color palette to reuse again. You can add and subtract additional color markers as needed to create just the right effect.

Work with Gradients *(continued)*

④ Double-click a color stop.

The Color Palette opens.

⑤ Click a color.

The gradient bar changes color.

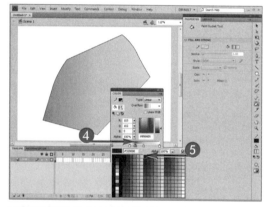

⑥ Repeat step **5** to change another color stop.

● You can drag the icons left or right to adjust the color intensity and bandwidth.

To add another color stop to the gradient, you can click below the gradient bar.

To remove a color stop, you can click-and-drag it off the panel.

Flash adjusts the gradient.

Note: *You can continue modifying the gradient by adding color markers, assigning colors, and dragging the markers to change the intensity.*

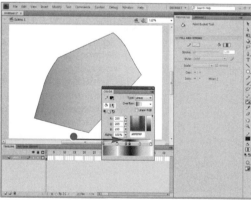

Save the new gradient

1 Click the Panel menu button.

2 Click Add Swatch.

Flash adds the gradient to the Swatches panel.

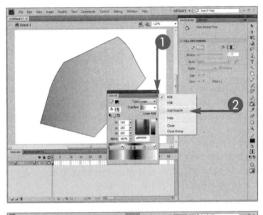

3 Click Window.

4 Click Swatches.

● The Swatches panel appears, showing the new gradient.

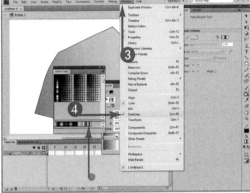

How do I control where the highlight in the center of a radial gradient appears?

▼ When using the Paint Bucket tool, you control where the highlighted center of a radial gradient fill appears by where you click the shape. Click left of center to make the fill highlight appear on the left, click right of center to make the fill highlight appear on the right, and click the center to make the fill highlight appear in the center.

Can I make changes to an existing gradient in the palette?

▼ Yes. Start by selecting the gradient to which you want to make modifications, and then open the Color panel to view the gradient swatch you want to edit. You can now make changes to the color markers or shades of color and save the edits as a new gradient color swatch.

Can I delete a custom gradient I no longer need?

▼ Yes. Click Window and then click Swatches to display the Swatches panel. Click the gradient swatch you want to delete. Click the Swatches Option menu at the top of the panel and then click Delete Swatch. Flash permanently deletes the gradient from all Color palettes.

Transform a Gradient Fill

You can use the Gradient Transform tool on the Tools panel to transform gradient and bitmap fills. Gradient fills blend two or more colors, and bitmap fills use an image or pattern as the fill rather than a color. There are two types of gradient fills: linear and radial. The Gradient Transform tool enables you to change the placement and appearance of linear, gradient, and bitmap fills.

By default, a radial fill changes color from a focal point outward. With the Gradient Transform tool, you can change the position of the focal point, thus changing

how the gradient appears on the object. With a linear fill, one color blends into another. Linear fills change color either horizontally or vertically.

When working with radial, linear, and bitmap fills, you can reposition, rotate, and resize the fills both horizontally and vertically. You have two additional options when you are working with a bitmap image: You can skew as well as tile a bitmap. A bitmap tile repeats the image vertically and horizontally. To tile a bitmap within a shape, use the Size control to make the bitmap smaller.

Transform a Gradient Fill

Modify a linear fill

1 Click the Gradient Transform tool.

Note: The Gradient Transform tool shares space with the Free Transform tool on the Tools palette.

2 Click the gradient fill you want to edit.

Edit control points appear on the fill.

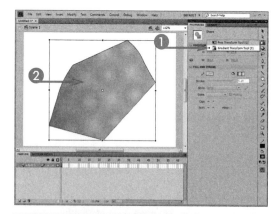

3 Drag control points to achieve the look you want.

- Repositions the focal point.
- Repositions the gradient.
- Changes the width of the gradient.
- Changes the size or radius of the gradient.
- Rotates the gradient.

Flash changes the radial gradient.

Note: You may need to zoom in or out to better view the edit control points.

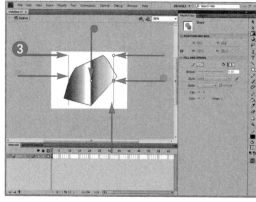

Modify a bitmap fill

1 Click the bitmap fill.

A bounding box and edit point controls appear around the fill.

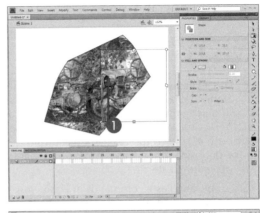

2 Drag control points to achieve the look you want.

● Changes the size of the fill vertically or horizontally.

● Rotates the bitmap fill.

● Skews the bitmap fill.

● Repositions the bitmap fill.

Flash makes the adjustments you specified.

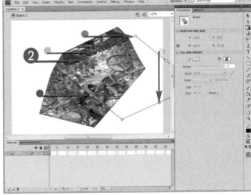

PART V

What does the Lock Fill modifier do?

▼ You can use the Lock Fill modifier to lock a gradient or bitmap fill and make the fill appear to extend across the Stage. For example, if you have several shapes across the Stage, you can lock the fill and have the gradient or bitmap fill each shape with a different portion of the gradient, much like a mask effect. To use the Lock Fill modifier, simply select a gradient or bitmap fill, click the Paint Bucket tool, and then click the Lock Fill modifier. The modifier tool button toggles the feature on or off. You can now use the Paint Bucket tool to fill objects on the Stage with the fill you selected.

What kinds of modifications can I make to a linear fill?

▼ You can rotate, reposition, or resize a linear fill. Linear fills work like bitmap fills, except that there are fewer options. When working with a linear fill, you click the Gradient Transform tool and then click the linear fill. Edit points appear on the fill. You can use the Rotation control to rotate the fill clockwise or counterclockwise. You can use the Width and Height controls to resize the bitmap, and you can use the Center Point control to reposition the linear fill. You can press and hold the Shift key as you rotate a linear gradient to constrain the rotation of the gradient to multiples of 45 degrees.

Move and Copy Objects

You can easily reposition objects on the Flash Stage to change the layout. Flash enables you to quickly move an object from one area to another. You can also make copies of an object. For example, you may need to move an object from the left to the right side of the Stage, or you may want to copy an object to create a new object.

The Cut, Copy, and Paste commands in Flash work the same way as they do in other programs. In Flash, the Cut, Copy, and Paste commands are available on the Edit menu. Copying an object allows you to paste a duplicate of the object. Cutting an object removes the object from the Stage so that you can paste it somewhere.

You can move an object by selecting and dragging it around the Stage. Dragging an object is the quickest way to place the object where you want it. You can press and hold the Shift key while you drag to restrict your movements to straight up, straight down, or at a 45-degree angle.

Move and Copy Objects

Move an object

1. Select the object you want to move.

2. Click-and-drag the object to a new position.

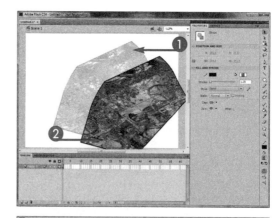

3. Release the mouse button.

   ● Flash moves the object to the location you selected.

Cut or copy an object

① Select the object you want to cut or copy.

Note: *See the section, "Select Objects with the Selection Tool," to learn how to select an object.*

② Click Edit.

③ Click either Copy or Cut.

Flash copies or cuts the object you selected to the Clipboard.

④ Click Edit.

⑤ Click Paste in Center.

The object appears in the center of the Stage.

Note: *If you want to place the copy on top of the original, click the Paste in Place command.*

What other methods can I use to move objects that are located on the Stage?

▼ You can select an object and then use the arrow keys to move the object up, down, left, or right. The arrow keys move your object one pixel at a time.

You can also select an object and use the X and Y fields in the Property Inspector to position the object. The X field determines the location of your object along the horizontal axis of your screen. The Y field determines the location of your object along the vertical axis of your screen. You can type values into these fields to specify exactly where to position your object.

Are the Cut, Copy, and Paste keyboard shortcuts the same in Flash as they are in other programs?

▼ Yes, whether you are using Windows or Mac OS, the keyboard shortcuts work the same way in Flash as they do in most other programs. Press Ctrl+X (⌘+X) to cut an object and place it on the Clipboard. Press Ctrl+V (⌘+V) to paste an object. Press Ctrl+C (⌘+C) to place a duplicate of a selected object on the Clipboard. Objects you place on the Clipboard can be pasted into Flash or into another program.

PART V

Copy Attributes

You can use the Eyedropper tool to quickly copy attributes from one object to another. Copying attributes, rather than reassigning them one at a time, can save you time and effort. The Eyedropper tool copies fills and strokes, and it enables you to apply those fills and strokes to other objects.

Much like a real-life eyedropper, the Eyedropper tool absorbs the formatting you have applied to a particular fill or stroke. Position the Eyedropper tool over a stroke, and a tiny pencil appears next to the Eyedropper icon. The pencil icon lets you know that you have placed the Eyedropper tool over a stroke.

When you click the Eyedropper tool, it absorbs the formatting applied to the stroke.

Position the Eyedropper tool over a fill, and a tiny paintbrush appears next to the Eyedropper tool. The paintbrush icon lets you know that you have placed the Eyedropper tool over a fill.

After you have picked up the attributes you want to copy, the Eyedropper tool becomes an Ink Bottle icon if you clicked a stroke, or a Locked Paint Bucket icon if you clicked a fill. You can then position the Eyedropper tool over the Stage and drop the formatting onto another stroke or fill.

Copy Attributes

1 Click the Eyedropper tool.

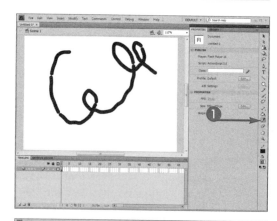

2 Click the element whose attributes you want to copy.

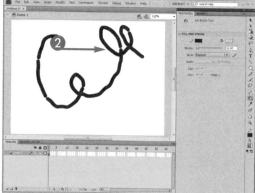

❸ Click the object to which you want to apply the attributes.

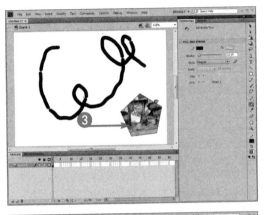

Flash copies the attributes.

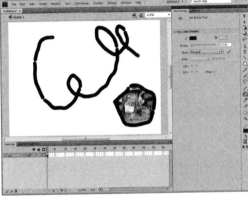

What is the purpose of the Ink Bottle tool?

▼ You use the Ink Bottle tool to change the format of strokes. You click the Ink Bottle tool and then use the Property Inspector to select stroke attributes. After you have selected the stroke attributes, you can click any stroke and the attributes of that stroke become the ones you selected. For example, if you select the Ink Bottle tool and then select the color blue and a ragged line, any stroke you click on the Stage becomes a blue, ragged line. The Ink Bottle tool, when used in conjunction with the Eyedropper tool, copies the attributes of one stroke to another stroke.

My Ink Bottle and Eyedropper tools do not work. Why not?

▼ You cannot use the Ink Bottle or Eyedropper tool on grouped objects. You must ungroup the objects by clicking Modify, and then clicking Ungroup before trying to copy stroke or fill attributes from a grouped object to another object on the Stage, and before changing attributes by using the Ink Bottle tool.

Can I copy attributes before I draw a stroke or fill on the Stage?

▼ Yes. You can use the Eyedropper tool to copy the attributes of an existing stroke or fill. You can then select a tool and draw on the Stage. The object you draw has the same attributes as the stroke or fill you selected with the Eyedropper tool.

Group
Objects

Y ou can work on multiple items at the same time by placing the objects in a group. A group enables you to treat the items, regardless of object type, as a single unit. Any edits you make affect all items in the group. For example, you can group lines and shapes together and reposition the entire lot in one fell swoop.

Like objects that you create using the Object Drawing model, items you group on the Stage do not interact with other lines or shapes outside the group. One of

the prime benefits of grouping several objects is that you can move or copy them all at once on the Stage instead of moving or copying one object at a time. Grouping is also helpful when you want to keep related objects together, such as the elements that create a logo. For example, your logo might include a background box, a text box, and several freeform lines. After you design or create the logo on the Stage and layer the objects the way you want them, you can turn the objects into a group. You can ungroup objects again to edit them individually.

Group Objects

Create a group

1 Select all the objects you want to include in a group.

Note: *See the section, "Select Objects with the Selection Tool," to select items on the Flash Stage.*

You can select multiple items by pressing and holding the Shift key while clicking each item.

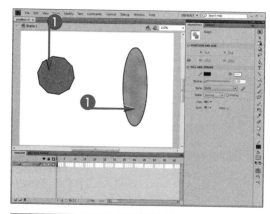

2 Click Modify.

3 Click Group.

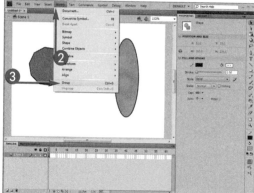

Flash groups the objects together and surrounds them with a bounding box.

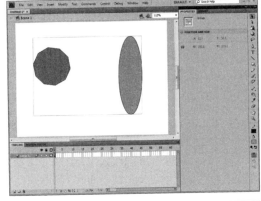

Ungroup a group

1 Select the group.

2 Click Modify.

3 Click Ungroup.

Flash ungroups the objects.

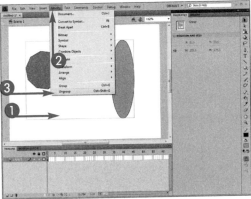

How can I avoid accidentally changing a group?

▼ If you worry about accidentally moving or changing a group, you can lock it. After selecting the group, click Modify, click Arrange, and then click Lock. To unlock the group again, click Modify, click Arrange, and then click Unlock.

How is grouping different from stacking?

▼ Grouping sticks objects together so that they act as one object. Stacking allows you to move different grouped objects to the background or foreground, or somewhere in between.

Can I have a group of one?

▼ Yes. You can turn one object into a group to keep it from interacting with other shapes and lines on the Stage. Any single object you create using the Object Drawing model is automatically grouped.

How do I edit items in a group?

▼ Double-click the group you want to edit. Everything else on the Stage dims except for the items in the selected group. After making your edits, double-click anywhere outside the group.

Stack Objects

Flash stacks grouped objects and symbols in the order in which you create them. Flash places each new grouped object or symbol above any previously created grouped objects or symbols. When objects overlap, objects higher in the stacking order appear to be on top of objects lower in the stacking order. You can change the stacking order of grouped objects. In fact, you can control exactly where an object appears in the stack.

Flash places all ungrouped objects on the same level — at the bottom of the stack. To move ungrouped objects up in the stacking order, you must group them or change them into a symbol.

You can select objects and then use menu commands to change the stacking order. If you select several groups and symbols that you want to move in tandem, they maintain their relative stacking order as they move in front of or behind other groups and symbols.

You can also use layers to control the stacking order of objects. See Chapter 27 to learn more about layers.

Stack Objects

① Select the group you want to reorder.

Note: *See the section, "Select Objects with the Selection Tool," to select items on the Flash Stage.*

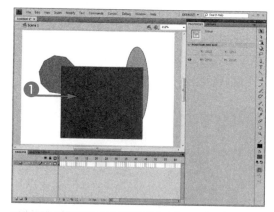

② Click Modify.

③ Click Arrange.

④ Click a command that tells Flash where you want to send the object.

To send an object to the very back of the stack, click Send to Back.

To bring an object to the very front of the stack, click Bring to Front.

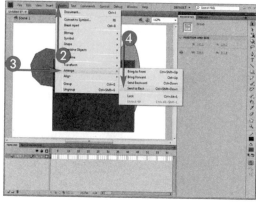

The object now relocates in the
stacking order.

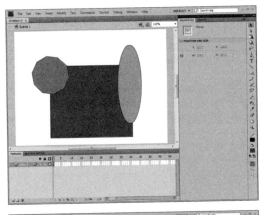

 Repeat steps **2** to **4** to reverse the
stacking order.

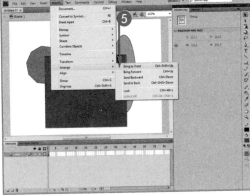

**Is there a shortcut to moving an object
up or back a layer in the stacking order?**

▼ Yes. You can use keyboard shortcuts to
quickly reposition an object in a stack.

Press Ctrl+Up Arrow (⌘+Up Arrow) to
move an object up one level in the stack.

Press Ctrl+Shift+Up Arrow (⌘+Shift+Up
Arrow) to move an object directly to the
top of the stack.

Press Ctrl+Down Arrow (⌘+Down Arrow)
to move an object down one level in the
stack.

Press Ctrl+Shift+Down Arrow
(⌘+Shift+Down Arrow) to move an object
directly to the back of the stack.

**Can I stack elements of objects drawn
using the Object Drawing model?**

▼ No. You cannot apply the stacking
commands to elements within objects
created using the Object Drawing model.
You cannot stack imported artwork with
objects drawn using the Merge Drawing
model. You can, however, break apart the
objects and then apply the stacking
commands.

Align Objects

U sing the Align panel, you can control precisely where an object sits on the Stage. You can open and display the Align panel for as long as you need it. Like the other panels available in Flash, you can move, resize, and collapse the panel as needed to free up workspace. Using the Align panel, you can align objects left, right, or center, either horizontally or vertically. You can use the Align panel to make two or more objects match in size. You can make them the same width, the same height, or the same width and height. You can also use the Align panel to evenly space and distribute objects. You can

make object alignments reference other objects or reference the Stage.

The alignment commands come in handy when you are trying to position several objects on the Stage, and dragging them around manually does not seem to create the results you want. Although the Flash rulers and grid can help you line objects up on the Stage, applying alignment options is much faster and easier.

To align an object, select the object you want to align, click Window, and then click Align to open the Align panel. You can also find alignment commands on the Modify menu on the main menu bar.

Align Objects

Align objects with other objects

1. Click Window.

2. Click Align.

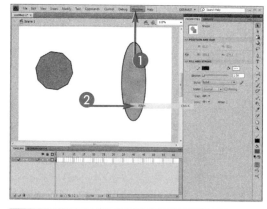

The Align panel opens.

3. Select the objects you want to align.

Note: See the section, "Select Objects with the Selection Tool," to select items on the Stage.

4. Click an alignment option.

This example horizontally aligns the objects, by clicking a horizontal alignment.

Flash aligns the objects.

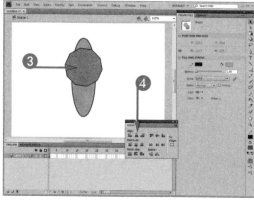

⑤ To align vertically, click a vertical alignment.

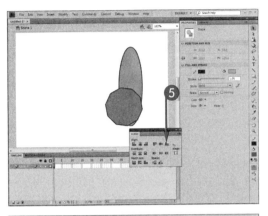

Align objects with the stage

① Select the objects you want to align.

Note: See the section, "Select Objects with the Selection Tool," to select items on the Stage.

② Click the To stage button.

③ Click an alignment option.

Flash aligns the objects to the Stage.

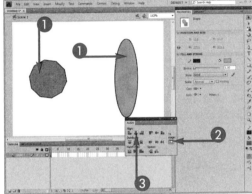

How can I use the Match Size buttons in the Align panel?

▼ You can use the Match Size buttons to make two or more objects the same size on the Stage. For example, if you have two circles of differing sizes, you can select them both and click the sizing option you want to apply. You can make the two objects equal in width, equal in height, or both.

How can I use the Space buttons?

▼ You can use the Space buttons in the Align panel to create equal spacing between two or more objects. You can space the objects evenly, vertically, or horizontally on the Stage.

What do the Distribute buttons do?

▼ You can use the Distribute buttons in the Align panel to equalize space between two or more objects and their outer edges. You can distribute objects along their vertical or horizontal centers, or top, bottom, left, or right edges.

Undo with the History Panel

The History panel saves each action you perform as you use Flash. You can use the History panel to undo one or more actions or to redo one or more actions. When you redo actions, you can apply the actions to the same object or to a different object.

When you open the History panel, the panel shows a list of the steps you have performed in the current movie, in the order you performed them. A slider located on the left side of the History panel points to the last step you performed. If you undo actions and then perform another action, you cannot redo the undone actions. Flash removes them from the History panel.

By default, Flash supports 100 levels of undo. You can use the Preferences dialog box to reset the levels of undo to any number between 2 and 9999.

You can clear the history list by clicking Clear History on the History panel's options menu. Clearing history does not undo your actions, but after you clear history, you cannot redo cleared actions. Closing a document also clears history. However, you can save steps so that you can use them in the current document or another document.

Undo steps

1 Click Window.

2 Click Other Panels.

3 Click History.

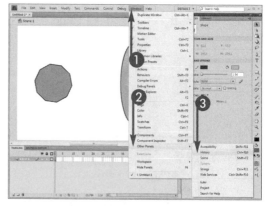

The History panel opens.

4 Drag the arrow back to the step before the last step you want to undo.

Note: You can also click to the left of the step before the last step you want to undo.

Flash undoes the steps.

To replay steps, or repeat the steps again, you can click-and-drag over the text of the steps you want to replay and click the Replay button.

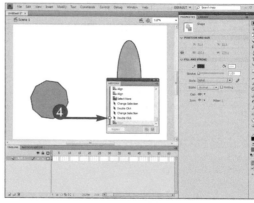

Automate tasks

1 In the History panel, click-and-drag over the steps you want to save.

2 Click the Save icon.

The Save As Command dialog box appears.

3 Type a command name.

4 Click OK.

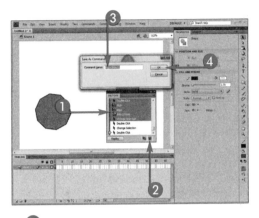

5 To execute a saved task, select an object.

6 Click Commands.

7 Click the command name you created in step **3**.

Flash executes the command.

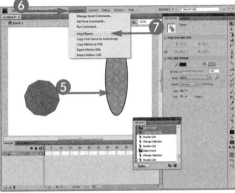

Can I rename and delete saved commands?

▼ Yes, you can use the Manage Saved Commands dialog box to rename or delete a task you have saved. To open the Manage Saved Commands dialog box, click Commands and then click Manage Saved Commands. To rename a command, click the command name and then click the Rename button. The Rename Command dialog box appears. Type the new name and then click OK.

To delete a command, click the command and then click Delete. You are prompted with the message, *Deleted commands cannot be undone. Are you sure you want to continue?* Click Yes. Flash deletes the command.

Can I use the menu to undo, redo, and repeat commands?

▼ Yes. To undo the last command you executed, click Edit, and then click Undo. To redo the command you just undid, click Edit, and then click Redo. If you execute a command and you want to repeat the action on another object, click Edit, and then clickRepeat. You can apply the Undo, Redo, and Repeat commands multiple times.

How do I reset the levels of undo?

▼ A small number of undo levels does not give you flexibility. A large number of undo levels uses more memory. To reset the levels of undo, click Edit, and then click Preferences to open the Preferences dialog box. In the Category box, click General. Type a value between 2 and 9999 in the Levels text box.

Add Text with the Text Tool

You can use the Text tool located on the Tools panel to add text to a Flash document. You can even animate text the same way you animate a graphic object.

You can use three types of text in Flash: static, dynamic, and input. Static text, the default text property, is text that does not change as the movie plays. Dynamic text can be altered as the movie plays and is controlled by ActionScript. Input text creates a field into which your user can type his own text. See Chapter 35 to learn more about dynamic and input text.

You add text to the Stage by using text boxes, which you can reposition or resize as needed. There are two types of text boxes: extending text boxes and fixed text boxes. To create an extending text box, click the Stage where you want the box to appear and start typing. To create a fixed text box, define the text box size by clicking and dragging to create the box's dimensions on the Stage. When you create a text box on the Stage, Flash applies the text attributes or formatting you assigned to previously added text boxes.

Add Text with the Text Tool

Add an extending text box

1 Click the Text tool.

2 Click the Stage.

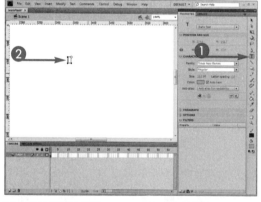

A text box appears on the screen.

3 Type your text.

Flash adds your text to the Stage.

You can click anywhere outside the text box to deselect the text object.

Note: *If you choose the Selection tool, you can double-click a text box to switch to Edit mode and make changes to the text; if you choose the Text tool, you can click the text box and make edits directly.*

Note: *See the section, "Format Text," to learn how to assign text attributes.*

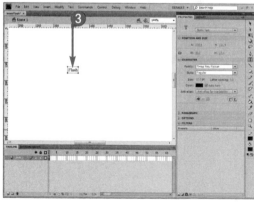

Add a fixed text box

Note: *Use fixed text boxes to type lines of text that you want to stay within the boundaries of the width of the box.*

1 Position the mouse pointer over the Stage, and click-and-drag the width you want to use for your text box.

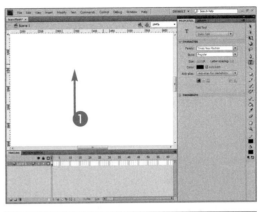

2 Type your text.

Flash adds your text to the Stage.

Note: *See the section, "Format Text," to learn how to assign text attributes.*

You can click anywhere outside the text box to deselect the text object.

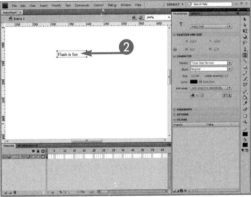

What is the difference between an extending text box and a fixed text box?

▼ When you type text into an extending text box, the text does not wrap; the width of the text box keeps expanding as you type. Press Enter to move to a new line. With a fixed text box, you specify a width. Text you type that reaches the end of the block wraps to the next line. To discern which method you are using, look at the icon in the upper-right corner of the text box. Extending text boxes display a circle, and fixed text boxes display a square.

How do I turn an extending text box into a fixed text box, and vice versa?

▼ Using the Text tool, click inside the text box and then position the mouse pointer over the circle in the upper-right corner of the text box. The mouse pointer becomes a double arrow. Drag the double arrow to the right and release the mouse button. The extending text box becomes a fixed text box. To turn a fixed text box into an extending text box, position the mouse pointer over the square in the upper-right corner of the text box. The mouse pointer becomes a double arrow. Double-click to change the fixed text box to an extending text box.

Format Text

Using the Property Inspector, you can easily format text in your Flash document to change the appearance of words and characters. All of the controls for changing text attributes are located in one convenient panel, where you can quickly change the font, font size, font color, and spacing.

You can choose text attributes before you start typing text or apply formatting to existing text. Leave the Property Inspector open to keep the formatting controls handy as you work with text on the Stage.

The Property Inspector offers many of the same formatting controls you find in other Adobe design programs. For example, you can select bold or italic text from the Style menu. When you click the Font drop-down menu, you see the names and samples of available fonts you can use.

Regardless of which attributes you assign to your text, it is important to make the text legible. Although special effects can add pizzazz to any message, the effects should never take precedence over the readability of your text.

Format Text

Format with bold and italics

1 Select the text or text box you want to edit.

2 Click the Style drop-down menu.

3 Select a style.

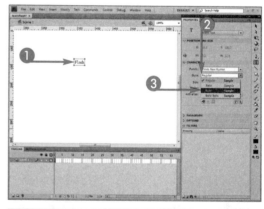

The text changes appearance.

● You can click the Text (fill) color box to open the Color palette and choose another color for the selected text.

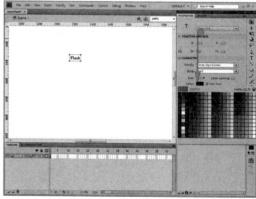

Change the font and size

① Select the text or text box you want to edit.

You can click the Text tool to select text within the text box.

You can click the Selection tool and click the text box to select the entire box for editing.

② Click the Family drop-down menu and select a font.

A list of available fonts appears, along with a sample box.

The text changes to the font type you selected.

③ Type a new font size in the Size field.

The text size changes.

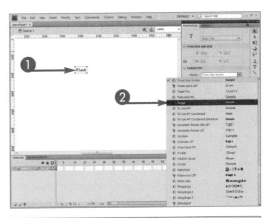

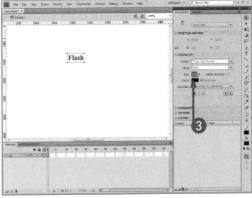

What are device fonts?

▼ When you work on an (X)HTML document, you are limited to the fonts that your user has on his computer, as there is no widely available method to embed font information into regular Web pages. Flash, however, does embed fonts, and so you can use any font you want in your movie. Unfortunately, the embedded font information adds to the overall file size. If you plan to use one of the commonly installed fonts, such as Arial, Times New Roman, or Courier, you can reduce your file size by using a device font. In this case, the font is not embedded, and so the font information on your user's computer is used instead. Flash includes three device fonts: _sans, _serif, and _typewriter.

Do I have to use the Property Inspector to format text?

▼ No. You can also use the Text options on the main menu to format your text. By using the Text options, you can change your font and font size, or make your text bold, italic, and more.

Can I use a gradient as a font color?

▼ No. If you want to apply a gradient to text, you must first break the text apart and apply the gradient to the fill. See the section, "Break Apart Text," to learn more.

Align and Kern Text

Y ou can control the position of text within a text box by using the alignment options in the Paragraph section of the Property Inspector or on the Text menu. Alignment options include setting horizontal controls for the positioning of text, such as left, center, right, or fully justified.

Left alignment moves the text to the left side of the text box. Right alignment moves the text to the right side. Center alignment centers the text between the left and right edges of the text box. Fully justified alignment spaces out the text evenly between the left and right edges so that both margins are flush with

the edges of the text box. To learn how to set margins for text boxes, see the section, "Set Text Box Margins and Indents."

Another way to control the positioning of text is with *kerning*. Kerning refers to the spacing between characters. By changing the kerning setting, which changes the space between characters, you can make your text aesthetically more pleasing. You can find kerning controls in the Property Inspector. To apply alignment or kerning options to a text box, you must first select the text.

Align and Kern Text

Align text

① Select the text or text box you want to edit.

You can click the Text tool to select text within the text box.

You can click the Selection tool and click the text box to select the entire box for editing.

② Click Paragraph.

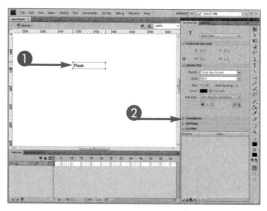

The Paragraph panel opens.

③ Click a Format button to specify the alignment you want.

Flash aligns the text.

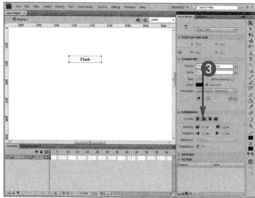

Kern text

1 Select the text or text box you want to edit.

You can click the Text tool to select text within the text box.

You can click the Selection tool and click the text box to select the entire box for editing.

2 Click the Auto kern check box to deselect it.

3 Drag on the Letter spacing value to change it.

Drag the spinner to the left to decrease the value, and to the right to increase it.

Flash kerns the characters in the text box.

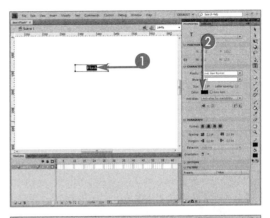

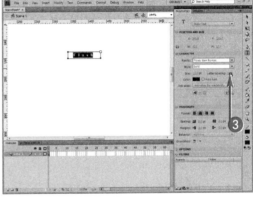

How do I create vertical text?

▼ You can create vertical text that flows from left to right as you create each line of text, or vertical text that flows from right to left as you create each line of text. To create vertical text, click the Text tool and then click the Change Orientation of Text icon located in the Property Inspector. A pop-up menu appears. Click Vertical, Left to Right, or Vertical, Right to Left. Click the Stage to create an extending text box, and then begin typing. To change existing text to vertical text, your text must be in an extending text box.

Does the Property Inspector save my current formatting settings?

▼ The Property Inspector retains your last formatting settings as long as you have Flash open. If you add another text box to the Stage, the text will have the attributes you previously assigned. The next time you launch Flash and open the Property Inspector, the default settings are in effect until you change them.

How do I copy attributes from one text box to another?

▼ Click the Selection tool and then click a character in the text box containing the text to which you want to copy attributes. Click the Eyedropper tool on the Tools panel and then click the text box containing the attributes from which you want to copy. Flash copies the attributes.

Set Text Box Margins and Indents

You can set margins and indents within text boxes for greater control of text positioning in your Flash documents. You can find margin and indent commands in the Format Options dialog box. This dialog box is accessible through the Paragraph section of the Property Inspector.

Margins define the distance between the edge of the text box and the text inside. For example, if a text box appears next to another graphic object on the Stage, you may want to specify a margin within the text box to make sure the text does not appear too close to the bordering graphic. You can define left and right margins, as well as top and bottom margins.

Indents are used to control where a line of text sits within the margins. For example, you might choose to indent the first line in a paragraph by several pixels or points.

In addition to margin and indent controls, the Property Inspector also has controls for line spacing. Line spacing is the distance between lines of text. You can increase the line spacing to add space between lines, or decrease the spacing to bring the lines closer together.

Set Text Box Margins and Indents

Set margins

1 Click the Selection tool.

2 Click the text box you want to edit.

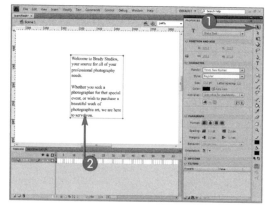

3 Type values to set the margins.

You can type a value in the Margins field.

Alternatively, you can click-and-drag on the current value to set the desired value.

Flash adjusts the margins.

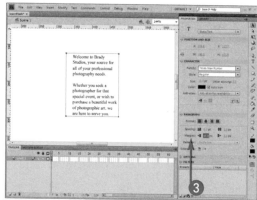

Set and indent and line spacing

1 Click the Text tool.

2 Click at the beginning of the text line you want to indent.

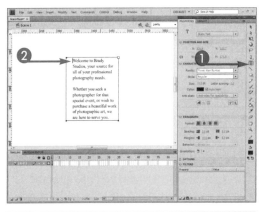

3 Type an indent value in the Spacing field.

Alternatively, you can click-and-drag on the current value to set the desired value.

4 Type a line spacing value in the Line spacing field.

Alternatively, you can click-and-drag on the current value to set the desired value.

Flash changes the indentation and line spacing.

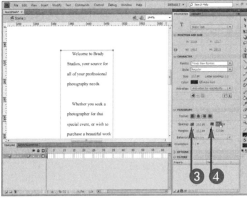

How do I change the margin's unit of measurement?

▼ By default, Flash assumes that you work with pixels as your unit of measurement, but you can change the unit of measurement to points, inches, centimeters, or millimeters. Click Modify, and then click Document. The Document Properties dialog box appears. Click the down arrow for the Ruler Units field and select a unit. Click OK. When you open the Format Options dialog box, the indent and margin values reflect the unit of measurement you defined.

Should I use the Line Spacing slider to set superscript or subscript characters in Flash?

▼ No. You cannot use Line Spacing on individual characters — only entire lines. To set superscript or subscript characters, first select the text you want to superscript or subscript. Next, display the Property Inspector. Click the down arrow for the Character Position field; a list of choices appears. Click Superscript or Subscript. Flash superscripts or subscripts the characters you selected.

Can I make text selectable?

▼ Yes. Selectable text is text that the user can copy or cut. Once the user has copied or cut the text, he can then paste the text into another document. In Flash, you can make static, horizontal text selectable by selecting the text and clicking the Selectable button on the Property Inspector panel.

Move and Resize Text Boxes

Y ou can move text boxes around on the Flash
Stage or resize them as needed. Text boxes
are as mobile and scalable as other objects
that you add to the Stage.

You can position a text box anywhere on the Stage.
Alternatively, you can move a text box off the Stage
onto the Pasteboard. Nothing you place on the
Pasteboard appears in your Flash movie. However, you
can move items to the Pasteboard and move them
back onto the Stage when you need them.

When you select a text box to resize, small handles
appear on the corners of the box. You can use these
handles to resize the box horizontally. If you activate
the Free Transform tool on the Tools panel, Flash
displays small handles on both the corners and sides
of the tool box, enabling you to scale and rotate the
box. When you resize a text box, depending on the
direction you choose to scale the box, Flash resizes the
text. Flash overrides any font sizes you have previously
set. If you want the text set at a certain size, you must
manually change the font size.

Move and Resize Text Boxes

Move a text box

1 Click the Selection tool.

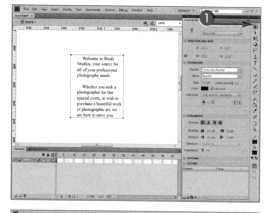

2 Click-and-drag the text box to a new location
and release the mouse button.

Flash moves the text box.

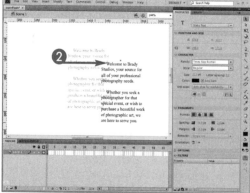

Resize a text box

① Click the Free Transform tool.

② Click the text box you want to edit.

A bounding box with handles appears around the text box.

③ Position your mouse pointer over a handle.

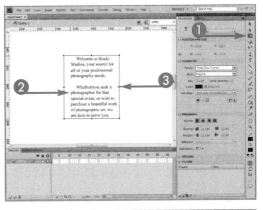

④ Click-and-drag a handle.

You can use a side handle to change the size of the box horizontally.

You can use a top or bottom handle to change the height of the box.

You can use a corner handle to change all sides of the box proportionately.

Flash resizes the text box.

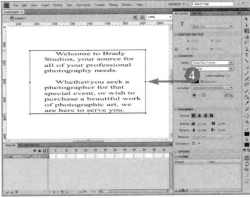

Can I resize the text box without distorting the text?

▼ Yes. Instead of using the Free Transform tool, you can click-and-drag the corner handles on the text box using the Text tool. This resizes the box while leaving the text size alone.

Can I spell-check text?

▼ Yes. Click Text and then click Spelling Setup to open the Spelling Setup dialog box. You can use the Spelling Setup dialog box to select the spell-check options you want to use.

You can spell-check your document by clicking Text and then clicking Check Spelling. If you have spelling errors in your document, Flash offers a list of suggestions. You can accept a suggestion, or you can ignore, change, or delete the misspelled word. If it is a word you use often, but it is not in the Flash dictionary, you can add it to your personal dictionary.

Break Apart Text

You can use the Break Apart command to turn text into graphics and then manipulate the text with the various Flash drawing and editing tools. For example, you can break text into separate blocks and distribute them to different layers in your animation, or you can break text apart to make modifications on each character in a word.

When you apply the Break Apart command to a text block, Flash treats each character of text as an object or graphic shape. You can apply the command once

to turn text into individual objects, an object for each character in the text. You apply the command a second time to convert the text into shapes. You can then modify the text shapes just as you modify other shapes you draw in Flash.

After you apply the Break Apart command to a text block, you can no longer make edits to the text, such as changing the font or font size. For that reason, be sure that you apply all of your text formatting before applying the Break Apart command.

Break Apart Text

① Click the Selection tool.

② Click the text box you want to edit.

③ Click Modify.

④ Click Break Apart.

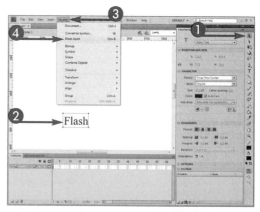

● Flash breaks the text into character blocks, where each character is an object you can manipulate.

When you click Modify and then click Break Apart a second time, Flash turns each character into a fill, and you can manipulate the characters as you would any other fill.

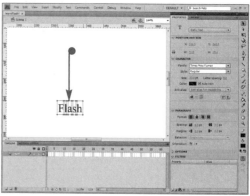

Distort Text

You can use the Free Transform tool's Envelope modifier to distort the appearance of text in a Flash project. For example, you can make the text appear as a wave or exaggerate the size of some letters while keeping the other letters the same, or you can make the text seem to follow a path.

In order to use the Envelope modifier, you must apply the Break Apart command to your text box. After you apply this command to a text block, you cannot edit or format the text again.

The Envelope modifier allows you to enclose the text shape with an envelope of edit points and then use the points to control the shape effect. The Envelope modifier uses two types of edit points: regular edit points and tangent points. Regular edit points are square handles and, when manipulated, can change the corners and sides of an object. Tangent handles are circles that adjust additional points along the edges of a selected object. Experiment with dragging both types of edit points to create different distortions with your text.

Distort Text

① Apply the Break Apart command twice to the text box you want to edit.

Note: To break apart text, see the section, "Break Apart Text."

② Click the Free Transform tool.

③ Click the Envelope button.

Edit points appear around the text shape.

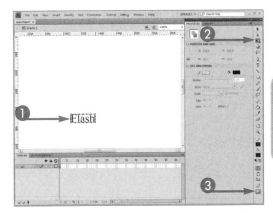

④ Click-and-drag an edit point to change the text shape.

⑤ Release the mouse button.

Flash modifies the text shape.

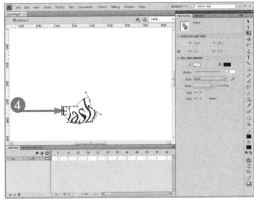

27

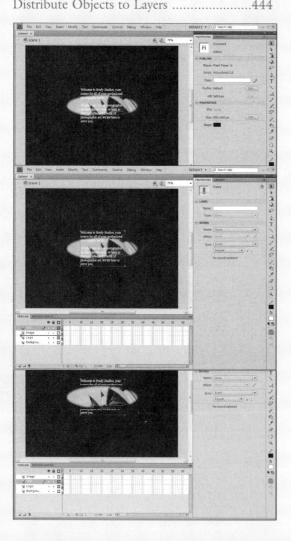

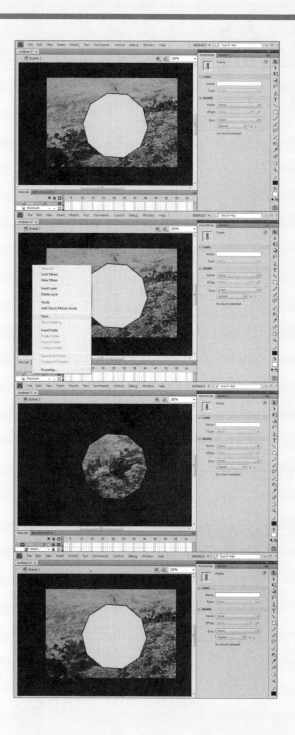

28

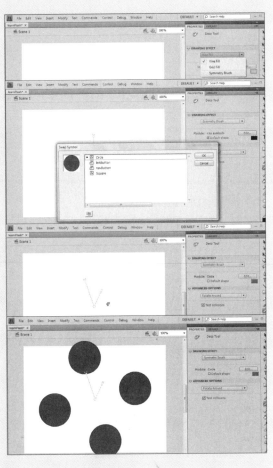

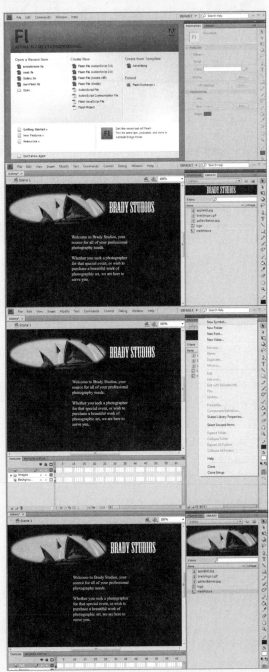

Add and Delete Layers

Layers can help you organize the objects you use in your Flash projects. When you open a new document, the Flash Timeline has a single layer. As your project becomes bigger, it is likely to have more objects. Instead of placing all of the objects on a single layer, which makes them difficult to locate and edit, you can add layers to the Timeline, and organize and place the objects on these separate layers.

Layers are similar to transparent sheets stacked on top of each other. Each layer lets you see through to the layer below until you add an object. On the Stage,

objects you place on higher layers appear to be in front of objects placed on lower layers. When creating your Flash document, you can place backgrounds on the bottom layer and add other objects to higher layers to create the perception of depth.

You click a layer to make it active; a pencil icon appears next to the active layer's name. You can add layers to the Timeline or delete layers you no longer need. Additional layers do not affect the file size, and so you can add as many layers as your project requires.

Add and Delete Layers

Add a layer

1 Click the layer above which you want to insert a new layer.

2 Click the New Layer icon.

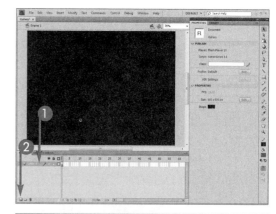

● Flash inserts a new layer.

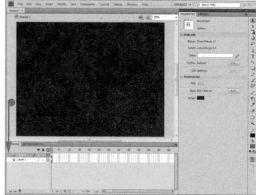

Delete a layer

1 Click the layer you want to delete.

2 Click the Delete Layer icon.

Flash deletes the layer.

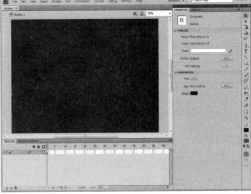

Are there other methods I can use to insert a layer?

▼ Yes. You can click the layer above which you want to insert a layer and then, on the main menu, click Insert, click Timeline, and then click Layer. Flash inserts a new layer. Alternatively, you can right-click the layer above which you want to add a layer and then click Insert Layer.

Are there other methods I can use to delete a layer?

▼ Yes. You can click the layer you want to delete and then drag it over the Delete Layer icon on the Timeline. Alternatively, you can right-click the layer you want to delete and then click Delete Layer.

Can I delete several layers at the same time?

▼ Yes. To delete contiguous layers in a stack, press and hold Shift and click the first layer you want to delete. While still holding down the Shift key, click the last layer you want to delete, and then click the Delete Layer icon. If the layers are noncontiguous, press and hold Ctrl (⌘), click each layer you want to delete, and then click the Delete Layer icon.

Work with Layers on the Timeline

Controlling layers is easy with the Flash Timeline. You can quickly rename, hide, or lock a layer, and the Timeline has buttons and toggles you can use to control a layer.

For example, you may want to hide a layer to remove the layer objects from view on the Stage so that you can focus on other objects you want to edit. If you leave the layer in view and click an object on the layer by mistake, you may change something you did not want to change.

The bar above the layer names has three icons that help you set the status of each layer. Each icon indicates a specific setting for the column below it. For example, the eye icon indicates whether the layer is visible. The lock icon tells you whether you have locked the layer. The outline icon enables you to view a layer's contents as outlines on the Flash Stage. You can toggle the status of all three icons on and off. You can also quickly rename layers by typing a new name directly on the layer name list.

Work with Layers on the Timeline

Rename a layer

1 Double-click the layer name.

The Name field changes to edit mode.

2 Type a new name.

3 Press Enter.

Flash changes the layer's name.

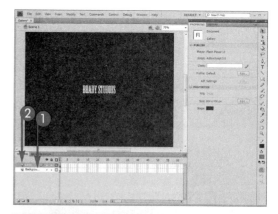

Hide a layer

1 On the layer you want to hide, click the Show/Hide Layer icon.

Flash hides all the objects on the layer.

Note: To show the layer, click the icon again.

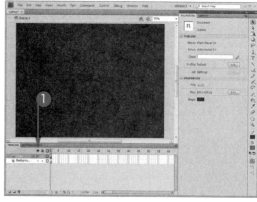

Lock a layer

1 On the layer you want to lock, click the Lock/Unlock Layer icon.

The bullet changes to a lock.

Flash locks the layer and you cannot edit the contents.

Note: To unlock the layer, click the icon again.

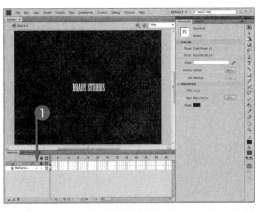

Change to Outline view

1 On the layer you want to show as outlines, click the View Layer as Outlines icon.

The square changes to an outline of a square.

Flash changes any objects appearing on the layer to outlines on the Stage.

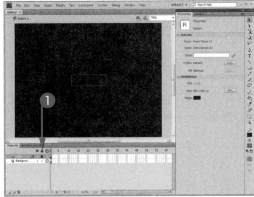

Can I hide multiple layers?

▼ Yes. The Show or Hide All Layers icon is also a toggle button. To hide all layers, click the Show/Hide All Layers icon. To show all layers, click the Show/Hide All Layers icon again, or right-click (Ctrl+click) while the mouse pointer is over a layer and then click Show All on the context menu. To hide all layers except one, right-click (Ctrl+click) the layer you want to show and then click Hide Others on the context menu.

Can I lock multiple layers?

▼ Yes. The Lock/Unlock All Layers icon located above the stack is a toggle button. To lock all layers, click the Lock/Unlock All Layers icon. To unlock all layers, click the Lock/Unlock All Layers icon again. To lock all layers except one, right-click (Ctrl+click) the layer you want to remain unlocked and then click Lock Others on the context menu.

How do I show all layers as outlines?

▼ You can choose to view the contents of all layers as outlines. The Show All Layers as Outlines icon at the top of the stack toggles the outline feature for all layers on and off. Click it once if you want to show all layers as outlines; click it again if you do not want all layers to show as outlines.

Stack Layers

To rearrange how objects appear in your Flash project, you can stack Flash layers the same way you might stack objects in a drawing. Each Flash layer acts like a transparent sheet. You can see through the sheet to the layer below until you add an object. Objects on higher layers appear to be in front of objects on lower layers.

For example, if you have a layer containing a background scene, you can move it to the bottom of the layer stack. Any objects you place on layers above the bottom layer appear to be in front of the background. Stacking layers in this manner creates the illusion of depth in your movie.

You can change the order of layers by moving them up or down the stack list. The layer at the top of the list is at the top of the stack, and the layer at the bottom of the list is at the bottom of the stack. All other layers appear in the middle, in the order listed.

You can change the position of locked and hidden layers.

Stack Layers

① Click the layer you want to move.

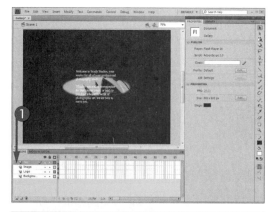

② Drag the layer up or down to its new location in the stack.

A thick black line indicates the position where the layer will be moved.

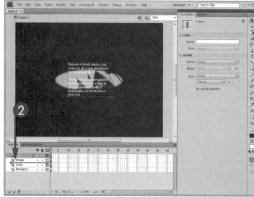

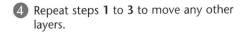

3 Release the mouse button.

● Flash moves the layer to its new position.

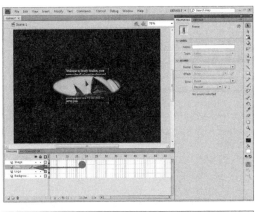

4 Repeat steps **1** to **3** to move any other layers.

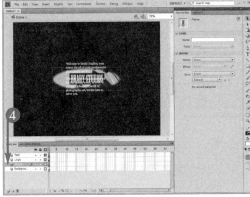

I cannot see all of my layers. Why not?

▼ The more layers you add to the Timeline, the longer the list of layer names becomes, and so not all the layers stay in view. Use the scroll bar at the far right end of the Timeline to scroll up and down the layer list to view other layers. You can also use Flash layer folders to organize layers on the Timeline. See the section, "Organize Layers into Folders," for information on organizing your layers for viewing.

How can I see more layers at a time in my Timeline?

▼ You can resize the Timeline to see more of your layers. Position the mouse pointer over the top border of the Timeline until the mouse pointer becomes a double-sided arrow. Click-and-drag the border up to increase the size of the Timeline. This enables you to see more of the layers on the Timeline.

Can I copy the contents of a layer?

▼ Yes. First, create a new layer by following the steps in the section, "Add and Delete Layers," and then click the layer you want to copy. Click Edit and then click Copy. Click the new layer, click Edit, and then click either Paste in Center, or Paste in Place. Flash copies the contents of the first layer and places them in the second layer.

Organize Layers into Folders

You can use layer folders to organize the numerous layers you use in a Flash project. Layer folders act just like the folders on the hard drive of your computer. For example, if you have several layers pertaining to a particular animation sequence, you can place all the related layers into one layer folder on the Flash Timeline. This makes it much easier to find a layer for editing. Flash identifies folders with a folder icon next to the folder name.

Layer folders can expand and collapse so that you can view or hide the layer folder content. You can tidy up the Timeline by collapsing folders that contain layers you are not currently using. You can also put layer folders inside other layer folders.

By default, Flash names layers in the order you create them, starting with Folder 1, continuing with Folder 2, and so on. You can rename a folder so that the folder name describes its contents. Layer and folder names can use upper- and lowercase letters and spaces. It is a good practice to name all the layers and folders that you use in your project.

Organize Layers into Folders

Create a folder

1. Click the layer above which you want to add a folder.
2. Click the Insert Layer Folder icon.
   - Flash adds a layer folder to the Timeline.

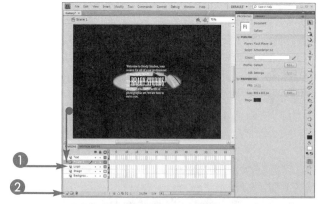

Move a layer to a folder

1. Click the layer you want to move into a folder.
2. Drag the layer over the folder.
3. Release the mouse button.
   - Flash places the layer in the folder.

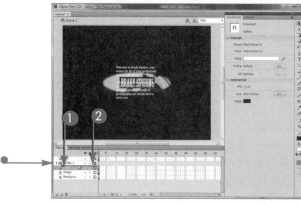

Rename a folder

1 Double-click the folder name you want to change.

The Name field changes to edit mode.

2 Type a new name.

3 Press Enter.

Flash changes the name of the folder.

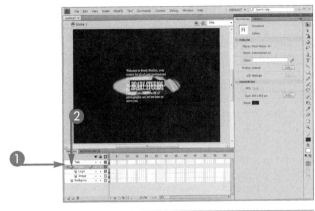

Expand and collapse a folder

1 Click a layer folder's Expand icon to expand the folder and view its contents.

2 Click a layer folder's Collapse icon to collapse the folder and hide its contents.

You can also right-click (Ctrl+click) the folder name and activate the Expand Folder or Collapse Folder commands.

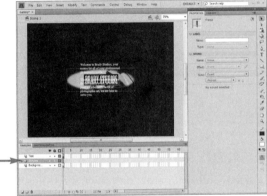

Can I change the stacking order of a folder?

▼ Yes. You can move layer folders the same way you move layers. Drag the folder name up or down on the Timeline to change the stacking order of the folder. See the section, "Work with Layers on the Timeline," to learn more.

How do I remove a layer from a folder?

▼ Display the content of the layer folder, drag the layer you want to remove from the folder, and then drop the layer where you want it to appear in the layer stacking order. To remove the layer completely from the Timeline, right-click (Ctrl+click) the layer name and click Delete Layer.

Can I lock and hide layer folders?

▼ Yes. You can lock and hide layer folders just as you can lock and hide layers. Locking a folder locks all the layers included within the folder. Click the dot under the Lock/Unlock All Layers icon next to the folder to lock a folder. Flash locks the folder and any layers associated with the folder.

How do I delete a layer folder I no longer need?

▼ To delete a layer folder, click the folder name to select it and then click the Delete icon. Flash warns you that deleting the folder will also delete the contents of the folder.

Add and Create a Mask Layer

Y ou can use mask layers to hide parts of underlying layers. The mask is like a window that lets you see through to the layers below, while other parts of the layers are hidden, or *masked*.

You might create a mask layer such as a filled star shape that acts like a window to the layer below. The window — or star shape — lets you see anything directly beneath, but the remainder of the mask layer hides anything that lies outside the window. A mask

layer can contain multiple fill shapes, but it cannot contain a fill and a symbol or grouped object, or multiple symbols and grouped objects. You can group several layers together under a single mask.

Mask layers appear with a unique icon on the Timeline. You can link a mask layer only to layers directly below it. You need to modify the properties of the lower layers to set them as masked. You can only view the masking effect if the mask and masked layers are locked.

Add and Create a Mask Layer

① Click the layer to which you want to add a mask.

② Click the New Layer button.

Flash adds a new layer.

③ Using the drawing tools, draw a fill shape on the Stage over the area you want to view in the layer below.

④ Right-click (Ctrl+click) the new layer.

⑤ Click Mask.

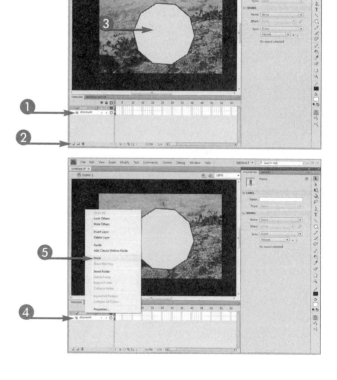

Flash converts the layer to a mask layer.

● The layer below the mask is converted to a masked layer, and both layers are locked.

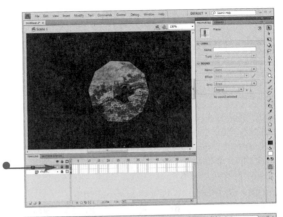

6 Click the lock icon on the mask layer to unlock it.

The layer unlocks.

You can now see the shape on the mask layer, rather than the mask effect.

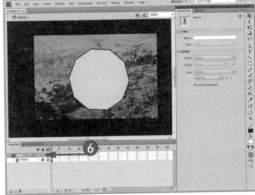

What sort of fill should I draw for my mask shape?

▼ You can use any kind of fill color or pattern to create a mask. Regardless of what makes up your fill, Flash treats the shape as a window to the linked layers below. For that reason, you should use a transparent fill rather than a solid one so that you can see through the fill to position the fill exactly where you want it on the Stage. Therefore, the fill color you use on the mask layer's objects is irrelevant.

I cannot see the mask effect. Why not?

▼ The layer may be unlocked. You must first lock the mask layer and each masked layer to see the mask effect. You can also see the effect if you preview the movie — click Control and then click Test Movie. The Flash Player window opens and runs the movie.

Can I convert a mask layer into a normal layer?

▼ Yes. Right-click (Ctrl+click) the mask layer and then click Properties. The Layer Properties dialog box appears. Click Normal and then click OK. Flash resets the layer to normal and removes the mask.

PART VI

Distribute Objects to Layers

The Distribute to Layers command distributes objects to different layers in your document, enabling you to animate each object separately. You can use the Distribute to Layers command to create layered animations. For example, you can use it to assist you in animating individual letters in a text block.

Using the Distribute to Layers command in conjunction with the Break Apart command, you can separate individual pieces of text, distribute the characters to different layers, and animate them separately. The Break Apart command literally breaks

apart the selected object into editable pieces. For example, if you apply the command to a text block, you can break each character into a separate text block. When you apply the Distribute to Layers command to the text, Flash moves each character to a separate layer and makes the character the layer name.

Objects you distribute using the Distribute to Layers command do not have to be on the same layer. Once you have used the Distribute to Layer command, the layer on which the objects existed originally is empty, and so you can then delete this layer.

Distribute Objects to Layers

① Select a text block.

② Click Modify.

③ Click Break Apart.

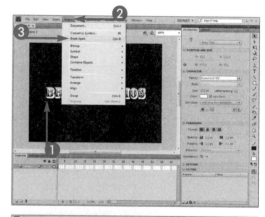

Flash breaks the text into individual letter blocks.

④ Click Modify.

⑤ Click Timeline.

⑥ Click Distribute to Layers.

Note: You must select all objects you want to distribute to layers before applying the command.

● Flash distributes each object to a separate layer.

After I distribute my objects, how do I tell which object is on which layer?

▼ When you click a layer in the Timeline, any object on that layer is selected. To see what shapes are on what layers, you can click on each layer in the Timeline and note what becomes selected on the Stage.

I have several objects, and I want to distribute some, but not all, of the objects to other layers. What should I do?

▼ Use the Selection tool to select the objects you want to distribute to other layers. To select some objects while not selecting others, press and hold Shift as you click each object you want to select. If you want to select everything on a particular layer, click the layer name.

An Introduction to Symbols

In Flash, a *symbol* is a reusable element that you can store in the Flash library. You can repeatedly reuse a symbol throughout your movie by inserting an *instance* of the symbol in the frame in which you want it to appear. An *instance* is simply a copy of the original symbol. Drawings you create using the tools in Flash, text, and imported graphics can all be converted to a symbol.

Flash Symbols

The primary purpose of using symbols in Flash is animation. When you convert an object to a symbol, you are able to apply a *motion tween* to it. Motion tweening is the easiest and most efficient way to animate in Flash. See Chapter 29 to learn how to create animation.

Another reason to use symbols is that they save file space. When you create a drawing in Flash or import a graphic, it adds to the file size of the finished product. If you need to reuse the object in your movie, it adds its file size each time it is used. Symbols, however, are only added once: They can be used as many times as you want in the movie without a corresponding increase in file size.

Storing Movie Elements

Every file you create in Flash has a library that stores elements you want to reuse in your project. You can manage these elements from the Library panel by organizing them into related folders, much like organizing files on the hard drive of your computer.

You can open, close, expand, and collapse the Library panel as you work with various symbols and instances in your document. The Library panel lists the symbols alphabetically. You can drag symbols from the panel and drop them onto the Stage to use in a frame. You can also add and delete symbols as needed. See the section, "Using the Flash Library," to learn more about using this organizational feature in Flash.

Editing Symbols

All instances of a symbol are copies of the object in the library. Each instance is linked back to the original, and so any changes made to the original are applied to all instances. There are certain edits that can be made to individual instances, such as their position on the Stage, their scale, and their rotation. However, more complex edits, such as changing the shapes that make up the symbol, must be made to the actual symbol.

You can either edit symbols in place, where you still have a visual reference to other objects on the Stage, or you can edit them individually on their own Stage.

Types of Symbols

You can reuse symbols to create animation in your Flash movies. Every time you reuse a symbol, you must specify how you want the symbol to behave. Flash classifies symbols into three types: graphics, buttons, or MovieClips.

Graphic symbols

You can create graphic symbols using the Flash drawing tools or by importing graphics from other programs to use in Flash. You can make graphic symbols as simple as a basic shape or as complex as a highly detailed drawing. You can also turn text into graphic symbols that you can manipulate and animate in your movies.

Graphic symbols have their own Timeline that closely resembles the Timeline of the main movie. However, the graphic symbol's Timeline is synchronized with the movie's Timeline, so while a graphic symbol can contain its own animation, that animation cannot play independently of the movie.

Button symbols

You can add interactivity to your movie through buttons. Like graphic symbols, buttons have their own Timeline. However, the button's Timeline is very different from that of the movie and the other symbol types, as it only contains four special frames, which enable you to create effects when the user mouses over the button or clicks it.

You can create a button by drawing shapes on the Stage or importing graphics and then converting them to a symbol, or you can draw shapes or import graphics directly into the button. You can also use other symbols, such as graphics or MovieClips, within buttons.

You can control what actions Flash takes when the user interacts with a button through ActionScript. See "Create a Button" later in this chapter, to learn how to create buttons.

MovieClip symbols

By far the most powerful symbol type is the MovieClip. Like graphic symbols, MovieClips have their own Timeline, which looks like the main movie's Timeline. However, unlike graphics, the Timeline of a MovieClip is independent of the main movie's Timeline; a MovieClip can also contain its own animation that is independent of the main movie's animation.

MovieClips can be created by converting existing drawings or imported graphics to a symbol, or by drawing or importing graphics directly onto the MovieClip's Timeline. You can also use graphic symbols, buttons, or other MovieClips within a MovieClip. MovieClips can also be created through ActionScript code.

Like buttons, MovieClips can respond to user actions, and so you can have them react when the user moves his mouse over the clip, clicks it, or even presses a key on his keyboard.

Using the Flash Library

You can use the Flash library to organize and store the items you create in Flash and the elements you import from other programs. When you first start a Flash file, the library is empty. As you add elements to your movie, such as symbols and imported assets, you can use the Library panel to manage the elements, insert instances, and more.

You can use the Library panel to preview an item, sort items, delete an item, view item properties, create new folders to organize items, or create new symbols. Like other panels found in Flash, you can resize, move, and hide the panel to suit the way you work. You can expand and collapse the panel, view the window in the wide or narrow state, or close the panel completely when it is not in use.

Each item listed in the library has an icon next to the item name that identifies the object type, such as graphic or button symbol. A preview window at the top of the Library panel allows you to view a selected item. The item list pane of the panel displays the name of each item, the type of item, the number of times you have used the item, linkage information, and the date you last modified the item. You can use a shared library when you want to use assets from one library in multiple Flash movies.

Open and close the library

1 Click Library.

● The Library panel appears.

Note: *By default, the Library panel is docked on the right side of the screen.*

● When the panel is docked, you can click the Collapse to Icons button or click the panel's title bar to collapse the Library panel.

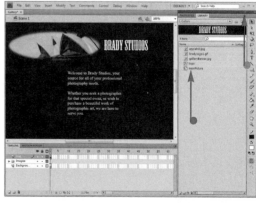

● You can click the Panel Menu button to open a menu of commands related to library tasks and items you can select from.

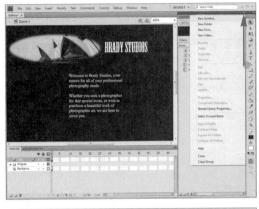

● You can preview an item in the library by clicking the item.

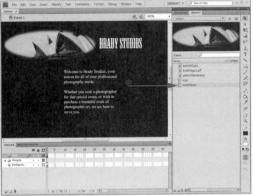

Can I rename a library item?

▼ Yes. To rename an item, you can use any one of the following four methods: First, you can double-click the item name, type the new item name, and press Enter (Return). Second, you can click the item name and then click the Properties icon to open the Symbol Properties dialog box. You then type the new name and click OK. Third, you can right-click the item and click Rename from the context menu. You then type the new item name and press Enter (Return). Fourth, you can click the item name. You then open the Panel menu, choose Rename, type the new item name, and press Enter (Return).

What is the common library?

▼ The common library stores buttons, MovieClips, and sounds that you can use in any Flash movie. To access the common library, click Window, click Common Libraries, and then click the library you want to use. You can create your own common library by creating a file with the items you want to make common, and placing the file in the Libraries folder under the Flash application. In Windows, the full path to the Libraries folder is Program Files\Adobe\Adobe Flash CS4\en\Configuration\Libraries.

continued

Using the Flash Library *(Continued)*

Y ou can sort the Library item list by name, type, use count, linkage, or date modified by clicking the column head. To expand or decrease the size of a column, you click-and-drag the line that separates the columns.

You can also organize items into folders. You might want to put all of the graphics related to a movie clip or button into a single folder. You use the New Folder button to create a folder. To place an item in a folder, you can drag the item over the folder. To toggle a

folder between open and closed, you can double-click the folder. You can also open and close a folder by clicking the folder to select it and then clicking Expand Folder or Collapse Folder on the Library panel menu. You can expand or close all folders by clicking Expand All Folders or Collapse All Folders on the menu.

In addition to symbols, you can store imported graphics, sound clips, and video files in the library. You can play sounds and MovieClips by clicking the Play button in the Preview window.

Using the Flash Library *(continued)*

Create a new folder

① Open the Library panel.

Note: See the previous section to learn how to open the Library panel.

② Click the New Folder icon at the bottom of the Library panel.

③ Type a name for the folder.

④ Press Enter (Return).

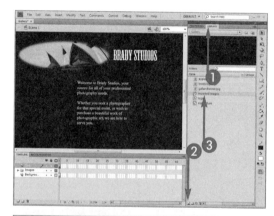

Flash creates a new folder.

⑤ Click-and-drag the item you want to place in the new folder.

⑥ Release the mouse button.

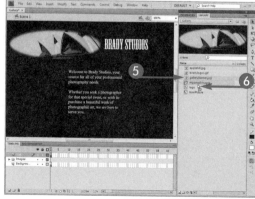

The item moves into the folder.

⑦ To view a folder's contents, click the arrow next to the folder name.

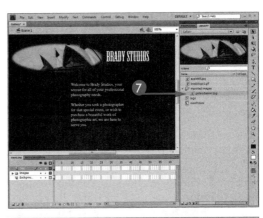

Delete a symbol

① In the Library panel, click the symbol you want to delete.

② Click the Delete icon.

Flash deletes the symbol from the library.

Is there an advantage to deleting unused items from my library? If so, how do I do it?

▼ You can reduce the size of your FLA file by deleting unused items from the library. Open the library panel menu and click Select Unused Items on the menu. Flash finds and selects all unused items. Click the Delete icon to delete the unused items. You do not need to delete unused items to reduce the size of an SWF file because unused items are not included in an SWF file. You can also find unused items by updating your use count and then sorting items by the Use Count field.

How do I sort a column in the library?

▼ To sort a column, click the column heading. Flash sorts the library by the column. You can click the Toggle Sorting Order button to toggle the sort order from ascending to descending or from descending from ascending. Flash then changes the sort order.

Can I use items from the library of another Flash movie in my current movie?

▼ Yes. Click File, click Import, and then click Open External Library. Locate the Flash movie whose content you want to use and click Open. The file's library opens. Drag the items from the library onto the Stage or into the library window of your current movie.

Create a Symbol

Most of the elements you plan to use in your movies will be symbols. You can use graphic symbols for simple or static objects, buttons to add interactivity, and MovieClips for complex animation sequences.

You can convert existing objects on your Stage to a symbol by clicking the Convert to Symbol menu item, found in the Modify menu, or by using the keyboard shortcut F8. Any items on the Stage can be converted to a symbol.

When you convert an item, a dialog box appears that allows you to name the symbol, select the symbol type, and set the registration point. The registration point is a reference marker on the symbol. It is used for setting the location of the symbol on the Stage.

You can also create an empty symbol. When you do this, Flash opens the symbol in its editing mode, with a new, blank copy of the Stage and the symbol's Timeline visible. The cross-hair marker in the center of the symbol's Stage represents its registration point. You can use Flash's drawing tools, import graphics, or insert other symbols onto the symbol's Stage.

Create a Symbol

Convert to a symbol

1 Select one or more shapes on the Stage.

2 Click Modify.

3 Click Convert to Symbol.

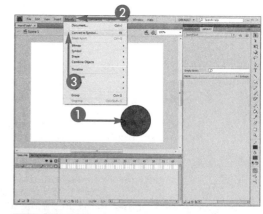

The Convert to Symbol dialog box appears.

4 Type a name for the symbol.

5 Click here and select a symbol type.

6 Click OK.

The object is converted to a symbol.

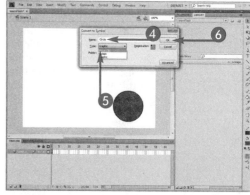

Create a new symbol

1 Click Insert.

2 Click New Symbol.

The Create New Symbol dialog box appears.

3 Type a name for the symbol.

4 Click here and select a symbol type.

5 Click OK.

Flash changes to the symbol-editing mode.

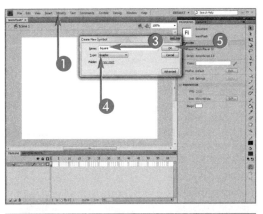

6 Create the symbol content.

You can draw with the drawing tools, or import a graphic by clicking File, and then clicking Import.

Note: *See Chapter 24 to learn how to use the drawing tools and how to import graphics.*

7 Click the scene name to exit symbol-edit mode.

The symbol is created.

You can also click the Edit menu and then click Edit Document to return to the main Timeline.

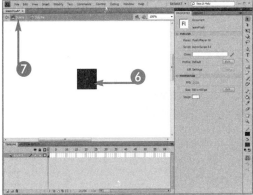

Are there any rules for naming symbols?

▼ No, there are no specific rules. However, Flash designers have established a set of best practices or guidelines for symbol names.

First and foremost, the symbol name should be descriptive of its purpose. You should be able to glance at the library and, from the name alone, be able to determine how and why you would use the symbol.

Second, the symbol name should begin with a capital letter. This is due to how symbols are treated in ActionScript; see Chapter 34 for more information.

Third, most Flash designers and developers prefer to not use spaces in their symbol names. While it is technically allowed, leaving them out makes writing ActionScript a bit easier.

Can I make a copy of a symbol?

▼ Yes, you can duplicate a symbol by using one of two methods: Use the Library panel or select an instance on the Stage. To use the Library panel to duplicate a symbol, click the symbol name in the Library panel, and then select Duplicate from the Library panel menu. To duplicate the symbol by selecting an instance, select an instance of the symbol on the Stage, and then, on the main menu, click Modify, click Symbol, and then click Duplicate Symbol. When you duplicate an image by selecting an instance, Flash makes a duplicate of the symbol and replaces the instance on the Stage with an instance of the duplicate symbol.

Insert an Instance

Y ou can reuse a symbol from the library by placing an instance of the symbol into your movie. Creating and using instances of a symbol can dramatically reduce the size of your Flash movie. An *instance* is a copy of a symbol, and each symbol can have an unlimited number of instances on the Stage.

Using instances of a symbol reduces the file size of your movie because saving instances of an image requires less space than saving a complete copy of an image each time you use it. You create an instance by

opening the library and dragging the symbol from the library onto the Stage.

Most of the time, you place instances of symbols on their own layer. Instances can exist on a single layer with other instances, but it is generally easier to control the stacking order of objects if they exist on separate layers. You can also place instances on the same layer as drawn objects, but the symbols are always on a higher level than the drawn objects. In order for drawn objects to lie on top of symbol instances, they must be on separate layers.

Insert an Instance

① Click the Library panel.

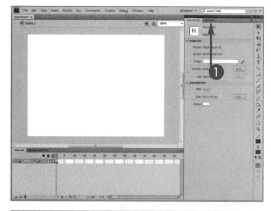

The library opens.

② Click the symbol you want to use.

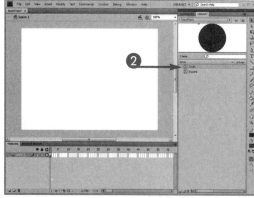

3 Drag the symbol from the library onto the Stage.

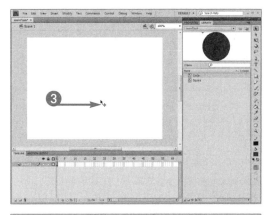

● An instance of the symbol appears on the Stage.

You can reposition or edit the instance, as needed.

Note: *See the next section, "Modify an Instance," to learn more about editing an instance.*

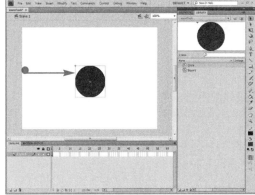

Can I break the link between an instance and a symbol?

▼ Yes, you can break the link between an instance and a symbol by selecting the instance, clicking Modify, and then clicking Break Apart. The instance breaks into an ungrouped collection of shapes and lines. This is useful if you need to make substantial changes to an instance or if you want to change the instance into a new symbol.

Can I change an instance of one symbol to an instance of another symbol?

▼ Yes. You select the instance of one symbol, click the Swap button in the Property Inspector to open the Swap Symbol dialog box, select the other symbol, and then click OK.

Can I delete an instance?

▼ Yes. To delete an instance, select the instance and then press the Delete key or the Backspace key. If you want to use the main menu to delete an instance, select the instance, click Edit, and then click Clear. Deleting an instance in no way affects the actual symbol or any other instance on the Stage.

Modify an Instance

You can change the properties of an instance to use it in different ways in your project. Changing properties enables you to use a single symbol in a variety of ways. Each instance of a symbol has its own properties, which are separate from the original symbol.

You can change the position of an instance by simply dragging it to a new location on the Stage. You can use the Free Transform tool to resize or rotate an instance.

You can also change the properties of an instance by using the Property Inspector. You can set the X and Y coordinates, which reposition the symbol relative to its registration mark, or you can resize it by adjusting the width and height settings. You can also change the color of the instance, as well as adjust the tint, Alpha, or brightness. Adjusting the tint allows you to mix the symbol's current color with a new color. Adjusting its Alpha lets you control its transparency. Brightness refers to the relative lightness or darkness of an image. Black has a brightness of −100 percent. White has a brightness of +100 percent. You also have an advanced option that allows you to set both the tint and Alpha together.

Modify an Instance

① Select the instance you want to modify.

② Click Properties.

③ Set values for X and Y.

Note: You can either drag (scrub) to a new value, or click to enter one manually.

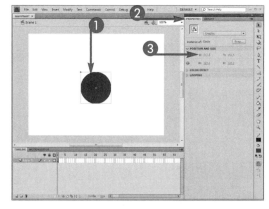

The symbol repositions on the screen.

④ Click Color Effect.

⑤ Click here and select Tint.

⑥ Select a new color.

⑦ Drag the Tint slider to set the percentage of the new color.

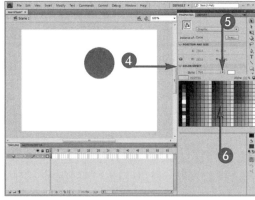

The color changes.

8 Click here and select Alpha.

9 Drag to adjust the transparency.

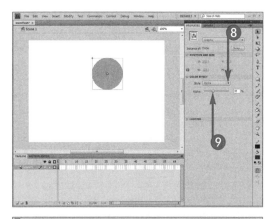

The instance becomes semi-transparent.

10 Type a new value for width.

11 Type a new value for height.

The symbol resizes.

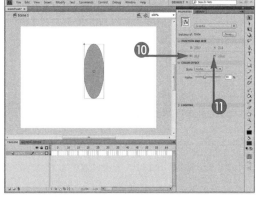

Can I flip an instance?

▼ Yes. Flipping changes the orientation of an instance. For example, flipping horizontally changes the orientation of an instance that faces right so that it faces left, or vice versa. Flipping vertically changes the orientation of an image that faces down so that it faces up, or vice versa. To flip an instance horizontally, select the instance and, on the main menu, click Modify, click Transform, and then click Flip Horizontal. To flip an instance vertically, select the instance and, on the main menu, click Modify, click Transform, and then click Flip Vertical.

Can I align symbols?

▼ Yes, you can use the Align panel with symbols, just as you would with drawn objects. Simply select the symbols you want to align, open the Align panel by clicking Window, and then clicking Align, and then click the desired alignment buttons.

When I enter X and Y coordinates for a symbol, it does not move to the place I had expected. Why not?

▼ The X and Y coordinates on the Property Inspector reference the registration point of the symbol. Therefore, if you have a symbol with a registration point in the top-right corner, setting both the X and Y coordinates to zero places the symbol in the top-right corner of the Stage. However, if the registration point is in the center, then those same coordinates place the center of the symbol on the top-right corner of the Stage, causing part of the symbol to be off the Stage.

Edit a Symbol

You can edit your symbols when you need to make changes to the original. Any change you make to the symbol affects all instances of the symbol. Flash provides three ways to edit a symbol: Edit in Place, Edit in New Window, and Edit mode, also called the symbol-edit mode in Flash.

If you use Edit in Place, the item you edit must be on the Stage. With Edit in Place, you can edit the symbol while viewing all the other items that are on the Stage. As you edit the symbol, the other items appear dimmed.

If you use Edit in New Window, Flash provides you with a new tab window in which you can edit your symbol. The only thing that appears on the Stage is the symbol, and you can see the Timeline associated with the symbol at the top of the screen. You can close the tab to return to the movie.

When you edit the symbol in Edit mode, Flash opens the symbol's Timeline. You can switch back to the Stage view by clicking the scene name.

Regardless of the edit mode you choose, the symbol appears on the Stage with its registration point displayed, and you can use all the tools on the Tools panel to make changes to the symbol.

Edit a Symbol

Edit in place

① Double-click the instance you want to modify.

Note: You can also right-click an instance and click Edit in Place.

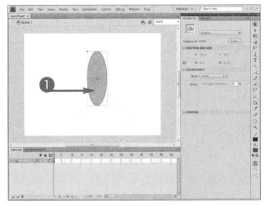

Flash changes to the Edit in Place mode.

② Use the Property Inspector, menu, library, or tools in the Tools panel to make changes to the symbol.

Note: See Chapter 24 to learn how to edit objects.

③ When finished with your edits, click the scene name to exit the Edit in Place mode.

Flash changes all instances of the symbol.

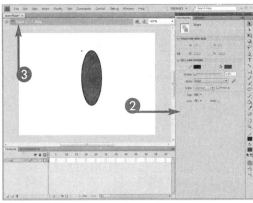

Edit in a new window

① Double-click the symbol's icon in the Library panel.

Note: *You can also right-click an instance and click Edit in New Window.*

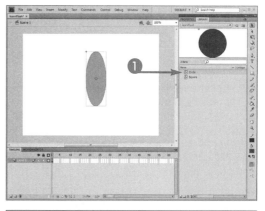

Flash changes to the Edit in New Window mode.

② Use the Property Inspector, menu, library, or tools in the Tools panel to make changes to the symbol.

Note: *See Chapter 24 to learn how to edit objects.*

③ Click the scene name to exit the Edit in New Window mode.

Flash makes the changes to all instances of the symbol.

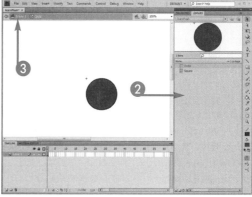

How do I edit a symbol using the Edit mode?

▼ To edit a symbol using the Edit, or symbol-editing, mode, select an instance of the symbol you want to edit. Then, on the main menu, click Edit, and then click Edit Symbols. The symbol appears alone on the Stage. Edit the symbol as necessary and then exit the symbol-editing mode by clicking Edit, and then clicking Edit Document, or by clicking the scene name above the Stage. When you are in symbol-editing mode, the name of the symbol you are editing appears above the Stage area.

How can I change a symbol's registration point?

▼ All symbols, groups, instances, type blocks, and bitmaps have a registration point, indicated by a cross-hair icon. Flash uses the registration point when you are positioning an object or applying transformations. When positioning an object, the registration point is used as the X and Y coordinates. When applying a transformation, it may be used as the point of origin. You can set the registration point when you create a new symbol. While editing your symbol, you can change the location of the registration point by moving the object relative to the cross hairs.

Introduction to Flash Buttons

You can use rollover buttons to enable users to interact with your Flash movies. A rollover button is a simple button that changes in appearance when the user positions the mouse pointer over it, and changes appearance again when the user clicks it. You can create buttons in Flash that are static or animated.

Buttons are a distinct symbol type in Flash. Buttons use four specific frames that control the various points of interaction with the mouse. You can assign actions to your buttons that instruct Flash on how to react when the user activates the button.

Buttons are a popular way to add interactivity to Web pages and forms as well as to movies. For example, you can include movie control buttons that allow users to stop the movie or start playing it again.

Buttons as Symbols

You can turn any symbol you create in Flash into a button symbol, or you can create a new button from scratch. You might custom-make a button shape that includes items specific to the interactive task the user performs. Flash even comes with predrawn buttons that you can use, found in the Buttons library among the common libraries on the Window menu. You can also use different symbols for different stages of the button. For example, the button may appear as a gray box when inactive, but may change to a different color when the user positions the mouse pointer over the button.

When you create a button, you need to think about how you want the button to behave when the user interacts with it. Do you want it static or animated? Do you want it to make a sound? What do you want to happen when the user positions the mouse pointer over the button, clicks the button, and releases the button? You can make buttons as complex or simple as you want. You must also determine the purpose of the button. When you activate the button, what happens? Does it play a movie, stop a movie, or open a form?

Button frames

There are four frames to a button: Up, Over, Down, and Hit. A Timeline of a button does not actually play like other Flash Timelines, but rather jumps to the appropriate frame directed by the user's mouse action.

The Up frame is what the button looks like when not in use. The Over frame is what the button looks like when the user positions the mouse pointer over it. The Down frame is what the button looks like when the user clicks it. The final frame, Hit, is not actually visible to the user at all. Rather, it defines the area of the button that the user can interact with or click.

Up frame

You use the Up frame to display the inactive button. This is the frame the user sees when the mouse pointer is not positioned over the button. By default, the Up frame already has a keyframe in the button's Timeline when you first create the button.

Down frame

The Down frame displays what the button looks like when the user clicks it. You can once again change the button's appearance or add a sound to the Down frame to indicate that the button has been activated.

Over frame

The Over frame displays what the button looks like when the mouse pointer is positioned over the button. For example, you might make the button turn a different color or emit a sound when the user positions the mouse pointer over it to indicate that the button is active.

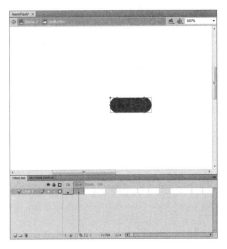

Hit frame

The Hit frame defines the clickable button area or boundary as a whole. This frame is often the same size and shape as the image used in the Over or Down frames. The Hit frame differs from the other button frames in that the user never actually sees it.

To learn more about creating buttons to use in your Flash movies, see the following sections in this chapter. To learn how to add actions and behaviors to buttons, see Section IX of this book.

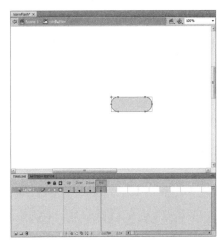

Create a Button

You can create button symbols to add interactivity to your Flash movies. Users click buttons to cause actions to occur. For example, users can click a button to open a Web page.

Buttons have four frames: Up, Over, Down, and Hit. The Up frame is how the button appears when the mouse pointer is not positioned over the button. The Over frame is how the button appears when the pointer is positioned over the button. The Down frame is how the button appears when users click the mouse while the pointer is positioned over the button.

The Hit frame defines the area that responds to user actions; it is not visible to users. Make sure your Hit frame is at least large enough to encompass the graphics used in the other three states. You can make the Hit frame larger than the other states.

To define the appearance of a button state, you can create or import a graphic for each frame. You can also leave some of the frames empty. Each frame inherits its appearance from the frame before, and so if you place a graphic in the Up frame and the Over frame, the Down frame has the same appearance as the Up frame.

Create a Button

Create a new button symbol

① Click Insert.

② Click New Symbol.

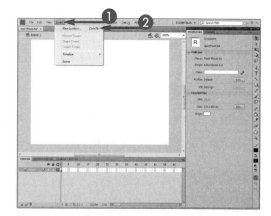

The Create New Symbol dialog box appears.

③ Type a name for the new button.

④ Click here and select Button.

⑤ Click OK.

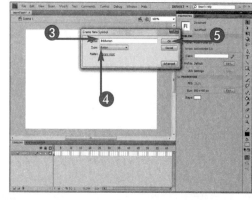

Create the up state

Flash changes to symbol-editing mode, and four button frames appear. You can now create a button state for each frame.

Flash automatically inserts a blank keyframe in the Up frame.

6 Create or place the Up state object on the Stage.

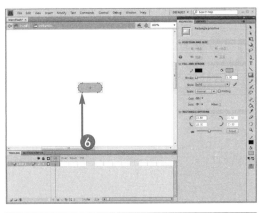

Create the Over state

7 Click the Over frame.

8 Insert a keyframe.

Flash duplicates the object from the Up keyframe.

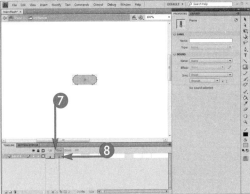

How do I preview a button?

▼ While in symbol-editing mode, click the button's Up frame and press Enter (Return). Watch the Stage as Flash plays through the four button frames. Any changes made to frames appear during playback. You can also drag the playhead over each of the symbol's button states to see how the symbol appears in each state.

Does Flash have premade buttons I can use?

▼ Yes. Flash has a library of buttons. To display the Buttons library, click Window, click Common Libraries, and then click Buttons. The Buttons Library panel appears. This panel works like the regular Library panel. Double-click a folder name to see a list of button types. You can preview a button by clicking its name. To use a button from the library, simply drag it from the Library panel onto the Stage.

Can I use a button from another Flash file?

▼ Yes. If you have stored a button symbol in another Flash file, you can open the other file's library window and place an instance of the symbol on the Stage. Click File, click Import, and then click Open External Library. The Open As Library dialog box appears. Double-click the Flash file you want to use. The associated library window opens onscreen. You can now use any button symbol you have stored in the library.

Create a
Button *(Continued)*

You can use any graphic or movie clip to define the appearance of a button state. You use movie clips to create animated buttons. See Chapter 29 to learn more. You can make even the simplest button more exciting by adding a few variations to each button state. You can duplicate the same object and use the object in each button frame with minor changes so that the button appears different in each state. For example, each state can be a different color or shape.

You use ActionScript to define the action that occurs when users click the button. Buttons are a popular way to add interactivity to Web pages and forms. You can create movie-control buttons that allow users to stop a movie and start playing it again. In addition, you can use buttons that analyze user input, respond to user input, load a movie, or perform a myriad of other tasks. See Section IX for details on writing ActionScript to control your buttons.

Create a Button *(continued)*

⑨ You can edit the object, as needed, if you want it to change in appearance between the button states.

In this example, a color change is applied to the button.

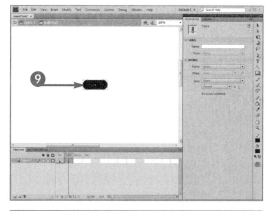

Create the Down state

⑩ Click the Down frame.

⑪ Insert a keyframe.

You can press F6 to quickly insert a keyframe.

Flash duplicates the object from the Over keyframe.

You can edit the object, if desired. In this example, another color change is applied to the button.

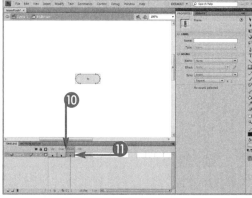

Create the Hit state

⑫ Click the Hit frame.

⑬ Insert a keyframe.

You can press F6 to quickly insert a keyframe.

Flash duplicates the object from the Down keyframe.

Users cannot see the object contained in the Hit frame.

⑭ Click the scene name to return to document-editing mode.

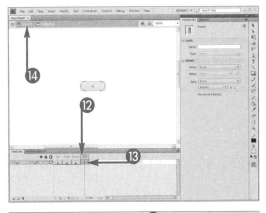

Place the button on the Stage

⑮ Click Library.

⑯ Click-and-drag the button from the library to the Stage.

The newly created button appears on the Stage.

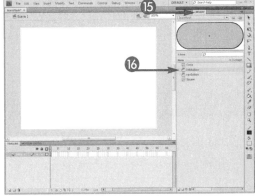

How do I test my button?

▼ Flash disables buttons by default, making it easier for you to work with them as you create your movie. To enable a button for testing, click Control, and then click Enable Simple Buttons. A check mark appears next to your selection on the menu. When you position your pointer over the button, the Over state appears. When you click while the pointer is over the button, the Down state appears. You can also preview the movie.

How do I select an enabled button?

▼ To select an enabled button, use the Selection tool to draw a rectangle around the button. To move an enabled button, select it and use the arrow keys to move it around the Stage. To disable a button after enabling it, click Control, and then click Enable Simple Buttons again. When you are creating a movie, it is best to leave your buttons disabled and only enable your buttons for testing.

Can I use layers when creating a button?

▼ Yes. The button's Timeline works just like the main Timeline in document-editing mode. You can add different layers to your button to organize various objects. For example, if your button includes a text block, you may want to place the text on its own layer; or, if your button uses a sound, you can place the sound clip on a separate layer. See Chapter 27 to learn more about using layers in Flash.

Draw Instances with the Deco Tool

Flash CS4 Professional has introduced a new way to add instances of symbols to your Stage through the Deco tool. The Deco tool allows you to quickly add multiple instances of a symbol in predefined patterns.

By default, the Deco tool creates a vinelike pattern that fills whatever stroke it is placed in. If it is added outside a stroke, it fills the entire Stage.

You can customize the Deco tool by using your own symbols in place of the default leaves and flowers. You can control the angle at which the vines grow, the color of the vines, and other settings.

You can also use the Deco tool to create instances of symbols in a grid pattern or in symmetrical patterns. Both of these settings make creating repeating patterns much easier than in previous versions, where you had to calculate the grid or symmetry manually.

You can also animate with the Deco tool. If this option is checked, Flash creates a frame-by-frame animation showing the brush as it draws the pattern.

Draw Instances with the Deco Tool

1 Click the Deco tool.

2 Click here and select a drawing effect.

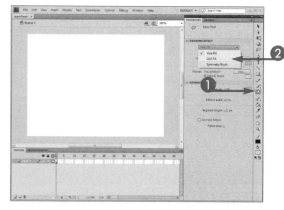

3 Click Edit.

The Swap Symbol dialog box appears.

4 Select a symbol.

5 Click OK.

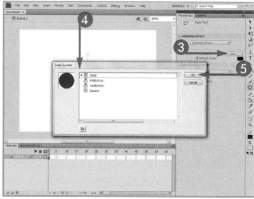

466

6 Click on the Stage.

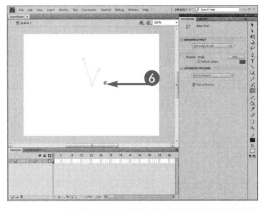

The Deco tool brush draws the pattern using the settings you specified.

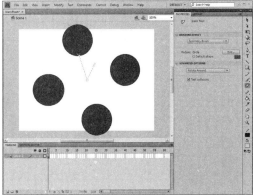

Can I use any symbol for the Deco tool?

▼ Yes. You can use movie clips, graphics, or buttons for any of the shapes used by the Deco tool. In general, smaller symbols work better when using the Vine Fill mode, and simple geometric shapes work best in the grid and symmetry modes.

How do I get the Deco tool to stop drawing once it starts?

▼ You can press the Escape key on your keyboard to stop drawing. The tool attempts to fill the available space, and the Vine Fill mode in particular can be quite slow, and so you may need to press Escape to stop the drawing once you have the desired results.

Are the objects created by the Deco tool grouped?

▼ Yes. Flash automatically groups the symbols when you create instances with the Deco tool.

PART VI

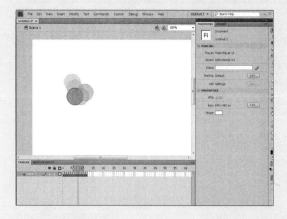

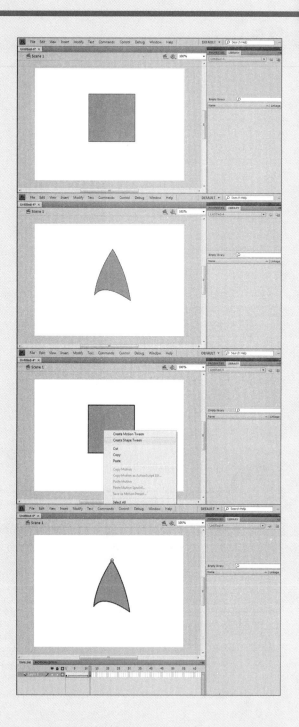

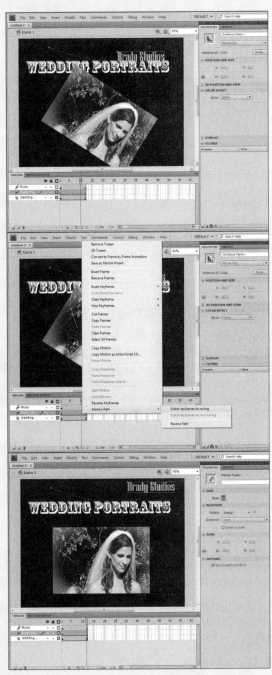

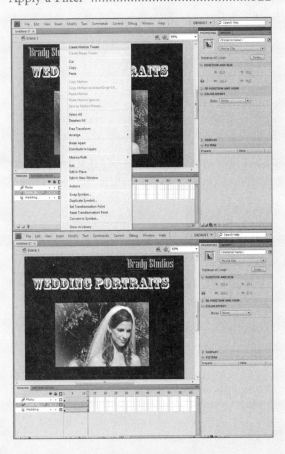

Introduction
to Animation

One of the most exciting aspects of Flash is its animation features. You can animate objects, synchronize the animation with sounds, add backgrounds, animate buttons, and much more.

Using Animation

You can use Flash animation to present a lively message or to simply entertain. Animation you create in Flash can make a Web site come to life. For example, you can create a cartoon to play in the banner for your site, or animate buttons for the user to click. You can create interactive presentations with instructions on how to complete workplace tasks, or make an online tutorial for clients that explains your latest product developments and applications.

You can create animation effects for all kinds of elements associated with Web pages, such as an animated preloader timer that displays how long it takes to complete a download, or an animated cursor that users can click to view different parts of your Web site. You can use Flash animation to enhance an online storefront, present training modules and company presentations, and create all manner of rich Internet applications.

Animation Basics

Animation is simply a change that occurs between two or more frames in a movie. Animation effects use frames to hold illustrated objects or scenes. The object or scene changes slightly from frame to frame to create the illusion of movement.

The change can be the slight movement of an object from one area on the screen to another, or it can be a change in the color, intensity, size, or shape of an object. Any change you make to an object from one frame to another makes the object appear to be animated during playback of your movie.

For example, you might create an animation of a ball bouncing. Each frame displays a snapshot of the ball in various bouncing positions. When you play the animation back, each frame appears briefly before the next frame replaces it. The effect is a ball that seems to bounce.

Animation History

The illusion of movement onscreen relies on a simple scientific principle. At the back of the human eye are a series of cones. These receive the optical information coming into the eye and transmit that information to the brain. Each time a new image comes into the eye, these cones need to reset themselves. If a series of static images are presented in quick succession, the cones do not fully reset between images. This effect, known as *persistence of motion*, fools the brain into believing that the objects are in motion.

The first full-length animated motion picture was Walt Disney's *Snow White and the Seven Dwarfs*, released in 1937. In these early days of animation, Disney and other animation pioneers painted objects and scenes on cels. A *cel*, which is short for *celluloid*, is a transparent sheet commonly used for hand-drawn animation. The cels were stacked to create an image. A movie camera then took a snapshot of that image to create a single frame. The animators reused some of the same cels for the next frame, such as backgrounds, and changed other cels to create an object's movement across the foreground. The end result was a strip of film that, when played back through a projector, created the illusion of movement. These techniques remained in common usage until nearly the end of the century, and many animators still prefer this traditional, hand-drawn method.

Flash and other computer-animation tools use similar principles today to create animation. Instead of transparent cels, you add content to frames and layers in a digital Timeline, and then stack the layers to create depth. Any time you want the content to change, you can add *keyframes* to the Timeline and vary the position or appearance of the content. When the animation or movie is played back, the content appears to move.

Instead of using a film projector for playback, Flash movies use the Flash Player application. Flash Player is a special program designed for viewing Flash content.

Using frames and layers, you can create simple or sophisticated animation effects for your Web site or Flash files to distribute to others.

Types of Animation
You can apply animation in one of two ways in Flash: You can create animation manually frame by frame, or you can let Flash help you create the illusion of motion through a process called tweening.

Frame-by-frame animation, as its name implies, involves creating the simulation of movement by subtly changing the content's appearance from frame to frame. This animation method gives you a great deal of control over how the content changes across the Flash Timeline. You determine how much of a change appears from one frame to the next, whether the change is very slight or very pronounced. While you maintain a lot of control with frame-by-frame animation, it can be extremely time-consuming to create. In addition, Flash movies that use frame-by-frame animation are considerably larger than those that use tweening, and require more processing on the end-user's computer. Therefore, this type of animation should only be used when absolutely necessary.

Tweening is the other method of animation in Flash. With tweening, you can simply specify the beginning and ending states of the object, and have Flash do all of the work of drawing everything in between. In fact, the term *tween* is derived from in between. If you watch the end credits of a traditional hand-drawn animated movie, you may see credits for Tweeners — people who did the same work for the movie as Flash does for you. Compared to frame-by-frame animation, tweening is faster and easier to create and edit and consumes less file size.

You can create motion tweens and shape tweens in Flash. Motion tweens can only be applied to symbols and text blocks, and are a good choice when you need to have an object move from one place on the Stage to another. Shape tweening involves morphing one shape into another, and can only be done on drawn shapes, not symbols. Most of the animation you create in Flash is done through motion tweens.

Introduction to Frames

Frames are the backbone of your animation effects. You can use frames to create the illusion of motion and change across time. When you start a new Flash file, it opens with a single layer and hundreds of placeholder frames in the Timeline. You can add frames to each layer you add to the Timeline. Before you start animating objects, you need to understand how frames work.

Frame Rates

The number of frames you use in your Flash movie combined with the speed at which they play determines the length of the movie. By default, new Flash files you create use a frame rate of 24 frames per second, or 24 fps. You can set a frame rate higher or lower than the default if needed.

The default frame rate is well suited for playing movies on the Web. Television and video use a frame rate of 29.97 fps, and film uses 24 fps. The maximum possible frame rate in a Flash movie is 120 fps; the minimum is 0.01.

You can change the frame rate using the Properties panel or the Document Properties dialog box. To view the set frame rate at any time, simply look at the bottom of the Timeline. The frame rate is listed along with the current frame and elapsed time information.

Constructing Animation

You can use the Timeline at the top of the Flash program window to build your animation sequences frame by frame and layer by layer. The Timeline contains frames you can use to add and create animation content, and layers to organize movie elements and create depth in your animation. When you click a frame in any layer, the Flash Stage displays any content associated with the selected frame. You can use as many frames and layers as you want to build your movies.

You can work with several different types of frames in the Flash Timeline: placeholder frames, keyframes, static frames, and tweened frames. Frames appear as tiny boxes in the Timeline. By default, the frames appear in Normal size; however, you can use the Timeline Frame View menu to change the appearance of frames in your Timeline. For example, you may prefer viewing larger frames in the Timeline so that they are more readable.

You can further organize your movie into manageable sections by creating *scenes*. A Flash movie can consume hundreds of frames. By breaking the animation into smaller sections, you can easily work on just the section you want. For example, your movie might include an introduction scene, different scenes for the main movie, and a final scene for credits. Each scene uses its own Timeline. You can work on each scene independently without disturbing objects in other scenes. When playing back the movie, Flash plays the scenes in the order you specify. You can use the Scenes panel to organize scenes and control the order in which they play.

Placeholder Frames

A *placeholder frame* is merely an empty frame. It has no content. In other words, when you click an empty frame, no content appears on the Stage. With the exception of the first frame in a new layer, the remaining frames are all placeholders until you assign another frame type.

Keyframes

You use *keyframes* to add content to your movie. A keyframe also defines a change in animation, such as an object moving or taking on a new appearance. Because keyframes are the only frames that define key changes in a movie, they are crucial in creating your animation effects. By default, Flash inserts a blank keyframe for you in the first frame of every new layer you add to the Timeline. A blank keyframe has no content on the Stage. A hollow bullet denotes a blank keyframe on the Timeline.

When you add content to a blank keyframe, it becomes a regular keyframe and its status changes on the Timeline. Keyframes containing content on the Stage are identified by a solid bullet in the Timeline. You can add and delete keyframes as needed by using the Insert menu on the menu bar, right-clicking the frame to view a context menu, or pressing the F6 key.

A keyframe that you add duplicates the content from the previous keyframe. This technique makes it easy to tweak the contents slightly to create the illusion of movement between frames. You can convert existing frames into keyframes, or choose to add new keyframes.

You can also delete or clear the content of any keyframe.

Static Frames

Static or regular frames display the same content as the previous frame in the Timeline. Static frames must be preceded by a keyframe. Static frames are used to hold content that you want to remain visible until you add another keyframe in the layer. You can use static frames to control how quickly or slowly the content changes between two keyframes, or the perceived speed in which the animation occurs. For example, if only one static frame appears between two keyframes, the change happens quite quickly. If you add several static frames between two keyframes, the change appears to happen more smoothly during playback. You can add frames when you need to slow down the animation change, or remove frames when you need to speed up the effect.

Tweened Frames

One way to create animation in a movie is to allow Flash to calculate the number of frames between two keyframes to create movement. Using a process called *tweening*, Flash determines the in-between positions of the animated object from one keyframe to the next, and spaces out the changes in the tweened frames between the two keyframes. Motion-tweened frames appear shaded in blue on the Flash Timeline and contain a motion-tween arrow. Shape-tweened frames appear shaded in green on the Timeline and contain a shape-tween arrow.

PART VII

Set Movie Dimensions and Frame Rate

You can specify the size and frame rate of a movie before you begin building the animation. You can use either the Document Properties dialog box or the Properties panel to set both the movie screen size and frame rate. Taking time to set the movie dimensions and frame rate now will save you time and prevent headaches later. If you resize the movie after you have created it, you may find yourself having to reposition elements on numerous layers to make things fit.

The vertical and horizontal dimensions of the Stage determine the size of your movie, which in turn specifies the size of the screen used to play the movie when published. You can make your movie any size, but most users prefer to keep the size relative to the largest objects in the movie.

The play speed of a movie is measured by the number of frames per second, or *fps*. By default, Flash assigns a frame rate of 24 fps, a good setting for animation delivered over the Web. You can set a higher or lower rate as needed, but setting the rate too high causes the images to blur, while setting it too low may cause the animation to appear choppy.

Set Movie Dimensions and Frame Rate

① Click Modify.

② Click Document.

You can also double-click the frame rate on the Timeline to open the Document Properties dialog box.

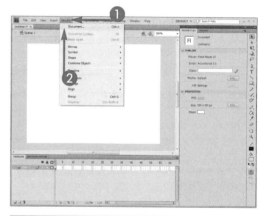

The Document Properties dialog box appears.

③ Type the number of frames per second you want the movie to play in the Frame rate text box.

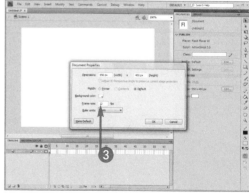

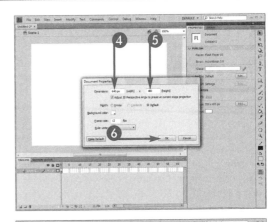

④ Type a width value in the width text box.

⑤ Type a height value in the height text box.

⑥ Click OK.

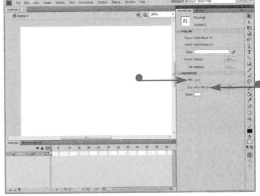

● The Flash Stage adjusts to the new dimensions you assigned.

● The new frame rate is set.

What is a good frame rate for my movie?

▼ The frame rate controls how quickly Flash displays images in a movie. If the images are displayed too quickly, they appear as a blur. If the images are displayed too slowly, they appear jerky. The default frame rate of 24 fps works well for most projects. If you set a higher frame rate, slower computers struggle to play at such speeds. If you are confident your target audience uses a high bandwidth and the latest version of Flash Player, you can use a higher frame rate.

You may find it easier to calculate the timing of your movie by reducing the frame rate to a factor of 10 fps, as it is generally easier to calculate multiples of 10 than of 24 or other numbers.

Can I vary the frame rate throughout my movie?

▼ No. After you set a frame rate, that rate is in effect for the entire movie. You can, however, vary the speed of animation sequences by adding or removing frames. If a sequence seems to go too fast, you can add regular, or *static*, frames between the keyframes to slow it down. See the next section to learn more about adding frames.

Where can I find the frame rate for my movie?

▼ You can quickly view a movie's frame rate by looking at the frame rate display at the bottom of the Timeline. The frame rate is listed along with the current frame number and elapsed time. You can also view the frame rate in the Properties panel. Click anywhere outside the Stage area to see the frame rate field in the Properties panel.

Add Frames

You can insert frames to add content and length to your Flash movies. When you add a new layer or start a new file, Flash gives you one blank keyframe in the Timeline and many placeholder frames. Adding frames is as easy as adding pages to a document. Flash lets you specify exactly what kind of frame to add and allows you to add as many frames as you need. You can add keyframes, regular frames, and blank keyframes, and you can add more than one at a time.

You add keyframes to define changes in the appearance of your animation, such as changing the

placement or color of an object. When you add a keyframe, Flash copies the contents of the previous keyframe, which you can then edit to create a change in the animation sequence.

You can also add regular frames to repeat the content of the keyframes preceding them. Regular, or static, frames help extend the animation sequence between keyframes. You can also add regular frames to slow down the change that occurs between two keyframes. For example, in an animation sequence of a bouncing ball, you can add regular frames to a bounce sequence to make the effect seem to slow down.

Add Frames

Add a keyframe

1 Right-click the frame on the Timeline that you want to turn into a keyframe.

2 Click Insert Keyframe.

You can also press F6 on the keyboard or click Insert, then click Timeline, and then click Keyframe.

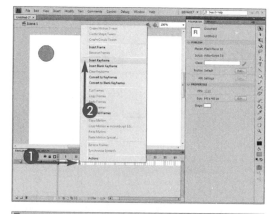

● Flash inserts a keyframe, marked by a solid bullet in the Timeline.

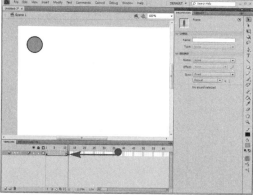

Add a regular frame

1 Right-click a frame where you want to insert a new frame.

2 Click Insert Frame.

You can also press F5 on the keyboard or click Insert, then click Timeline, and then click Frame.

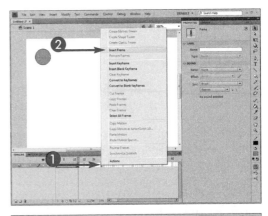

● Flash inserts a frame.

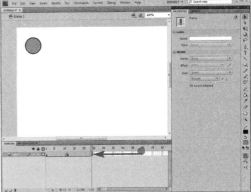

How can I determine how long my movie is?

▼ The Timeline displays the total length of the movie next to the current frame rate. When you are adding frames, you can figure out the number of frames you need to add to achieve a certain amount of time by multiplying the amount of time required by the frame rate. For example, to create a 5-second animation at the default 24 fps frame rate, you would need to add a total of 120 frames (24 x 5 frames). At 10 fps, the same 5-second animation would require only 50 frames.

What is the maximum number of frames I can have in my movie?

▼ Flash movies can contain up to 16,000 frames. At the default 24 fps rate, that would mean your Flash movie would run for 666.67 seconds, or just over 11 minutes.

Does adding additional frames increase the size of my file?

▼ Yes, although the exact increase in file size depends on the objects being placed on the Stage in each additional frame. Adding frames with simple, nonanimated shapes does not add as much size to the file as adding frames with complex objects, imported graphics, and animation.

Select Frames

Y ou select frames on the Flash Timeline to add, move, or edit the content of frames. You must also select frames if you want to remove them from the Timeline. You can use a couple of selection techniques when working with frames.

You can select a single frame, multiple frames, or all the frames on the Timeline. In fact, you can select multiple frames on multiple layers. When you select multiple frames, they can be contiguous or non-contiguous. You can select multiple contiguous frames by holding the Shift key while you select them, or by clicking and dragging across the frames you want to

select; you can select noncontiguous frames by pressing and holding the Ctrl key while you make your selection.

When you select a single frame, it appears highlighted on the Timeline and the frame number appears on the status bar at the bottom of the Timeline. The playhead also appears directly above the selected frame. When you select multiple frames, Flash highlights the frames you selected, and the number of the last frame in the group appears on the Timeline status bar. Any content of the layer that is associated with the frame is selected on the Stage.

Select Frames

Select a single frame

① Click a frame to select it.

Flash highlights the frame on the Timeline.

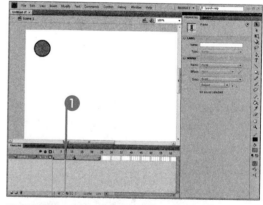

Select contiguous multiple frames

① Click the first frame in the range of frames you want to select.

② Press and hold the Shift key and click the last frame in the range.

Flash selects all of the frames in the range you selected.

You can also click the first frame and drag to the last frame you want to select.

Note: *To select noncontiguous frames, press and hold the Ctrl (⌘) key while clicking frames.*

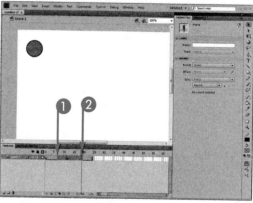

Add Frame Labels

Rather than needing to refer to frames by number, you can add labels to frames. The label appears on the Timeline, providing a visual reference to help you identify portions of your movie. Labels can also be used in ActionScript to move the playhead to that frame.

You can add a label to any keyframe in your movie. However, it is considered a best practice to create a layer that specifically holds the labeled keyframes. That way, you can separate the labels from the individual content on the frames, so if you decide later that you do not need the visual components

and you delete the layer, then the labels are not deleted.

You can use any characters for your labels, including spaces. When you create your labels, it does not matter whether you capitalize the label or not, but you should be consistent, as ActionScript forces you to reference the label using the same case in which it was created.

The Timeline displays a small flag in the labeled frame. If there is enough room between the labeled keyframe and the next keyframe on that layer, the label displays on the Timeline as well.

Add Frame Labels

① Click the keyframe you want to label.

② Click Properties.

③ Type a label for the frame.

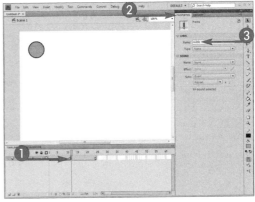

● The label appears in the Timeline.

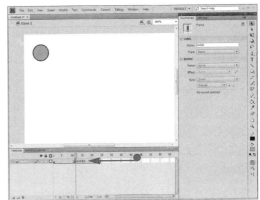

Delete Frames or Change Keyframe Status

You can remove frames you no longer need or change them to a type of frame that you can use. For example, you may decide a particular animation sequence between two keyframes runs too slowly during playback. You can remove several regular in-between frames to speed up the sequence; or you might make a drastic change in your animation and decide you no longer need a particular keyframe in the sequence.

You can use the Remove Frames command to remove a single frame or several frames completely from the Timeline. To remove a keyframe from the Timeline,

you must select both the keyframe and all the in-between frames associated with it; otherwise, the Remove Frames command removes the last regular frame before the next keyframe, rather than the actual keyframe.

Instead of removing a keyframe completely, however, you can change the status of the keyframe by using the Clear Keyframe command. This command removes the keyframe status of the frame and demotes it to a regular frame. When you change the status of a keyframe, all in-between frames are altered as well. To clear a frame's content only, you can apply the Clear Frames command.

Delete Frames or Change Keyframe Status

Delete frames

① Click the frame, or range of frames, you want to delete.

② Right-click the selected frame or frames.

③ Click Remove Frames.

Flash removes the frame, and any existing frames to the right move over to fill the void.

Note: *You can also press Shift+F5 on your keyboard.*

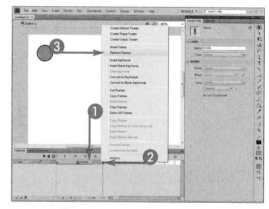

Clear frames

① Select the frame or range of frames you want to clear.

Note: *See the section, "Select Frames," to learn how to select frames in the Timeline.*

② Right-click the selected frame or frames.

③ Click Clear Frames.

Flash removes the content from the selected frames.

Note: *If you clear a keyframe, Flash changes the keyframe to a blank keyframe in the Timeline.*

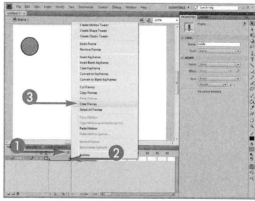

Change keyframe status

1 Right-click the keyframe you want to change.

2 Click Clear Keyframe.

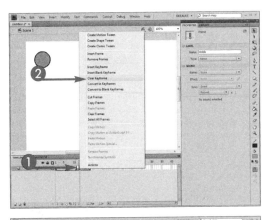

● Flash converts the keyframe to a regular frame, and changes the frame to match the contents of the previous keyframe.

Note: You cannot change the status of the first keyframe in a layer.

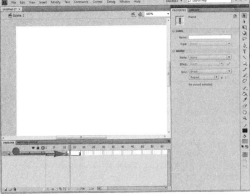

Can I remove a range of frames?

▼ Yes. Select the range of frames you want to delete by clicking the first frame in the group and then dragging to highlight the remaining frames. Once all the frames in the range are selected, you can apply the Remove Frames command. See the section, "Select Frames," earlier in this chapter to learn more about frame-selection techniques.

If I delete a keyframe, is the frame label removed as well?

▼ Yes. Any time you remove a keyframe from the Timeline, its associated frame label is removed as well. To learn more about adding labels to frames, see the section, "Add Frame Labels," earlier in this chapter.

Can I undo a frame deletion?

▼ Yes. If you click the Edit menu and then click Undo immediately after removing a frame, Flash undoes the action. You can also use the History panel to undo your actions. See Chapter 25 to learn more about this feature.

What does the Convert to Keyframes command do?

▼ If you click the Convert to Keyframes command in the context menu, Flash converts the selected frame into a keyframe. You can use this command to create a change in animation content in the middle of an existing animation sequence. If you click the Convert to Blank Keyframes command, Flash turns the selected frames into blank keyframes and you can add new content.

Create Frame-by-Frame Animation

Perhaps the simplest form of animation that most people have encountered is the small flip-books that can be found in novelty stores. These contain a series of images that change slightly from page to page, and when you flip through the book quickly, it appears as though the image is being animated.

Before computer animation, movie special effects used a similar technique. In the 1960s, Ray Harryhausen used a process called stop-motion photography in films such as *Jason and the Argonauts* and *Sinbad and the Eye of the Tiger.* He would first create clay models

of monsters, living skeletons, and other creatures; then he would snap a photograph of the object, move it slightly, snap another photograph, and repeat this process. It could often take many hours to create a few seconds of animation.

You can create a similar effect in Flash using *frame-by-frame* animation. You can create frame-by-frame animation by creating an object in a keyframe. Then, you can create another keyframe, usually in the next frame, and slightly manipulate the object. You can repeat this process to create the animation effect.

Create Frame-by-Frame Animation

1 Click the first keyframe you want to animate.

2 Add the object you want to animate to the Stage.

You can add an instance of a symbol from the library to animate, or you can use the drawing tools to create an object.

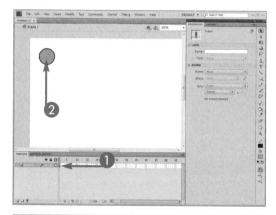

3 Add a keyframe to the next frame in the Timeline where you want to continue the animation.

You can press F6 to quickly insert a keyframe, or click the Insert menu, click Timeline, and then click Keyframe.

Note: *You can continue the animation in the very next frame, or space out the animation with a few regular frames in between.*

Flash inserts a keyframe that duplicates the contents of the first keyframe.

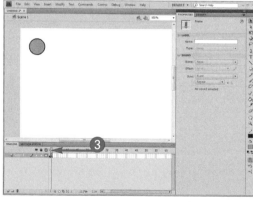

④ Change the object slightly to create the animation effect.

You can move the object slightly on the Stage, or change the appearance of the object, such as its color or size.

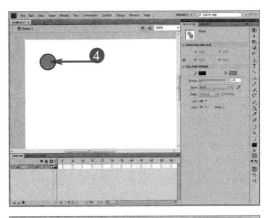

⑤ Add a third keyframe to the next frame in the layer where you want to change the animation.

You can press F6 to insert a keyframe, or use the Insert menu to add a keyframe.

Flash inserts a keyframe that duplicates the contents of the second keyframe.

⑥ Change the object appearance or position again slightly so that it differs from the previous keyframe contents.

⑦ Repeat steps **3** to **6** to complete the animation.

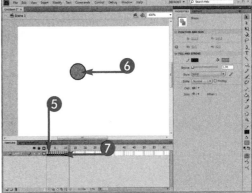

Creating frame-by-frame animation seems very time-consuming and complicated. Is there an easier way?

▼ Frame-by-frame animation is definitely the hardest, most time-consuming way to create animation. It also results in the largest file sizes. That said, it also gives you the finest level of control over the animated effects you create. Motion and shape tweening are much easier ways to create animation, but offer less control. You will discover as you work through your projects that the ideal solution is to use a combination of all three techniques to achieve the effect you want.

Am I limited as to what kinds of objects I can use in my animation?

▼ No. When you create frame-by-frame animation, you can use anything: drawn objects, symbols, imported graphics — even video. You can also freely switch between them; for example, you could have a symbol in one frame and replace it with a drawn object in the next.

How can I control the speed at which my frame-by-frame animation plays?

▼ You can increase or decrease the frame rate of the movie to speed up or slow down the animation as a whole. Alternately, you can add additional static frames between the keyframes to slow down individual sequences, or remove static frames between keyframes to speed them up.

PART VII

Preview Flash Animations

You should preview your Flash documents to ensure your animations work properly. You can preview your documents in the authoring environment, in the test environment, or in a Web browser.

You can easily test your movie in the Flash-authoring environment, which is the Stage area in the Flash program window, by pressing Enter (Return). This causes the playhead to progress through the movie, and most animations play. Button functionality is disabled when previewing this way, and ActionScript-driven animation

does not play. You can press Enter or Return again to stop playing the movie.

While viewing the movie in the authoring environment gives you an idea of what it will look like, it is a good idea to frequently test your movie in Flash Player, so that you can see precisely how the movie will look to your users, as well as interact with buttons and see ActionScript events. You can preview your movie in Flash Player by clicking Control, and then clicking Test Movie on the main menu, or by using the keyboard shortcut Ctrl+Enter.

Preview Flash Animations

Play a movie

① Click Control.

② Click Play.

You can also press Enter (Return) to play the movie.

Flash plays your movie on the Stage.

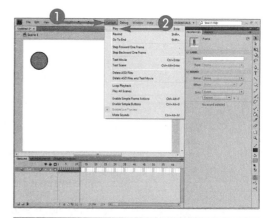

③ Press Enter (Return).

The animation stops.

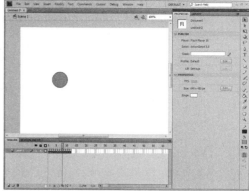

Preview in Flash Player

① Click Control.

② Click Test Movie.

You can also press Ctrl+Enter or ⌘+Return.

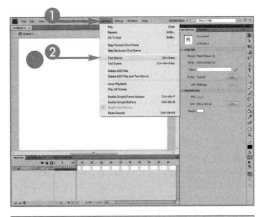

Flash Player opens and plays the movie.

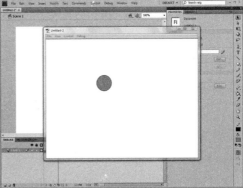

Why should I use the test environment?

▼ When you view your movie in the Flash Player window, you are seeing your movie as others will see it. When you click File, and then click Save, Flash saves the movie you are authoring in FLA format. To view your animation on the Web, your file must be in SWF format. Clicking Control, and then clicking Test Movie creates a SWF file, moves you to the test environment, which is the Flash Player window, and plays the SWF file.

How do I test my movie in a Web browser?

▼ To test your movie in a Web browser, click File, click Publish Preview, and then click Default. Flash opens and plays your movie in your default Web browser. You can also test your movie in a Web browser by clicking File, clicking Publish Preview, and then clicking HTML. You should always test your movie in a Web browser before posting it on the Web.

View Multiple Frames with Onion Skinning

When creating frame-by-frame animation, it can be difficult to position objects in each new keyframe because you cannot see where they are in previous or subsequent frames. Fortunately, Flash provides a feature, called *onion skinning,* to solve this problem. When you turn the feature on, a number of frames appear before and after the current frame. The objects on those frames are semi-transparent, as if viewed through the translucent layers of an onion.

Onion skinning offers two modes of display: dimmed content or outlined content. The objects in the frames surrounding the current frame appear dimmed — the default option — or as outlined objects, but regardless of the choice, the contents of the current frame are fully displayed. This allows you to see multiple frames and how their movements relate to the current frame.

You can change the number of frames visible before and after the current frame by dragging the brackets, which are visible at the top of the Timeline to either side of the playhead.

View Multiple Frames with Onion Skinning

Turn on onion skinning

① Click a frame in your animation sequence.

② Click the Onion Skin button at the bottom of the Flash Timeline.

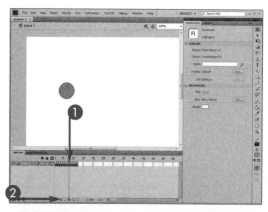

● Flash displays dimmed images from the surrounding frames and places onion skin markers at the top of the Timeline.

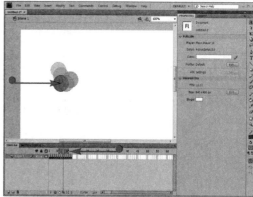

Turn on onion skinning outlines

1 Click a frame in your animation sequence.

2 Click the Onion Skin Outlines button.

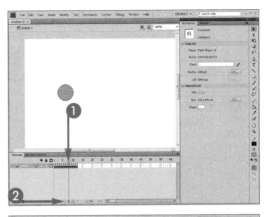

● Flash displays outlines of the images from the surrounding frames and places onion skin markers at the top of the Timeline.

Control the number of visible frames

1 Click-and-drag the brackets on the Timeline.

Flash displays more or fewer frames as onion skins.

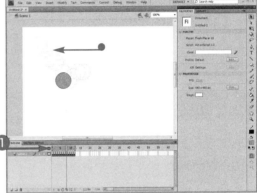

Can I edit the onion skin frames?

▼ Yes. Flash includes an Edit Multiple Frames feature to allow you to edit the frames visible when you turn on onion skinning. You can enable the feature by clicking the button to the right of the Onion Skin button.

How do I make the onion skin markers stay in place?

▼ If you click another frame, the onion skin markers move in position relative to the frame you are in. To keep them anchored in their original locations, click the Modify Onion Markers button and then click Anchor Onion. This command keeps the markers from adjusting when you click different frames.

Can I apply onion skinning to all the frames and layers in my movie?

▼ Yes. You can enable the Onion All feature from the pop-out menu on the Timeline. This causes Flash to onion-skin all the frames in all the layers in your movie.

Create Animation with a Motion Tween

While frame-by-frame animation offers you the most control, it is far easier and more efficient to animate with tweens. Rather than needing to position or otherwise modify an object on each frame, you can simply create the initial frame and the ending frame of an animation sequence and let Flash fill in the frames in between. The term *tween* is derived from in between. Flash offers two types of tweens. The first is a motion tween. The second, shape tweening, is discussed in the next section.

Motion tweens are the most efficient type of animation available in Flash, primarily due to the fact

that motion tweens use symbols. Other animation types typically use drawn objects on the Stage, which must be re-created in memory in each frame. Symbols are only stored once in the library, and thus do not require additional memory when they are used repeatedly, such as in a motion tween.

You need to create a keyframe and place the symbol in its starting position on the Stage. Then, you can add a tween to the symbol through a right-click menu. When you reposition the symbol on the Stage, Flash adds the necessary frames to create the animation.

1. Add an instance of a symbol to the Stage.

Note: See Chapter 28 for details on creating symbols.

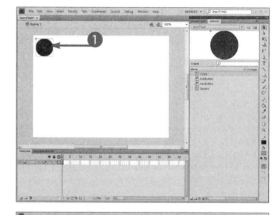

2. Right-click the symbol.
3. Click Create Motion Tween.

④ Move the symbol to a new location on the Stage.

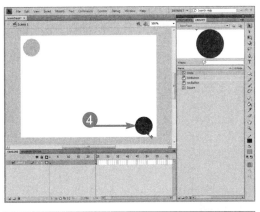

Flash creates the tween.

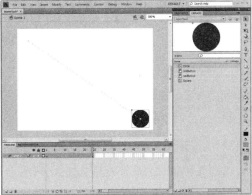

Can I change the length of the animation?

▼ Yes. Flash automatically adds a keyframe in frame 24, creating a 2-second sequence. You can position your mouse over the right edge of that keyframe and drag to change the length of the sequence. If you drag to the left, you shorten the sequence, whereas if you drag to the right, you lengthen it.

How can I add additional movement to the symbol?

▼ To have the symbol continue animating beyond the second keyframe, you can simply add another keyframe and then position the symbol in the location at which you want the symbol to arrive. You can continue doing this as much as you want. See the section, "Add Frames," earlier in this chapter, for details on how to add keyframes.

What does the line with the dots that appears on the Stage represent?

▼ The line shows the path of the animation. See the next section for information on how to manipulate the animation with this line.

PART VII

Change the Path of an Animation

When you create a motion tween, you see a green line with a series of dots appear on the Stage. This line represents the path the symbol takes from its starting to its ending position.

By default, the line is straight, but you can manipulate the path to have your symbol travel along a curve. You can manipulate the path with the Selection tool by simply moving your mouse cursor near the edge of the line and dragging, which causes the line to curve and the symbol to follow the curved path. Once the line is curved, you can move the symbol to a new location on the Stage. The line remains curved, but the radius of the curve changes to accommodate the new position.

The dots along the line represent the symbol's position at each frame. The number of dots corresponds to the number of frames along the tween; as Flash defaults to a 24-frame animation, the line initially contains 24 dots. If you lengthen or shorten the animation, you see the number of dots change accordingly.

Change the Path of an Animation

① Click the Selection tool.

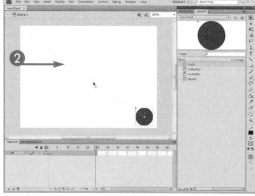

② Position your mouse near the edge of the line.

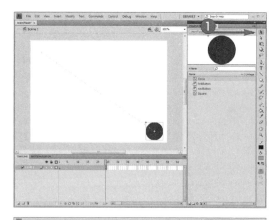

③ Drag the line to create a curve.

Flash curves the line.

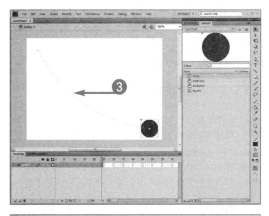

④ Press Enter (Return).

The animation plays, with the symbol following the curve.

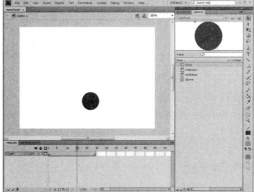

Can I get the symbol to rotate as it animates?

▼ Yes. The Properties panel provides additional controls when you apply a motion tween. If you click a frame along the tween, the panel displays a series of settings to control the animation. You can click Orient to Path to have the symbol maintain its alignment with the path, or you can scrub the time indicator next to Rotate to have the symbol spin that number of times. You can control the direction of the spin through the drop-down menu below that.

Can I have the symbol speed up as it nears the end of the animation?

▼ Yes. You can use the Ease control on the Properties panel to control the starting and ending speed of the symbol. A positive ease number creates an ease-out effect, whereby the symbol slows over the course of the animation, whereas a negative value creates an ease-in effect, whereby the symbol speeds up. You can control this more precisely through the Motion Editor, which is discussed later in this chapter.

PART VII

Create a Shape Tween

You can use shape tweens to create morphing effects in your movies. Whereas motion tweens can only be applied to symbols, shape tweens can only be applied to drawn objects.

You need to add two keyframes to your Timeline to create a shape tween. In the first keyframe, you can draw any shape you want. In the second keyframe, you delete the first shape and replace it with the second shape. When you return to the first keyframe, you can set the object to shape tween. You can use

onion skins to position the second object relative to the first — see the section, "View Multiple Frames with Onion Skinning," to learn how to use onion skins.

You can control the morphing effect by adding shape hints. A shape hint defines a specific spot on the first symbol that remains in place to the second symbol. Each hint is represented by a circle with a letter. You can position the circle in the first keyframe, and then position the corresponding circle in the second keyframe to force the spot in the first keyframe to move to the spot on the second.

Create a Shape Tween

Morph objects

① Use the drawing tools to draw a shape.

Note: *Be sure that the Object Drawing model is turned off.*

② Insert a keyframe.

See the section, "Add Frames," to learn how to insert keyframes.

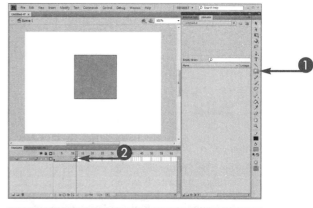

Flash inserts a keyframe.

③ Delete the object.

④ Draw a new object in the same position as the first.

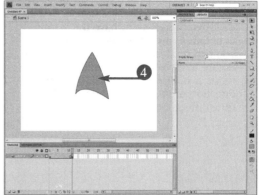

5 Click the first keyframe.

6 Right-click the shape.

7 Click Create Shape Tween.

The tween is created.

8 Press Enter (Return).

The animation plays.

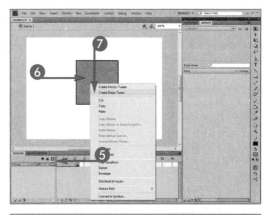

Add shape hints

1 Click Modify.

2 Click Shape.

3 Click Add Shape Hint.

4 Position the hint.

5 Position the hint on the second object.

6 Press Enter (Return).

The animation plays.

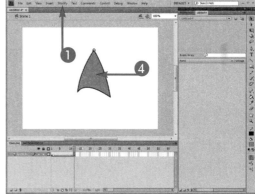

How many shape hints can I use on a single object?

▼ Because shape hints are referenced by letters in the English alphabet, you are limited to 26 per object. Rarely, however, will you need this many; most of the time, you will need no more than three or four shape hints.

When I right-click the object, the Create Shape Tween option is grayed out. Why is this?

▼ You can only apply shape tweening to drawn objects on the Stage. If you attempt to add a shape tween to a symbol, the option becomes grayed out. Also, if you draw a shape using the Object Drawing model, it is grayed out unless you ungroup the shape.

Can I change other properties of the shape during a tween?

▼ Yes. If you position the second shape somewhere on the Stage other than where the first object is, it moves as it morphs. If the second shape is a different color from the first shape, the color gradually shifts from the first to the second.

Modify Animation with the Motion Editor

For many years, software used by video artists to create animation for film has included tools to fine-tune animation. These tools, such as Adobe After Effects, allow the artists to control individual aspects of the animation, such as setting a scaling animation to ease in while the position animation remains at a constant speed.

With Flash CS4 Professional, Adobe has added the Motion Editor to the program, giving you the same control over your animations as you would have in tools such as After Effects. When you open the Motion Editor panel and select a tween, you see five sections of controls: Basic motion, Transformation, Color effect, Filters, and Eases. You can click the arrow next to any of the categories to expand or collapse its controls. From the Motion Editor, you can add keyframes and new effects to your animation.

The right portion of the panel displays a representation of the Timeline. You can scroll to see the elapsed frames; a label appears every five frames. When you have an effect in place, it is represented in the Timeline portion of the panel as a line showing its progress.

① Click a tween.

② Click Motion Editor.

If you do not see the Motion Editor panel, click Window, and then click Motion Editor.

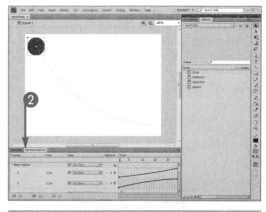

③ Click the Go to Next Keyframe button.

The playhead advances to the end of the animation.

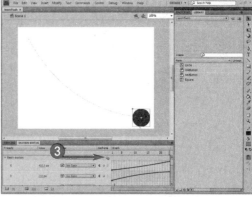

④ Click the arrow next to Transformation.

The Transformation controls appear.

⑤ Click the Add or Remove Keyframe button.

A Transformation keyframe is added.

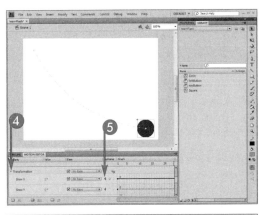

⑥ Click-and-drag to scrub the Skew value.

The value changes, creating a skew effect within the animation.

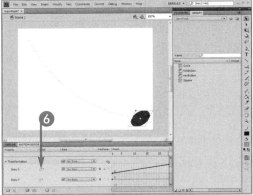

What does the Simple(Slow) option in the Ease drop-down menu do?

▼ The drop-down menu next to the effect name displays the easing value for the animation, which can be controlled by adding an ease effect to the animation. The settings for easing are at the bottom of the Motion Editor. You can click the plus sign to add a new Ease. You see a series of preset easing values, or you can create your own.

Can I change the color of an object over time?

▼ Yes. The Motion Editor includes a section for Color effects. Like easing, you can click the plus sign next to Color effects to add an Alpha effect, which changes the transparency of the symbol, or a Brightness effect to lighten or darken the symbol, or a Tint effect to change the color. You can also choose Advanced to control the color values precisely.

What are filters?

▼ Filters allow you to add effects such as drop shadows to your animation. Applying and animating filters is covered in Chapter 30.

Move and Copy Frames

You can move and copy the frames in your movie to change the sequence of your movie. For example, you might want to move a sequence of frames forward or backward on the Timeline, or you may want to copy multiple frames and paste them elsewhere on the Timeline so that the sequence plays twice.

The Copy Frames and Paste Frames commands found on the Edit menu allow you to edit the frames, whereas the standard Copy and Paste commands merely affect the objects on the Stage.

You can also use drag-and-drop to move frames, which allows you to drag frames around on the Timeline and drop them into new locations. You can also drag a frame to another layer. You can select multiple frames and relocate them as a group by dragging them around the Timeline. In order to drag-and-drop frames, you need to click once to select the frame, and then click-and-drag a second time to move them. If you simply click-and-drag without first selecting the frame, you merely end up selecting the frames across which you drag.

Copy a frame

1 Click a frame or click and drag to select the frames you want to copy.

Note: *You may need to click the Timeline tab to display it.*

Flash highlights the frames on the Timeline.

2 Click Edit.

3 Click Timeline.

4 Click Copy Frames.

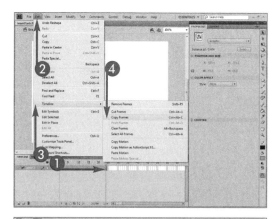

5 Click the frame into which you want to paste.

6 Click Edit.

7 Click Timeline.

8 Click Paste Frames.

Flash pastes the copied frame into the selected frame.

Move a frame

1 Select the frame or frames you want to move.

Flash highlights the frames on the Timeline.

2 Drag and then drop the frame at the new location on the Timeline.

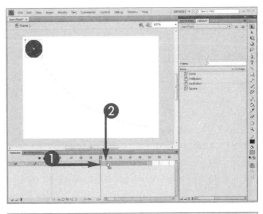

Flash moves the frame or frames.

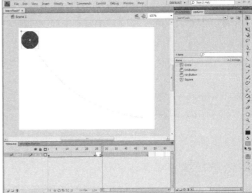

Can I use the drag-and-drop technique to copy frames?

▼ Yes. First, select the frame or frames you want to copy. Press and hold the Alt (Option) key, and then drag the frame or frames and drop them into the new location on the Timeline. Flash duplicates the frames.

Can you explain Cut Frames, Copy Frames, and Paste Frames?

▼ The Cut Frames, Copy Frames, and Paste Frames commands work a lot like the Cut, Copy, and Paste commands, except that you use them exclusively with frames. When you cut frames, Flash removes the frames from the Timeline and makes them available for you to paste into another location. When you copy frames, Flash copies the frames and makes them available for you to paste into another location.

Can I move an entire movie from one file to another file?

▼ Yes. To start, on the main menu, click Edit, click Timeline, and then click Select All Frames. Then click Edit, click Timeline, and click Copy Frames. Flash copies the entire document. Open the new file. Click the frame into which you want to paste and click Edit, click Timeline, and then click Paste Frames. Flash pastes the movie into the new file.

PART VII

Create an Animated Movie Clip

You can create animation that resides within a movie clip symbol. Movie clips have a Timeline that is identical in structure to the Timeline of the main movie. In fact, the main movie is nothing more than a special type of movie clip.

You can use any techniques discussed previously to create animation within the movie clip. The animation in a movie clip can use frame-by-frame, shape tweening, or motion tweening. The main concept to understand about movie clips is that while their Timeline looks like the main movie's Timeline, the two are independent from one another. Therefore, if the main movie stops playing, the movie clip continues. More importantly, if the main movie never technically began playing, because it only contains a single frame, animated movie clips play by themselves within the movie.

As with any other symbol, movie clips can be made up of multiple layers. They can contain graphic symbols, buttons, drawn objects, and other movie clips — even other animated movie clips. In this case, each clip's animation would play independently from the other clips.

Create an Animated Movie Clip

① Click Insert.

② Click New Symbol.

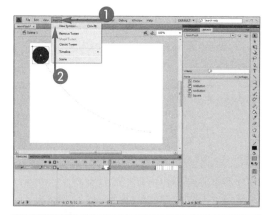

The Create New Symbol dialog box appears.

③ Type a name for the symbol.

④ Click here and select Movie Clip.

⑤ Click OK.

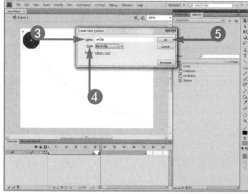

The symbol opens in Editing mode.

6 Add an animated sequence to the movie clip.

Note: See the previous sections in this chapter for information on how to create animated sequences.

7 Click Scene 1.

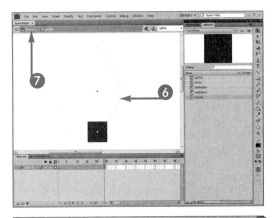

The main movie's Timeline reappears.

8 Click Library.

9 Drag the movie clip to the Stage.

The movie clip is inserted into the movie.

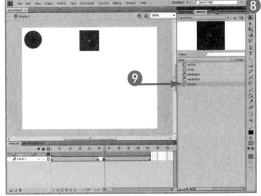

Are there any limits to what I can do in a movie clip?

▼ No. The main Stage is technically nothing more than a special instance of a movie clip. Therefore, anything that can be done in the main movie's Timeline can be done in a movie clip's Timeline.

Can I have as many layers as I want in a movie clip?

▼ Yes. Movie clips, as with any other type of symbol, can be made up of as many layers as needed. They can contain any number of other symbols, of any type, or any number of drawn objects.

Create Animated Buttons

You can create animated buttons for added impact. Although simple geometric shapes make excellent buttons, you can add animations to frames. If the image of a button stays the same for all four frames in the Timeline, the button looks the same regardless of how users interact with the button; in other words, users cannot distinguish between button states. Animating the object used for each button state tells users the status of the button. Users can see a change when they position the mouse pointer over a button and when they click the button.

Creating an animated button requires up to four different shapes or animations. You cannot animate the frames as you would in the normal movie. Instead, you need to add a movie clip that contains its own animation to one or more of the frames. When the button activates the frame, the movie clip plays through its animation as long as the button's frame is active.

One common technique is to have a simple, static shape — often just a graphic symbol — in the button's Up frame. Then, you can replace that symbol with a movie clip that animates the graphic in the Over frame, and switch back to the static symbol for the Down frame.

Create Animated Buttons

Create a new button

① Create a new button symbol.

Note: *See Chapter 28 to learn how to create a new button.*

Flash changes to symbol-editing mode and displays four button frames.

② Insert a symbol from the library.

Note: *You can also draw a new shape.*

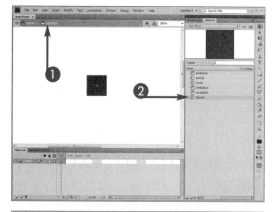

③ Click the Over frame.

④ Insert a blank keyframe.

You can press F7 to quickly insert a blank keyframe.

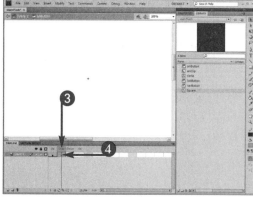

⑤ Create a new object or place an existing object on the Stage to use as the Over state.

Note: The object must differ from the object placed in the Up frame in order to create an animated button.

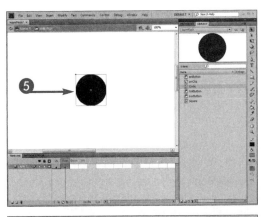

⑥ Click the Down frame.

⑦ Insert a blank keyframe.

You can press F7 to quickly insert a blank keyframe.

⑧ Insert a symbol or drawing on the Stage.

Note: You can use the same symbol as you used in one of the other frames, or a different one.

⑨ Click Scene 1.

Flash returns to the Stage, and the button is created.

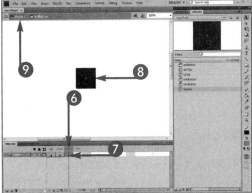

Why do I need to draw a shape in the Hit frame?

▼ Although the Hit frame is invisible to users, it defines the active area of the button and is essential to the button's operation. You must make the object you draw big enough to encompass the largest object in the other button frames. If you do not, users may click an area of the button that does not activate it. If you have trouble guessing how large an area to define, you can use the Onion Skin feature to see outlines of the shapes in all the other frames. Click Onion Skin again to turn the feature off.

Should I add my movie clip to another layer in my button Timeline?

▼ You can use as many layers and layer folders as you need with a button to keep the various elements organized, including movie clips you add to the button.

Can I use an animation clip from another Flash file?

▼ Yes. Click the File menu, click Import, and then click Open External Library. Locate the Flash file containing the clip you want to use, and then double-click the filename. This opens the other file's library on-screen, and you can drag the clip you want to use onto the Stage.

Create Realistic Motion with the Bone Tool

You can use the new Bone tool in Flash CS4 Professional to create realistic character animation. Relying on a technology known as *Inverse Kinematics*, the Bone tool allows you to connect objects at joints so that as you move one piece, the others move accordingly.

To use the Bone tool, simply drag from one joint to another. Flash creates the necessary links between the objects. For example, if you were drawing a human shape and wanted to use the Bone tool to enable realistic movement of the arms, you would create an

object for the upper arm and another for the lower arm, and then use the tool to drag from the shoulder — the top point of the upper arm shape — to the elbow at the top of the lower arm shape.

When you use the Bone tool, Flash automatically places the shapes associated with the bones on their own layer, called an *Inverse Kinematics pose layer*. These layers are named Armiture_1, Armiture_2, and so forth, although you can rename them as needed. They are also marked with a special icon.

Create Realistic Motion with the Bone Tool

Create bones

1 Draw a series of shapes or insert some symbols.

Note: *See Chapter 24 for details on drawing shapes, and Chapter 28 for details on creating and inserting symbols.*

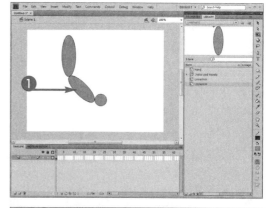

2 Click the Bone tool.

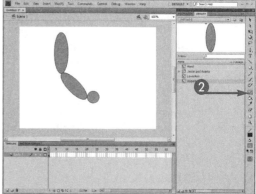

③ Click-and-drag to connect joints on your shapes.

Flash draws bones to show the connections and moves the shapes to a new Armature layer.

④ Repeat step **3** to create additional bones.

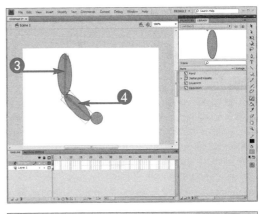

⑤ Click the Selection tool.

⑥ Move the lower shape on the Stage.

The connected shapes move as well.

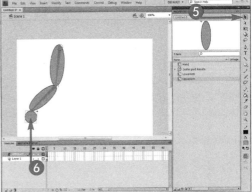

What kinds of objects can I use with the Bone tool?

▼ The Bone tool can be used on drawn shapes, grouped shapes, or symbols. If you connect drawn shapes, the areas nearest the joints distort when they are moved. Grouped shapes and symbols do not distort. Normally, you choose whether or not to use symbols, based on the type of animation you want to apply, but with the Bone tool, the decision is based solely on whether or not you want the objects to distort.

What is the purpose of the Bind tool?

▼ The Bind tool, which can be found by pressing and holding your mouse button down on the Bone tool, can be used to edit the points used by bones for connections. When you click on a drawn object that uses bones with the Bind tool, a series of yellow and red boxes appear, designating the connection points. You can add or remove connection points using the tool.

PART VII

continued

Create Realistic Motion with the Bone Tool *(Continued)*

O nce you add bones to your objects, you can insert additional poses to create animation. Poses function like keyframes in that they define specific points where you control the placement of the objects connected to joints. If the poses are separated by more than one frame, Flash automatically tweens the frames.

You cannot add keyframes to an Inverse Kinematics pose layer, only poses, although the functionality is the same. You can add a pose to the layer by right-clicking the frame and selecting Insert Pose. You can

then use the Selection tool to reposition the shapes in the frame. You will most likely have other shapes or symbols on the Stage as well, and will also need to add frames or keyframes to those layers to complete the animation.

You cannot create bones that connect to objects that are already tweened. If you have a shape to which you have applied a motion or shape tween, you need to remove the tween before you can apply bones and animate with Inverse Kinematics.

Create Realistic Motion with the Bone Tool

Animate with bones

① Right-click a frame on an Inverse Kinematics pose layer.

② Click Insert Pose.

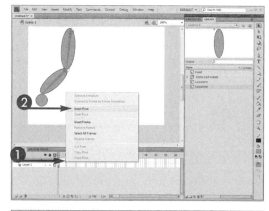

● A pose keyframe is added to the Timeline. The separating frames are shaded dark green.

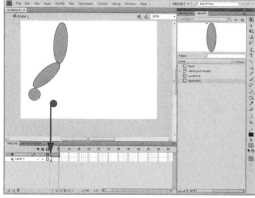

③ Click the Selection tool.

④ Reposition the shapes.

⑤ Repeat steps **1** and **2** to add additional poses.

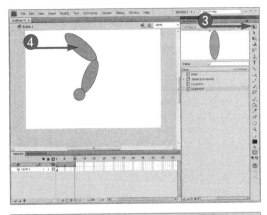

⑥ Press Ctrl+Enter.

Flash Player opens and plays the animation.

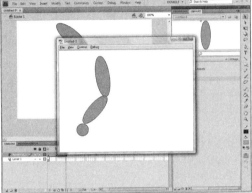

Can I add more than one bone to a single shape?

▼ Yes, although you cannot add more than one connection point for the bones. Therefore, you may occasionally need to add joints at unrealistic points. For example, if you want to animate both arms connecting to a torso, you need to connect the arms not at the shoulder joint, but rather in a central location closer to the neck, as each shoulder on the torso shape cannot be a separate connection point.

When I try to use the drawing tools, I get an error. Why is this?

▼ Most likely, you have the Inverse Kinematics pose layer selected. You cannot draw directly on a pose layer. You therefore need to either select a different layer or add a new layer to add additional art to the drawing. If you want to add additional shapes to the Inverse Kinematic animation, you need to draw them on a separate layer and then connect them with the Bone tool.

Rotate Movie Clips in 3D

You can rotate and move movie clip instances in 3D in Flash CS4 Professional using the new 3D tools. Flash allows you to rotate movie clips in 3D space using the 3D Transform tool.

When you click a movie clip with the 3D Rotation tool, a 3D axis overlay appears on the shape. The X or vertical orientation is represented in red, the Y or horizontal orientation is green, and the Z or 3D orientation is blue. You can drag the shape along any of these axes and see it transform accordingly.

You can reposition the 3D axis overlay on the shape by dragging the small circle at its center. Repositioning the overlay allows you to adjust the point around which the object will be transformed; by default, it is centered.

Rotate Movie Clips in 3D

① Insert a movie clip onto the Stage.

Note: See Chapter 28 for details on creating and inserting movie clips.

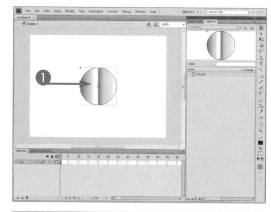

② Click the 3D Rotation tool.

The 3D axis overlay appears on the movie clip.

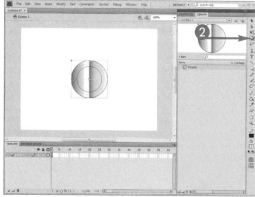

③ Drag one or more of the axes.

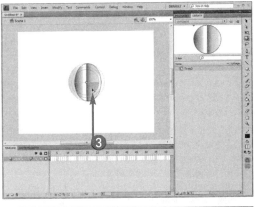

The shape rotates in 3D.

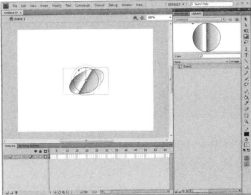

Can I use anything other than a movie clip?

▼ No. All of the 3D tools in Flash rely on movie clips. If you click on a drawn shape or other symbol type with the 3D Rotation tool, the shape simply becomes selected. You can convert it to a movie clip and use the tool at that point. See Chapter 28 for details on converting shapes to movie clips.

If I have a movie clip nested inside another movie clip, can I rotate the inner one relative to the outer one?

▼ Yes. By default, the 3D Rotation tool is set to Global space, meaning that objects are rotated relative to the Stage. You can, however, switch the tool to the Local setting, causing the shapes to rotate relative to a parent movie clip. You can toggle the setting on and off by clicking the 3D Rotation tool and then clicking the Global button in the Options section of the Tools panel. You can temporarily toggle the setting by pressing and holding the letter D on your keyboard while you drag with the 3D Rotation tool.

PART VII

Move Movie Clips in 3D

You can move objects in 3D space using the 3D Translation tool. The tool shares its space with the 3D Rotation tool on the Tools panel.

When you click a movie clip using the 3D Rotation tool, a 3D axis overlay appears on the shape. The overlay consists of two arrows, where the red arrow represents the X or horizontal axis and the green arrow represents the Y or vertical axis. The center point represents the Z or 3D axis.

When you drag along any of these axes, the shape distorts along the appropriate axis. Therefore, if you drag along the Z axis, the shape either grows or shrinks, depending on the direction of the drag: Dragging up moves the shape away from the camera, and so it shrinks; dragging down moves it toward the camera, causing it to grow. However, you see that as the shape grows or shrinks, it does so while maintaining its perspective.

The 3D overlay is positioned by default at the center of the symbol. You can drag it to a new location. Doing so changes the point relative to which the perspective changes.

Move Movie Clips in 3D

① Click the 3D Rotation tool.

② Click 3D Translation Tool.

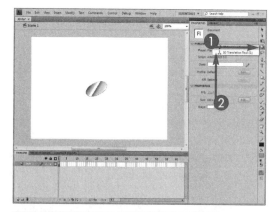

③ Click a movie clip instance on the Stage.

Note: *See Chapter 28 for details on creating movie clips.*

The 3D Overlay appears.

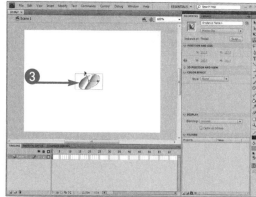

④ Click-and-drag the red arrow.

The symbol shifts in perspective.

⑤ Click-and-drag the green arrow.

The symbol shifts in perspective.

Can I use the 3D Rotation tool and the 3D Translation tool on the same symbol?

▼ Yes. When using the 3D Translation tool on a flat symbol, it appears that dragging along the X and Y axes only moves the shape left or right, or up or down. However, if you first use the 3D Rotation tool to change the perspective of the symbol along one of the axes, then you are better able to see the effects of moving the symbol along the X and Y axes with the 3D Translation tool.

Can I create actual 3D shapes in Flash?

▼ While it is possible to draw shapes and manipulate them with the 3D tools so that they appear to be 3D, Flash can only technically draw flat shapes. You need a 3D drawing application such as AutoCAD or Autodesk Maya to draw true 3D shapes. It is then possible to import these shapes into Flash.

Can I animate in 3D?

▼ Yes. You can create 3D animation by simply using the 3D Rotation and 3D Translation tools in keyframes. However, keep in mind that the tools can only be applied to movie clips, and so you can use either motion tweening or frame-by-frame animation, but not shape tweening.

Rotate Objects in a Motion Tween

You can use the Properties panel to create a motion tween that rotates an object a full 360 degrees. For example, you might animate a corporate logo that seems to spin in place, or you might illustrate a moving vehicle with wheels that rotate. When controlling a tweened rotation, you tell Flash which direction to rotate the object, and Flash creates the necessary frames to create the effect.

The Rotation section of the Properties panel allows you to control the rotation. You can set the number of times the symbol rotates by scrubbing the value. You can also scrub to set the number of degrees by which it rotates. You can further control the rotation by setting the direction to either CW for clockwise or CCW for counterclockwise. If you have curved the path along which the object animates, you can check the Orient to Path option to have the object rotate along the path instead.

Use the None option to remove a rotation effect from a motion tween sequence. You can apply motion tweens only to symbols in your movies.

① Create a motion tween.

Note: See Chapter 29 to learn how to build a motion tween in your movie.

② Click the tween on the Timeline.

③ Click-and-drag the Rotate value.

Dragging to the left decreases the value.

Dragging to the right increases the value.

4 Click-and-drag to set the degrees by which the object will rotate.

Dragging to the left decreases the value.

Dragging to the right increases the value.

5 Click here and set the direction for the rotation.

6 To test the rotation, click the first frame in the animation sequence and press Enter (Return).

Flash rotates the tweened object.

Can I only use scrubbing to set the value for the number of times the object rotates or the angle of rotation?

▼ No. If you click directly on the current value, a text box displays where you can enter the value you want. You can also press and hold the Shift key while you scrub to change the values in increments of 10, rather than 1.

How can I remove rotation if I no longer want it?

▼ The simplest method of removing the rotation is to set the Direction to none. You can also select the Orient to Path option to have the symbol rotate relative to the path. If you turn this option on and then off, any previous rotation settings are lost.

Can I rotate in 3D?

▼ Yes. The new 3D Rotation tool in Flash allows you to create 3D Rotation effects. See Chapter 29 for details on how to use the 3D Rotation tool.

Animate Symbols Along a Path

When you create a motion tween in Flash, you see a line drawn on the Stage. This line represents the path along which the symbol will animate. The dots along the line represent the symbol's place at each of the frames of the animation.

You can adjust the curvature of the line so that the animation occurs along a path. With the Selection tool, you can simply click-and-drag the edge of the path to curve it. You can click on either end of the line

with the Selection tool to adjust the control handles and more dramatically adjust the path's curvature. You can use the Free Transform tool on the path to change its width or height.

You can add additional points along the path by clicking a frame and then moving the symbol to a new location. Flash automatically adds a new keyframe at that point and adjusts the path accordingly. You can then use the Selection tool to make more changes to the curvature of the path.

Animate Symbols Along a Path

1 Add a symbol to the Stage.

Note: See Chapter 28 for information on adding symbols.

2 Right-click the symbol.

3 Click Create Motion Tween.

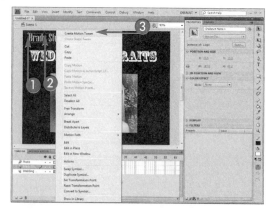

Flash adds a motion tween to the symbol.

4 Click the Selection tool.

5 Move the object to a new location.

6 Move your mouse near the edge of the path.

7 Click-and-drag to curve the path.

8 Click the Selection tool.

9 Click either the first or last point on the path.

Control handles appear.

10 Adjust the handles to change the curve.

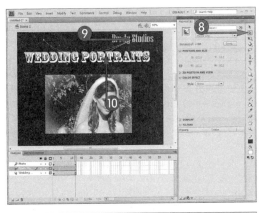

The curve is adjusted.

11 Click at a point in the Timeline during the tween.

12 Click the Selection tool.

13 Move the symbol on the Stage.

Flash adds an additional keyframe to the animation.

What happened to the Guide Layers I used in older versions of Flash?

▼ Prior to Flash CS4, designers had to add a special kind of layer, called a Guide Layer, in order to animate along a path. While Guide Layers still exist in Flash CS4 for backward compatibility, they are no longer needed, as all tweens include a path by default, and the path can be edited directly on the Stage.

Can I draw more complex paths to use for my animations?

▼ Yes. You can create a new layer and use the Pen or Pencil tool to draw a path. Then, you can select the path, cut it to your Clipboard, and then paste it onto the tweened layer. Flash applies the path you are pasting as the path for the symbol. Note that you cannot use closed paths, such as the outline of a circle, rectangle, or polygon. The path must have a clear starting and ending point.

Use Roving Keyframes

You can adjust the position of an object within a tweened span by simply selecting the object and moving it to a new location. Flash automatically adds a new keyframe and adjusts the path of the object accordingly.

Using this ability to automatically create new keyframes, however, can often result in uneven timing for your animation. For example, if you have a tween that lasts 24 frames, and you reposition the symbol at frame 19 so that it is farther from the end point, it will have the first 19 frames to travel a short distance, and

then need to go a long way in the final 5 frames, causing it to appear to speed up.

You can solve this problem with roving keyframes. When you reposition an object within a tween, you can tell Flash that you want the timing of the animation to remain constant, so that it evens out the timing throughout the animation to ensure that the symbol remains at a constant speed. You can add as many additional keyframes within the tween as you want, and Flash ensures that your symbol moves consistently along the new path.

① Click within a tween span.

Note: See Chapter 29 for information on how to create a tween.

② Move the symbol to a new location.

③ Right-click the tween span.

④ Click Motion Path.

⑤ Click Switch keyframes to roving.

The keyframes are converted and the timing is evened out.

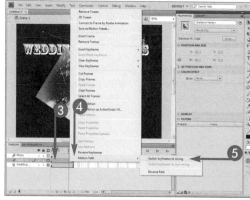

Ease Animation

When you create an animation, the symbol moves from one keyframe to the next at a constant rate of speed. You can increase or decrease the speed at which it moves by adding new keyframes, or you can use easing.

You can apply easing to any tween. When you ease, you tell Flash that you want the symbol to start moving quickly at the beginning of the animation and then gradually slow down as it approaches the end, or you can have it start off slowly and then gradually speed up.

You control easing on the Properties panel. When you have applied a tween, you see an Ease section on the panel. You can scrub the value to the right to ease the tween in, meaning that the symbol begins slowly and gradually speeds up, or scrub to the left to ease out, whereby the symbol slows down over the course of the animation. Maximum values for each setting are 100. You can press and hold the Shift key while you scrub to increase the value by increments of 10 instead of 1. You can also click directly on the value to enter a value manually, with negative values representing an ease in.

Ease Animation

① Click a tween span on the Timeline.

Note: See Chapter 29 for details on creating tweens.

② Click-and-drag to scrub the ease value.

Drag to the right to create an ease in effect.

Drag to the left to create an ease out effect.

③ Press Enter (Return).

The animation plays, showing the easing effect.

Motion Tween Opacity, Color, and Brightness

By using the Color section in the Properties panel, you can tween the opacity, color, and brightness of an instance. Opacity, referred to as *Alpha* in Flash, is the level of transparency of an object in your movie. By default, all objects are 100 percent opaque. You can change the level of transparency by using the Alpha control. For example, you might want the object to appear to fade out at the end of an animation or fade in at the beginning of the animation. Alternatively, you might want the object to become somewhat transparent so that viewers can see a background layer behind the object.

You can also tween the color and brightness of an object by using the Color field. Tweening the color makes the color change over time; tweening the brightness makes the brightness change over time.

The example in this section shows you how to apply an Alpha value setting to the start of the motion tween, making the astronaut appear to fade in. You can apply these same principles to the last frame in a tween to make the object fade out instead.

Note: See Chapter 29 to learn how to make a motion tween.

Motion Tween Opacity, Color, and Brightness

1 Create a motion tween animation.

Note: *See Chapter 29 to learn how to make a motion tween.*

2 Click the symbol on the Stage.

3 Click the arrow to toggle open the Color Effect section.

4 Select Alpha from the Style drop-down menu.

5 Drag the slider to set a new Alpha setting.

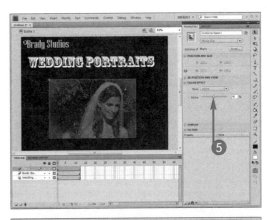

Flash applies the new Alpha setting; if one did not already exist, a keyframe is added to the Timeline.

6 With the first frame in the motion tween selected, press Enter (Return).

Flash plays the animation, showing the Alpha tween effect.

When I select Tint and choose a color, I do not get the color I expect. Why not?

▼ The Tint setting is used to blend the symbol's current color with the newly selected color. You can drag the Tint slider to control how much blending occurs: A setting of 0 percent preserves the original color entirely, while a setting of 100 percent replaces the original with the new color.

Can I tween the opacity, color, or brightness of text?

▼ Not directly. These settings only apply to symbols. However, you can convert the text to a symbol by selecting the text, clicking Modify, and then clicking Convert to Symbol. The Convert to Symbol dialog box appears. In the dialog box, click Button, Movie clip, or Graphic, and then click OK. You can now tween the opacity, color, or brightness of your text by using the same steps you would use to tween any other instance.

Reverse Frames

You can reverse your motion tween with the Reverse Frames feature. This feature literally reverses the order of frames in your movie. For example, if you create a motion tween that makes an object move from left to right, you can reverse the frame sequence, making the object move from right to left. You can use the Reverse Frames feature when you want to repeat the animation sequence in reverse without having to re-create the entire animation. You can use the Reverse Frames command on all types of motion tweens, including tweens that change the color, size, skew, rotation, or opacity of an object.

You can either reverse the frames of an existing tween to simply change the order in which the animation occurs, or you can copy the existing tween, paste it into the Timeline after the current animation, and then reverse the new frames. This way, you can have an object, for example, move from the right side of the Stage to the left and then back to the right.

Reverse Frames

1 Click within a tween span.

Note: *See Chapter 29 to learn how to create tweens.*

Flash selects the span.

2 Right-click the selected frames.

3 Click Copy Frames.

Flash copies the frames.

4 Click the frame into which you want to paste the frames.

5 Right-click the frame.

6 Click Paste Frames.

Flash pastes the frames into the Timeline.

⑦ Right-click the newly copied frames.

⑧ Click Reverse Frames.

Flash reverses the frames.

Note: *You may need to add frames to other layers.*

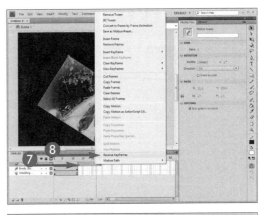

⑨ To see the effect, press Enter (Return).

Flash plays the animation.

How do I undo a reverse?

▼ You can immediately undo the Reverse Frames command if you click the Edit menu and then click Undo. Make sure you do this immediately after you realize you are not happy with the animation results. If you do not apply Undo immediately, you can always right-click within the reversed frames and select Reverse Frames again to put them back in their original order.

Will other effects that I apply to the tween be preserved when I reverse the frames?

▼ Yes. Any effects you applied, such as adding Alpha or tint effects, are preserved and also play in reverse order. If you modify the path, it is preserved exactly as it was originally.

Copy Motion Tween Information

You can use the Copy Motion command to copy motion tween information from one instance of a symbol to another.

Motion tween information includes data about the changes in position of the object on the Stage, such as the horizontal (x) and vertical (y) positions. Motion tween information includes horizontal and vertical scale information, changes in rotation and skew, changes in color, and changes in filters or blend modes.

You can only copy motion applied to symbols or groups, and you can only paste it onto similar objects. If you attempt to paste motion copied from a symbol onto a drawn object, Flash asks if you want to have the object converted to a symbol before it pastes the effect. The object is then converted to a MovieClip.

You can edit the animation after you paste motion from another shape. This allows you to use the animation applied to one object as the starting point for animation on another.

Copy Motion tween Information

① Select all the frames containing the motion tween information you want to copy.

Note: See the section, "Create a Motion Tween," to build motion tween animation effects.

② Right-click (Ctrl+click) the selected frames and click Copy Motion.

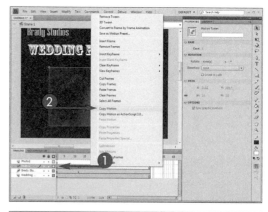

③ Select the instance to which you want to apply the motion tween information.

④ Right-click (Ctrl+click) the selected instance and click Paste Motion.

Flash copies the motion tween information and applies it to the instance.

Save Motion as a Preset

In Flash CS4, you can now save animation effects as a Motion Preset. This causes the sequence to be saved in the Motion Presets panel and to be available to any other Flash movies you create, thus allowing you to create animated sequences once and then easily reuse them, either on the same project or on others.

Flash also comes with a series of Motion Presets that you can apply to your project. You can access them in the Motion Presets panel by clicking Window, and then clicking Motion Presets. The panel contains a

Default Presets folder with the presets that ship with the program. You can simply click a preset, and then click Apply to add it to the currently selected symbol on the Stage.

By default, when you save your own presets, they are added to a Custom Presets folder. While you cannot rename this folder, you can organize presets that you create by adding new folders into the Custom Presets folder. You can then drag presets you create into this folder. Your own presets can be renamed and organized at any time.

Save Motion as a Preset

① Right-click an existing tween span.

Note: See Chapter 29 for details on creating a tween.

② Click Save as Motion Preset.

The Save Preset As dialog box appears.

③ Type a name for the preset.

④ Click OK.

The preset is saved.

To view the preset, you can open the Motion Presets panel.

Apply a Filter

You can use filters to add visual effects and alter the appearance of symbols in your Flash movies. For example, you might add a blur to an animated graphic that moves across the screen. You can add filters to text, movie clips, and buttons. You can use the Filters section of the Properties panel to add and manage filters that you assign. You can assign multiple filters to the same object.

Filters in Flash apply similar effects to the layer styles in Photoshop. You can add blurs, drop shadows, bevels,

and glows. Each of these has a wide variety of settings that you can adjust to achieve the look you want.

All filters can be animated. They move with their associated objects, and so if you apply a shadow to a symbol and then motion tween it to another part of the Stage, then the shadow moves seamlessly with the symbol. If you apply a filter to a keyframe and then change its settings in another keyframe, the filter animates from one group of settings to the other.

Apply a Filter

Add a filter

1 Click a symbol on the Stage.

2 Click the arrow next to Filters to expand that section.

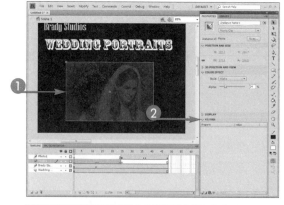

3 Click the Add Filter button.

4 Click a filter.

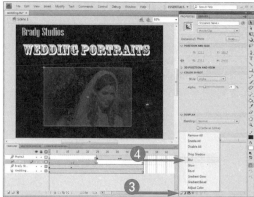

Flash adds the filter.

5 Make adjustments to the settings until the filter appears to your specifications.

Flash assigns the filter settings to the object.

Remove a filter

1 On the Filters tab, click the filter you want to remove.

2 Click the Delete Filter button.

Flash removes the filter.

Can I save a filter I have modified to reuse it again later?

▼ Yes. You can store edited filters as presets in Flash and reuse them in your project. First create and edit a filter, then click Presets, and then click Save As. The Save Preset As dialog box appears. Type a name for the filter and click OK. The next time you want to use it, click Presets, and then click the name of the filter.

Can I disable a filter but keep it assigned to the object?

▼ Yes. From the Filters panel, you can click the check mark in front of the filter name in the filters list to disable a filter. Flash replaces the check mark with a red X. The filter is still assigned, but disabled. When you play or test the movie, the filter does not appear. You can enable the filter again by clicking in front of the filter name to remove the red X.

Do filters impact the performance of my movie?

▼ Yes. For best results, keep filters to a minimum and use the filter's controls to adjust the quality and strength of the filter. Lower settings can improve the playback performance on slower computer systems.

PART VII

31

Add Sound

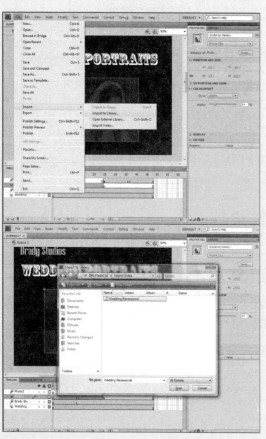

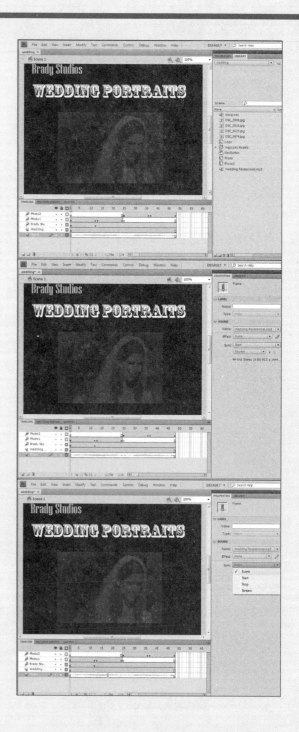

32

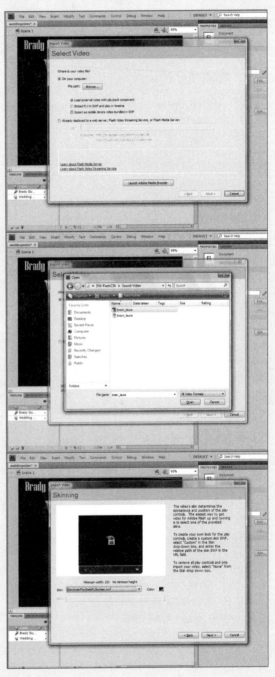

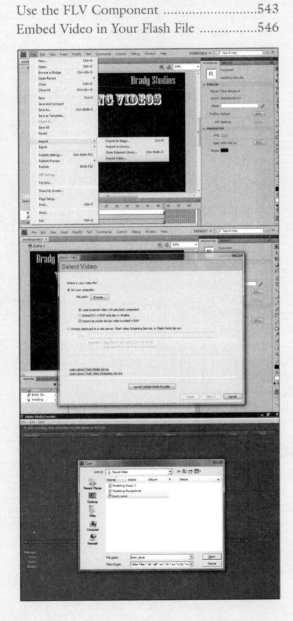

Introduction to Flash Sounds

You can improve your users' experience by adding sound to your Flash movies. You can add short sound effect clips or background music. Sounds can also include voice narrations, musical scores, and sound effects.

You can assign a sound that continues to play throughout your Flash movie, or synchronize a sound to play with specific frames. You can also assign sound clips to buttons.

Understanding Digital Sounds

Although not visible to the naked eye, sounds are made of waves that vary in frequency and amplitude. Digital sounds are visually represented as *waveforms*. Waveforms appear as vertically stacked lines of varying heights resembling the output from a seismic chart of an earthquake. The more intense the sound, the taller and denser the waveform line measurement.

For computer usage, sounds are transformed into mathematical equations, called *digital sampling*. Digital quality is measured by how many samples exist in a single second of the sound, called the *sampling rate*. Sampling rates are expressed in *kilohertz* (kHz). Higher sampling rates result in larger files and clearer sounds. Typically, sampling size is measured in 8, 16, or 24 bits. The *bit rate* is the amount of data that is streamed or encoded for each second that plays in a sound file. Higher bit rates result in higher-quality sound waves.

Like graphics, sounds can consume large amounts of disk space and RAM, and stereo sounds use twice as much data as mono sounds. You can set compression options for reducing event sounds and streaming sounds when publishing and exporting your Flash files.

Compression simply reduces the overall file size of an audio clip. Keep in mind that the more you compress a sound and lower the sampling rate, the smaller the sound file and the lower the sound quality. It may take some experimentation to find the right balance between file size and sound quality in your own Flash movies.

Types of Sounds

All sounds that you add in Flash, whether music, narration, or sound effects, fall into two categories: event driven and streamed. An action in your movie triggers event-driven sounds, and these types of sounds must be downloaded completely before playing in your movie. You assign an event sound to start playing on a specific keyframe, and it continues to play independently of the Timeline for your movie. If the event sound is longer than your movie, it continues to play even when your movie stops. You can use event sounds when you do not want to synchronize a sound clip with frames in your movie.

Streamed sounds download as they are needed, and start playing even if the entire clip has not yet finished downloading. Flash synchronizes streamed sounds with the frames of your movie and attempts to keep any animation in sync with the streamed sounds.

When assigning event or streamed sounds, you can use the options in the Property Inspector to specify the sound type. Flash offers four sync options — event, stream, start, and stop — based on what you want the sound to do.

Sound File Formats
Flash recognizes a large variety of sound file formats. You can import WAV, AIFF, MP3, System 7 Sounds (Mac), Sun AU, Sound Designer II (Mac), and QuickTime file formats into your movies. You need to install QuickTime 4 or later to support some of the sound file formats. When importing sounds, Flash works best with 16-bit sounds.

You can export the audio you use in your Flash movies in MP3 format, or you can compress it as ADPCM, MP3, or RAW. You can find compression options in the Publish Settings dialog box. You can check the file format for any sound clip using the Sound Properties dialog box. The dialog box offers detailed information about the sound clip, including file size and compression assigned to the clip.

If you create Flash content for mobile devices, you can publish your Flash movie with device sounds, which are encoded in the device's native file format. Device sound formats include MIDI, MFi, and SMAF.

Adding Sounds in Flash
You can import sounds from other sources to use in your Flash movies. Flash stores imported sounds in the library. You add sound clips in the same way that you add other frame content. Although you can only add one sound per frame in Flash, you can use multiple layers for different sounds. For example, you can add new sounds to the same frame, but assign them to different layers. To help keep your movie organized, it is a good practice to add sounds to their own layers in a movie.

Controlling Sounds
You can use the Property Inspector to control sounds in a movie, such as changing the sound type and creating sounds that repeat, or *loop*. You can also apply sound effects to fade sound in or out, or appear to emanate from the left speaker channel or right speaker channel. You can also find a few rudimentary features for editing sounds in Flash using the Edit Envelope dialog box. The dialog box allows you to set beginning and end points for a sound and control the volume of a sound while it plays in a movie.

However, you should keep in mind that Flash is not designed to be an audio-editing tool. If your movie sounds require more detailed editing, use a sound-editing program, such as Adobe Soundbooth CS4 or Apple Logic Pro 7, to modify the sound clip before importing it for use in Flash.

You can also use ActionScript and built-in behaviors to control how a sound plays in a movie. To learn more about using ActionScript, see Chapter 33.

Import a Sound File

Although you cannot record sounds in Flash, you can import sounds from other sources for use in your Flash movie. For example, you can import an MP3 file and add it to a movie, or you can import a recording that plays when users click a button. Flash supports popular sound file formats such as MP3, WAV, and AIFF.

When assigning sounds in Flash, you place them in keyframes; but, before you can add a sound to a frame, you must import it. When you import a sound, Flash stores it in the library. You can use copies, called

instances, of the sound as many times as necessary throughout your movie. You can also use sounds that are in other Flash files. Even though you can drag a sound from the library and drop it on the Stage, it obviously does not have a visual representation. Rather, a waveform representation of the sound appears on the Timeline on the layer in which you added the sound. You may need to increase the size and number of frames on your Timeline layers to see the waveform.

Import a Sound File

① Click File.

② Click Import.

③ Click Import to Library.

The Import to Library dialog box appears.

④ Click the sound file you want to import.

⑤ Click Open.

Flash imports the sound file and places it in the library.

Note: *See the next section, "Assign a Sound to a Frame," to learn how to add a sound to your Flash movie.*

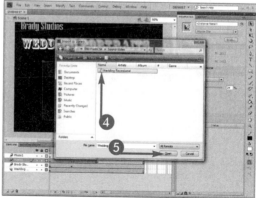

Assign a Sound to a Frame

Y ou can enliven any animation by adding a single sound effect or an entire soundtrack. You can take instances of sounds from the library, insert them into frames on the Timeline, and use them throughout your movie. Flash displays sounds as waveforms in Flash frames.

Sound files are imported into the Flash library. Flash gives you no visual representation of the sound on the Stage. Instead, a *waveform* — an image of

vertical lines representing the digital sampling of the sound — appears in the Timeline frame. Depending on the length of the sound, it may play through several frames of your movie.

There are two methods you can use to assign a sound to a frame: You can drag an instance of the sound from the library onto the Stage, or you can choose the sound from the Sound drop-down menu in the Property Inspector. The method you choose depends on which feature is more readily available.

Assign a Sound to a Frame

1 Create a new layer.

2 Click Library.

3 Click-and-drag the sound from the library and drop it onto the Stage.

Flash adds the sound to the frame, and the waveform for the sound appears in the frame.

To test the sound, press Enter (Return).

Assign a Sound to a Button

Y ou can use sound to call attention to the buttons in your movie. For example, you can add a clicking sound that users hear when they click a button. If your buttons are part of a graphic or page background, adding a sound to the Over frame of the button helps users find the button on the page.

If you add multiple sounds to your buttons, you make them even more interesting. You can add a different sound to each button frame, such as a chime effect

that plays when users roll over the button with the mouse pointer, and a click effect when users actually click the button. It is not necessary to add a sound to the Hit state because users never see or interact with the Hit state.

When assigning a sound to a button, you should create a separate layer for the sound. You add layers to the button Timeline the same way you add layers to the main Timeline.

Assign a Sound to a Button

① Create a button.

Note: See Chapter 28 for details on creating buttons.

② Click the Insert Layer icon.

Flash adds a new layer to the button Timeline.

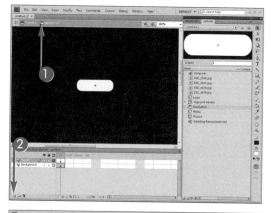

③ Click the frame into which you want to insert the sound.

④ Press F6.

● Flash inserts a keyframe.

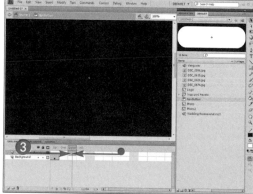

⑤ Drag the sound to the Stage.

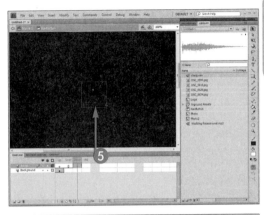

⑥ Add frames as needed to the other layer or layers to finish designing the button.

The button is created with the sound.

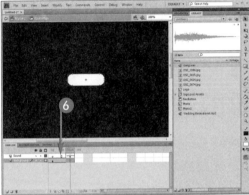

To which button frame should I assign a sound?

▼ The most practical frames to use when assigning button sounds are the Over and Down frames; however, you can also assign a sound to the Up frame. You might want the button to beep when users roll over the button with the mouse pointer. This alerts users to the button. If this is the case, assign the sound to the Over frame. Alternatively, if you want the button to make a sound when users actually click it, assign the sound to the Down frame. Do not assign a sound to the Hit frame. The Hit frame defines the button's active area.

I want to share my imported sounds with other Flash files. Is there an easy way to do this?

▼ Yes. You can create a library of sounds that you can use in other Flash projects. Create a Flash file that contains all the sounds you want to share in the library. When you save the file, save it to the Libraries folder located among the Flash program files and folders. When you restart Flash, the new sample file is added to the list of common libraries under the Window menu.

Create Event Sounds

Y ou can create Event sounds that are triggered by an event, action, or behavior. An Event sound can be triggered when the playhead reaches the frame containing the Event sound, or by Flash actions or behaviors you assign to symbols.

Event sounds play until they are explicitly stopped. The sound must completely download before it begins playing. By default, Flash treats all sounds you add to the Timeline as Event sounds.

You can use Event sounds to include background music in your movie. However, keep in mind that if

the sound file is longer than your movie, the sound keeps playing until it ends or encounters a Stop command. If your movie happens to loop and the Event sound does not stop by the time the movie reaches its starting point again, Flash plays two instances of the sound at the same time. This overlapping of sounds is usually undesirable. As a result, you should accurately check the length and timing of your Event sounds before including them in loops. Alternatively, you could use a Start sound. To learn more about Start sounds, see the section, "Assign Start Sounds."

Create Event Sounds

① Click a frame containing the sound you want to change.

Note: See the section, "Assign a Sound to a Frame," earlier in this chapter to learn how to add sound clips to your movie.

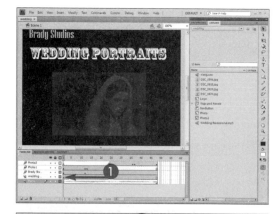

② Click Properties.

③ Click the Sync drop-down menu.

PART VIII

④ Click Event.

Flash changes the sound to an Event sound.

⑤ Click the first frame in your movie or the frame containing the sound.

⑥ Press Enter (Return).

Flash plays the movie, including the newly assigned sound.

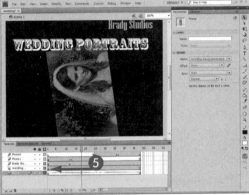

What types of sounds work best as Event sounds?

▼ You can assign an Event sound to start playing in a specific keyframe and then continue to play independent of the Timeline for your movie. If the Event sound is longer than your movie, it continues to play even when your movie stops. For best results, designate short sounds as Event sounds. Sound effects, such as a handclap or a bell ringing, work well as Event sounds. Long sounds, such as an entire song, work best as Streamed sounds. You can use Event sounds when you do not want to synchronize a sound with frames in your movie.

How do I unassign a sound?

▼ To remove a sound, you can use the Property Inspector. Click in any frame the sound occupies, and open the Property Inspector. Go to the Sound field and click None. Flash removes the sound from the Timeline. You can also remove a sound by selecting all the frames the sound occupies and clicking Edit, clicking Timeline, and then clicking Clear Frames, or by deleting the layer that contains the sounds.

Can I rename a sound?

▼ Yes. To rename a sound, open the Library window and double-click the sound you want to rename. Type a new name and press Enter (Return). Flash assigns the new name to the sound.

Assign Start Sounds

You can use the Flash Start sound control to play an instance of a sound in your movie. Start sounds are particularly useful when your movie or your sound loops. Start sounds act like Event sounds, with one important difference: Only one instance of the sound plays at a time. Therefore, if an instance of the sound happens to be playing, which can happen if your movie loops or you have set your sound to loop, the Start sound does not restart itself. By using a Start sound, you can avoid the problem of overlapping sounds that sometimes occurs with Event sounds.

You can use the Sync field in the Property Inspector to turn an Event sound into a Start sound. Remember that all sounds you add to movie frames are classified as Event sounds by default. Flash offers four Sync options: Event, Stream, Start, and Stop. You choose an option based on what you want the sound to do. In addition to options for changing the sound status, the Property Inspector also offers options for looping and editing the sound.

Assign Start Sounds

① Insert a keyframe where you want to add a sound in your movie.

You can press F6 to quickly insert a keyframe, or you can right-click (Ctrl+click) a frame and click Insert Keyframe.

② Click Properties.

③ Click the Name drop-down menu.

④ Click the sound you want to assign.

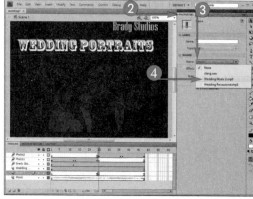

Flash assigns an instance of the sound in the frame.

⑤ Click the Sync drop-down menu.

⑥ Click Start.

Flash assigns the sound Start status.

⑦ To test the sound, click a frame at the beginning of the movie or the Start sound keyframe.

⑧ Press Enter (Return).

When the playhead reaches the frame with the Start sound, the sound plays.

Can I change a sound's Sync type?

▼ Yes. You can easily change a Sync type for any sound in your movie. Simply click in any frame that contains the sound for which you want to change the Sync type, open the Property Inspector, and choose another Sync type. Flash has four Sync types: Event, Stream, Start, and Stop. This chapter explains each Sync type.

What does the Loop option do?

▼ Selecting Loop causes the sound to loop continuously in your movie. The sound continues to play even after your movie ends.

The Loop option is located in the Property Inspector. You can set your sound to loop a specified number of times by selecting Repeat and typing the number of times you want the sound to loop in the Text box.

Can I increase the height of my sound layer?

▼ Yes. Enlarging a layer that contains a sound enables you to view the waveform image of the sound on the Timeline. To increase the layer height, right-click (Ctrl+click) the layer name and click Properties. This opens the Layer Properties dialog box. Click the Layer Height and choose a percentage. Click OK to close the dialog box and apply the new height setting.

Assign Stop Sounds

You can stop a sound before it reaches the end by inserting a Stop sound property. A Stop sound is simply an instruction that tells Flash to stop playing a specific sound. For example, if your animation ends in a particular frame but your sound goes on much longer, you can place a Stop sound in the frame in which you want the sound to stop playing.

You use the Property Inspector to assign a Stop status to a sound. The Sync field includes the synchronization types Event, Start, Stop, and Stream.

You can assign these synchronization types to any sounds in your movies. You use Stop sounds in conjunction with other Sync types. You set the frame in which you want the sound to start to Event, Start, or Stream, and then you set the frame in which you want the sound to end to Stop. For example, if you have a long sound clip playing as a background sound in your movie, you can stop it at a certain point using the Stop property.

You can also use Flash actions and behaviors to control sounds in your movies. See Chapter 34 to learn more about actions and behaviors.

Assign Stop Sounds

① Insert a keyframe where you want to add a Stop sound in your movie.

You can press F6 to quickly insert a keyframe, or you can right-click (Ctrl+click) a frame and click Insert Keyframe.

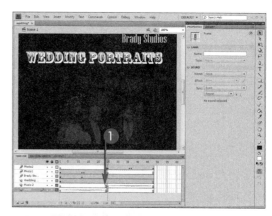

② Click Properties.

③ Click Sound.

④ Click here and select the sound you want to stop.

Flash assigns an instance of the sound in the frame.

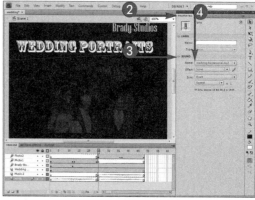

5 Click the Sync drop-down menu.

6 Click Stop.

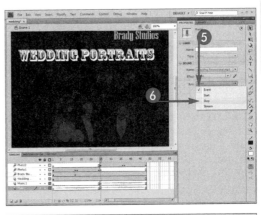

Flash assigns the sound Stop status.

7 To test the sound, click a frame at the beginning of the movie or before the Stop sound keyframe.

8 Press Enter (Return).

When the playhead reaches the frame with the Stop sound, the sound stops.

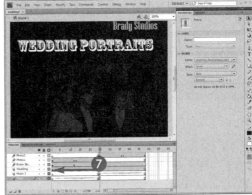

Can I coordinate the start and end of a sound with an animation?

▼ Yes. You can determine when you want the sound to start and when you want the sound to stop. Sounds start in the keyframe in which you place them. Creating a keyframe, selecting the sound, and then selecting Stop in the Sync field immediately stops the playback of the sound. By coordinating the animation with the frames in which the sound starts and stops, you can synchronize the sound with the animation. Remember, dragging the playhead across the Timeline lets you see precisely what is happening in each frame of the animation.

Can I stop all the sounds playing in my movie?

▼ Yes. You can precisely control your sound through ActionScript. See Chapter 34 for more details on using ActionScript in your movies.

Assign Streaming Sounds

Y ou can use *streaming* sounds to synchronize the sound with an animation. This enables users to hear the sound as soon as the movie starts because Flash breaks the sound into smaller units for easier downloading. Streaming sounds are good for long sound files, such as musical soundtracks. The sound starts streaming as the page downloads, and so users do not have to wait for the entire file to finish downloading.

With streaming sounds, Flash synchronizes the frames in your movie with the sound. If your sound is a bit slow in downloading, the frames slow down as well.

The synchronization forces Flash to keep your animation at the same pace as your sound. Because streaming sounds are synchronized with the animation, they are an excellent choice when you create talking characters. Occasionally the sound may play much faster than Flash can display the individual frames, resulting in skipped frames. When your movie ends, the streaming sound also stops.

You can use the Property Inspector to turn a sound into a streaming sound. The Sync drop-down menu includes the four synchronization types you can assign to sounds in your movies, including the Stream sound type.

① Click on a frame with a sound.

Note: See the section, "Import a Sound File," to learn how to import sounds into Flash.

You can press F6 to quickly insert a keyframe, or you can right-click (Ctrl+click) a frame and click Insert Keyframe.

② Click the Sync drop-down menu.

③ Click Stream.

Flash assigns the sound-streaming status.

Loop Sounds

The Loop property enables you to make a sound play over and over again. You can choose to loop Event sounds, Start sounds, and Streaming sounds. When you loop a sound, you are using only one instance of the sound.

You can also repeat a sound using the Repeat property. To set the number of times you want a sound to repeat, assign Repeat in the Properties panel. The number you type dictates how many times the sound repeats. If you type **1** or leave the default setting to 0, the sound plays through one time. If you type **5**, Flash loops the sound five times from start to finish.

If you specify a loop setting that exceeds the length of your movie, the sound continues to play even after your movie stops. For that reason, it is important to test your loop setting to make sure it is compatible with the running time of your movie. Alternatively, you can place a Stop sound at the end of your movie to stop the sound.

Use caution when looping streaming sounds because when you do this, Flash adds frames to a movie, thus creating a larger file size.

Loop Sounds

① Click a frame containing the sound you want to loop.

② Click here and select Loop.

When you play the movie, Flash loops the sound.

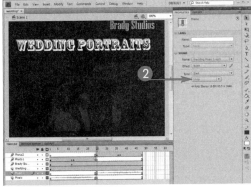

Add Sound Effects

Y ou can use sound effects to improve the way sound integrates into your movie. Sound effects enable you to fade sounds in or out, make sounds move from one speaker to another, change where sounds start and end, or adjust the volume at different points in the sound. You can make your sound files smaller by defining the exact point at which a sound starts and ends.

You can apply premade sound effects to your movie. You choose the effect in the Effect field of the Properties panel. You can also customize sound effects

by using the Edit Envelope dialog box. When you import a sound into Flash, the file includes information about the length, volume, and speaker settings for the sound. You can fine-tune these settings by using the Edit Envelope dialog box. This dialog box also displays your sound as a waveform with both left and right audio channels. You can click the waveform in either channel and drag edit points, called *envelope handles*, to adjust the volume of the sound. You can also use the Edit Envelope dialog box to adjust the length of a sound.

Add Sound Effects

Apply premade sound effects

① Click a frame containing the sound to which you want to apply a sound effect.

② Click the Effect drop-down menu.

③ Click the effect you want to apply.

To test the effect, press Enter (Return), and Flash plays the sound.

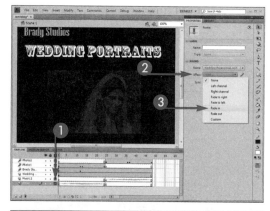

Create custom sound effects

① Click a frame containing the sound you want to edit.

② Click the pencil icon.

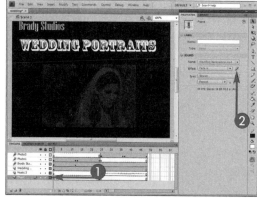

The Edit Envelope dialog box appears.

③ Click inside an audio channel to add an envelope handle.

④ Click-and-drag the envelope handle down to decrease, or up to increase, the volume.

You can add up to eight handles.

⑤ Click the Play Sound button to play the sound.

⑥ Click the Stop Sound button to stop the sound.

● You can click Seconds to set the time units to seconds.

● You can click Frames to set the time units to frames.

● You can click Zoom In or Zoom Out to change the magnification level.

● You can drag the Time In and Time Out bars to adjust the start and end points of the sound.

⑦ Click OK.

Flash applies the changes you have made to the sound you selected.

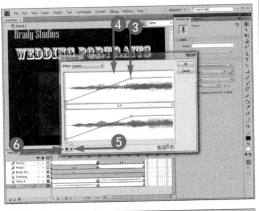

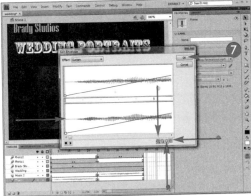

What are audio channels?

▼ Flash audio channels simulate stereo audio channels and determine the volume of a sound or which speaker a sound should play in. You can also use channels to make the sound move from one speaker to the other. The top waveform box in the Edit Envelope dialog box represents one channel; the bottom box represents the other channel. You can use Flash audio channels to control the sounds in your movie.

Can I change the panning for a sound channel?

▼ Yes. Panning enables you to shift sound from one speaker to another speaker. To create a custom panning effect, open the Edit Envelope dialog box and adjust the volume by dragging envelope handles in each channel in opposite directions. As you decrease the volume in the left channel, this technique increases the volume in the right channel, or vice versa.

Can I access other sound editors while in Flash?

▼ While testing your movie, you may want to edit a sound using another sound editor. In the Library window, click the sound you want to edit and then click the Options menu. Click Edit With and locate the sound-editing program you want to use. You can then edit the sound using the other program. When you save the sound file, Flash updates every instance of the sound.

Convert Video to Flash Video

I n order to work in video in Flash, you need to convert it from whichever format it was created in to the Flash Video format. Flash Video files provide a small file size while maintaining quality. Flash Video is commonly referred to as FLV, after the file extension used with converted movies.

You need to use the Adobe Media Encoder in order to convert video from its original source format to FLV. The Media Encoder is included along with Flash, and is either accessible from the first screen of the Import

Video dialog box, or directly from the operating system through the Start Menu or the Dock.

The Media Encoder allows you to select a source video. You can either choose to encode it as FLV, to use in Flash movies; the new F4V format, which offers higher-quality conversion than FLV; or the H.264 format for use on the Apple iPhone. You can select from a list of presets for the size and quality of the movie, and select a path to which the resulting file is saved.

Convert Video to Flash Video

1 Click File.

2 Click Import.

3 Click Import Video.

The Import Video dialog box appears.

4 Click Launch Adobe Media Encoder.

The Adobe Media Encoder launches.

5 Click Add.

The Open dialog box appears.

6 Click the video you want to convert.

7 Click Open.

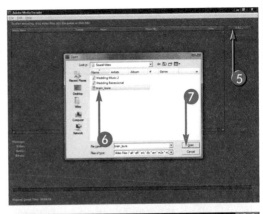

8 Select a format.

9 Select a preset.

10 Click Start Queue.

The video is converted to FLV format.

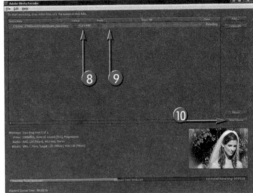

Can I convert more than one video at a time?

▼ Yes. The Adobe Media Encoder is designed to allow you to add a series of videos to a queue and then encode them all at once. The process of encoding video, particularly long or high-quality movies, can be both time and processor intensive, and so you can add your videos to the Media Encoder, start the queue, and then leave your computer to do the work while you do other tasks. You may also choose to have the computer work overnight on the encoding.

What formats can I convert to FLV?

▼ The Media Encoder accepts almost every type of common video format, including AIFF, AVI, MPEG, MOV, and many more. A detailed list of the supported file formats can be found in the Media Encoder help file.

Use the FLV Component

The preferred method of inserting Flash Video into a Flash movie is to use the FLV or Playback Component. Components are special Movie Clips that are included with Flash and contain prebuilt functionality. The FLV Component greatly simplifies the process of inserting Flash Video into a movie.

You need to convert your video to the FLV format before you can use the component. See the previous section, "Convert Video to Flash Video," for details on how to convert to FLV.

Flash includes a wizard that steps you through the process of loading the FLV into the component. You

can access the wizard by clicking File, clicking Import, and then clicking Import Video. The wizard provides a simple, three-step process for conversion. You can select a video on your hard drive and configure the look and feel of the control buttons. Once you complete the wizard, Flash places an instance of the playback component on the Stage. Components are included with Flash to simplify common tasks. The Playback Component includes all of the visual elements and code necessary to control the video. You can then simply save the file, upload both it and the FLV file to your Web server, and enjoy the video.

Use the FLV Component

Note: If the Import Video dialog box is already open, skip to step 4.

① Click File.

② Click Import.

③ Click Import Video.

The Import Video wizard appears.

④ Click Browse.

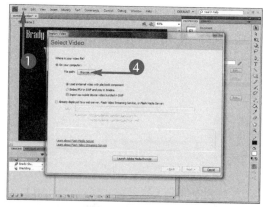

The Open dialog box appears.

⑤ Select the video you want to use.

Note: Be sure to select an FLV video.

⑥ Click Open.

⑦ Click Next.

8 Select a skin.

9 If desired, select a color for the skin.

10 Click Next.

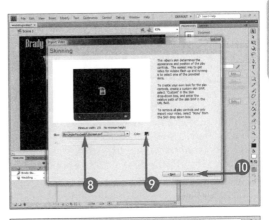

The Finish Video Import screen appears.

11 Click Finish.

The wizard closes, and an instance of the component is placed on the Stage.

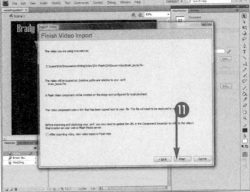

When the wizard finished, a progress dialog box appeared saying that it was getting metadata. What is that?

▼ *Metadata* is a term that describes data or information about a file. In the case of video, the metadata contains information such as the frame rate and pixel dimensions of the video file.

Can my video be transparent or semi-transparent?

▼ Yes. The Flash Video format includes support for an Alpha channel to provide transparency. In order to have transparent video, however, you need to shoot the video in front of a green or blue screen. You may have seen this technique in the extra features on DVD movies. Then, you need to edit the video in a tool such as Adobe Premiere Pro, where you can designate the green or blue background as a chroma key, or Alpha channel. When you convert the file to FLV, the Media Encoder recognizes the channel and makes it transparent when imported into Flash.

Embed Video in Your Flash File

You can embed a video into your Flash movie. This gives you the ability to make the individual frames in your video an integrated part of your Flash movie. Embedded videos reside on the Timeline. Embedded videos work best with files that last ten seconds or less and do not contain sound.

Embedded video files can increase the size of your Flash movie dramatically, making the download of the SWF file over the Web very slow. You may experience problems synchronizing the audio with the video if your video file is longer than ten seconds.

When you import your video using the embedded video option, you can choose to import it as an embedded video, a movie clip, or a graphic. You can also choose to place an instance on the Stage, increase the number of frames if necessary, separate the sound from the video, and set the video quality. The frame rate for the video and the frame rate for the Flash document must be the same. If the frame rates differ, the playback of the video may not be smooth. Before the embedded video can play, the entire video must download.

① Click File.

② Click Import.

③ Click Import Video.

The Import Video wizard appears.

④ Click Browse.

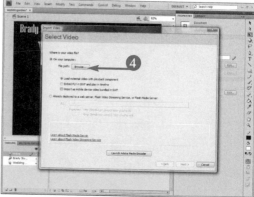

The Open dialog box appears.

5 Click the file you want to import.

Note: You can only embed Flash Video files with an .flv extension. See the section, "Convert Video to Flash Video," for details on converting to FLV.

6 Click Open.

7 Click Next.

Note: If your video is on a Web server, choose the Already deployed to a Web server, Flash Video Streaming Service, or Flash Media Server option and enter the URL.

The Select Video screen appears.

8 Click Embed FLV in SWF and play in Timeline.

9 Click Next.

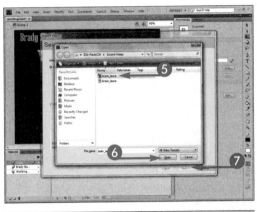

What is the difference between importing an embedded video as an embedded video, as a movie clip, or as a graphic?

▼ If you import your video as an embedded video, each frame of the embedded video occupies a frame on the main Timeline. If you import your video as a movie clip, the video has its own Timeline that is independent of the main Timeline. If you import your video as a graphic, the video is a static image and you cannot use ActionScript to interact with the video. When you import an embedded video, choose Increase Number of Frames in the wizard to ensure that Flash has enough frames to place the entire video in the movie.

What types of video files can I import into my Flash movie?

▼ You can only import FLV files into Flash movies as of Flash CS4. The first screen of the Import Video wizard provides a button to launch the Adobe Media Encoder, which can be used to convert almost any other format of video to FLV. See the section, "Convert Video to Flash Video," for details.

How do I make sure my video frame rate is the same as my document frame rate?

▼ Flash sets the document frame rate to the video frame rate by default. To check the frame rate setting, in the Encoding screen click the Show Advanced Setting button. The frame rate should be set to Same As Source.

Embed Video in Your Flash File *(Continued)*

When importing a video to embed, the Import Video wizard offers you several pages of options for controlling how a video is embedded into your document. For example, you can use the Embedding page of the wizard to specify a symbol type for the video and control how the video appears on the Stage, or if you want the Flash Timeline to expand to include all the necessary frames to match the video.

You can also specify whether or not you want to include the audio from the video. Choosing to not include audio greatly reduces the file size of the movie, but it may impact the ability of users to understand what is taking place in the video. The final screen of the wizard provides a summary of your choices.

Using a component to play external video is generally better than embedding. However, there are times when embedding video can be helpful.

Embed Video in Your Flash File *(continued)*

The Embedding screen appears.

⑩ Select Embedded video.

Note: Select Movie clip if you want to import the video as a movie clip; select Graphic if you want to import the video as a graphic.

⑪ Click Place instance on stage.

⑫ Click Next.

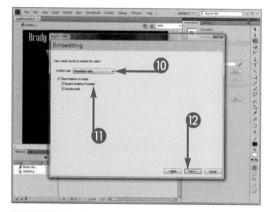

The Finish Video Import screen appears.

⑬ Click Finish.

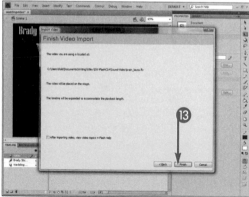

The Flash Video Encoding Progress dialog box appears, and Flash imports and encodes the video, and then embeds it in your document.

Depending on the file, the encoding process may take a few minutes.

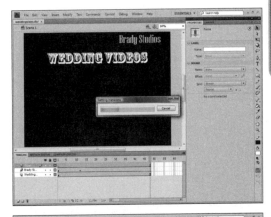

The video is placed on the Stage.

How do I play an embedded video clip?

▼ You can use the Control menu's commands to play the Flash file and view the clip. Click Control, and then click Play to see the entire Flash Timeline, including the video clip. You can also view the clip in the Flash Player window. To do so, click Control, and then click Test Movie.

Can I edit the video clip's size on the Stage?

▼ Yes. To change the clip-viewing window size, click the Free Transform tool and click the Scale modifier. You can then adjust the clip object's handles to resize the clip's appearance. You can also move the clip around on the Stage just like any other object you place on the Stage.

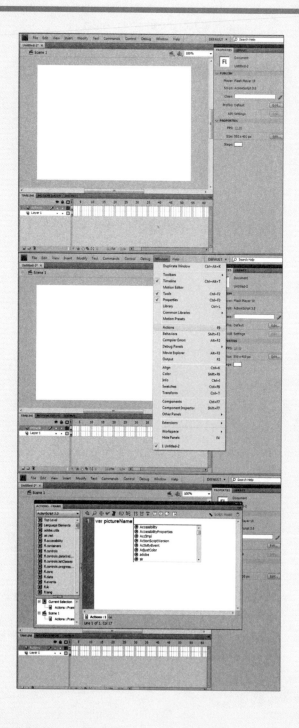

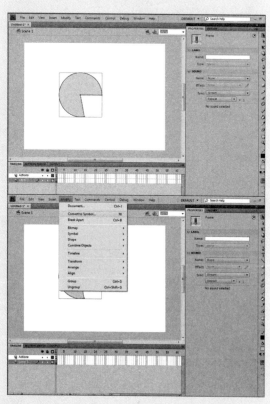

34
Use ActionScript in Your Movie

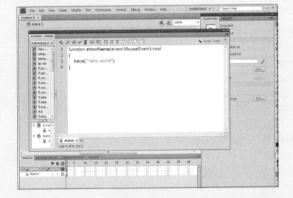

35
Work with Text in ActionScript

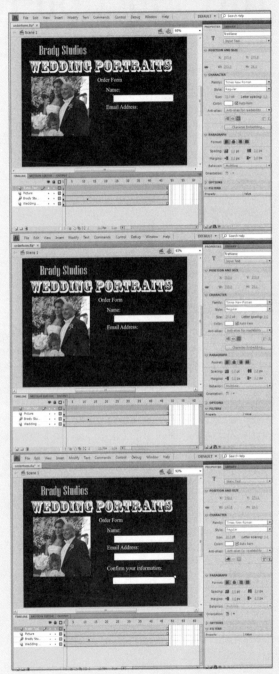

Introduction to Flash ActionScript

You can add interactivity to your Flash movies using ActionScript. By adding interactivity, you can allow users to interact with a movie, triggering an immediate change in the movie. For example, a user might click a button to activate another movie clip or jump to a Web page, or you might set up a movie to stop when it reaches a certain frame. Interactivity can be as simple as a button press or as complex as an e-commerce site or an online videogame.

What Is ActionScript?

ActionScript is an object-oriented programming language based on scripts. Scripts are simply short statements that tell Flash what to do. ActionScript statements are composed of code based on the ActionScript language. When you assemble several statements, you create a script. You can also control parts of the script by specifying parameters. For example, you can write a script that tells Flash to go to and play a particular frame in your movie. When assigning this action, you set the parameter for the action by designating a particular frame in your movie.

With ActionScript, you can write instructions that tell Flash to respond to mouse clicks and key presses a user might perform while viewing a movie, or you can request information from the user and have your Flash movie respond to the information the user provides. You can also use ActionScript to animate objects in your movie, and you can combine statements to produce sophisticated interactive elements for your movies.

ActionScript Versions

As a Flash developer, you can choose to work in any of the three versions of ActionScript: 1.0, 2.0, and 3.0. ActionScript 3.0 is the newest version and has been thoroughly redesigned to support today's growing Web design needs. ActionScript 3.0 is based on ECMAScript — which is the same standard JavaScript is based upon — and works best for users familiar with object-oriented programming. ActionScript 3.0 executes much faster than previous versions, and is designed to allow developers to create highly complex Flash files.

ActionScript 2.0 is simpler than 3.0, but is slower to execute in Flash Player. ActionScript 1.0 is the simplest form of ActionScript and is not as commonly used today. Flash Player 9 supports all three versions of ActionScript.

Because of its many advantages and increased functionality, this book focuses on using ActionScript 3.0 to build interactivity. To run movies created with ActionScript 3.0, your users must use Flash Player 9 or later.

Assigning ActionScript Versions

When you start a new file in Flash, you have the option of choosing which version of ActionScript to base the file on. The Welcome Page and the New Document dialog box list both ActionScript 3.0 and ActionScript 2.0. You can also use the Publish Settings dialog box to change which version of ActionScript is associated with the file. You can assign only one version of ActionScript to a file.

Using ActionScript in Flash

Unless you are writing scripts in an ActionScript text file, all ActionScript 3.0 instructions are attached to keyframes in your movie. As such, it is good practice to manage ActionScripts by placing them in one easy-to-locate place in your movie. You should create a new layer and place all ActionScript in the first keyframe of the new layer. After you establish a location for your scripts, you can open the Actions panel and start adding ActionScript. Most developers make this layer the top-most layer in the Timeline to make it easy to find.

The Actions panel is the perfect tool for adding ActionScript to your movie. The panel includes a text editor for adding and editing script, a toolbox of common scripting codes, and a navigator area for viewing what scripts are assigned to what items in a movie. The Actions panel even offers a Script Assist mode to help you add actions without having to know a lot about writing scripts. However, if you are an experienced developer, you may prefer to use the special authoring environment for writing your code. You can write your own scripts separately from your Flash movies in an external Script window. You can use the external Script window to write ActionScript, Flash Communication, or Flash JavaScript files. See the Flash Help files to learn more about using the Script window.

If your Flash projects require form elements and user interface controls, such as check boxes, radio buttons, and list boxes, you can use components. Components are prebuilt, complex movie clips. Although prebuilt, components still require you to add some ActionScript coding of your own. Components are available in ActionScript versions 2.0 and 3.0.

continued

Introduction to
Flash ActionScript *(Continued)*

Flash ActionScript programming is built on objects, classes, properties, and methods. Understanding how each building block works can help you understand how to add scripts and produce interactivity in your movies.

Understanding Objects and Classes

Object-oriented programming, or OOP, is a very common programming paradigm, used by most modern languages. In OOP, programmers organize code into objects, which mimic real-world concepts such as shopping carts or encapsulate specific businessmodels, such as a process to add a new customer to a database. As ActionScript 3.0 is an object-oriented programming language, understanding the basic terminology and concepts of OOP are vital to your success in using it.

As OOP is designed to mimic real-world situations, it can be helpful to think of a real-world analogy to apply to the terms. The following examples compare OOP concepts to the design and construction of a new housing community.

The main building block in OOP is a *class.* A class defines an object, but does not represent an actual instance of the object. Before you can start using objects, you have to create them as a class. In the housing analogy, a new community cannot be built out of thin air. Before any construction can begin, the developer must plan out, or in a sense, define, each model of house he plans to build. To do this, he has a set of blueprints drawn up, one for each house model. These blueprints can be thought of as classes. You cannot actually live in a blueprint, just as you cannot actually use a class in a program; rather, each provides the definition for the actual objects.

Objects are *instances* of classes. Just as you must build a house based on a blueprint before you can live in it, you must also work with an instance of a class in order to use it. When you create an instance of a class, you are creating an object, an actual thing that you can use in the program. When you create an instance of a class in OOP, you *instantiate* it.

If you have ever placed an instance of a movie clip or a button on the Stage in Flash, you have used objects. In fact, when you convert artwork in Flash to a symbol, you are actually creating a class; when you drag the symbol to the Stage, you are creating an instance of that class — an object.

The Button class in Flash is unique in that instances of it can only be created visually on the Stage. MovieClips, dynamic Text Fields, and components are examples of classes that you can instantiate either visually on the Stage or through code. The remaining classes, of which there are several dozen, can only be instantiated through code.

In addition to the predefined classes, you can also create your own. As has already been mentioned, you are actually creating a new class every time you create a new symbol. Specific business-logic needs or processes, such as a shopping cart in an e-commerce application, also need to be defined as custom classes. Creating custom classes is beyond the scope of this book, but is an important topic for further exploration once you understand the basics of ActionScript.

Classes in ActionScript are organized into *packages.* Each class is defined in its own ActionScript file, and a package is nothing more than a folder that contains a group of related classes.

Understanding Properties and Methods

A real-world object has properties — the things that make up the object. For example, a house can be defined by its square footage, the number of bedrooms and bathrooms it contains, the direction it faces, its color, and many other attributes. In OOP, these attributes are known as *properties.* Properties can be seen as the nouns of an object. Just as you would describe your house by the properties listed above, you can describe a MovieClip by its shape, its color, its transparency or Alpha, and its location on the Stage.

If you live in a modern housing subdivision, you are aware that your community only contains three or four models of houses. These were created from the sets of blueprints commissioned by the developer. Each instance of a particular model of home shares a group of common properties, such as the square footage and number of rooms. However, each house is also unique from the others in the neighborhood. While you may live in the same model of home as your neighbor, your house is most likely of a different color, or may be located on a different side of the street. Certainly, your house has a unique address.

Instances of objects in ActionScript also share many properties while having other unique properties. You can create as many instances of a particular MovieClip on the Stage. Each instance shares the same basic shape as each other instance. However, you can position each instance in a different place on the Stage, so that their x and y properties are different. You can scale each instance in order to set different xScale and yScale properties.

In addition to defining objects through properties, you also want to do things to properties. In your home, you can enter and exit, cook dinner, sleep, watch TV, and work on the computer. Similarly, you need to be able to add and remove products from a shoppingCart class that you define for your e-commerce application. MovieClips can be animated on the Stage. The actions that you can perform to objects are known as *methods.* Just as properties can be seen as the nouns of an object, methods can be seen as the verbs of an object.

Most of the time, all instances of an object use a common set of methods. While it is possible to define custom methods for individual instances of an object, doing so is beyond the scope of this book.

Static classes

Before continuing, it is important to understand a special type of class in ActionScript. These classes, known as *static classes,* cannot be instantiated. Instead, you can simply access their properties and methods directly. Static classes are used for cases where having individual instances does not make logical sense. One example of a static class is Math. The Math class contains a set of properties that define mathematical constants, such as Pi, and a set of methods to perform mathematical calculations, such as sine. While it makes sense that you can have more than one instance of a MovieClip on the Stage and thus need instantiation to control each one separately, it also makes no sense to need to instantiate the Math class: Pi is always Pi, and so you do not need a separate instance. Other examples of static classes include the Stage, as you cannot have more than one Stage in a movie; Mouse, because you cannot use more than one pointer device at a time; and Keyboard, as the same applies to keyboards.

continued

Introduction to
Flash ActionScript *(Continued)*

ActionScript is an event-driven language: Something has to happen in your Flash movie in order for any ActionScript code to execute. Events in Flash include the user moving his mouse over an object, clicking, or typing on the keyboard, or the playhead entering a frame.

Understanding Events, Event Listeners, and Event Handlers

At any given moment, a Flash movie is broadcasting hundreds, or possibly thousands, of events. The vast majority of these events are ignored. In fact, all events are ignored unless you write code to tell Flash Player to do something when a specific event occurs. This code is made up of two parts: event listeners and event handlers.

You can tell Flash Player to have a specific object listen for a specific event by adding an *event listener* to the object. The event listener instructs Flash Player to run a block of code when the event occurs. The code to be executed is the *event handler.*

Functions

Good programmers understand the importance of reusing code. Functions allow you to encapsulate blocks of code that you want to reuse. By using functions, you can save yourself time and energy, as you only have to write, and debug, code once.

ActionScript includes a host of prebuilt functions to handle common situations. Methods are, in fact, nothing more than functions that are defined as part of a class. You can also create your own functions, a topic which is discussed in more detail later in this chapter. Event handlers are a special type of function.

Arguments

An *argument* — also referred to as a *parameter* — is a value that you pass into a function. A well-written function only relies on data that is expressly passed to it as an argument, and never attempts to read or manipulate variables created outside of the function. Arguments are declared in the parentheses that follow the function name.

Data Types

ActionScript 3.0 is what is referred to as a *strongly typed* language. That means that whenever you declare a variable, you should tell ActionScript what kind of data it will hold. Some common data types are `Number` and `String`, although any class can be used as a data type, and so `MovieClip` is a data type as well. You declare the data type by typing a colon after the name of the variable, and then typing the data type, as in `userName:String`.

Functions can be written to either return a value to the script that called them or to simply perform processing and not return a value. If the function returns a value, then the data type of the returned value should be indicated following the parentheses for the argument. If the function does not return a value, then you type **void,** which simply means that the function returns nothing.

ActionScript Syntax

Like spoken languages, ActionScript has rules of punctuation and grammar you must follow, and these rules comprise the syntax of the scripting language. The remaining information in this section shows you the basics for writing code. If you run into any difficulties, be sure to consult the Flash Help files. The Help files are an excellent source for helping you learn more about using ActionScript in your Flash files.

Using semicolons

Each ActionScript statement ends in a semicolon. A statement is generally a single line of code. For example, a statement that declares a variable might look like this:

```
var myVar:String = "Hello World";
```

While the details of declaring variables are discussed in the section, "Create Variables," you should note that the line is a single statement and thus ends in a semicolon.

Using curly braces and parentheses

Sometimes, ActionScript code is too complex to be expressed in a single statement. In these cases, you create a code block. A code block begins with a line that defines the block, and then the code that will execute. The executable code is enclosed within curly braces. For example, a function declaration is written as a code block:

```
function myFunction():void

{

    return true;

}
```

You should always be careful that you close any curly brace you open. Unbalanced braces cause the script to return an error, but the error message often gives you the wrong line number. It is a good habit to always add both the opening and closing curly braces at the same time, and then go back and add the code between them.

The same rules apply to the use of parentheses: You must always be sure to close any parentheses you open. Parentheses are used to call functions and group mathematical operations.

Whitespace and casing

ActionScript is, for the most part, whitespace-insensitive, which simply means that it does not usually matter whether or not you have spaces in your code. As an example, the function declaration earlier could be written with the opening curly brace on the first line or on a separate line as shown. Many developers prefer to put it on the first line, while many others prefer to have it on its own line — the choice is yours. The code also executes properly if you do not indent the line of code within the curly braces; however, ensuring that your code is readable saves untold amounts of time when debugging, and so it is always recommended that you use whitespace to make your code easy to read. One important exception to this rule is that variable and function names cannot contain spaces.

ActionScript is case-sensitive. If you declare a variable with all lowercase letters, then you must always use all lowercase letters to refer to that variable.

Functions, variables, keywords, properties, and methods that are built into ActionScript are always expressed with *camel casing*, whereby multiword names begin with a lowercase letter, and then use an uppercase letter for the first letter of each additional word. As an example, the property that allows you to scale an object is `scaleX` — note that the **X** is uppercase. Classes in ActionScript are all defined using Pascal casing, which follows the same concept as camel casing except that the first letter is also capitalized, such as MovieClip. In order that the code you write matches the code built into the language, you should follow this same technique in your code: Use Pascal casing for custom classes you define, and camel casing for everything else.

Dot Syntax

ActionScript uses *dot syntax* to separate an object name from a property, function, or method. For example, you would set the `xScale` property for an instance called `myButton` by writing `myButton.xScale`.

Using the Actions Panel

You can use the Actions panel to write, format, and edit the ActionScript you include in your FLA file, or authoring file. There are three parts to the Actions panel: the Actions toolbox, the Script Navigator, and the Script pane.

The Actions toolbox contains a list of ActionScript statements organized by category. You can use the Actions toolbox to add code to the Script pane. You can click-and-drag the code to the Script pane, or you can double-click a code to add it to the Script pane.

The Script Navigator provides a hierarchical listing of all of the movie clips, buttons, and frames in your document that have scripts associated with them. You can click an element to view the associated ActionScript in the Script pane.

You use the Script pane to type and edit your scripts. The Script pane is a full-featured editor that helps you format your code. It has a toolbar that provides buttons that enable you to add script, find and replace text, insert a target path, check syntax, show code hints, debug your code, and turn on Script Assist.

Using the Actions Panel

Open the Actions panel

① Click the frame to which you want to add ActionScript.

② Click Window.

③ Click Actions.

You can also press F9 to quickly display the Actions panel, or click the Edit ActionScript button in the Properties panel.

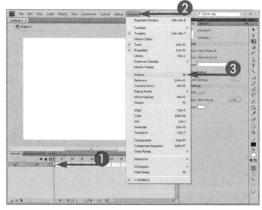

The Actions panel opens.

● The Actions toolbox lists categories, subcategories, and ActionScript code.

● You can use the Script pane to add and edit scripts.

● The Script Navigator pane lists all the elements by level in your movie, with the current selection at the top.

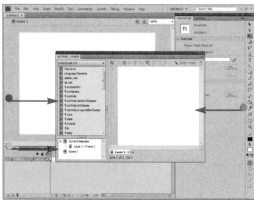

- You can drag the splitter bar, or border, to change the size of the Actions toolbox and Script pane.

- You can click the name of the object for which you want to see any associated code.

- You can click the Panel menu to view a context menu of related commands.

- You can use the tool buttons to work with scripts you add to the Script pane.

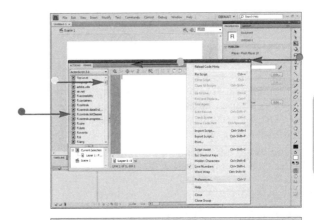

Using the Actions toolbox

④ Click a class category to see associated subcategories or codes.

- You can click a subcategory to see a list of codes.

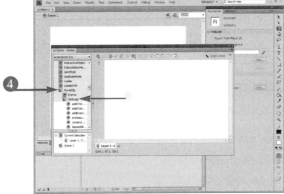

Can I leave the Actions panel open and still view my Timeline?

▼ Yes. You can minimize the panel if you need to view the Timeline or Stage, and then maximize the panel again when you need to add or edit scripts. You can use several techniques to minimize the panel. You can click the panel's title bar or click the panel's Minimize button to quickly minimize the panel. You can drag the title bar to move the panel around the screen. You can click the title bar again, or click the Maximize button to maximize the panel.

What are the Go to Line, Find and Replace, Find Again, Print, and Check Syntax options on the Actions Panel menu for?

▼ You use Go to Line to move to a specified line in your script; you use Find and Replace to find a string of characters; you use Find Again to continue your search; and you use Print to print your script. Click Check Syntax to have Flash check your script for syntax errors.

What does the Auto Format icon do?

▼ By clicking the Auto Format icon, you can format your code for increased readability. You can also set Auto Format options in the Preferences dialog box. You open the Preferences dialog box by clicking the Panel menu and then selecting Preferences. You can then choose to use automatic indentation as well as choose a tab size.

Assign ActionScript to a Frame

You use the Actions panel to add ActionScript to keyframes in your movie. Frames can include multiple scripts, but you can write ActionScript in only one frame at a time.

When you assign an ActionScript, it appears in the Script pane on the right side of the Actions panel. As soon as you assign an ActionScript to a frame, the frame is marked with a tiny icon of the letter *a*.

Almost all of the ActionScript you write is in frame 1. Because Flash cannot execute code until the playhead

reaches a frame, code you place in other frames may not be available throughout the movie. By placing the code in frame 1, you ensure that it will execute when the movie first plays.

You should always create a unique layer for your scripts. While you can add the script to any keyframe, adding it to a frame that also contains visual elements can lead to confusion, as you have to search for your code. If all or most of the code is on frame 1 of a specifically named Actions layer, it is easy to find.

Assign ActionScript to a Frame

① Click the Insert Layer icon.

Flash inserts a new layer.

② Rename the layer **Actions**.

Note: See Chapter 27 for details on adding and naming layers.

③ Select the keyframe in frame 1 of the layer.

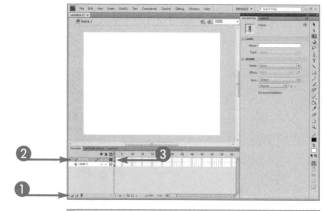

④ Display the Actions panel.

Note: See the section, "Using the Actions Panel," to learn how to open the panel.

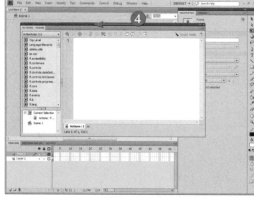

5 Type **trace("Hello, world");**.

Flash adds the ActionScript to the Script pane.

● Flash also adds a tiny letter *a* to indicate that an action is assigned to the frame.

Note: See the section, "Trace Variables," for more information on the trace command.

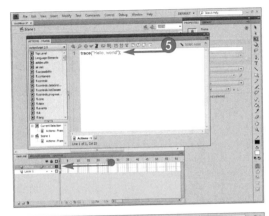

6 Press Ctrl+Enter to test the movie.

When you play the movie in the Flash Player, Flash carries out the frame action you assigned.

● In this example, the words, Hello world, appear in the Output panel.

Can I assign actions to anything besides a layer?

▼ In ActionScript 1.0 and 2.0, you could add code to instances of buttons and movie clips. This led to many Flash movies containing what is referred to as spaghetti code — messy code that is very difficult to edit.

With ActionScript 3.0, you can only write code on keyframes on a Timeline. You now use event listeners and event handlers to associate code with specific symbol instances.

Can I assign actions to regular frames?

▼ No. You can add ActionScript only to a keyframe. If you try to assign ActionScript to a frame that is not a keyframe, Flash automatically assigns the actions to the previous keyframe in the Timeline. By default, the first frame in the Timeline is a keyframe.

Can I share my ActionScript code with other Flash applications?

▼ One of the reasons you want to keep your code in a central location is so that you can share your code with other Flash applications. You can create your code in an external file by using your favorite code editor or by selecting ActionScript file in the New Document dialog box. The filename for your file must be appended with .as. You use the import statement to include ActionScript from an external file in your current document. If you choose to create your file by using the ActionScript file option in the New Document dialog box, code hinting and other editing tools are available to help you create your file.

PART IX

Name an Instance on the Stage

In order to reference an instance of an object on the Stage in your code, you need to name it. Each instance must then have a unique name. All of the classes that are built into ActionScript use Pascal case, whereby you begin the name with a capital letter, and combine multiple word names into a single word, capitalizing the first letters of each of the former words. When you create a symbol, you are creating a new class; therefore, you should use Pascal case to name your symbols.

Instance names should use camel casing. Once again, you combine multiple words into a single word, but in camel casing you do not capitalize the first letter. Your instance name should contain some reference to the symbol name, but needs to also contain something that makes it unique, such as adding a number. For example, if you have a MovieClip symbol called Box, then you might create instances called box1, box2, and so forth. Buttons are most often named based on their purpose. As an example, you might have a button called NavButton, and then create instances called navHome, navAbout, and so forth.

Name an Instance on the Stage

① Use a drawing tool to draw a shape or shapes on the Stage.

② Click the Selection tool.

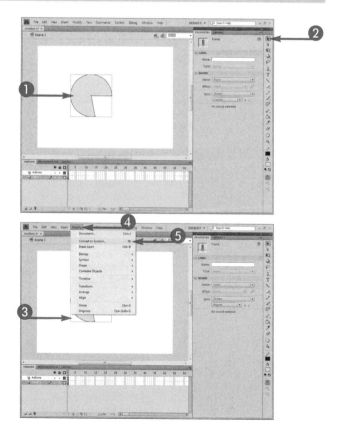

③ Select the shape.

④ Click Modify.

⑤ Click Convert to Symbol.

You can also press the F8 key.

The Convert to Symbol dialog box appears.

6 Type a name for the symbol.

7 Click here and select the type.

Note: You can only use a movie clip or a button.

8 Click OK.

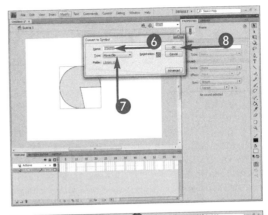

9 Open the Properties panel.

10 Type a name for the instance.

Flash assigns the new name.

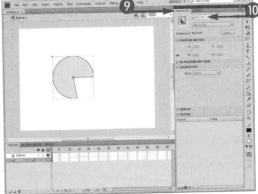

What kinds of objects can be given instance names?

▼ You can provide an instance name for movie clips, buttons, text fields, and components. Because drawn objects, imported bitmaps, graphic symbols, and other assets cannot be controlled through ActionScript, they cannot be given an instance name.

Can I reuse instance names in the same movie?

▼ Each element on the Stage at any given time must have a unique instance name. Unfortunately, Flash does not warn you when this occurs, and allows you to use the duplicate name. However, only one of the objects — the one added to the Stage last — is affected by the code, and so this should be avoided.

You said instance names are case-sensitive. What if I use the wrong casing when referencing a name?

▼ Flash returns an error if you reference an instance using a different case than when you created it. For example, an instance named firstname is different from one named firstName.

Create Variables

Variables allow you to store information to use later in your script. For example, you can store a customer's name as a variable. In ActionScript, variables are declared using the `var` keyword, followed by the variable name. The name should be descriptive for easy reference. The variable name must begin with a letter and can only contain letters, numbers, and underscores. The variable name is case-sensitive throughout your script, and so you should be consistent in what case you use.

You should always declare a data type for the variable you are creating. You declare the data type by setting it after a colon, which follows the variable name. If the variable contains words or phrases or other alphanumeric characters, you should set the data type to `String`. If the data is numeric, then you typically use the `Number` data type. A complete list of available data types appears in the code hinting in the Actions panel; a description of each data type can be found in the help file.

You can give a variable a value when you create it by typing an equal sign and the value. String values must be quoted; numeric values must not be quoted.

Create Variables

① Click the Insert Layer icon.

② Rename the layer **Actions**.

Note: See Chapter 27 for information on naming layers.

③ Click Window.

④ Click Actions.

The Actions panel opens.

Note: You can also press F9 to open the panel.

5 Type **var pictureName.**

6 Type a colon.

A list of data types appears.

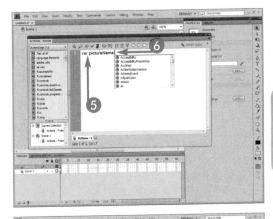

7 Type **String.**

You can also press Enter (Return) once the code hints select String.

8 Type an equal sign.

9 Type a value.

10 Type a semicolon.

The variable is created.

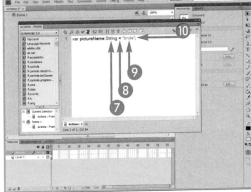

Do I have to give the variable a value when I create it?

▼ No. Sometimes, it makes sense to give a value to the variable when you create it, but at other times it does not. It is legal to create a variable without providing a value, and then set the value later.

Can I create a variable that simply stores a true or false value?

▼ Yes. ActionScript, like other programming languages, supports a data type called Boolean. Named for mathematician George Boole, Boolean data is either true or false. When you create a Boolean variable, you can set it to either value. Note that true and false are keywords in ActionScript, and so you do not put them in quotes.

Are there more specific numeric data types?

▼ Yes. The Number type can hold any kind of number, but ActionScript also supports int for integers. Note that most data types are actually classes, and so they need to be capitalized, but int, as a subtype of Number, is written in all lowercase letters.

Trace Variables

One of the biggest challenges in programming is debugging. As you work on your scripts, you will encounter many times when you create a variable that is used in the processing of the code but does not result in any actual output to Flash Player. If your code does not function as you expect, it might be because one of these variables is being set to a value other than that which you expect.

You can use the `trace` command to display these variables. When you trace a variable, its value appears in the Output panel when you run the movie. You can trace variables, literal values, and other data.

While tracing is an important debugging tool, you would not want a final movie to contain them, as they would confuse your user. You will most likely simply delete the `trace` statements after you have debugged your code, but you can also tell Flash to not export `trace` commands when you publish the movie. Publishing your Flash movie is covered in Chapter 36.

Trace Variables

Note: You need to open the Actions panel to complete the following steps. See the section, "Using the Actions Panel," for more details.

① Create a variable.

② Assign the variable a value.

Note: See the previous section for information on creating variables.

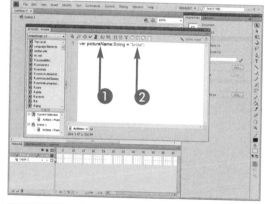

③ Type **trace**.

④ Type a parenthesis.

⑤ Type the name of the variable you created in step **1**.

⑥ Close the parenthesis.

⑦ Type a semicolon.

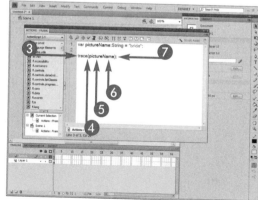

8 Click Control.

9 Click Test Movie.

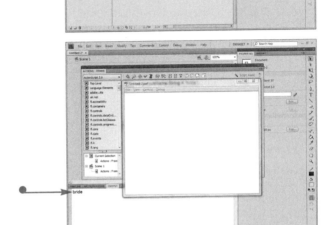

The movie opens in Flash Player.

● The Output panel opens, displaying the value of the variable.

How do I display a literal string with a `trace` command?

▼ You can have the `trace` command display a literal value by placing the value in quotes inside the command's parentheses:

```
trace("This will be displayed");
```

I do not see the code hints appear. What am I doing wrong?

▼ Possibly nothing. The Flash ActionScript panel does not provide code hinting at all times. When you start a new statement, for example, code hinting does not appear. If code hints disappear while you are using them, which can happen if you use the Backspace or Delete key to remove code you were typing, you can reshow them by holding the Ctrl or ⌘ key and pressing the Spacebar.

Add Comments to Your Code

You can add comments to your code. Comments help you to understand what is happening in your code. You can add a comment at the top of the script to explain the overall purpose of the code, and you should add a comment to any point in the code that does not make sense on its own. Comments are always ignored by Flash Player.

Comments also help future developers understand your thought processes. If someone else has to take over development of your project at a later date, they will appreciate seeing comments to help them get up to speed. If you are taking over development of an existing project, you will likewise be thankful if the developer before you left comments.

Comments can also be useful for debugging. If you cannot find a problem in your code, you can comment out the code, one statement or section at a time, until the problem goes away. As soon as it does, you know that whatever section or statement you commented out last was the culprit and you can more easily fix it.

You can add a single-line comment by placing two forward slashes before the comment. You can create a multiline comment by typing a slash and an asterisk, the comment, and then an asterisk and a slash.

Add Comments to Your Code

Add a single-line comment

Note: You need to open the Actions panel to complete the following steps. See the section, "Using the Actions Panel," for more details.

1 Type two forward slashes.

2 Type a comment.

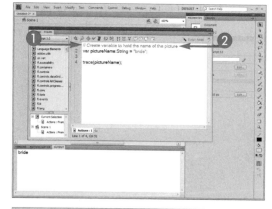

Add a multiline comment

1 Type a slash and an asterisk.

2 On a new line, type a comment.

3 On another line, type an asterisk and a slash.

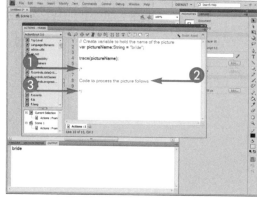

Test the movie

1 Click Control.

2 Click Test Movie.

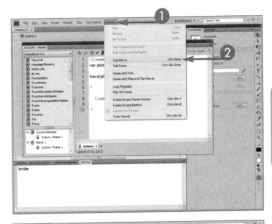

PART IX

Flash Player opens and the movie plays.

The comments are ignored and do not change the appearance or functionality of the movie.

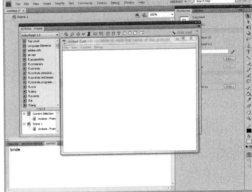

Can I add a comment on the same line as code?

▼ Yes. You can use a single-line comment at the end of a line of code:

```
var userName:String;
//stores user name
```

Does every line or block of code need to be commented?

▼ No. If the purpose of the code is clear from reading it, there is no need to add a comment. You only need to add comments for those lines or blocks of code whose function may be unclear, and where the comment adds clarification.

Why is the text of my comment turning gray?

▼ One of the things that the ActionScript panel does to help you is code coloring. Comments turn gray; ActionScript keywords turn blue; literal strings turn green. You can control the colors used in the code by clicking Edit, clicking Preferences, and then clicking ActionScript.

Create a Function

Y ou can organize your code into logical, reusable blocks by creating functions. Functions allow you to organize your code and to reuse blocks of code as many times as needed.

You create functions in your code with the `function` keyword, followed by the name of the function. Function names should be in the form *verbNoun*; for example, a function that adds numbers might be called `addNumbers`.

Following the name of the function is a pair of parentheses. You can send data into the function as

arguments by placing the names of the arguments within the parentheses; arguments are discussed in the next section. Following the closing parenthesis, you place a colon and a declaration of the data type of the information to be returned from the function. If the function does not return any information, the type is *void*. See the section, "Return a Value from a Function," later in this chapter for more details. Finally, you have a pair of curly braces. All of the code for the function is placed within the braces.

Create a Function

Note: You need to open the Actions panel to complete the following steps. See the section, "Using the Actions Panel," for more details.

1 Type **function.**

2 Type the name of the function.

3 Type a pair of parentheses.

4 Type a colon.

5 Type **void.**

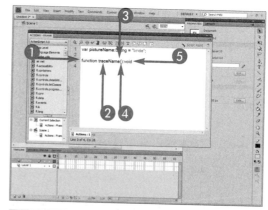

6 Type a left curly brace.

7 Type the code to be executed by the function.

8 Type a right curly brace.

The function is complete.

Note: See the next section for information on calling and using functions.

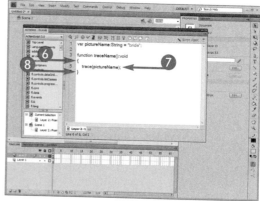

Call a Function

You can use a function in your code by *calling* it. You call a function by typing the name of the function followed by parentheses. You can call a function from almost anywhere in your script. Function calls can be on their own lines, or they can be set as a value for a variable. You can even call functions from within other functions.

Some functions take arguments. Arguments are data that the function needs in order to perform its calculations. If the function takes arguments, you need to send the data when you call the function. These argument calls are placed between the

parentheses after the name of the function. You need to be sure that the data being sent to the arguments is of the data type expected by the function, or else an error occurs. See the next section for information on creating a function that takes arguments.

Sometimes, functions simply execute a block of code. Other times, they may perform calculations that result in a value being generated by the function. In these cases, you need to call the function by setting it as the value of a variable; the variable then holds the value returned from the function.

Call a Function

Note: *You need to open the Actions panel to complete the following steps. See the section, "Using the Actions Panel," for more details.*

① Create a function.

Note: *See the previous section, "Create a Function," for more details.*

② Below the function, type the name of the function followed by a set of parentheses and a semicolon.

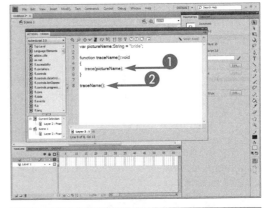

③ Press Ctrl+Enter.

● The movie plays and the function executes.

Pass Arguments to a Function

A function can read and write variables created outside of the function. However, doing so is not considered to be a best practice for writing code. One of the important concepts behind using functions is that they are portable; that is, the function is written in such a way that it can be moved from one script to another and continue to work. If the function directly manipulates variables from the surrounding script, it is reliant on that script.

Instead, you should always pass data needed by the function to it in the form of *arguments*. Arguments are simply variables that are passed into the function by the calling code and then used by it.

You create arguments by naming them within the parentheses on the line that creates the function. Each argument should be given a specific data type. Once defined, the arguments can be used in the function as normal variables.

You can define arguments as being optional by giving them a value when you create them so that they have a default value. You are required to pass data for any argument that is not given a default value.

Pass Arguments to a Function

Create arguments

Note: You need to open the Actions panel to complete the following steps. See the section, "Using the Actions Panel," for more details.

① Type **function**, followed by the name of the function.

② Type a left parenthesis, the name for an argument, a colon, and a data type, and then a right parenthesis.

③ Type a colon and then type **void**.

④ Add the curly braces.

⑤ Between the braces, write the code for the function, using the arguments.

The function is created.

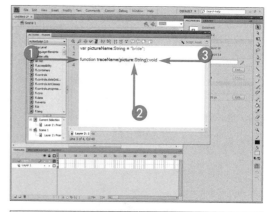

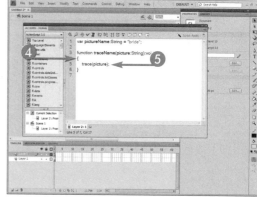

Call the function

6 Below the function, type the name of the function and a left parenthesis.

7 Provide a list of data to match the argument list.

8 Type a right parenthesis and a semi-colon.

The function is called.

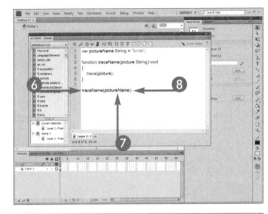

9 Press Ctrl+Enter to test the movie.

The movie plays and the function executes.

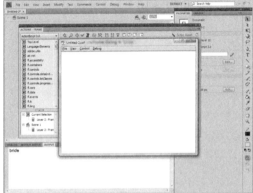

Can the arguments be listed in any order?

▼ Most of the time, the order in which you list arguments when you define the function is irrelevant. The only rule you have to keep in mind is that any optional arguments must come last in the list — you cannot list any required arguments after any optional ones. When you call the function, you must list the arguments in the exact order that they are defined in the actual function.

How many arguments can a function take?

▼ There is no limit to the number of arguments that can be defined for a function. You need to define as many arguments as are necessary to provide the data needed for the function to execute.

Can arguments be of any data type?

▼ Yes. You can create arguments using simple data types such as String or Number, or complex data types such as Array or even MovieClip. They can use literally *any* data type.

Return a Value from a Function

ome functions are designed to simply perform a task. For example, if you have an e-commerce application, you need a function to add items to a shopping cart. When called, all the function does is add an item. It performs the action and then allows the rest of the script to continue to execute. Other times, you need the function to execute its code and then return a result to the code that called it. For example, a calculator application needs a function to add numbers to one another. Once the calculation is complete, it stands to reason that you need the result to be sent back to the calling code.

You can have functions send data back to the code that called it by adding a *return* statement to the function. This statement takes a variable and sends it back to the code that called the function. The *return* statement must be the final line of the function; any code placed after the *return* statement fails to execute.

Return a Value from a Function

Create the function

Note: *You need to open the Actions panel to complete the following steps. See the section, "Using the Actions Panel," for more details.*

① Type **function**, followed by the name of the function.

② Type a left parenthesis.

③ Add arguments with data types.

④ Type a right parenthesis.

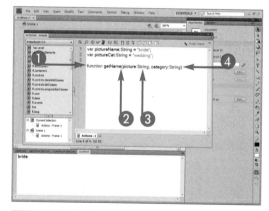

⑤ Add a left curly brace.

⑥ Between the braces, write the code for the function.

⑦ As the last line of the function, type **return** and the name of the variable being returned.

⑧ Add a right curly brace.

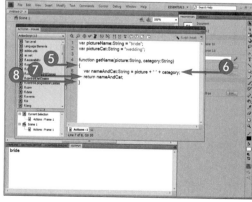

9 After the parentheses on the function definition, add a colon and a data type of the return variable.

The function is created.

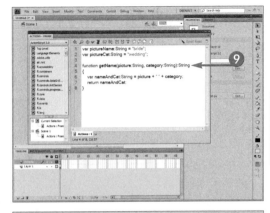

Call the function

10 Below the function, declare a variable.

Note: See the previous section, "Create Variables," for details.

11 Set the data type to match the type set in step **6**.

12 Type an equal sign.

13 Type the function name, parentheses, the values for the arguments and a semicolon.

The function is called.

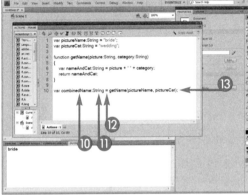

Can functions return more than one value?

▼ Functions can only have a single `return` statement. If you need to return more than one value from the function, you must use a complex data type such as an Array or Object. A thorough discussion of these data types is beyond the scope of this book.

Can I have code that determines the value of the `return` statement based on criteria?

▼ Yes. Functions can contain almost any code, including ActionScript `if-else` statements. See the following section for details on creating `if-else` statements in code.

Make Decisions in Code

ActionScript, like other programming languages, includes the ability to have the script execute different blocks of code based on differing criteria. This allows your code to provide a basic level of intelligence.

You can make decisions in your code using `if-else` statements. The `if` statement follows a fairly simple syntax:

```
if(condition) {
    Code to execute if condition is true
}
```

The condition needs to be an ActionScript expression that evaluates to either true or false. For example, if you have a variable x and a variable y, you can test to see if x is greater than y with: `if(x > y)`. If x is greater than y, the code within the `if` statement executes. If not, the code continues below the `if` block.

You can add an `else` clause after the closing curly brace of the `if` statement, with its own set of braces, to provide code that executes if the original expression is false. The `else` clause does not take an expression.

Make Decisions in Code

Create an If statement

Note: You need to open the Actions panel to complete the following steps. See the section, "Using the Actions Panel," for more details.

1. Type **if**.

2. Type a left parenthesis.

3. Type an expression.

4. Type a right parenthesis.

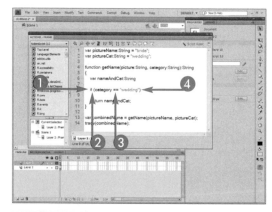

5. Type a left curly brace.

6. Type the code to execute if the expression is true.

7. Type a right curly brace.

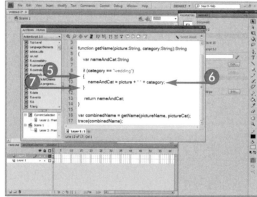

8 After the closing curly brace, type **else**.

9 Type a left curly brace.

10 Type the code to execute if the expression is true.

11 Type a right curly brace.

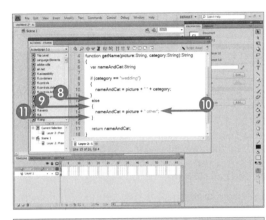

12 Press Ctrl+Enter to test the movie.

The movie runs.

● In this example, the statement, bride wedding, appears in the Output panel.

How do I test to see if two variables have the same value?

▼ To test for equality in ActionScript, you use two equal signs, as follows:

```
if(x == y)
```

A very common mistake while learning code is to forget that a single equal sign sets the value of the variable on the left to the value on the right, while a double equal sign tests for equality. Be careful to double-check your `if` statements to be sure that you are using double equal signs.

Can I call a function within an `if` statement?

▼ Yes. Within the code of the `if` statement, you can have any legal ActionScript statements, including function calls. You can also call a function in the expression of the `if` statement, as long as the function returns a value that can be used to determine whether the expression is true.

Can I test for more than one value?

▼ Yes. Between an `if` and an `else` statement, you can add as many `else if` statements as you want. `Else if` statements follow the same syntax as the `if` statement, and so they take an expression to evaluate.

Create Event Handlers and Listeners

No code in ActionScript can execute without an event occurring. Events include the playhead entering a frame; a MovieClip or other object being created; external data being loaded; or the user interacting with the movie by moving their mouse, clicking on something, or typing a key on the keyboard.

At any given time, there may be hundreds of events occurring in the movie, but they are all ignored unless you write code for them. Code to control events has two parts: an *event handler* and an *event listener*.

An event handler is a function that you create to respond to the event. The event handler always takes an argument, which is the event itself, and never returns a value. See Chapter 33 for details on functions, arguments, and retuning values.

In theory, any object in your movie can be made to respond to any event. Therefore, it is necessary to instruct Flash Player as to which object should be made to respond to which event. You can do this through the addition of an event listener, which is simply a line of code that reads, `"When this event occurs on this object, call that event handler."`

Create Event Handlers and Listeners

Create an event handler

Note: You need to open the Actions panel to complete the following steps. See Chapter 33 for more details.

1. Type **function.**

2. Type a name for the function.

3. Type a left parenthesis.

4. Type **event:MouseEvent.**

5. Type a right parenthesis.

6. Type a colon and **void.**

7. Type a left curly brace.

8. Type the code to execute when the event occurs.

    In this example, a string of text is displayed in the output window.

9. Type a right curly brace.

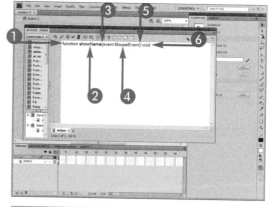

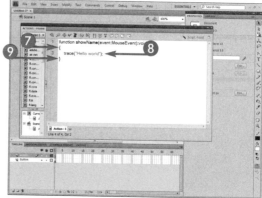

Create an event listener

① On the Stage, create an instance of a symbol.

Note: See Chapter 28 for details.

② Use the Properties panel to give the instance a name.

Note: See Chapter 33 for details on naming instances.

③ In the Actions panel, type the instance name and a period.

④ Type **addEventListener(**.

⑤ Type **MouseEvent.CLICK** and a comma.

⑥ Type the name of the handler created above and a closing parenthesis.

Test the movie

① Press Ctrl+Enter.

The movie plays.

② Click the symbol.

The event listener triggers the event handler.

In this example, the text is displayed in the output window.

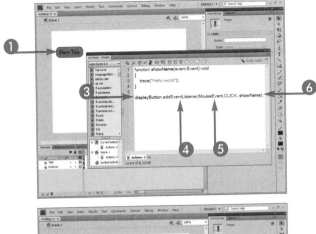

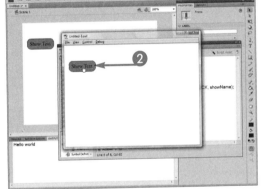

What other event types are there?

▼ ActionScript supports dozens of event types. You can always use `Event`, which is a generic event that responds to anything. However, it can be helpful to use more specific event types. For example, you might use `MouseEvent`, which includes subtypes including `CLICK`, `MOUSE_OVER`, `ROLL_OVER`, and several more. Or you could use `KeyboardEvent`, which includes subtypes `KEY_DOWN` and `KEY_UP`. Using a more specific event type gives you greater control over the events in your movie.

Should I always write my event handler before I write the event listener?

▼ Because your ActionScript code is compiled into the final movie, it does not necessarily execute in a linear order. Therefore, you can write them in any order. However, it has become an accepted best practice to place your event handlers, along with other functions, at the top of your code, and any listeners below them.

Will the event handler always have a return type of void?

▼ Yes. Event handlers cannot return values. See Chapter 33 for details on functions and return types.

Stop a Movie

When you play a Flash movie, it plays through all of its frames, and then loops back to the beginning and starts over, again playing through all of the frames. You can control this behavior with the ActionScript `stop()` command.

When the code encounters a `stop()` command, it freezes the playhead for the current Timeline. If the command is placed in a frame on the main Timeline, the movie stops. However, you should keep in mind that MovieClips have an independent Timeline, and so a `stop()` command on the main Timeline does not

stop a MovieClip; instead, the command needs to be added to that MovieClip's Timeline as well.

You can place the command directly within the code on a particular frame, or you can use an event handler to have something in the movie trigger the action. For example, you may want to provide a button that the user can click to stop the movie at any time. In this case, you would place the `stop()` command within an event handler, and add an event listener to the button to trigger the action. See the previous section for details on using event handlers and listeners.

Stop a Movie

① Add a button to the Stage.

Note: *See Chapter 28 for details on buttons.*

② Name the instance.

Note: *See Chapter 33 for details on naming instances.*

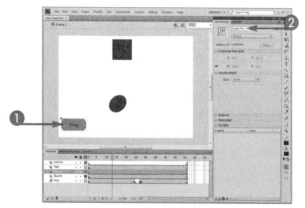

③ Press F9 to open the Actions panel.

④ Add an event handler.

Note: *See the previous section for details on creating event handlers.*

⑤ In the handler code, type **stop();**.

⑥ Add an event listener for the button.

Note: *See the previous section for details on creating event handlers.*

The stop action is added to the movie.

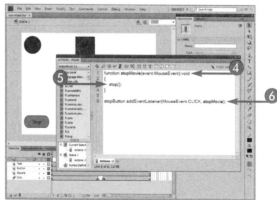

Go to a Specific Frame

Normally, Flash movies begin at frame 1 and play through to the end of the movie, up to 16,000 frames later. However, you can use ActionScript to tell the movie to jump to a specific frame at any time.

ActionScript includes two commands that allow you to navigate to specific frames: gotoAndPlay and gotoAndStop. The former jumps to the frame indicated and then continues to play from there, while the latter simply jumps to the indicated frame

and then stops. With either, you need to tell it to which frame you want to jump. You can provide a frame number or a frame label. While either works, labels are preferred. If you end up adding new frames before the one to which you are jumping, the label moves with it and causes your script to continue to work. If you reference the frame by number and then add new frames, the script jumps to the wrong place in the movie. See Chapter 29 for details on labeling frames.

Go to a Specific Frame

Note: You need to open the Actions panel to complete the following steps. See Chapter 33 for more details.

1. Type **gotoAndStop** and a left parenthesis.

2. Type a frame number or label.

Note: In this example, frame 24 has been labeled next.

3. Type a right parenthesis and a semicolon.

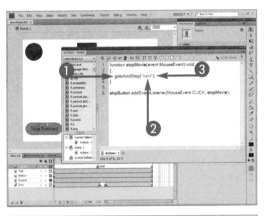

4. Press Ctrl+Enter.

The movie plays.

5. Click the button.

The movie jumps ahead.

In this example, the code is in frame 1, causing the movie to jump to frame 24 immediately.

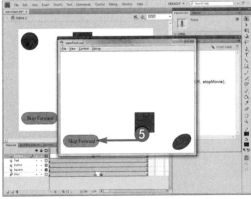

Drag-and-Drop Movie Clips

You can use ActionScript to create movie clips that users can drag around the screen. You can use draggable movie clips for games you create in Flash, user interfaces that require drag-and-drop actions, slider bars, and much more. Working with the Actions panel, you can type a specific script that tells Flash to start dragging a movie clip instance when the user clicks the clip object. When the user releases the mouse, Flash stops the dragging action.

Creating a drag-and-drop script involves creating a series of objects — usually MovieClips — to drag. Each

needs a unique instance name. You need to use two event handlers. The first enables the object to be dragged, while the second enables it to be dropped. Usually, you want to rely on the `MouseEvent.MOUSE_DOWN` event for dragging and the `MouseEvent.MOUSE_UP` event for dropping.

If you have more than one object that you plan to drag-and-drop, you need to have the event handler determine which object should be used. All event handlers are passed an Event object. This object contains a target property that identifies the object that initialized the event.

Drag-and-drop movie clips

Create and name an instance

1 Place an instance of a MovieClip on the Stage.

Note: See Chapter 28 to learn how to create movie clips.

2 Assign an instance name.

Note: See Chapter 33 for details on assigning instance names.

Create a script

1 Create a new layer.

2 Rename the layer Actions.

3 Press F9 to open the Actions panel.

4 Type **function dragPicture(event:Mouse Event):void.**

5 Type a left curly brace and press Enter (Return).

6 Type **event.target.startDrag();.**

7 Type a right curly brace and press Enter (Return).

8 Repeat steps **1** to **4**, replacing `dragPicture` with `dropPicture` and `startDrag` with `stopDrag`.

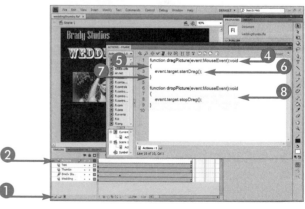

Add event listeners

① Type **picture.addEventListener(Mouse Event.MOUSE_DOWN, dragPicture);**.

② Type **picture.addEventListener(Mouse Event.MOUSE_UP, dropPicture);**.

Note: In both cases, be sure to use the name of the instance you created in the subsection, "Create and Name an Instance."

Note: If you have multiple objects to drag, repeat steps 1 and 2 for each instance.

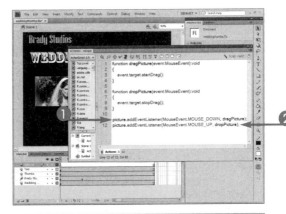

Test your movie

① Press Ctrl+Enter.

Flash Player appears.

② Drag the movie clip object.

The object appears as a draggable movie clip.

PART IX

How can I make the cursor look like a hand when I mouse over it?

▼ If you use a MovieClip as the object you are dragging, the cursor remains as a standard arrow. This may confuse users, as many will not think that they can click on something if they do not see a hand cursor. You can fix this by setting the buttonMode property of the MovieClip to true:

`clip.buttonMode = true;`

As you might infer from this, the hand cursor appears automatically if you use a button symbol instead of a MovieClip.

Do I have to force my users to hold down the mouse button while they drag?

▼ No. You can use any event to drag. MouseEvent.MOUSE_DOWN and MouseEvent.MOUSE_UP are the most common, but you could create a situation whereby you use the MouseEvent.CLICK event to start the drag and the MouseEvent.DOUBLE_CLICK event to end it. It would be possible to use MouseEvent.CLICK for both, but that would require much more complex code than is covered in this book.

Animate with ActionScript

You ou can create animation in Flash using either the Timeline, with keyframes and tweens, or ActionScript. (See Part VII for details on animating with the Timeline.)

Animation in ActionScript simply involves changing a property of an object over time. You can even animate if your movie has only a single frame, as Flash still loops over the movie — playing that frame over and over and executing any code repeatedly.

You can move objects on the Stage by manipulating the x or y properties. You can change the size of

objects with the xScale and yScale properties, or have an object fade in and out by changing the alpha property. As all of these are numeric properties, you can simply add or subtract from their value.

As with other code in ActionScript, your animation needs to be triggered by an event. In the case of animation, you will most likely use the Event.ENTER_FRAME event, which is triggered at the movie's frame rate; for example, if your frame rate is 12 frames per second, the event occurs 12 times per second.

Animate with ActionScript

Create and name an instance

1 Place an instance of a MovieClip on the Stage.

Note: See Chapter 28 to learn how to create movie clips.

2 Assign an instance name.

Note: See Chapter 33 for details on assigning instance names.

Create a script

1 Create a new layer and name it Actions.

2 Rename the layer Actions.

3 Press F9 to open the Actions panel.

4 Type **function animateClip(event: Event):void.**

5 Type a left curly brace.

6 Type **event.target.x = event.target.x + 1;.**

7 Type **event.target.y = event.target.y + 1;.**

8 Type **event.target.alpha = event.target. alpha -0.01;.**

9 Type a right curly brace.

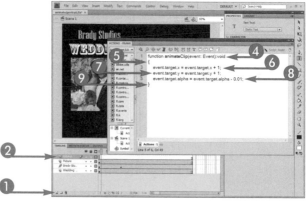

Add event listeners

1 Type *clip*.addEventListener(Event.
ENTER_FRAME, animateClip);.

*Note: Replace the clip with the name of the
instance you want to drag.*

*Note: If you have multiple objects to
animate, repeat step **1** for each
instance.*

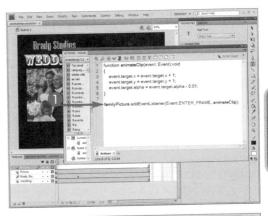

Test your movie

1 Press Ctrl+Enter.

Flash Player appears.

The object animates.

In this example, the object moves
down and to the right, gradually
fading out.

Why does the alpha **property need to
subtract 0.01, instead of a percentage?**

▼ The alpha property in ActionScript is
expressed as a value between 0 for
transparent and 1 for opaque. By
subtracting .01 from it, you are saying that
it will take about 100 iterations of the
event to disappear. At a frame rate of 12
fps, that would be approximately 8
seconds, although the alpha will become
too low to be seen after about 6 seconds.
Unfortunately, the Properties panel
expresses this alpha value as a
percentage.

**Is there an easier way to write the code
that adds or subtracts one from the
current value of a property?**

▼ Yes. The expression variable =
variable +1 says that you want to add 1
to the current value of the variable. A
shorthand for this is variable++. A
shorthand for subtracting 1 from the
current value is variable--. You can add
or subtract an arbitrary value by writing
variable += value or variable-=
value.

So the code in the example above could
be written as follows:

```
event.target.x++;
event.target.y++;
event.target.alpha -= .01;
```

Create Input Text Boxes

F lash supports three types of text boxes. *Static text boxes* have their text entered when you initially create them on the Stage, and that text cannot be changed when the movie runs. *Input text boxes* serve as form fields, allowing the user to enter information into Flash Player. *Dynamic text fields* cannot be modified by the user, but you can use ActionScript to add or change their text as the movie plays.

You can use the Text tool to create any type of text box. Then, you can use the Properties panel to set the behavior of the box. If you want an input text box, you select that option in the panel. You would most likely want to add a static text field next to the input field to provide a label for the input field.

You can control the appearance of the input text box in the Properties panel. The panel provides a Show Border Around Text option that draws a box around the field; without it, the field is completely invisible, so unless you have a background image to use, you want to check this option. You can also select from a range of other formatting options.

① Click the Text tool.

② Click-and-drag to create a text box on the Stage.

③ Click the Text type drop-down menu.

④ Click Input Text.

Flash changes the text box to an input text box.

5 Type an instance name for the box.

- You can click the Show Border Around Text button to add a border around the text box.

- You can assign formatting, such as a font, font color, and size for the text box.

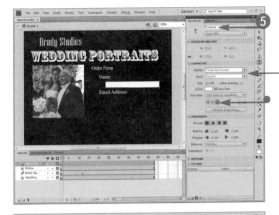

- You can assign paragraph-level formatting, such as alignment, by using these properties.

What does the Line Type field enable me to do?

▼ In the Line Type field, you can select from Single Line, Multiline, Multiline No Wrap, or Password. Select Single Line to display user input on a single line. If the text is too long to fit in the text box, the text box scrolls. Select Multiline to display the user input on multiple lines and have the input wrap at the end of the box. Select Multiline No Wrap to display the user input on multiple lines and have the input wrap when the user presses Enter. Select Password to have asterisks appear as the user types.

How do I use character embedding?

▼ By default, Flash embeds fonts for static and dynamic text fields, but not input fields. If you use a font that is not on the user's computer, Flash substitutes another font. If you want the font you selected to appear, you can embed the font in your Flash document. You use the Character Embedding dialog box to embed a font. If you want to embed only certain characters, type the characters in the Include These Characters field. To choose a range of characters, click an option on the list or Ctrl+click to select several options. To embed all the characters that are currently in the field, click Auto Fill. Click Don't Embed if you do not want to embed fonts.

Create Dynamic Text Boxes

I f you want to display the text that your user enters in an input field, and so have text change in response to any other events that might occur in your movie, you can use a dynamic text box. Like input and static text boxes, dynamic text boxes can be created using the Text tool.

In the Properties panel, you use the Instance Name field to name your dynamic text box. Click the Show Border Around Text button to display a border around your dynamic text box. Click Selectable to give users

the ability to click-and-drag to select the text so that they can copy and paste it. You can also choose the font you want to use, the font size, the font color, a line type, a rendering method, and whether you want to render the text as HTML.

Dynamic text boxes automatically use an embedded font, but if you choose to display the text in Arial, Times New Roman, or some other common font, you can reduce the file size of your finished movie by choosing to use a device, or nonembedded, font. You can select this option in the Properties panel.

Create Dynamic Text Boxes

① Click the Text tool.

② Click-and-drag to create the field on the Stage.

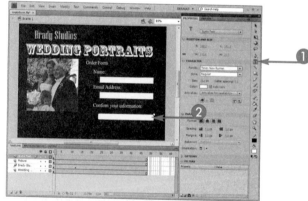

③ Click the Static Text type drop-down menu.

④ Click Dynamic Text.

Flash changes the text box to a dynamic text box.

⑤ Type the instance name.

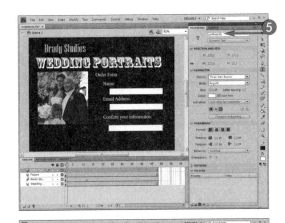

⑥ You can click the Character Embedding button to control whether or not the font is embedded.

The text field is created.

What does font rendering do?

▼ Font rendering allows you to control anti-aliasing. Anti-aliasing is a technique by which Flash Player blurs the edges of text to create rounded corners and make the text more readable. However, it can add to the file size. Very small text, such as text below 10 points, does not need to be anti-aliased, whereas large text, such as that used for headers, should always be anti-aliased. The Use Device Fonts option uses the fonts installed on the user's computer. Bitmap Text (No Anti-alias) displays text that is not anti-aliased. Anti-alias for Animation causes Flash to ignore alignment and kerning information and makes the animation smoother. Anti-alias for Readability makes fonts easier to read if they are not being animated.

What happens if I select Render Text as HTML?

▼ If you choose Render Text as HTML when you choose Dynamic Text or Input Text in the Properties panel, Flash creates or saves HTML formatting tags. This enables you to save the font name, style, color, size, and hyperlinks associated with the text. To render text as HTML, you must assign the text an instance name, select Render Text as HTML in the Properties panel, and use the Actions panel to set the `htmlText` property to a value that includes HTML.

Read and Write Text with ActionScript

Y ou can use ActionScript to read text that your users enter in input text fields and to display that text in dynamic fields. In order for ActionScript to reference either type of field, you need to give them an instance name. Note that static text fields cannot be given instance names, and thus cannot be read or written to in ActionScript.

You can access the information your user provides in an input field by calling the `text` property of the field. For example, if your field's instance name is `userName`, you would read it through `userName.text`.

Likewise, you can write to a dynamic field using the same `text` property. You can write the data from an input field to a dynamic field by setting one's `text` property to the other. For example, to display the data input into a field called `userName` into a dynamic field called `displayUser`, you would type **displayUser.text = userName.text.**

You also need some sort of button that users can click when they finish typing. See Chapter 34 for details on writing code to trigger buttons.

Read and Write Text with ActionScript

① Create an input text field and give it an instance name.

Note: See the section, "Create Input Text Boxes."

② Create a dynamic text field and give it an instance name.

Note: See the section, "Create Dynamic Text Boxes."

③ Create a button symbol, place it on the Stage, and give it an instance name.

Note: See Chapter 28 for details on creating and naming buttons.

④ Create a new layer named Actions.

Note: See Chapter 27 for details on creating and naming layers.

⑤ Click F9 to open the Actions panel.

⑥ Type **function setText(event:MouseEvent):void.**

⑦ Add a left curly brace.

Note: See Chapter 34 for details on creating event handlers.

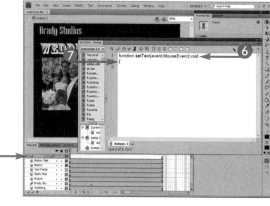

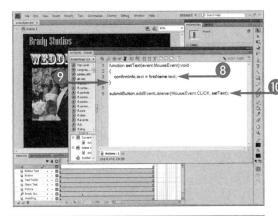

⑧ Type **dynamicField.text = input Text.text;.**

Note: Replace dynamicField and inputText with the names of the fields that you set in steps 1 and 2.

⑨ Type a right curly brace.

⑩ Type **submitbutton.addEvent Listener(MouseEvent.CLICK, setText;.**

Note: See Chapter 34 for information on event listeners.

⑪ Press Ctrl+Enter to test the movie.

Flash plays the movie.

⑫ Type text in the input field.

⑬ Press the Submit button.

● Flash displays the text in the dynamic field.

Can I remove the text from the input field when my user presses the button?

▼ Yes. In your event handler, you can simply set the field's `text` property to an empty string, represented by two double-quotation marks:

```
inputField.text = ""
```

When I type a lot of text in the input field, it is cut off when it displays in the dynamic field. Can I have the dynamic field resize to fit the text?

▼ Yes. You can simply set the dynamic field's `autoSize` property to true to have it expand or contract based on the amount of text being placed in it:

```
dynamicField.autoSize = true;
```

Note that true is a keyword in ActionScript, and so it is not in quotes.

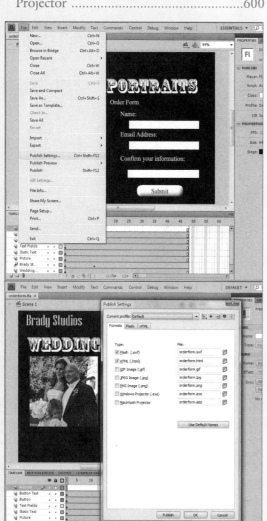

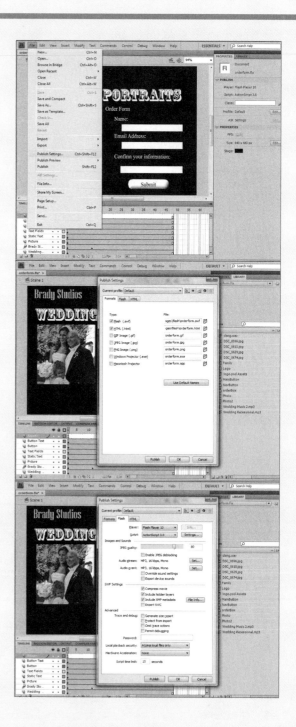

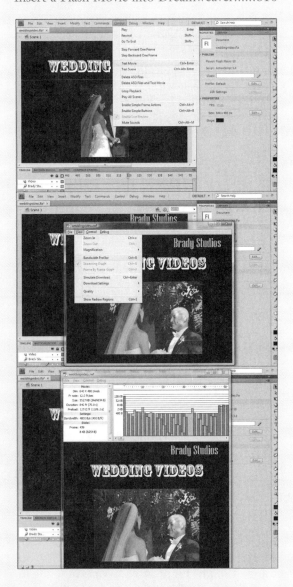

Understanding Flash Formats

U nlike many other programs with which you may be familiar, Flash uses a variety of different formats for its files, depending on the authoring environment in which the files are created and the current stage of the project. It is important to have an understanding of these formats before you try to publish your movie to your Web site so that you do not become confused.

SWF files

The final output format of almost all Flash movies is SWF. The format is often pronounced *swiff*, after the extension. Prior to the release of Flash MX, which was version 6 of the program, the file extension officially stood for Shockwave Flash, but as of MX, Macromedia began phasing out the Shockwave platform and changed what the extension stood for along the way. Today, Adobe says that the extension does not stand for anything.

SWF files can only be run in Flash Player: Flash CS4 Professional, the authoring environment, cannot play SWF files. The process of publishing a Flash movie can be seen as the process of converting the authoring tool's file into a SWF. SWF is not an editable format; you need to use some other format to make any changes to the file, and then convert that file to SWF.

Flash Authoring Files

While you are working in the Flash CS4 Professional authoring environment, which is most commonly referred to as Flash, you are creating and saving a FLA file (which uses the .fla filename extension). This is the editable version of your movie. Just as Flash cannot play a SWF file, Flash Player cannot read the FLA format. For most designers, the process of publishing their movie involves converting their editable FLA file into a noneditable SWF file.

Other Flash Formats

Over the last several years, the Flash platform has grown to include a variety of applications and formats. Following is a brief overview of the other applications and formats within the platform.

Flash Video

If you want to play video in your Flash movie, you need to convert the video to FLV format (which uses the .flv filename extension). The only video format that can be played in Flash Player is FLV. Flash CS4 Professional includes the Adobe Media Encoder, which can convert video files from a variety of formats. Many video-editing tools are also able to export to FLV format.

ActionScript Files

If you have a Flash movie that contains large amounts of ActionScript, you can export the script into one or more external files. These files are saved with an .as filename extension, but can be read by ActionScript as if they were still a part of the original movie. Externalizing ActionScript not only helps to make your movie easier to edit, but it also enables you to reuse your code by including the ActionScript file in other movies as well.

Flash Project Files

A new addition to Flash CS4 is the ability to create a set of source files for your movie that is stored not in a binary FLA file, but rather a text-based XFL file (which uses the .xlf filename extension). The biggest disadvantage to the FLA format is that it can only be read by the Flash authoring tool. The new XFL format, in contrast, is actually a compressed ZIP file that contains a collection of XML-based files that describe the source. It is hoped that in the future other applications will be able to read the format. For example, it might be possible to open the file in a future version of Photoshop and edit the graphics in the file without the need to reimport them into Flash as you do today. As a brand-new format, XFL does not currently have many applications, but it opens up many new possibilities for the future of Flash.

Flash JavaScript

Flash JavaScript files allow developers to extend the functionality not only of Flash movies, but rather the Flash authoring environment itself. Experienced JavaScript developers can use the language to add new panels, customize the interface, or store commands that save them from having to perform repetitive tasks. These files have a .jsfl filename extension.

Adobe Integrated Runtime

The Adobe Integrated Runtime, or AIR, represents a shift from the traditional thinking of how Flash movies work and how users interact with them. Instead of thinking of Flash as an animated environment for the Web, AIR allows developers to create desktop applications using Flash. These applications are downloaded and installed just like any other application, they can be launched from the Windows Start menu or the Dock on Macintosh computers, and they can do anything a traditional desktop application can do, including accessing the local file system and printing.

While any Flash movie can theoretically be compiled as an AIR application, they are more likely to be created as AIR applications from the start, as the needs of a desktop application are often very different from the needs of the Web; as such, the details of authoring for AIR are well beyond the scope of this book. Flash CS4 Professional includes all of the necessary settings to publish your movie to AIR.

Flex

Adobe Flex, which uses the .mxml extension, is a platform for creating Flash-based applications in a more developer-centric, code-based environment. While Flex is not suited for heavy animation work, it is a far superior environment for creating user interfaces and entire Web sites. Flex applications are created by combining an XML-based markup language called MXML — which is primarily responsible for creating the visual aspect of the application — with ActionScript 3.0, which handles the programmatic logic of the application. Flex is also a good tool for working with AIR.

Flash Components

Components allow you to quickly implement common tasks. For example, you do not need to understand the complexities of creating a player for Flash Video files, because Flash comes with a component that lets you simply point to the FLV file and be done. Other components that come with Flash include common user interface widgets such as scroll bars and multi-line text fields.

You can create your own components as well. These are saved as SWC files. Like the new XFL format, SWC is actually a zipped file that contains the SWF and AS files that are necessary to implement the component. Flash Components use the .swc filename extension.

Important Non-Flash Formats

Several formats that are not directly created or read by Flash are important to your Flash work. You almost certainly use graphics files, which are generally JPEG, GIF, PNG, or Photoshop PSD files. You may add sound to your movie, most likely using the MP3 format. Finally, if you want your movie to be able to play as traditional video, say on a TV set, you can export to the QuickTime MOV format.

Publish Your Movie to a SWF

You use the Publish Settings dialog box to publish your document. By default, Flash is set up to publish your document in Flash format with an .swf filename extension and an accompanying HTML file, but you can choose to publish in other formats, including GIF, JPEG, or PNG, or self-playing Windows or Mac files.

Depending on the format you select, the Publish Settings dialog box may provide a tab with publishing options you can set. The Publish Settings dialog box also assigns default names, but you can override the settings and enter your own unique filenames. In

addition, you can choose the directory in which you want to save your published document.

When publishing your document in the Flash format, you can set several options, including the version of ActionScript you will use, the minimum version of Flash Player you require your users to run, and the load order, which controls whether the movie's layers are created bottom-up or top-down. You can also select options such as Generate Size Report, Omit Trace Actions, Protect from Import, Debugging Permitted, and Compress Movie, and set the quality of exported JPEG graphics.

Publish Your Movie to a SWF

① Click File.

② Click Publish Settings.

The Publish Settings dialog box appears.

③ Click the type of file you want to publish.

Flash and HTML are selected by default.

You can use the default name or you can type a new name in the File field.

Depending on which format you select, additional tabs appear with options related to that format.

④ Click the Directory icon for the file type you want to publish.

The Select Publish Destination dialog box appears.

⑤ Select the directory in which you want to save your file.

By default, Flash saves your file in the directory in which you saved the FLA file.

⑥ Click Save.

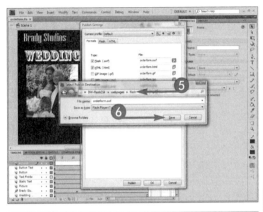

⑦ Click Publish.

Flash publishes your files.

⑧ Click OK.

The Publish Settings dialog box closes.

How does the Publish feature differ from the Export Movie feature?

▼ You use the Publish feature when you want to publish your document on the Web or as a stand-alone application. Flash saves the publish settings with the document. The Export Movie feature is similar to the Publish feature, except the publish settings are not saved with the document.

Do I always have to publish a movie through the Publish Settings dialog box?

▼ No. If you want to publish your movie using the last settings you set in the Publish Settings dialog box, you can click File on the main menu and then click Publish. Flash bypasses the Publish Settings dialog box, but does not give you a chance to name the file.

In looking at the list of versions of ActionScript, I see something called Adobe AIR and something else called Flash Lite. What are these?

▼ The Adobe Integrated Runtime, or AIR, allows you to create desktop applications. See the previous section for a more-detailed discussion of AIR. Flash Lite is a specialized version of a SWF file that plays on a cell phone or other portable device.

Change Flash Publishing Options

Y ou can use the Publish Settings dialog box to change many of the settings that Flash uses when you publish a SWF file. The settings appear as a tab in the dialog box when you have Flash selected as a format.

You can set the minimum version of Flash Player that your user will need in order to play your movie. For usage statistics on Flash Player, see the Flash Player Census at www.adobe.com/products/player_census/flashplayer/. The site includes details on how many people are using the player, broken down by version,

operating system, and other criteria. You can also set the version of ActionScript you are using. You need to be sure that the code you wrote matches the version selected here; all of the code in this book is written in ActionScript 3.0.

You can also set the compression for JPEG images and audio files. You have choices to compress the movie, include hidden files, and specify several advanced settings. You can also password-protect your file. You can add file information. This information is read by search engines and may improve your search rankings.

Change Flash Publishing Options

① Click File.

② Click Publish Settings.

The Publish Settings dialog box appears.

③ Click Flash.

The Flash settings tab displays.

- You can set the version of Flash Player here.

- You can set the ActionScript version here.

- You can use these settings to control JPEG compression and audio options.

4 Click File Info.

A dialog box appears, displaying information about the file.

5 Type a title, author, and description.

6 Click OK.

The settings are saved.

What do the Advanced options do?

▼ The Generate Size Report option creates a text file that details the size, frame-by-frame, of the file. The Protect from Import option, along with the password, prevents the SWF file from being opened in other Adobe programs such as Authorware or Director. Omit Trace Actions removes any trace commands that you might have in your ActionScript. Finally, the Permit Debugging option allows users with the debug version of Flash Player to debug problematic ActionScript.

What is Local Playback Security?

▼ This setting controls how Flash Player interacts with external resources. The Access Local Files Only option means that Flash Player can only access files on the user's local computer, and cannot retrieve additional assets from a network, while the Access Network Only option means the opposite.

Publish the Movie to a Stand-Alone Projector

You can create a Flash movie that plays in its own Flash Player window without a browser or another application. Viewers of the file do not need to install Flash Player. When you publish a movie in Windows Projector or Macintosh Projector format, Flash publishes the movie as an executable file with an .exe or .app extension.

You can easily place the files on compact discs and distribute them, or you can send them as e-mail file attachments. You must publish the projector file to a

format appropriate to the computer platform of the end user. For example, if you want to create a Flash movie projector file for a Mac user, make sure that you publish the file to a Mac projector format (APP) instead of a Windows projector format (EXE).

Depending on the size of your movie, the Flash projector file may be quite large, and so you might need to compress the file by using a program such as WinZip before sending it as an e-mail attachment.

Publish the movie as a projector

1 Click File.

2 Click Publish Settings.

The Publish Settings dialog box appears.

Note: If you have previously published your file, the selections from your last publication appear in the dialog box.

3 Select Windows Projector and/or Macintosh Projector as the format type.

● If you do not want to publish your movie on the Web, deselect Flash and HTML.

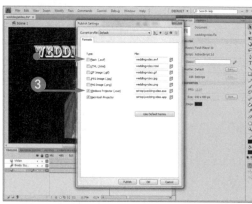

④ Click Publish.

Flash publishes your movie as a projector.

⑤ Click OK.

The Publish Settings dialog box closes.

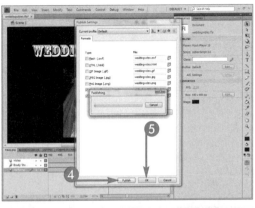

Play the movie

① Test the movie by double-clicking its name.

The Flash Player window appears and plays the movie.

② Click the Close button to close the window when the movie stops.

The movie closes.

Can I create a Macintosh projector file in Windows?

▼ Yes. Select the Macintosh Projector option in the Publish Settings dialog box. Flash creates a file with an .hqx extension. After creating the HQX file, you must apply a file translator such as BinHex to the file before a user can view it on a Macintosh computer.

What is the difference between a SWF file and a projector file?

▼ When you save a file as a projector file, you are making an executable copy of your Flash movie. This file does not require a player or plug-in. It comes with everything necessary to run the movie. A regular SWF file packs only the movie data, not the player. Regular SWF files require Flash Player to view the movie.

Do I need to worry about licensing my projector file?

▼ Adobe allows free distribution of its Flash Player and projector products. If you are distributing your movie for commercial purposes, however, you need to check the Adobe Web site for information about crediting Adobe. Visit www.adobe.com/support/programs/mwm. You need to include the "Made with Adobe" logo on your packaging and give proper credits on your credit screen.

PART X

Test Movie Bandwidth

You can use the Flash Bandwidth Profiler to help you determine which movie frames might cause problems during playback on the Web. File size and the user's data-transfer rate affect how smoothly and quickly your movie downloads and plays. With the Bandwidth Profiler you can test your movies for maximum effect. The feature works within the Flash Player window.

With the Bandwidth Profiler, you can test a variety of different modem and broadband connection speeds and gauge which frames in your movie use the most bytes. This information helps you to see exactly where

your movie might slow down during playback. For example, you can use the Bandwidth Profiler to simulate different modem speeds, such as comparing how long a movie takes to download at 56K (4.7 kilobytes per second) versus through DSL (32.6 kilobytes per second).

When you activate the Bandwidth Profiler, it opens as a window at the top of the Flash Player window. The left section of the Profiler displays the different status areas you can check, such as the movie's dimensions and speed, or the frame state. The right section displays a Timeline and a graph detailing frame data.

Test Movie Bandwidth

Open the Bandwidth Profiler

① Click Control.

② Click Test Movie.

Flash Player opens and starts playing the movie.

③ Press Enter (Return) to stop the movie.

④ Click View.

⑤ Click Bandwidth Profiler.

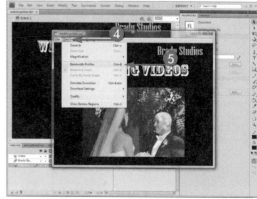

The Bandwidth Profiler appears at the
top of the Flash Player window.

● The left side of the Profiler shows
information about the movie, such
as file size and dimensions.

● The bars on the right represent
individual frames and the total size,
in bytes, of data in the frame.

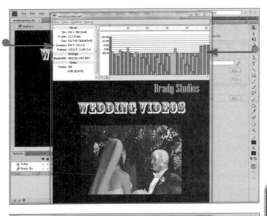

6 Drag the scroll bar to view the rest of
the movie.

**Can I customize the download speed I
want to test?**

▼ Yes. To customize the modem speed, click
View, click Download Speeds, and then
click Customize. The Custom Modem
Settings dialog box appears. You can then
set a speed to simulate in the test. For
example, you can change an existing
speed's bit rate by typing another bit rate,
or you can enter a custom speed in a User
Setting field and a bit rate to test for that
speed. Click OK to save your changes.

**Can I save the test settings for use with
another movie?**

▼ Yes. Just leave the Bandwidth Profiler open
in the Flash Player window. You can open
another movie from the Flash Player
window, or you can return to the Flash
Player window at a later time and use the
same Profiler settings. To open another
movie without leaving the Flash Player
window, click File, and then click Open.
Double-click the movie you want to view,
and it begins playing in the Flash Player
window.

continued

Test Movie Bandwidth *(Continued)*

Y ou can use two different views in the Flash Bandwidth Profiler to see how the frames play in your movie: Streaming Graph mode or Frame By Frame Graph mode. The default view is Streaming Graph mode. Depending on the view you select, the right section of the Profiler displays data differently.

A vertical bar on the graph represents a single frame in the movie. The bars correspond with the frame number shown in the Timeline. In Streaming Graph mode, the alternating blocks of light and dark gray show the relative byte size of each frame, and the stack indicates how much data must download, or stream, into a browser window. Streaming Graph

mode shows you the real-time performance of your Flash movie.

In Frame By Frame Graph mode, Flash profiles each frame side by side. If a frame's bar extends above the bottom red line of the graph, the Flash movie pauses to download the frame's data. Frame By Frame Graph mode shows you which frames are causing delays during movie downloads.

If you decide your movie needs to be optimized for greater speed, simplifying graphics by using symbols and grouped objects can help, as well as avoiding custom colors and too many gradient effects. Also, limit the number of fonts you use with any text in your movies.

Test Movie Bandwidth *(Continued)*

Change the Graph view

⑦ Click View.

⑧ Click Frame By Frame Graph.

Flash displays the Profiler in Frame By Frame Graph mode.

● You can use the scroll bar to scroll through the movie's Timeline and view other frames.

Close the Profiler

9 To close the Profiler, click View.

10 Click Bandwidth Profiler.

The Bandwidth Profiler bar closes.

Does the Bandwidth Profiler test the exact modem speed?

▼ No. The Bandwidth Profiler estimates typical Internet connection speeds to estimate downloading time. Modem speeds are typically never at full strength. For example, on the low end of the scale, a 28.8 Kbps modem can download 3.5 kilobytes of data per second under perfect conditions, but in real life, there are no perfect connections when connecting to the Internet. Even higher-speed connections are subject to heavy broadband traffic that slows down connection speeds. Flash gears each test speed setting in the Profiler toward real-life connection speeds.

How do I view a specific frame in the Bandwidth Profiler?

▼ Use the scroll bar arrows to move left or right in the Profiler Timeline at the top of the Profiler graph. To view a specific frame, drag the playhead to the frame, or click the playhead where you want it to go.

Is there a faster way to open the Bandwidth Profiler?

▼ Yes. You can press Ctrl+B (⌘+B) in the Flash Player window to display the Profiler.

Create an (X)HTML Page in Flash

Your browser cannot play a Flash movie directly. Instead, you need to create an (X)HTML page that includes the necessary code to call Flash Player and have it run the movie. You can select HTML as the publishing format in Flash, and it creates your SWF file and an HTML file that you can use to display your SWF file.

When publishing to HTML format, Flash generates all the necessary HTML code for you, including the tags you need to view your document in most browsers. Flash bases the HTML document it creates on a template that contains basic HTML coding. By default, Flash assigns the Flash Only template. You can choose another template, or, if you know HTML code, you

can customize a template or create your own template.

The HTML tab in the Publish Settings dialog box has a variety of options for controlling how your movie plays in the browser window. You can detect the Flash version, set the movie dimensions, set playback options, and specify the quality, window mode, HTML alignment, scale, and Flash alignment for your document.

When setting dimensions, you can choose from Match Movie, Pixels, or Percent. Match Movie makes your movie the size you specified in the Document Properties dialog box; Pixels enables you to specify the size of your movie in pixels; and Percent enables you to specify the percentage of the browser window your movie should occupy.

Create an (X)HTML Page in Flash

1 Click File.

2 Click Publish Settings.

The Publish Settings dialog box appears.

● Make sure the HTML format is selected.

3 Click the Flash tab.

Flash displays options associated with generating a SWF file.

④ Set any Flash format options you want to change on the Flash tab.

Note: See Chapter 36 for details on these settings.

⑤ Click the HTML tab.

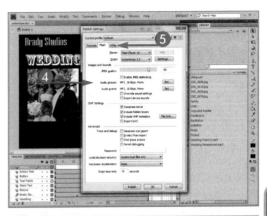

Flash displays options associated with generating an HTML file.

⑥ Select a template.

⑦ Click the Detect Flash Version option.

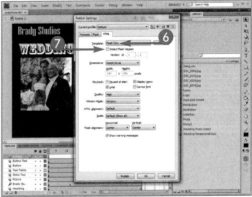

What is an HTML template?

▼ An HTML template is an HTML file that contains tags that enable you to play your Flash SWF file on the Web. Flash Professional 8 has ten templates from which you can choose. To obtain information about a template, choose the template and then click the Info button.

You can set up your own HTML templates or customize existing templates. Flash looks for all HTML templates in the HTML folder, so be sure to save your HTML templates in the HTML subfolder within the Flash application folder on your computer system. Your template must include a line that starts with the title code $TT, such as $TTMy Template.

What does the Detect Flash Version option do?

▼ Flash Player comes preinstalled with most Web browsers. There are several versions of Flash Player. Flash Professional CS4 uses Flash Player 10. If you choose Detect Flash Version, the HTML file you generate can detect the version of Flash Player that is installed on the user's computer. If the version of Flash Player installed is not compatible with the SWF file you have created, the user is directed to a Web page with a link to the most recent version of Flash Player. Not all templates enable you to detect the Flash version.

continued

Create an (X)HTML Page in Flash *(Continued)*

Y ou can use the Playback options to control how a movie plays. You can specify whether the movie is paused at Start, loops continuously, displays the Flash Player menu, or uses device fonts. If the movie is paused at Start, users have to press a button to start the movie. If you choose Display Menu, when users right-click (Ctrl+click) while the movie is playing, a shortcut menu appears.

You can choose the Device Font option if you want to substitute anti-aliased fonts for fonts that are not on the user's system. This option applies only to static text. *Anti-aliasing* smooths the edges of objects in your

Flash movie and gives objects a crisp, clean appearance. However, anti-aliasing also slows down the processing time of your Flash movie. You use the Quality option to determine the trade-off between anti-aliasing and playback speed. The order of the quality values from lowest to highest is Low, Auto Low, Auto High, Medium, High, and Best. In general, the higher you set the quality value, the higher the quality of the images in your movie and the slower the processing time. If you select the Show Warning Messages option, the program warns you of errors in your template.

⑧ Select a movie dimension option.

If you select Pixels or Percent, type a value in the Width and Height fields.

⑨ Select playback options.

The Loop and Display Menu options are selected by default.

⑩ Select a quality setting.

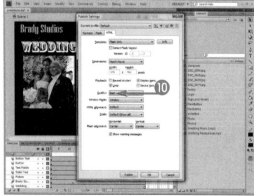

⓫ Select the horizontal alignment.

⓬ Select the vertical alignment.

⓭ Select the Show warning messages option.

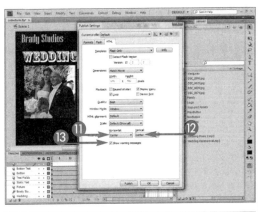

⓮ Click Publish.

Flash creates a SWF file and an HTML file.

⓯ Click OK.

The Publish Settings dialog box closes.

What does the Scale option do?

▼ You can set the Scale option if you have changed the document's width or height. Choosing Default displays the entire document and retains the original aspect ratio. Choosing No Border scales the document to fit within the boundaries you have specified, without changing the aspect ratio and without distorting the movie. Flash crops the movie, if necessary. Exact Fit displays the document using the width and height you have specified. Exact Fit does not preserve the original aspect ratio, and so the images in your movie may be distorted. If you choose No Scale, the document does not scale when users resize the Flash Player window.

What does the HTML Alignment option do?

▼ The HTML Alignment option enables you to tell Flash how you want to align your SWF file within the browser window. Choosing Default centers the SWF file. Choosing Left, Right, Top, or Bottom aligns the file with the left, right, top, or bottom of the browser window.

What does the Flash Alignment option do?

▼ You use the Flash Alignment option to set the alignment of a Flash document within the application window. You can set the horizontal alignment to Left, Center, or Right. You can set the vertical alignment to Top, Center, or Bottom. Flash crops the document, if necessary.

Insert a Flash Movie into Dreamweaver

While the ability of Flash to generate an (X)HTML page for your Flash movies can be helpful, you do not have much control over the appearance of that page. If your Flash movie is going to serve as your entire Web site, then you can use this feature. If instead you want to use the Flash movie as only a portion of your site, then you are better off creating your own (X)HTML document in Dreamweaver and then inserting the Flash movie into it.

You can create your document in Dreamweaver just as you would any other (X)HTML document. When you come to the point of inserting your Flash movie, you can click the Insert Flash button on the Insert bar. Then, you can simply select the SWF file you want to insert.

Dreamweaver's Design view cannot play Flash movies, and so they are instead represented by a gray box. However, if you either preview the page in a Web browser or use the Live View option, you can see your Flash movie play within your page.

Insert a Flash Movie into Dreamweaver

① Click File.

② Click Publish.

Note: See the previous sections for details on publishing the movie; you only need to publish to the SWF format.

Note: Be sure to select the folder that contains your Web pages for the publishing directory.

③ Open Dreamweaver CS4.

④ Open the file into which you want to insert your Flash movie.

Note: See Part 1 for information on opening Dreamweaver and Web pages.

⑤ Click Media.

⑥ Click SWF.

The Select File dialog box appears.

7 Select the SWF file you published in step **2**.

8 Click OK.

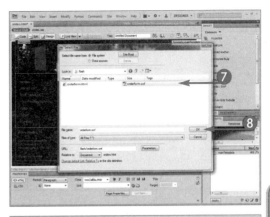

The Object Tag Accessibility Attributes dialog box appears.

9 Type a title for the Flash movie.

10 Click OK.

The Flash movie is inserted into the Web page.

Can I edit the movie in Dreamweaver?

▼ No. You can only edit the movie in Flash. However, if you click on the file in Dreamweaver, you can click the Edit button on the Property Inspector to launch Flash. If the FLA file is in the same directory as the SWF file, it opens; otherwise, Flash prompts you to find the FLA file.

How do I get the edited file back into Dreamweaver?

▼ Once you are done editing the file in Flash, simply republish it, using the same directory and filename as you did before. When you return to Dreamweaver, it has the new version of the file.

Do I need to upload anything special to get my movie to play on the Web?

▼ Yes. You need to upload the SWF file. Be sure that it is uploaded into the same location relative to the (X)HTML page as you have it on your local computer. You also need to upload the contents of the Scripts folder that Dreamweaver creates when you first insert the movie.

A

INDEX

You can master all kinds of topics visually, including these.

All designed for visual learners—just like you!

Read Less–Learn More®

Microsoft®
Office 2007

978-0-470-13547-1

Microsoft®
Windows Vista™

978-0-470-04577-0

Dreamweaver® CS3 and
Flash® CS3 Professional

978-0-470-17745-7

Visual®
An Imprint of ⑨**WILEY**